`mapt.io`

Mapt is an online digital library that gives you full access to over 5,000 books and videos, as well as industry leading tools to help you plan your personal development and advance your career. For more information, please visit our website.

Why subscribe?

- Spend less time learning and more time coding with practical eBooks and Videos from over 4,000 industry professionals

- Improve your learning with Skill Plans built especially for you

- Get a free eBook or video every month

- Mapt is fully searchable

- Copy and paste, print, and bookmark content

Packt.com

Did you know that Packt offers eBook versions of every book published, with PDF and ePub files available? You can upgrade to the eBook version at `www.packt.com` and as a print book customer, you are entitled to a discount on the eBook copy. Get in touch with us at `customercare@packtpub.com` for more details.

At `www.packt.com`, you can also read a collection of free technical articles, sign up for a range of free newsletters, and receive exclusive discounts and offers on Packt books and eBooks.

Contributors

About the author

Helder teaches, writes and develops applications with Java and Web technologies since 1995. In 1996 he wrote one of the first books in Portuguese about HTML and JavaScript, and since then he created hundreds of presentations, tutorials, and course materials on Java, Java EE, programming tools, patterns, techniques, methodologies, HTML, CSS, JavaScript, SVG, XML and related technologies, data visualization, Arduino and Internet of Things. He holds a masters degree in Computer Science. He also has a background in the visual arts and design and has some of his artwork in permanent museum exhibits. He lives in Brazil, where he works as an independent consultant, developer and instructor and a frequent speaker at technological events.

I would like to thank my wife, Ana Carolina, and my daughter, Marina, for their patience and inspiration. Many examples created for this book use data from public portals and scientific publications, for which I thank the researchers for sharing it. Finally, I must thank the creators of D3.js and the GitHub community that maintains it, since this book would not exist without them.

About the reviewers

Erina Dmello is an assistant professor in the Computer Science department of St. Francis College, Mumbai. Her enthusiasm for web technologies inspires her to contribute to freelance JavaScript projects, especially on Node.js. She has technically reviewed the books *JavaScript JSON Essentials* and *RESTful Web API Design with Node.js* for Packt Publishing. Her research topics were SDN and IoT, which, according to her, create amazing solutions for various web technologies when used together. Nowadays, she focuses on blockchain and enjoys fiddling with its concepts in JavaScript.

I would like to sincerely thank the Packt Publishing team for providing an opportunity for me as a reviewer, and also would like to acknowledge my family for their support and love.

Santosh Viswanatham is a software developer, maker, and an open source enthusiast who prefers mountains to beaches. He works as a web developer at Gaian Solutions and previously worked at Infosys Ltd.

Santosh has been volunteering for Mozilla for the past six years as a developer evangelist and participation leader, and previously as a featured add-ons board member, and an executive member of the FSA Board. He is a tech speaker at Mozilla and speaks about his favorite web stuff, including browser extensions, WebVR, PWA, DevTools, and CSS Grid. For his contributions to Mozilla, his name is listed in the credits of every shipped Firefox browser.

When he is not glued to his computer, you will find him reading books, watching movies, and trying not to cook badly.

I would like to thank my parents and my family members, who have always been supportive of my adventures and learning. I would like to express my gratitude to my colleagues and current employer, Gaian Solutions, for always inspiring me and providing wonderful and exciting learning opportunities with which to explore myself. Finally, a big thanks to all my friends, who motivate and help me to be a better person every day.

Packt is searching for authors like you

If you're interested in becoming an author for Packt, please visit authors.packtpub.com and apply today. We have worked with thousands of developers and tech professionals, just like you, to help them share their insight with the global tech community. You can make a general application, apply for a specific hot topic that we are recruiting an author for, or submit your own idea.

Table of Contents

Preface

This book was created as a guide to help you learn and explore D3.js. Its goal is to provide a learning path so that you obtain a solid understanding of its fundamental concepts, learn to use most of its modules and functions, and gain enough experience to create your own D3 visualizations.

Fundamental concepts are explained in each chapter and then applied to larger examples in step-by-step tutorials. There are hundreds of examples you can download and run.

Code listings are used throughout the book, but most of the time they focus on a specific feature and show only a fragment of the full code. But you can always download the full listing. All the code examples used in the book are available from a public GitHub repository (see details below). You can try out all the code examples as you learn. You can also use it in any way you like since it's free and open source.

This book covers the basic and advanced features of D3. By the time you finish reading this book, having practiced with the code examples, I believe you will have a very good and solid knowledge of this library.

Who this book is for

The ideal target audience of this book includes web developers and designers, data journalists, data scientists and artists who wish to create interactive data-driven visualizations for the Web.

Basic knowledge of HTML, CSS, and JavaScript is required. No previous SVG knowledge is necessary.

What this book covers

Chapter 1, *Introduction*, introduces the D3.js JavaScript library, describing its main features and concepts, and how it drives data to transform documents.

Chapter 2, *Technical Fundamentals*, covers fundamental standard web technologies used by D3, such as SVG, JavaScript (ES 2015) data structures, HTML Canvas and standard data formats such as JSON and CSV.

Chapter 3, *Quick Start*, includes a practical step-by-step introduction to D3.js exploring a bit of everything that will be covered later in this book. You will learn how to bind data to HTML and SVG elements and create a simple horizontal bar chart, with interactive features and animated transitions.

Chapter 4, *Data Binding*, covers most of the *d3-selection* module and describes data-binding strategies in detail using several examples. In this chapter, you will also learn how to load and parse external data files and use the *d3-dsv* and *d3-fetch* modules.

Chapter 5, *Manipulating Data and Formatting*, explores tools from six modules: *d3-array, d3-collection, d3-random, d3-interpolate, d3-format* and *d3-time-format*. You will learn how to transform data arrays, create new collections using grouping, generate random distributions, histograms, interpolate all kinds of data and format dates and numbers according to a locale.

Chapter 6, *Scales, Axes, and Colors*, shows how to create and configure axes for Cartesian or radial grids (*d3-axis*), and scales that convert data from an input domain to an output range (*d3-scale*). Color schemes, interpolators, and color manipulation tools are also covered in examples that use the *d3-color, d3-scale-chromatic* and *d3-interpolate* modules.

Chapter 7, *Shape and Layout Generators*, explores the generator functions from the d3-shape module used to create some classic chart types such as line, pie and stacked area charts. In this chapter, you will learn how to generate the data to render these charts in SVG or Canvas.

Chapter 8, *Animation and Interactivity*, covers event handling, transitions and interactive behaviors in D3, exploring the *d3-transition, d3-ease,* and *d3-timer* modules. This chapter also explores zoom (*d3-zoom*), drag (*d3-drag*) and brush (*d3-brush*).

Chapter 9, *Visualizing Hierarchical Data*, shows how to prepare a data set so that it can be used to represent a hierarchy, using nesting techniques and tools provided by the *d3-hierarchy* module to represent hierarchical data as a tree, dendogram (cluster), treemap, circle pack or partition.

Chapter 10, *Visualizing Flows and Networks*, explores the visualization of network and flow diagrams. You will learn how to create a Sankey diagram (*d3-sankey*), a chord/ribbon diagram (*d3-chord*), and a force-directed animation simulation (*d3-force*).

Chapter 11, *Visualizing Geographical Data*, explores the *d3-geo* module, which contains tools for operations in planar and spherical geometry. You will learn how to render interactive map visualizations using D3.js using different geographical projections.

To get the most out of this book

The best way to learn a library than coding with it. If you follow the examples in this book and try them out as you read, I'm sure that your learning path will be quick. Also, make sure you set up your browser's development environment as indicated in *Chapter 1: Introduction*, so that you can catch programming errors quickly. Errors are a great learning resource, as long as you can find them and fix them. If you get stuck, you can always rely on the code examples.

When writing this book, I did my best to provide the most accurate information possible. All code listings were tested, and additional efforts were made to guarantee that all code examples are properly referenced in the book and work as expected. This book is based on D3.js version 5.9.2. I expect that the code examples should continue working with any 5.x version but there is a small possibility that some code may not work as expected if you are using a later version.

Download the example code files

You can download the example code files for this book from your account at `www.packt.com`. If you purchased this book elsewhere, you can visit `www.packt.com/support` and register to have the files emailed directly to you.

You can download the code files by following these steps:

1. Log in or register at `www.packt.com`.
2. Select the **SUPPORT** tab.
3. Click on **Code Downloads & Errata**.
4. Enter the name of the book in the **Search** box and follow the onscreen instructions.

Once the file is downloaded, please make sure that you unzip or extract the folder using the latest version of:

- WinRAR/7-Zip for Windows
- Zipeg/iZip/UnRarX for Mac
- 7-Zip/PeaZip for Linux

The code bundle for the book is also hosted on GitHub at `https://github.com/PacktPublishing/Learn-D3.js`. In case there's an update to the code, it will be updated on the existing GitHub repository.

We also have other code bundles from our rich catalog of books and videos available at https://github.com/PacktPublishing/. Check them out!

Download the color images

We also provide a PDF file that has color images of the screenshots/diagrams used in this book. You can download it here:
http://www.packtpub.com/sites/default/files/downloads/9781838645571_ColorImages.pdf.

Conventions used

There are a number of text conventions used throughout this book.

CodeInText: Indicates code words in text, database table names, folder names, filenames, file extensions, pathnames, dummy URLs, user input, and Twitter handles. Here is an example: "This code applies the .red class to each element of a collection."

A block of code is set as follows:

```
<p>See results in console log.</p>
<div id="section">
    <p>Paragraph 1</p>
    <p>Paragraph 2</p>
</div>
<p>Paragraph 3</p>
```

Any command-line input or output is written as follows:

```
npm install d3
```

Warnings or important notes appear like this.

Tips and tricks appear like this.

Get in touch

Feedback from our readers is always welcome.

General feedback: If you have questions about any aspect of this book, mention the book title in the subject of your message and email us at customercare@packtpub.com.

Errata: Although we have taken every care to ensure the accuracy of our content, mistakes do happen. If you have found a mistake in this book, we would be grateful if you would report this to us. Please visit www.packt.com/submit-errata, selecting your book, clicking on the Errata Submission Form link, and entering the details.

Piracy: If you come across any illegal copies of our works in any form on the Internet, we would be grateful if you would provide us with the location address or website name. Please contact us at copyright@packt.com with a link to the material.

If you are interested in becoming an author: If there is a topic that you have expertise in and you are interested in either writing or contributing to a book, please visit authors.packtpub.com.

Reviews

Please leave a review. Once you have read and used this book, why not leave a review on the site that you purchased it from? Potential readers can then see and use your unbiased opinion to make purchase decisions, we at Packt can understand what you think about our products, and our authors can see your feedback on their book. Thank you!

For more information about Packt, please visit packt.com.

Introduction 1

This chapter will introduce the D3.js (data-driven document) JavaScript library, describing its main features, explaining how it works, and showing how it drives data to transform documents. D3 contains an integrated set of tools that will help you bind data to graphical elements in a web page, in order to create scatterplots, bar charts, line charts, hierarchical node-link diagrams, networks, chord diagrams, sunburst charts, thematic geographic maps, or any interactive data visualization you can imagine. But D3.js is also a huge library, and is famous for having a steep learning curve. The goal of this book is to provide a learning path that will help you grasp its fundamental data-driven concepts and become familiar with its essential API.

In this chapter, you will learn how to set up your environment and test it by creating a very simple D3 application. It also includes a general overview of D3's architecture, describing the relationships between its many modules and a brief description of each one.

This chapter will outline the following topics:

- D3 data-driven documents
- Using D3
- Modules microlibraries

D3 data-driven documents

D3, which stands for d*ata-driven documents,* is an open source JavaScript library used to create interactive web-based data visualizations. It provides a mechanism that connects arbitrary data to document elements, allowing their appearance and behavior to be driven by the data. Created by Mike Bostock, Jeff Heer, and Vadim Ogievetsky in 2001, it's currently used in hundreds of thousands of websites and is one of the most popular JavaScript data visualization libraries in the world.

If you have ever used interactive data applications from large news web portals such as *The New York Times, The Washington Post,* or *The Guardian,* there is a great probability that it was a D3 application. You may have also used one of the many charting libraries that are based on D3.

D3.js is also free and open source. You can use it in any project, commercial or not. Its source code is distributed in GitHub and is maintained by an active community of developers worldwide.

What is D3?

Yes, D3 is a JavaScript library, but no, D3 is not a charting library. There are no ready-to-use templates to create bar, pie, or line charts, for example. To create one of these charts, you have to draw all the lines, curves, and rectangles yourself using open standards such as SVG or HTML Canvas. D3, however, will do most of the hard work for you. It's not trivial to use pure SVG to draw a bar chart; you need to scale data values so they fit in the chart, then calculate where to place each bar, and finally, set the coordinates of each rectangle before drawing it. Using D3, starting with an array of data, you can render all the bars with half a dozen chained commands in a single line of code.

D3 is a data visualization library. There are layout generators for pie charts that compute angles, which you can then use to draw arcs for the slices. There are functions that take a flat object array and turn it into a hierarchically linked object structure with coordinates for each node. You can use that data to draw circles at each coordinate point and draw lines between two nodes, rendering a tree. But you can also use the data differently, it's up to you. D3 doesn't restrict your creativity in any way. It doesn't tie you to a proprietary framework. Everything is based on open web standards.

D3 is also not only a data visualization library. Visualization is provided by HTML, CSS, or SVG. D3 focuses on the data. It's actually a collection of integrated JavaScript tools for manipulating the data structures necessary to create data visualizations. The core of the library is a fluent API used to select and manipulate the DOM. It replaces the DOM and libraries such as JQuery. It includes the data-driven mechanism that gives D3 its name, allowing you to bind arbitrary data to DOM elements, and then perform style and attribute transformations based on that data. This API is also used to bind and dispatch events, and to generate animated transitions.

D3 also includes tools to load and parse different data formats, such as JSON and CSV, perform general data manipulation on objects and arrays; generate data sequences and random numbers, perform interpolation and locale formatting. The actual data visualization parts contain layout generators, scales, axis generators, map projections, shape generators, color schemes, and other tools that are applied to previously selected DOM nodes and data.

How does it work?

A simplified view of D3's architecture is illustrated as follows. As implied by the name of the library, it's the data that drives the documents that display D3 visualizations. By adding, changing, and removing data, you directly affect the way your chart appears on the screen:

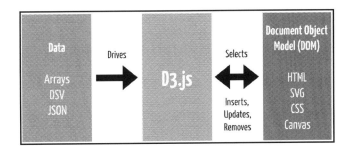

D3.js architecture

Data is usually provided as a JavaScript array, either generated locally or loaded from an external file. A typical D3.js script uses CSS selectors to select HTML or SVG elements and binds them to individual data items, removing, updating, or appending graphical elements automatically, when necessary.

You use CSS selectors to select one or more elements to create what D3 calls a selection object, which can then be used to apply styling and change the attributes of the selected elements. Binding an array to a selection object will map each data item to an element in the selection. These data items can be accessed in callback functions used in methods that set values for styles, attributes, and transforms.

You can also declare a selection of elements that don't exist in the DOM. Binding this selection to a data array will automatically create one element for each data item. You can then use the data to provide content, styles, and attributes for the new elements.

D3 also keeps data and their elements in sync. When updating with a smaller dataset, elements in excess are placed in a separate array, so you can remove them. If the dataset grows, existing elements are updated and missing elements are created and appended to fit the available data.

Using D3

All that you need to start using D3 can be found at d3js.org where you can download and install the library as a single JavaScript file, a collection of standalone microlibraries, a CDN link, or an NPM installation script. The site also includes the official documentation, which covers the library in great detail, with hundreds of tutorials for beginners and advanced users, and thousands of online examples.

The D3 site is a great place to start because you can try out several examples of data visualizations created with D3. Just click on any hexagon and it will lead you to a page showing a D3 application and its source code. Most are published in GitHub and published using the *Bl.ocks* platform (bl.ocks.org), which is a huge portfolio based on GitHub source code. Newer projects use the *Observable* platform (observablehq.com), which contains interactive tutorials where you can edit the code and see changes in real time. These platforms are very popular among the D3 community. Many of these tutorials were designed by creators and major contributors of the D3 library, such as Mike Bostock, Jason Davies, and Philippe Riviere.

Take some time to explore these examples and see what you can create using D3.

The D3.js website is a showcase of the many different data visualizations you can create using this library

Environment setup

You don't need a sophisticated development environment to use D3. If you already develop Web applications using npm, you can install it with:

```
npm install d3
```

You can also add the **d3.js** file to a local folder after downloading the full library (default bundle) as a ZIP from the official website. Then you can import it to your HTML file using the <script> tag and a local relative path; for example (for the minified version):

```
<script src="js/d3/d3.v5.min.js"></script>
```

If you have a permanent web connection, it's probably simpler to use a CDN link:

```
<script src="https://d3js.org/d3.v5.min.js"></script>
```

For very simple applications that don't load external files, you can simply open the page in your browser from the file system. It's better to load the page using a web server. If you are using a code editor, it may already have a launch configuration or plugin that always starts a web server when you choose to load a page. You can also install a simple web server using npm, by using the following command:

```
npm install http-server -g
```

The preceding command will install it globally. Then, you can move to the directory where your files are located and simply type the following:

```
http-server
```

Then you can load your files from http://localhost:8080.

You can also develop D3 using online code editors, such as *CodePen* (codepen.io) or *JSFiddle* (jsfiddle.net). It's also a great way to share your code.

Hello, world

Let's create a simple D3-powered data-driven visualization to test your configuration. Create a new HTML file in your development environment and import the D3 library, or import it into any HTML page using the <script> tag as shown in the last section. Then add an <svg> and a <script> block inside your page's <body> as follows:

```
<body>
    <svg id="chart" width="600" height="200"></svg>
    <script>
    </script>
</body>
```

Now add the following array inside the <script> block:

```
const array = [100, 200, 300, 350, 375, 400, 500];
```

We will use that array to generate a series of dots. Type in the following code (you can ignore the comments), which consists of a series of chained commands:

```
d3.select("#chart")       // selects the svg element by id (like JQuery)
  .selectAll("circle")    // declares the elements we would like to create
  .data([100])            // sets the data to drive the creation of the
                          // elements
  .enter()                // creates a selection to add elements per
                          // data item
  .append("circle")       // appends an element of this type to each
```

```
                        // data item
.attr("r", 10)          // sets "r" attribute
.attr("cy", 100)        // sets "cy" attribute
.attr("cx", d => d)     // sets "cx" attribute (same as function(d) {
                        // return d; }
```

If your configuration is working correctly, when you load the page containing this code in a browser, you should see a single dot on the screen:

A dot on a screen created with D3. Code: HelloWorld/1-intro-d3.html

If you inspect the dot with your browser's JavaScript development tools, you will notice that the following code was generated inside the SVG:

```
<svg width="600" height="200">
    <circle r="10" cy="100" cx="100"></circle>
</svg>
```

The preceding JavaScript code selects the `<svg>` element from the page and then selects all `<circle>` elements inside it. But there aren't any, so the selection is empty. The next line, however, contains a `data()` command with a one-element array: `[100]`. The `enter()` command binds the data to the selection creating a selection of `<circle>` placeholders the same size as the data array. In this case, it will only contain one placeholder. Finally, the `append()` command, called in the context of this selection, appends a `<circle>` element to it, making it a child of the `<svg>` element.

The last three commands set attribute values and the last one takes a function and returns the element received by the function, which is used as the attribute's value. This element is the value `100` that was stored in the array passed to the `data()` command.

The code is available in the `HelloWorld/1-intro-d3.html` file from the GitHub repository for this chapter.

Now let's make some changes. Replace the `[100]` in the `data()` command with `array`. It will now reference the seven-element array we created before:

```
.data(array)
```

Run the page again. What happened? Consider the following screenshot:

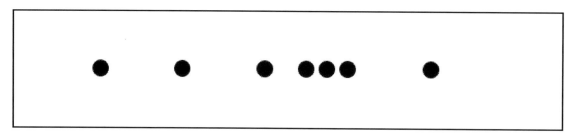

Several dots added to the screen with positions driven by the data. Code: HelloWorld/2-binding.html

Now there are seven dots on the screen; the same number of dots as the data array. And each dot is positioned at a different horizontal position (which was defined by the `cx` property of the `<circle>`) that is set using values from the data array. We used the data array to drive the position of each circle.

Now skip a line and add this code after the selection (see `HelloWorld/3-update.html`):

```
setTimeout(function() {
    d3.select("#chart").selectAll("circle")
        .data([50, 75, 125, 225, 325, 425, 450])
            .attr("r", 5)
            .attr("cx", d => d)
            .style("fill", "red")
}, 2000)
```

This code will run two seconds after the page loads and shows the circles in the positions defined by the first chain of commands. The function inside it selects the `#chart` SVG element again, and then all the circles inside it. But this time, these circles do exist. The `data()` command binds a new data array to the selection. No `enter()` command is called because there aren't any elements to be added.

The `attr()` commands are used to the circle's attributes. Only two `attr()` commands were called in the preceding code because we are only changing two attributes: the *radius* of the circle, and the *position*, which will now obtain its value from the new array. Besides that, we also used `style()` to change the color of the dots. If you run this file, two seconds later, the dots shrink, move to the left and become red:

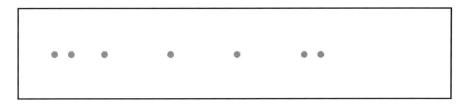

The dots changed color. size. and position after an update. Code: HelloWorld/3-update.html

One very nice feature of D3 is how simple it is to animate transitions. You just need to chain a `transition()` command before the attributes and styles that changed. The default transition takes a quarter of a second. Let's make it a little longer by configuring duration. Add the following line between the `data()` command and the first `attr()`, to add a one-second transition during the data update:

```
.transition().duration(1000)
```

Your page body should now look like this (see `HelloWorld/4-transition.html`):

```
<body>
<svg id="chart" width="600" height="200"></svg>
<script>
    const array = [100, 200, 300, 350, 375, 400, 500];

    d3.select("#chart")
            .selectAll("circle")
            .data(array)
            .enter()
            .append("circle")
            .attr("r", "10")
            .attr("cy", 100)
            .attr("cx", d => d)

    setTimeout(function() {
        d3.select("#chart").selectAll("circle")
            .data([50, 75, 125, 225, 325, 425, 450])
            .transition().duration(1000)
            .attr("r", 5)
            .attr("cx", d => d)
            .style("fill", "red")
    }, 2000)
</script>
</body>
```

Now, after two seconds, the dots will spend another second changing color, shrinking, and moving to the left. Congratulations! You created a full D3 application, complete with data updates and transitions.

Debugging D3

Although you don't need a full frontend modular development environment to create visualizations with D3.js, you still need a good debugger. Every browser comes with development tools that allow you to navigate a static page structure and generated DOM elements, and a console where you can interact in real time with the data used by the JavaScript engine in the real time.

The most important tool is the *JavaScript console,* where you will see any error messages. It's very common to get a blank page when you expected something else and to not have a clue on why your code doesn't work as expected. Sometimes it's just a comma you forgot, or the internet is down and some file was not loaded. If you have the JavaScript console open while you run your page, it will instantly tell you what's going on. It's also a good idea to use an editor with line numbering since most error messages inform the lines where the problem occurred:

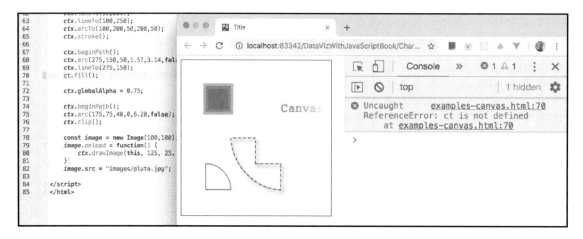

Debugging JavaScript with the JavaScript console

You can open the developer tools as a frame in your browser or as a separate window. Following are the menu paths for the JavaScript console in latest versions of the three most popular browsers:

- **Chrome: View | Developer | JavaScript Console**
- **Firefox: Tools | Web Developer | Web Console**
- **Safari: Develop | Show Error Console**

Many code fragments and examples can be tested by simply typing them in the JavaScript console. The console's context is the currently loaded page. You will be able to access the functions of any JavaScript library file that was loaded with the `<script>` tag, and any global variables declared in `<script></script>` blocks, so you can also use the console to experiment with D3. The console is a great way to learn D3 since you can run functions in real time and immediately see the results they produce. You can try out many code examples in this book using the JavaScript console.

Modules (microlibraries)

You don't have to always load the entire D3 library. D3 is a modular library, so if you are only using some D3 features, you can include only the parts that you are using. The minified default bundle is about 240 KB in size, but you may be able to create your chart using as little as 13 KB if you don't need many modules. An animated interactive bar chart, complete with tooltips, transitions, colors, and SVG graphics can be created with less than 24 KB loading just the following two modules:

```
<script src="https://d3js.org/d3-selection.v1.min.js"></script>
<script src="https://d3js.org/d3-transition.v1.min.js"></script>
```

But if you need axes, maps, and other features, you will require more modules and dependencies. In this case, either use the default bundle, or set up a development environment where you can install each module using *npm*, since it automatically includes any dependencies. For production, you can generate and export a custom bundle using a packing tool such as *Rollup*. To install any module using *npm*, use the following:

```
npm install module-name
```

For the examples in this chapter (and most of the book) we will import D3 using the `<script>` tag with the CDN URL to the default bundle.

Even if you always use the default *d3.js* bundle, you should be aware of the modules it contains, and of the modules that are not part of the default bundle, because they need to be imported separately in case you require their functions. All the official documentation is also organized per module, and knowledge of the modular structure will allow you to tune the performance of your D3 application, in case you decide to create a custom bundle. Modules have their own versioning systems. You might need to load a module separately if you wish to use a feature included in a new major version, not yet included in the default bundle.

The following diagram shows the modules available in D3.js version 5, indicating direct dependencies (transitive dependencies are not shown). For example, if you need to use a function from the *d3-scale* module, you should import all the direct dependencies: (*d3-array, d3-time-format, d3-collection, d3-format, d3-interpolate*) and the transitive ones:(*d3-time and d3-color*). In this case, you should either use `npm` or import the default bundle.

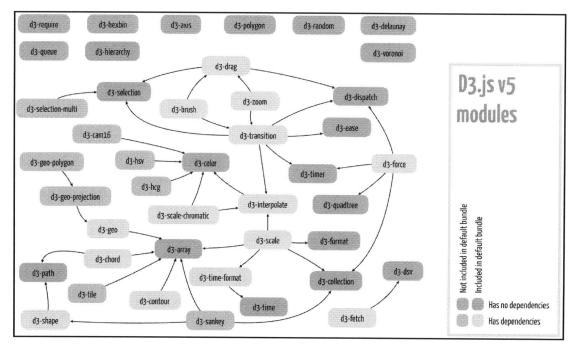

Modules (microlibraries) available in D3.js v5 showing direct dependencies. The orange and yellow libraries are included as part of the default bundle. The other libraries (pink and purple) have to be explicitly imported

The following tables contain a quick reference of all modules available in the current version, classified according to their purpose. In this book, we will be using functions from almost all of them.

Data manipulation

The following modules listed are used to generate, manipulate, transform, parse, and format data, in the form of numbers, text, arrays, objects, and files. They are all included in the default *d3.js* bundle:

Module	Bundled (d3v5)	Description
d3-array	Yes	Several array utilities that extend the basic ES6 functions, optimized for use with datasets. Dependencies: *none*.
d3-collection	Yes	Maps and sets optimized for use with datasets; functions for object collections and nesting data. Dependencies: *none*.
d3-random	Yes	Random number generators. Dependencies: *none*.
d3-dsv	Yes	Parser functions for delimiter-separated data. Dependencies: *none*.
d3-interpolate	Yes	Several functions for interpolating numbers, colors, strings, and so on. Dependencies: *d3-color*.
d3-scale	Yes	Generator functions to map data dimensions to graphical dimensions. Dependencies: *d3-array, d3-collection, d3-format, d3-interpolate, d3-time-format, d3-time*.
d3-time	Yes	API for operations with time (intervals, ranges, and so on). Dependencies: *none*.
d3-format	Yes	Locale-sensitive methods for number formatting. Dependencies: *none*.
d3-time-format	Yes	Locale-sensitive methods for date/time formatting. Dependencies: *d3-time*.

Modules with methods for manipulating, transforming, parsing, and formatting data

Document manipulation

These are core modules in D3 used to select and manipulate HTML or SVG elements by providing a concise API to the DOM. With these modules, you can select and filter elements (using CSS selectors), create elements, append, insert, or remove from the DOM tree, add attributes and contents, change styles or classes, connect event handlers, and join data. Practically any D3 application uses at least *d3-selection*.

Module	Bundled (d3v5)	Description
d3-selection	Yes	Contains the essential DOM API for selection and manipulation of DOM elements. Dependencies: *none*.
d3-selection-multi	No	Adds optional support for setting multiple attributes, styles, or properties in selections and transitions using an object syntax. Dependencies: *d3-selection, d3-transition*.

Modules with functions for selecting and manipulating graphical elements using the DOM

Interactivity and animation

The modules listed in the following table are used in dynamic visualizations when updating data, zooming, dragging, selecting and clicking charts and maps.

Module	Bundled (d3v5)	Description
d3-transition	Yes	Methods to configure the transition applied to a selection. Dependencies: *d3-interpolate, d3-ease, d3-dispatch, d3-selection, d3-timer, d3-color*.
d3-ease	Yes	Easing functions for animations. Dependencies: *none*.
d3-zoom	Yes	Apply transforms in HTML, SVG, or Canvas using mouse or touch. Also includes support for programmatic transforms. Dependencies: *d3-dispatch, d3-drag, d3-interpolate, d3-selection, d3-transition*.
d3-drag	Yes	Drag and drop SVG, HTML, or Canvas using mouse or touch. Dependencies: *d3-dispatch, d3-selection*.
d3-brush	Yes	Selects a one or two-dimensional region for detailing using the mouse or touch. Dependencies: *d3-dispatch, d3-drag, d3-interpolate, d3-selection, d3-transition*.

d3-quadtree	Yes	Partitions two-dimensional space recursively into squares. Used to calculate regions for brushing and zooming. Dependencies: *none*.
d3-timer	Yes	A queue for managing concurrent animations. Dependencies: *none*.
d3-dispatch	Yes	Mechanism for event dispatching to named callbacks. Dependencies: *none*.

Modules with methods for event handling and dispatching, animations, and interactions

Colors

The following table lists modules that contain representations for machine-friendly and human-friendly color spaces and color schemes.

Module	Bundled (d3v5)	Description
d3-color	Yes	Support for several color spaces. Supports RGB, HSL, Cubehelix, Lab (CIELAB), and HCL (CIELCH). Dependencies: *none*.
d3-scale-chromatic	Yes	Sequential, diverging, and categorical color schemes and palettes. Dependencies: *d3-color, d3-interpolate*.
d3-hsv	No	Support for the HSV color space. Dependencies: *d3-color*.
d3-hcg	No	Support for the HCG color space. Dependencies: *d3-color*.
d3-cam16	No	Support for the CIECAM16 color space. Dependencies: *d3-color*.

Modules with methods for operations with colors spaces and schemes

Asynchronous operations and packaging

These modules are used to load files using Ajax.

Module	Bundled (d3v5)	Description
d3-fetch	Yes	Methods for fetching files asynchronously using Ajax. Also includes parsing methods for several data formats. Dependencies: *d3-dsv*.
d3-queue	No	Supports queueing of concurrent asynchronous requests. Dependencies: *none*. This module is deprecated in favor of ES6 promises.
d3-require	No	Supports AMD for loading modules and dependencies. Dependencies: *none*.

Modules for Ajax operations and module packaging

2D geometry

The following modules listed contain a complete two-dimensional graphical API that can be used to create any type of visualization, from simple line, area, or pie charts to arbitrary paths and shapes.

Module	Bundled (d3v5)	Description
d3-shape	Yes	Generators and utility functions to create and manipulate arcs, curves, lines, areas, stacks, curves, pie charts, symbols, and links in SVG or Canvas. Dependencies: *d3-path*.
d3-axis	Yes	Generates SVG axes. Dependencies: *none*.
d3-path	Yes	A Canvas API that generates SVG paths (which can be rendered as a Canvas or SVG). Dependencies: *none*.
d3-polygon	Yes	Utility functions for two-dimensional polygons. Dependencies: *none*.

Modules with methods for primitive geometric SVG operations and generators for shape-based charts

Spherical geometry and geographic maps

The following table lists modules that are used to display information in geographic maps. They contain methods for spherical trigonometry, geographic projections, and other utilities.

Module	Bundled (d3v5)	Description
d3-geo	Yes	Generators for geographic paths and standard projections, spherical shapes, and trigonometric functions, transforms, streams, and other utilities. Dependencies: *d3-array*.
d3-contour	Yes	Creates contour polygons, which are commonly used for geographical density, bathymetry, or relief maps. Dependencies: *d3-array*.
d3-geo-projection	No	Additional projections for d3-geo. Dependencies: *d3-geo, d3-array*.
d3-geo-polygon	No	Several utility functions for spherical polygons. Dependencies: *d3-geo, d3-array, d3-geo-projection*.

Modules with methods for displaying data from geographical information systems (GIS)

Layouts

The following modules listed, include generator functions, utilities, and algorithms to create visualizations for complex relationships such as node-link hierarchies, graphs, trees, networks, flow diagrams, tiles, and Voronoi diagrams.

Module	Bundled (d3v5)	Description
d3-hierarchy	Yes	Generator functions for hierarchic layouts such as node-link, adjacency, and enclosure diagrams. Functions create stratifications, clusters, trees, dendrograms, treemaps, circle packs, and partitions. Dependencies: *none*.
d3-force	Yes	Implementation of a force simulation (uses the Stormer-Verlet method), used for interactive visualizations of graphs, networks, and hierarchies. Dependencies: *d3-collection, d3-dispatch, d3-quadtree, d3-timer*.
d3-chord	Yes	Generator function and utilities for creating chord flow diagrams. Dependencies: *d3-array, d3-path*.

d3-sankey	No	Generator function and utilities for creating Sankey flow diagrams. Dependencies: *d3-array, d3-collection, d3-shape.*
d3-tile	No	A layout for raster image-based tiles, normally used for displaying tiles of geographic maps behind a vector layer. Dependencies: *d3-array.*
d3-hexbin	No	Generator function and utilities for creating scatterplots of hexagonal bins, useful for color-encoded heatmaps. Dependencies: *none.*
d3-voronoi	Yes	Generator functions and utilities for creating Voronoi diagrams (nature-like diagrams that show regions in a plane that are nearest to a point). Dependencies: *none.*
d3-delaunay	No	Compute the Delaunay triangulation of a set of points; a simpler and faster method to create Voronoi diagrams. Dependencies: *none.*

Modules containing algorithms and generator functions for graphical layouts

Summary

This chapter provided a general introduction to the D3.js library, describing its architecture, modules, and showing how to set up a small D3 application that, although very simple, demonstrated one of the central paradigms in D3, which is driving the appearance of a visualization using arbitrary data.

The next chapter will consist of reference topics that cover fundamental technologies used by D3, such as SVG (an introductory tutorial), JavaScript (mostly a review of the fundamental data structures in ES 2015), and Canvas (a short reference). There is also a short section on data formats. If you are comfortable with all these topics, or if you want to start using D3 right away, you can skip them now and proceed to straight Chapter 3, *Quick Start.*

References

- D3.js documentation: d3js.org
- D3.js API reference: github.com/d3/d3/blob/master/API.md
- D3.js module repository: github.com/d3
- D3.js gallery: github.com/d3/d3/wiki/Gallery
- D3.js wiki: github.com/d3/d3/wiki
- Bl.ocks portfolios: bl.ocks.org
- Observable notebooks: observablehq.com

Technical Fundamentals

2

This chapter covers fundamental standard web technologies used by D3: SVG, JavaScript (ES 2015), HTML Canvas and standard data formats such as JSON and CSV. It is intended as a general reference to these topics.

Most data visualizations created with D3.js generate SVG graphics. Good knowledge of SVG is important to make the most of D3, but you only really need to know the basics. It's enough to know how to create simple shapes such as rectangles, circles, lines, and their attributes and styles. It's also useful to understand how to apply transforms, such as translate, scale and rotate. This chapter includes a quick refresher on SVG that covers these essential topics and a bit more, since the more SVG you know, the more graphical resources you will have to create data visualizations using D3.

All the code examples in this book use ES 2015 (ES6) JavaScript. You should have a working knowledge of at least ES5 JavaScript to be able to follow the code examples. This chapter provides a short description of the main ES6 features used in the code, as well as a brief review of the structures used to store data in JavaScript, such as strings, objects, arrays, maps, sets, and functions, including a list of the methods used to manipulate strings and arrays.

D3 uses SVG to generate most graphics, but it can also generate graphics in Canvas contexts. This is usually used for performance optimizations, but it's also a bridge to the integration with other contexts such as WebGL. This chapter contains a short reference of the main methods available in the Canvas 2D context and a Canvas version of the examples previously shown in SVG.

Outline of this chapter:

- Introduction to SVG
- Essential JavaScript data structures
- HTML Canvas
- Data formats

Scalable Vector Graphics (SVG)

SVG stands for *Scalable Vector Graphics*. It's an XML-based image format that describes graphics using geometrical attributes. Unlike HTML5 Canvas, which is another standard for vector graphics, SVG primitives are made of individual XML elements described using tags and attributes. It is also object-based and provides a DOM, which allows CSS styling, dynamic shape creation and manipulation, and coordinate transforms using JavaScript or CSS.

To control SVG elements with D3 you should understand basic SVG syntax and rules, how a document is structured, how each element is rendered, the effects caused by attributes and styles, as well as nesting and transformation rules.

All the code used in this section is available in the *SVG/* folder, from the GitHub repository for this chapter. You can see the results simply loading the pages in your browser.

SVG graphics context (viewport)

When SVG is embedded in HTML it creates a *viewport*: a default graphics context similar to the context created by Canvas. To create the viewport, all you need is to add an empty `<svg/>` tag inside your `<body>`. Since this is an HTML tag, you can style it with standard HTML CSS and set its size using `width` and `height` attributes (you can alternatively use CSS properties), as follows:

```
<style>
    svg {
        border: solid 1px lightgray;
        background-color: hsla(240,100%,50%,0.2)
    }
</style>
<body>
<h2>SVG viewport</h2>
    <svg width="600" height="300"></svg>
</body>
```

The following screenshot contains the result of the code above and the default coordinate system used by SVG, which starts on the upper-left corner of the viewport. You can change the orientation, scale and other aspects of the coordinate system configuring the `viewBox` attribute (see end of this section).

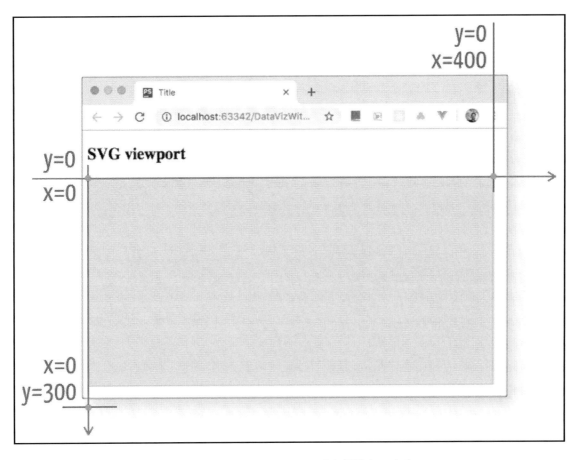

The SVG viewport embedded in an HTML page. Code: SVG/1-viewport.html.

You can also create an SVG element using the DOM API, or D3, which is much simpler. The result is identical (see `SVG-with-D3/1-viewport.html`):

```
<body>
    <script>
        d3.select("body").append("svg").attr("width", 400).attr("height",
300);
    </script>
</body>
```

Shapes

Shapes are positioned in the viewport using x and y coordinates. They described by XML tags like <rect>, <circle>, <ellipse>, <path>, <polygon> and others. You create SVG graphics by placing these tags inside the <svg> element. Each supports attributes that configure their position in the viewport, and specific properties for each shape, such as radii, vertices or dimensions.

A circle can be drawn in SVG using the <circle> element and at least the **r** attribute (radius). If you don't provide any other attributes, you will only see the lower-right quarter of the circle, since the default coordinates for its center will be (0,0).

You can place a circle anywhere, inside or outside the visible viewport, by providing explicit values for the cx and cy attributes, as shown above. Unlike CSS, SVG does not declare units. The values are expressed in absolute numbers and default to pixels (but you can change this). The following SVG places circles of different radii in different positions in the viewport.

```
<svg width="400" height="300">
    <circle r="25"></circle>
    <circle cx="250" cy="200" r="50"></circle>
    <circle cx="50"  cy="50"  r="20"></circle>
    <circle cx="400" cy="300" r="50"></circle>
</svg>
```

The result is shown in the following image:

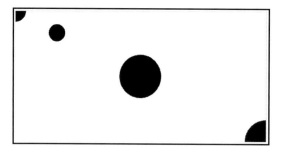

Drawing circles in the SVG coordinate system. Code: SVG/2-circle.html

You can obtain the same result using DOM or D3, as shown in the following code (see SVG-with-D3/2- circle.html):

```
<script>
    const svg = d3.select("body")
                    .append("svg")
```

```
            .attr("width", 400)
            .attr("height", 300);

    svg.append("circle").attr("r", 25);
    svg.append("circle").attr("cx", 250).attr("cy", 200).attr("r", 50);
    svg.append("circle").attr("cx", 50).attr("cy", 50).attr("r", 20);
    svg.append("circle").attr("cx", 400).attr("cy", 300).attr("r", 50);
</script>
```

Of course, this code could be much smaller if we had used D3's data-binding features or even standard JavaScript loops, but code duplication was maintained so you can compare it to the XML version. The `SVG-with-D3/` folder contains D3 examples like this for all the SVG XML code examples described in this section.

Fills and strokes

Shapes have default black fill colors and transparent stroke borders, unless you assign different color strings to the SVG attributes (or CSS properties) `fill` and `stroke`.

In the following SVG, three straight lines were drawn using the mandatory `x1/y1` and `x2/y2` attributes for `<line>` elements. They would be invisible it the `stroke` attribute wasn't present. A `stroke-width` has a default value of 1.

```
<svg width="400" height="300">
    <line x2="400" stroke="red"  stroke-width="5"/>
    <line y2="150" stroke="blue" stroke-width="5"/>
    <line x2="200" y2="150" stroke="black" stroke-width="1"/>
</svg>
```

As before, missing attributes use zero as default, so `x1` and `y1` are zero in all lines, which makes them all start at the top-left corner, which is the origin. Only half of the strokes for the red and blue lines are visible, since they are centered in the borders of the SVG:

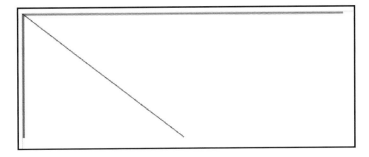

Drawing lines with different stroke colors and stroke-widths. Code SVG/3-lines-stroke.html

Besides width and color, you can control many other stroke attributes, such as transparency (`stroke-opacity`), dash arrays (`stroke-dasharray`), line caps (`stroke-linecap`) and others (see `SVG/5-rect-stroke.html`). If you only want to stroke a closed shape, you need to either redefine its fill to none, or set fill-opacity to zero, since closed shapes have opaque black fills by default.

SVG styling with CSS

You can also specify style rules using SVG CSS properties, which have the same names as the attributes. CSS properties, however, have precedence over XML attributes. Declaring a style with the same name as an attribute will override it. If you add the following style declaration in the `<style>` block of your page, the width of all lines will change to 20 pixels:

```
line {
    stroke-width: 20px; /* Overrides attr */
}
```

This result is shown below. The lines at the edges *seem* thinner because half of their width is outside the context:

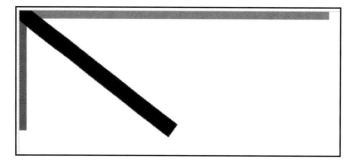

Overriding XML style attributes with CSS. Code: SVG/4-lines-css.html.

You can also apply CSS `class` and `style` attributes to different SVG objects. For example, consider the following CSS class declarations:

```
.reds {
    fill: red;
}
.semitr {
    fill-opacity: 0.5;
}
```

Since the following rectangles each belong to one or more of these classes, they will inherit the style properties declared for each class:

```
<svg width="600" height="200">
    <rect x="50" y="50" width="90" height="90" class="semitr"/>
    <rect x="200" y="50" width="175" height="100" rx="40" ry="40"
          class="reds semitr"/>
    <rect x="450" y="25" width="100" height="150" class="reds"/>
</svg>
```

One class applies the red fill, the other applies 50% transparency. The rectangle in the middle belongs to both classes, so it's both red and semi-transparent, as follows:

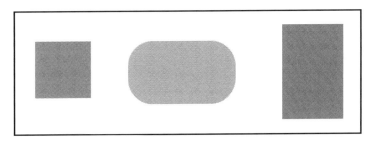

Applying CSS classes to SVG rectangles. Code: SVG/6-rect-css-class.html.

The `<rect>` element, used to create the squares and rectangles above, require two attributes: `height` and `width`, and can positioned in the viewport with `x` and `y`. Rounded corners can be applied by setting the `rx` and `ry` properties (radius of the corner).

Although HTML and SVG share many CSS properties, many, such as `fill` or `stroke`, only exist in SVG. In HTML you would use `background-color` and `color`, which don't work in SVG. When embedded in an HTML page, the `<svg>` element represents a graphics context in the HTML namespace, so to fill it you need to use `background-color`. But any elements declared *inside* the `<svg>` element, such as `<rect>`, are part of the SVG namespace where the CSS `background-color` property doesn't exist, and you need to use `fill`.

Transparency

When objects overlap in SVG, the code order determines which element will appear over the other. Preceding siblings are always overlapped by siblings that are declared after them. The CSS z-index property doesn't work in SVG. To move an object to the front, you have to modify the DOM tree.

You can see through objects that overlap by changing their transparency. You can apply opacity levels to fills and strokes separately, using `fill-opacity or stroke-opacity`, or for the entire object using `opacity`. All attributes require a value between **0** (invisible) and **1** (opaque). An alternative, which achieves the same result, is to use the alpha component in `rgba` or `hsla` color strings (for example, 'rgba(255, 0, 0, 0.5)').

The three squares below apply different transparency parameters on fills and strokes:

```
<rect x="50" y="50" height="100" width="100" rx="10" ry="10"
      stroke="red" stroke-width="10" fill-opacity="0"/>
<rect x="75" y="75" height="100" width="100" rx="10" ry="10"
      fill="gray" stroke="black" stroke-width="10" fill-opacity=".7"/>
<rect x="100" y="100" height="100" width="100" rx="10" ry="10"
      fill="yellow" stroke="blue" stroke-width="10" stroke-opacity=".6"/>
```

In the following code, two thin vertical rectangles appear behind a wide horizontal rectangle, and two other vertical rectangles appear in front of it:

```
<rect x="300" y="50" height="150" width="25"/>
<rect x="400" y="50" height="150" width="25" fill-opacity=".5"/>

<rect x="250" y="100" height="50" width="300"
      fill="red" stroke="orange" stroke-width="10" stroke-opacity=".5" />

<rect x="350" y="50" height="150" width="25"/>
<rect x="450" y="50" height="150" width="25" fill-opacity=".5"/>
```

The following image shows the result:

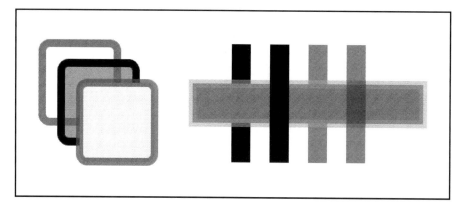

Drawing rectangles with different fills, strokes and transparency. Code: 7-rect-opacity.html.

Ellipses

Ellipses have a center in `cx` and `cy` like circles, but also have two radii, which are set with `rx` and `ry`. The following code creates three ellipses in different positions.

```
<svg width="600" height="300">
    <ellipse cx="150" cy="100" rx="150" ry="100"
             fill="yellow" fill-opacity="0.5"
             stroke="blue" stroke-width="1" stroke-dasharray="5 5"/>
    <ellipse cx="400" cy="150" rx="75" ry="125"
             fill="red" fill-opacity="0.2"
             stroke="red" stroke-width="5" stroke-opacity="0.5"/>
    <ellipse cx="400" cy="250" rx="150" ry="40"
             fill="black" fill-opacity="0"
             stroke="green" stroke-width="20" stroke-opacity="0.2" />
</svg>
```

The preceding code produces the following result:

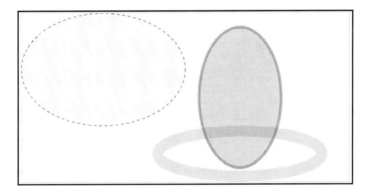

Ellipses created with SVG. Code: SVG/8-ellipse.html.

Polygons and polylines

Polygons (`<polygon>`) and polylines (`<polyline>`) render closed or open shapes using straight lines specified by a list of vertices passed in the `points` attribute. The only difference between them is that polygons close the shape. To close a polyline you need to repeat the initial coordinates. They also have a **fill-rule** attribute that controls the winding order, and determines if a hole will be drawn inside the shape when an outline crosses with itself.

The following code creates two polygons. The second one has a `fill-rule` that will reveal a hole:

```
<svg width="600" height="300">
  <polygon
      points="150,150 50,150 100,20 150,50 200,200 50,200 20,154 48,82
32,20"
      fill="blue"/>
  <polygon
      points="450,150 350,150 400,20 450,50 500,200 350,200 320,154 348,82
332,20"
      fill="red" fill-rule="evenodd"/>
</svg>
```

The result is shown as follows:

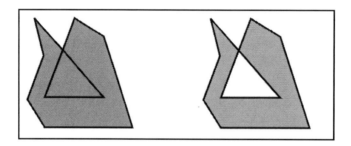

Polygons created with SVG. The second polygon uses fill-rule="even-odd" and reveals a hole.
Code: SVG/10-polygon.

Paths

With paths you can draw open and closed shapes mixing lines, curves and arcs using a compact drawing language in the d attribute of the `<path>` element. It can be used to create arbitrary paths mixing straight lines and curves:

```
<path d="M100,200 C200,50 300,100 300,200 L400,250 500,100"
      fill="yellow"
      stroke="red"
      stroke-width="4"/>
```

Don't worry about all those numbers and letters in the d attribute. It's the most important part of the path, but it can always be generated for you. Most of the shape generators you will use in D3 to create lines, pie slices and other arbitrary shapes generate path strings that you can use in the d attribute.

The simple `<path>` above renders the image below (the dots are added separately and show the control points):

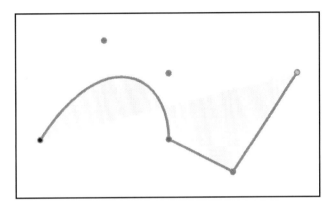

A curve described by a <path> element. Code: SVG/11-path-line.html.

Text

Unlike HTML, you can't simply insert text inside any element. You have to create text objects using the `<text>` element with text contents. You can position text using x and y attributes, but you must remember that y is actually the *baseline* (default). If y is zero or not present, only the parts of the text that extend below the baseline will be visible inside the graphics context.

This example places both text and a rectangle in the same position:

```
<rect x="0" y="0" height="36" width="200"/>
<text font-size="36" x="0" y="0" fill="lightgray">ghijklmnop</text>
```

The following illustration shows the result, at left. Note that only the parts of the text that extend below the baseline actually appear over the rectangle. The other two examples show text with a different baseline alignment: `alignment-baseline="middle"` and `alignment-baseline="hanging"`.

Drawing text in SVG and the baseline. Code: SVG/14-text.html.

You can also align text horizontally using the `text-anchor` attribute. The following illustration describes properties and values used to align text horizontally or vertically. If you intend to rotate text relative to its position, these parameters will affect the result.

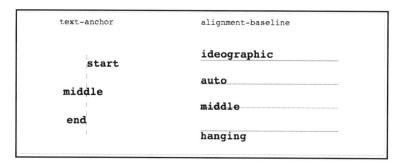

Properties for aligning text. Code: SVG/15-text-align.html.

It's best to configure baselines and alignments in CSS instead of using XML attributes.

If your text spans multiple lines, you can use the `<tspan>` element inside `<text>` to move words or letters to positions relative to the parent `<text>` element (see SVG/16-tspan.html).

Group containers

You can group several shapes in SVG with the `<g>` element. It's analogous to a `<div>` in HTML. This is an invisible element and it's positioned at the center of coordinates. CSS properties applied to a group affect all the objects it contains. You can also apply matrix transforms to groups to move, rotate and scale all its contents. A group container can also contain other group containers.

In the following SVG, circles and ellipses are in a group, and rectangles are in another. The color of the elements is each group is declared in CSS, and they are translated, scaled and rotated together:

```
<style>
    svg { border: solid 1px lightgray; }
    #bars { fill: red; }
    #round { opacity: .7; fill: blue; }
</style>
<body>
<svg width="600" height="300">
    <g id="bars" transform="translate(0,100) rotate(-90, 100, 150)">
        <rect x="100" y="150" height="20" width="150"></rect>
```

```
        <rect x="100" y="180" height="20" width="100"></rect>
        <rect x="100" y="210" height="20" width="200"></rect>
    </g>
    <g id="round" transform="translate(200,100) scale(.3) ">
        <circle cx="280" cy="220" r="50"></circle>
        <ellipse cx="150" cy="90" rx="80" ry="50"></ellipse>
    </g>
</svg>
</body>
```

The following screenshot shows the groups before applying any transforms or styles to their groups (at left), and after applying the transforms and styles from the code above (right):

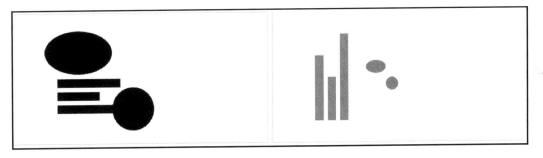

Applying styles and transforms to grouped shapes. Code: SVG/18-groups-transforms.html.

Styles applied directly to individual elements in the groups have precedence and will override any styles declared at the group level. Positions of elements inside the group are always relative to the coordinate system introduced by any transforms applied to the group.

Reusing objects: use and defs

An SVG can have a <defs> header containing shapes, groups and other elements that will not be displayed. Filters, clipping masks, gradients and reusable shapes are usually declared in the <defs> header. You will need to assign an id to each element you wish to reuse later.

The element can be displayed later declaring the <use> element outside the <defs> block. This element references an existing element by **id** using standard *xlink* notation.

In the following example, two rectangles are created at 0.0. Since they are in the `<defs>` header, they will not be displayed. Each is previously configured with colors, dimensions and position. Outside the `<defs>` header, each element is displayed twice when referenced by each `<use>` element, translating each one to a different position:

```
<svg width="600" height="200">
    <defs>
        <rect id="black"  x="0" y="0" width="20" height="20"
            fill="rgb(64,32,32)" />
        <rect id="white" x="0" y="0" width="20" height="20"
            fill="rgb(255,225,200)" />
    </defs>
    <g transform="translate(10,10) scale(3)">
        <use xlink:href="#black" />
        <use xlink:href="#white" transform="translate(20)"/>
        <use xlink:href="#white" transform="translate(0,20)"/>
        <use xlink:href="#black"  transform="translate(20,20)"/>
    </g>
</svg>
```

The result is shown in the following image. You can use this to create a checkerboard.

Reusing objects with <defs> and <use>. Code: SVG/22-defs-use.html.

You will rarely use `<defs>` and `<use>` in D3, but placing reusable code such as clipping masks, filters and gradients in a `<defs>` header is good practice.

Matrix transforms

Matrix transforms are used to scale, translate, skew or rotate any shape or group, or the entire SVG viewport. Transform commands are functions used in the `transform` XML attribute, in text notation and separated by spaces, for example:

```
<g transform="translate(100,100) scale(3) rotate(-90)"> ... </g>
```

The order is significant. If you call `scale(.5)` and then `rotate(90)`, the result will be different if you call them in the reverse order.

In `translate()`, `scale()` and `skew()`, the first parameter is an x coordinate value, and the second, if present, the y coordinate. In `rotate()`, the first parameter is an angle in degrees, and the next two parameters, if present, are the coordinates of the center of rotation (if not present, the object will rotate around 0,0 and may disappear from the viewport if the angle is big enough). Flipping an object can be achieved by scaling with negative values for x and/or y.

The `translate()` transform can be used to move groups to different positions. In this case, the x and y coordinates of each object should be considered relative to the group. When creating objects that will be treated as a group, you might also choose to position all objects at the origin (not declaring any x or y coordinates, or use only values relative to the group) to later control the position using `translate()`

You can also apply transforms as CSS styles, but you will need to use explicit units for degrees and distances, for example:

```
<g style="transform: translate(100px,100px) scale(3) rotate(-90deg)"> ...
</g>
```

Consider the following SVG drawing of a pair of SVG coordinate axes:

```
<g id="coords">
    <line x1="10" y1="10" x2="200" y2="10" />
    <line x1="10" y1="10" x2="10" y2="150" />
    <text x="200" y="20">x</text>
    <text x="20" y="150">y</text>
</g>
```

The following images show the results of applying translate, rotate/scale and skew to an image of the SVG coordinate axes, compared to the original object(in black):

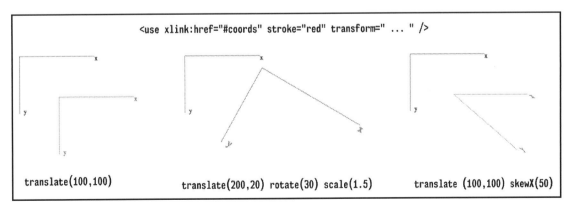

Applying transforms to shapes and groups. Code: SVG/19-translate.html. 20-scale-rotate.html. 21-skew.html.

Configuring the SVG viewport

You can configure the SVG viewport by changing the values in the `viewBox` attribute (which can also be used in some reusable SVG elements). The `viewBox` attribute contains four numbers separated by spaces. The first two are the center of coordinates, which default to **0 0**, and the last two are the `width` and `height`, which default to the declared or default height and width of the SVG. If present, this attribute can move the viewport to a different position and its scale.

For example, if you have an SVG with dimensions 400x300, the default viewport will be `0 0 400 300`. If you declare a `viewBox` of `0 0 800 600`, all the objects inside the SVG will be displayed at half the size, since a declared value of 100 is no longer 1/4 of the viewport's width, but 1/8. You can also change the origin of coordinates. For example, you can move it to the center of the SVG and position elements with negative coordinates if you have a `viewBox` of `-200 -150 400 300` (remember that the coordinates start at the top-left corner).

Consider the following SVG:

```
<svg width="400" height="300" viewBox="...">
    <line x1="0" y1="-300" x2="0" y2="300"/>
    <line y1="0" x1="-400" y2="0" x2="400"/>
    <rect x="-130" y="-130" height="20" width="200" fill="red"/>
    <rect x="130" y="-130" height="200" width="20" fill="blue"/>
    <rect x="0" y="100" height="20" width="200" fill="green"/>
    <rect x="-130" y="-65" height="200" width="20" fill="orange"/>
</svg>
```

The images below show what would appear on the screen, depending on the values you include for the `viewBox` attribute. The first one is the default.

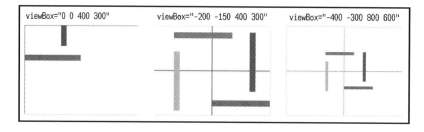

Scaling and translating the viewport with the viewBox attribute.
Code: SVG/26-viewBox-default.html. 28-viewBox-center.html. 28-viewBox-scaled.html

You may rarely use `viewBox` with D3 since you can achieve the same results using matrix transforms, which are simpler.

Gradients

Linear gradients are created perpendicular to a line, so it requires the same attributes as the `<line>` element. Radial gradients use circle attributes. Gradients should declare at least one child `<stop>` with a non-zero `offset` and `stop-color` different than black, since the default color is black and the default offset is zero. Typically, gradients declare two or more stop colors. Gradients are used used as a `fill` or `stroke` value. They are usually defined in `<defs>` with an `id` that can be referenced later using `url(#id)`.

The following SVG code declares two gradients and applies one of them to a square, and the other to a circle:

```
<svg width="600" height="300">
    <defs>
        <linearGradient x2="1" id="rainbow">
            <stop offset="0" stop-color="rgb(255,0,0)" />
            <stop offset="0.25" stop-color="rgb(255,255,64)" />
            <stop offset="0.5" stop-color="rgb(64,255,64)" />
            <stop offset="0.75" stop-color="rgb(64,64,255)" />
            <stop offset="1" stop-color="rgb(128,0,255)" />
        </linearGradient>
        <radialGradient cx="0.35" cy="0.35" r="1" id="glow">
            <stop offset="0" stop-color="rgb(255,255,255)" />
            <stop offset="0.5" stop-color="rgb(0,128,255)" />
            <stop offset="1" stop-color="rgb(128,0,255)" />
        </radialGradient>
    </defs>

    <rect x="0" y="0" width="200" height="200"
        fill="url(#rainbow)" transform="translate(50,50)"/>
    <circle cx="100" cy="100" r="100"
        fill="url(#glow)" transform="translate(300,50)"/>
</svg>
```

The result is shown in the following screenshot:

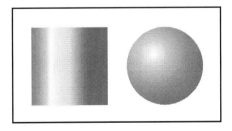

Linear and radial gradients. Code: SVG/23-gradient.html.

Clipping

A clipping mask is created with any shape declared inside the `<clipPath>` element. This is usually done in `<defs>`, setting an id for the clipping mask that can be referenced in the object that should be clipped, using `url(#id)` inside a `clip-path` attribute, as shown below:

```
<svg width="425" height="425">
    <defs>
        <clipPath id="poly">
            <circle r="139" cx="200" cy="199"/>
        </clipPath>
    </defs>

    <!-- Clipped image -->
    <image x="25" y="25"
           height="350" width="350"
           xlink:href="../Data/Images/pluto.jpg"
           clip-path="url(#poly)"/>
</svg>
```

The following SVG screenshots show the circular clipping mask above applied to an image. The SVG at left shows the original image and the clipped image is shown at right.

Clipping an image in SVG. Code: SVG/24-clipping.html.

Filters

SVG filters can be applied to any shapes, text or images. They are usually created in the <defs> header with an id that can be referenced via url(#id) using the filter attribute. The <filter> element can contain several different filter types and you can also create composite filters. The following example creates two different configurations for the <feGaussianBlur>filter, applied to a text element and a circle:

```
<svg width="600" height="300">
    <defs>
        <filter id="filter1">
            <feGaussianBlur stdDeviation="7" />
        </filter>
        <filter id="filter2" x="-100" y="-100" height="200" width="200">
            <feGaussianBlur stdDeviation="0,5" in="SourceGraphic" />
        </filter>
    </defs>
    <text id="text" font-size="40" fill="black" x="50" y="60"
        filter="url(#filter2)">Do you need glasses?</text>

    <g id="stardot" transform="translate(100,25) scale(0.5)">
        <polygon id="star" points="250,0 400,500 0,200 500,200 100,500"
            fill="red" fill-rule="evenodd"/>
        <circle  id="circ" cx="250" cy="283" r="75" fill="blue"
            filter="url(#filter1)" />
    </g>
</svg>
```

The result is shown as follows:

A Gaussian blur filter applied to different shapes. Code: SVG/25-filter.html.

An SVG example

The following code uses several SVG elements described in this section to draw some shapes, shadows, gradients and text:

```
<svg width="300" height="300">
    <defs>
        <filter id="shadow">
            <feDropShadow style="flood-color: green"
                          dx="5" dy="5" stdDeviation="3"/>
        </filter>
        <linearGradient id="grad" x1="0" y1="0" x2="100%" y2="0">
            <stop offset="0%" stop-color="magenta"/>
            <stop offset="100%" stop-color="yellow"/>
        </linearGradient>
        <clipPath id="circle">
            <circle r="40" cx="175" cy="75"/>
        </clipPath>
    </defs>

    <!-- rectangle -->
    <rect x="50" y="50" height="50" width="50"
          fill="red"
          stroke="blue"
          stroke-width="10"
          stroke-opacity="0.5"/>

    <!-- dashed shape -->
    <path id="path1"
          d="M150,200 L150,150 L100,150 C100,200 150,250 200,250 L200,200
Z"
          stroke-dasharray="5 2 1 2"
          stroke-width="2"
          stroke="blue"
          fill="none"
          style="filter:url(#shadow)"/>

    <!-- gray quarter-circle -->
    <path d="M0,0 L0,-100 A100,100 0 0,0 -100,0 L0,0 Z"
          transform="translate(100,250) scale(0.5) "
          stroke="red"
          stroke-opacity=".5"
          stroke-width="4"
          fill-opacity=".2"/>

    <text fill="url(#grad)" font-size="20" x="200" y="100">
        Scalable
        <tspan dy="20" x="200">Vector</tspan>
```

```
        <tspan dy="20" x="200">Graphics</tspan>
    </text>

    <image x="125" y="25" height="100" width="100"
        xlink:href="../Data/Images/pluto.jpg"
        clip-path="url(#circle)"
        opacity="0.75"/>

    <!-- raindow half-circle -->
    <path d="M100,200 C100,100 250,100 250,200"
        transform="scale(0.6) rotate(180,295,225) "
        fill="url(#grad)"/>
</svg>
```

Compare this code and the following image it generates it with an identical image created using D3 (`SVG-with-D3/29-example.html`) and HTML Canvas (`Canvas/1-canvas-svg-compare.html`):

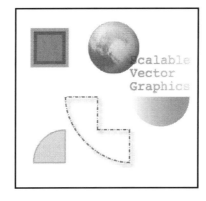

An image created using SVG. Code: SVG/29-example.html.

Essential Javascript data structures

Data used as sources for visualizations is usually organized in some kind of structure. The most common structures are probably *lists* (arrays) and *tables* (maps), stored in some standard data format. When using data from external sources, you usually need to clean it up, removing unnecessary values, simplifying its structure, applying bounds, etc. After that you can parse it and finally store it locally in a JavaScript array or JavaScript object that can be used by the chart.

Once your data is stored in a JavaScript data structure, you can transform it further applying mathematical operations on the stored values. It's useful to have a good knowledge of the main data structures used in JavaScript: arrays, objects, functions, strings, maps and sets, since your data will probably be in one of these formats. This section describes each one of them briefly and lists useful functions, methods and operators you can use to manipulate data stored in these formats.

You don't have to be a JavaScript guru. You just need to know essential JavaScript. How to declare constants and variables, perform basic mathematical, Boolean, string and attribution operations, call and create functions, manipulate objects and arrays, instantiate objects, use control structures, write callbacks, sort and filter datasets, use basic string manipulation functions, math functions, dates, generate random numbers.

If these are trivial tasks for you, you can skip this section.

All client-side applications, such as interactive Web graphics, depend on browser support. This book assumes that your audience uses browsers that support HTML5 Canvas and ES2015 (which include all modern browsers). All JavaScript examples use ES2015 syntax, which include:

- `const` and `let` instead of `var`
- Arrow functions (`d => d` instead of `function(d) { return d; }`) where appropriate
- Spread operators `[... iterable]`, chained expressions, maps, sets and promises
- Template strings literals, defined using backticks
- Iterable collections, such as maps and sets

Arrays

The main data structure you will use to store one-dimensional data is the JavaScript *array*. An array of values is all you need to make a simple bar chart or line chart. With an array of arrays you can create a scatterplot.

Arrays are created by declaring a list of items within brackets, or simply a pair of opening-closing brackets if you want to start with an empty array:

```
const colors = ["red", "blue", "green"];
const geocoords = [27.2345, 34.9937];
const numbers = [1,2,3,4,5,6];
const empty = [];
```

You can then access the items of an array using an *array index*, which starts counting from zero:

```
const blue = colors[1];
const latitude = geocoords[0];
```

Each array has a `length` property that returns the number of elements. It's very useful to iterate using the array index:

```
for(let i = 0; i < colors.length; i++) {
    console.log(colors[i]);
}
```

You can also loop over the elements of an array using the `of` operator (introduced in ES2015), when you don't need the index:

```
for(let color of colors) {
    console.log(color);
}
```

And you can use the `forEach()` method, which runs a function for each element and also allows access to the *index, item* and *array* inside the function:

```
colors.forEach(function(i, color, colors) {
    console.log((i+1) + ": " + color);
}
```

Multi-dimensional arrays are created in JavaScript as arrays of arrays:

```
const points = [[200,300], [150,100], [100,300]];
```

You can retrieve individual items like this:

```
const firstPoint = points[0];
const middleX = points[1][0];
```

JavaScript provides many ways to extract and insert data into an array. It's usually recommended to use methods whenever possible. The following table lists useful methods you can use on arrays. Some modify the array; others return new arrays and other types. The examples provided use the `colors` and `numbers` arrays as declared above. Try them out using your browser's JavaScript console:

Method	Description	Example

push (*item*)	Modifies the array adding an item to the end.	`colors.push("yellow");`
		`// ["red", "blue", "green",`
		`"yellow"];`

pop ()	Modifies the array, removing and returning the last item.	`const green = colors.pop();` `// ["red", "blue"];`

unshift (*item*)	Modifies the array inserting an item at the beginning.	`colors.unshift("yellow");`
		`// ["yellow", "red", "blue",`
		`"green"];`

shift ()	Modifies the array, removing and returning the first item.	`const red = colors.shift();` `// ["blue", "green"];`

splice (*p, n, i*)	Modifies the array, starting at position *p*. Can be used to delete items, insert or replace.	`const s = numbers.splice(2,3);`
		`// s = [3,4,5]`
		`// numbers = [1,2,6]`

reverse ()	Modifies the array, reversing its order.	`numbers.reverse();` `// [6,5,4,3,2,1]`
sort ()	Modifies the array sorting by string order (if no args) or by a comparator function.	`numbers.sort((a,b) => b - a);` `// numbers = [6,5,4,3,2,1]`
slice (*b,e*)	Returns a shallow copy of the array between *b* and *e*.	`const mid = numbers.slice(2,4)` `// mid = [3,4]`

filter (*function*)	Returns new array where the elements pass the test implemented by the function.	`const even = numbers.filter(n =>`
		`n%2==0);`
		`// [2,4,6]`

find (*function*)	Returns the first element that satisfies the test function	`const two = numbers.find(n =>`
		`n%2==0);`
		`// 2`

indexOf (*item*)	Returns the index of the first occurrence of item in the array.	`const n = numbers.indexOf(3);` `// 4`
includes (*item*)	Returns *true* if an array contains item among its entries.	`const n = numbers.includes(3);` `// true`

`lastIndexOf (item)`	Returns the index of the last occurrence of the item in the array.	`const n =`
		`colors.lastIndexOf("blue");`
		`// 1`

`concat (other)`	Returns a new array that merges the current array with another.	`const eight =`
		`numbers.concat([7,8]);`
		`// [1,2,3,4,5,6,7,8]`

`join()`
`join (delim)`
	Returns a comma-separated string of the elements in the array (an optional delimiter may be used)	`const csv = numbers.join();`
		`// "1,2,3,4,5,6"`
		`const conc = numbers.join("");`
		`// "123456"`

`map (function)`	Returns new array with each element modified by function.	`const squares = numbers.map(n =>`
		`n*n);`
		`// [1,4,9,16,25,36]`

`reduce (function)`	Returns the result of an accumulation operation using the values in the array.	`const sum =`
		`    numbers.reduce((a, n) => a +`
		`n);`

`forEach (function)`	Executes the provided function once for each element in the array.	`const squares = [];`
		` numbers.forEach(n =>`
		`squares.push(n*n)`
		`// squares = [1,4,9,16,26,36]`

JavaScript functions for array manipulation.

Strings

Strings are primitive types in JavaScript that can be created with single quotes or double quotes. There is no difference. It's only a matter of style. ES2015 introduced two new string features: *template literals* and *multiline strings*.

Multiline strings can be created adding a backslash at the end of each line:

```
const line = "Multiline strings can be \
reated adding a backslash \
at the end of each line";
```

Template literals are strings created with *backticks*. They allow the inclusion of JavaScript expressions inside ${} placeholders. The result is concatenated as a single string.

```
const template = `The square root of 2 is ${Math.sqrt(2)}`;
```

If you need to use a special character in a string, such as a double quote in a double quoted string, or a backslash, you need to precede it with a backslash:

```
const s = "This is a backslash \\ and this is a double quote \"";
```

There are several methods for string manipulation. They all return new strings or other types. No methods modify the original strings.

Method	Description	Example
startsWith(s)	Returns *true* if string starts with the string passed as a parameter	`const s = "This is a test string"` `const r = s.startsWith("This"); //` `true`
endsWith(s)	Returns *true* if string ends with the string passed as a parameter	`const s = "This is a test string"` `const r = s.endsWith("This"); //` `false`
substring(s,e)	Returns a substring between *start* (incl.) and *end* indexes (not incl.)	`const k = "Aardvark"` `const ardva = k.substring(1,6);`
split(*regx*) split(*delim*)	Splits a string by a delimiter character or regular expression and returns an array	`const result = s.split(" ");` `// result =` `//` `["This","is","a","test","string"]`
indexOf(s)	Returns the index of the first occurrence of a substring	`const k = "Aardvark"` `const i = k.indexOf("ar"); // i = 1`
lastIndexOf(s)	Returns the index of the last occurrence of a substring	`const k = "Aardvark"` `const i = k.lastIndexOf("ar"); // i` `= 5`
charAt(*i*)	Returns char at index *i*. Also supported as *'string'[i]*	`const k = "Aardvark"` `const v = k.charAt(4);`
trim()	Removes whitespace from both ends of a string.	`const text = "  data  "` `const r = data.trim(); // r = "data"`

	Returns an array as the result of matchin a regular expression against the string.	`const k = "Aardvark"`
		`const v = k.match(/[a-f]/g);`
		`// v = ["a", "d", "a"]`

match (*regx*)		

replace (*regx,r*)
replace (*s,t*)
	Returns new string replacing match of regexp applied to the string with replacement, or all occurrences of source string with a target string.	`const k = "Aardvark"`
		`const a = p.replace(/a/gi, 'u')`
		`// a = "uurdvurk"`
		`const b = p.replace('ardv', 'ntib')`
		`// b = "Antibark"`

JavaScript functions for string manipulation

Functions

Functions are typically created in JavaScript using the `function` keyword, using one of the forms below:

```
function f() {
    console.log('function1', this);
}
const g = function(name) {
    console.log('function ' + name, this);
}
f(); // calls f
g('test'); // calls g() with a parameter
```

The `this` keyword refers to the object that owns the function. If this code runs in a browser, and this is a top-level function created in the `<script>` block, the owner is the global `window` object. Any properties accessed via this refer to that object.

A function can be placed in the scope of an object, behaving as a method. The `this` reference in the following code refers to the `obj` object and can access `this.a` and `this.b`:

```
const obj = {a: 5, b: 6}
 obj.method = function() {
     console.log('method', this)
 }
object.method()
```

Arrow functions were introduced in ES2015. They are much more compact and can lead to cleaner code, but the scope of `this` is no longer retained by the object. In the code below, it refers to the global `window` object. Code that uses `this.a` and `this.b` will not find any data in the object and will return *undefined*.

```
obj.arrow = () => console.log('arrow', this)
 object.arrow()
```

Objects

An object is an unordered collection of data. Values in an object are stored as key-value pairs. You can create an object by declaring a comma-separated list of *key:value* pairs within curly braces, or simply a pair of opening-closing curly braces if you want to start with an empty object:

```
const color = {name: "red", code: ff0000};
const empty = {};
```

Objects can contain other objects and arrays, which can also contain objects. They can also contain functions (which have access to local properties and behave as methods):

```
const city = {name: "Sao Paulo",
              location: {latitude: 23.555, longitude: 46.63},
              airports: ["SAO","CGH","GRU","VCP"]};
const circle = {
    x: 200,
    y: 100,
    r: 50,
    area: function() {
        return this.r * this.r * 3.14;
    }
}
```

A typical dataset used by a simple chart usually consists of an array of objects.

```
var array2 = [
    {continent: "Asia", areakm2: 43820000},
    {continent: "Europe", areakm2: 10180000},
    {continent: "Africa", areakm2: 30370000},
    {continent: "South America", areakm2: 17840000},
    {continent: "Oceania", areakm2: 9008500},
    {continent: "North America", areakm2=24490000}
];
```

You can access the properties of an object using the dot operator or brackets containing the key as a string. You can run its methods using the dot operator:

```
const latitude = city.location.latitude;
const oceania = array2[4].continent;
const code = color["code"];
circle.r = 100;
const area = circle.area();
```

You can also loop over the properties of an object:

```
for(let key in color) {
    console.log(key + ": " + color[key]);
}
```

Properties and functions can be added to objects. It's common to write code that declares an empty object in a global context so that operations in other contexts add data to it:

```
const map = {};
function getCoords(coords) {
    map.latitude = coords.lat;
    map.longitude = coords.lng;
}
```

Objects can also be created with a constructor. You can create an object that contains the current date/time using:

```
const now = new Date();
```

JSON is a data format based on JavaScript objects. It has the same structure as JavaScript object but the property keys have to be placed within double quotes:

```
{"name": "Sao Paulo",
        "location": {"latitude": 23.555, "longitude": 46.63},
        "airports": ["SAO","CGH","GRU","VCP"]};
```

To use a JSON string in JavaScript you have to parse it.

Maps and sets

Besides arrays, ES2015 also introduced two new data structures: `Map`, an associative array with key-value pairs easier to use than simple objects, and `Set`, which doesn't allow repeated values. Both can be transformed to and from arrays.

You can create a new `Set` object using:

```
const set = new Set();
```

And add elements to it using:

```
set.add(5);
set.add(7);
```

If you try to add elements that already exist, they won't be included in the set:

```
set.add(1);
set.add(5);    // not added
set.add(7);    // not added
console.log(set.size); // prints 3
```

You can check if a `Set` contains an element:

```
console.log(set.has(3)); // false
```

And convert a `Set` object into an array:

```
const array1 = [... set]; // spread operator
```

A `Map` can be more efficient than using an object to store key-value pairs in an associative array:

```
const map = new Map();
map.set("a", 123)
map.set("b", 456);
```

You can then retrieve the value for each `key` using `get(key)`:

```
console.log(map.get("b"))
```

Or using iterative operations and the `keys()`, `values()` and `entries()` methods:

```
for (let key of map.keys()) {
    console.log(key, map.get(key))
}

for (let [key, value] of map.entries()) {
```

```
        console.log(key, value)
    }

    map.forEach ((k, v) => console.log(k, v))
```

Maps can be converted into arrays with the spread operator or `Arrays.from()`:

```
    const array2 = [... map.values()];   // an array of values
    const array3 = Array.from(map.values()); // an array of keys
```

HTML5 Canvas

Most of your D3 applications will render graphics using SVG, but several shape generators in SVG can also generate Canvas, and you may choose to use Canvas in all or part of your application to improve performance if you have memory problems due to excessive objects created in the DOM.

This section provides a brief overview of the Canvas API, listing the methods you are most likely to use and some examples that can be compared to the ones created for SVG.

To draw using Canvas you need to create a `<canvas>` element in your page. You can do that using plain HTML:

```
    <body>
        <canvas id="canvas" width="400" height="300"></canvas>
    </body>
```

Or using D3:

```
    d3.select("body").append("canvas").attr("width", 400).attr("height", 300);
```

If you declare the Canvas element in HTML, you can reference it by its ID using the DOM or D3:

```
    const canvas = d3.select("#canvas").node(); // node() returns the DOM
    object
```

Once you have a canvas object, you obtain a 2D graphics context and start drawing:

```
    const ctx    = canvas.getContext("2d");
```

Practically all the Canvas API consists of methods and properties called from the graphics context. Before drawing, you set properties such as `font`, `fillStyle`, `strokeStyle`:

```
ctx.fillStyle = "red";
ctx.strokeStyle = "rgba(255,127,0,0.7)";
ctx.lineWidth = 10;
```

And then *fill* or *stroke* rectangles and arbitrary paths containing lines and curves. The following commands will draw a red 50x50 pixel square with a 10 pixel wide yellow semi-transparent border at position 50,50:

```
ctx.fillRect(50,50,50,50);
ctx.strokeRect(50,50,50,50);
```

You can also draw other shapes, text and images on the same canvas. The context properties will not change unless they are redefined or a previously saved context is restored.

It's a good practice to save the context to the stack before applying properties or transforms, and restore it when you are done drawing an object. This allows you to always start with a clean context:

```
ctx.save();
ctx.transform(50,60);
ctx.scale(2);
// ...
ctx.restore();
// starting with a new context
```

Some essential Canvas commands are listed in the following tables below. All commands are methods or properties of the current Canvas context.

The following table lists properties that modify the state of a Canvas:

Property or method	Description
fillStyle	Sets the color to be used in `fill()` commands.
strokeStyle	Sets the color to be used in `stroke()` commands.
lineWidth	Sets the line width to be used in `stroke()` commands.
lineCap	Sets the style of the line caps: can be *butt* (default), *round* or *square*.
textAlign	Sets the alignment for text: can be *start* (default), *center*, *end*, *left* or *right*.
textBaseline	Sets the baseline for text: can be *middle*, *hanging*, *top*, *bottom*, *ideographic* or *alphabetic* (default).

`font`	Sets the font to be used in text commands, using the compact CSS font syntax.
`globalAlpha`	Sets the global opacity (0 = transparent, 1 = opaque) for the context.

`shadowBlur,`
`shadowColor,`
`shadowOffsetX,`
`shadowOffsetY`
	Sets shadow properties. Default shadow color is transparent black. Default numeric values are zero.

`setLineDash (`*dasharray*`)`	Sets the dash array (alternating line and space lengths) for strokes.
`translate (`*x,y*`)`	Sets the current translate transform for the context.
`scale (`*x,y*`)`	Sets the current scale transform for the context.
`rotate (`*angle*`)`	Sets the current rotate transform for the context.
`save ()`	Saves the state of the current context (pushes into a stack).
`restore ()`	Restores the state of the last context that was saved (pops it from the stack).

Methods and properties that modify the state of the Canvas context

The `fillRect ()` command is typically used to clear the entire canvas before redrawing, but you can also use it to draw arbitrary rectangles. The following table lists methods you can use to draw rectangles, draw text and images:

Method	Description
`fillRect (`*x,y,w,h*`);`	Fills a rectangle. Typically used to clear the Canvas on redrawing.
`strokeRect (`*x,y,w,h*`)`	Draws a border around a rectangle.
`fillText (`*text,x,y*`);`	Fills text at position *x*, *y* (depends on current `textAlign` and `textBaseline`).
`strokeText (`*text, x, y*`);`	Draws a border around text.
`drawImage (`*image, x, y, w, h*`)`	Draws an image at *x,y* with width *w* and height *h*.

Canvas context methods used to draw rectangles. text and images

A path is a series of commands to move to points, draw lines, curves or arcs. To draw a path you need to first call `ctx.beginPath()`, then call a sequence of commands that move to points, draw lines and curves, and when you are done you can close the path (if it's a closed path) and call `fill()` and/or `stroke()` to draw it using the current styles. The following table lists several commands you can use in a path:

Method	Description
`beginPath()`	Starts a path.
`closePath()`	Closes a path.
`moveTo(x,y)`	Moves the cursor to a position in the path.
`lineTo(x,y)`	Moves the cursor to a position in the path, drawing a line along the way.
`bezierCurveTo(`*c1x,c1y,c2x,c2y,x,y*`)` `quadraticCurveTo(`*cx,cy,x,y*`)`	Draws curves with one (quadratic) or two (Bezier) control points in a path.
`arc(`*x,y,r,sa,ea*`)`	Draws an arc by specifying the center, radius, start and end angles in a path.
`arcTo(`*sx,sy,r,ex,ey*`)`	Draws an arc by specifying the coordinates of the starting point, the radius and the coordinates of the ending point.
`rect(`*x,y,w,h*`)`	Draws a rectangle in a path with coordinates of top-left corner, width and height.
`clip()`	Creates a clipping region with the shapes drawn by the path that will affect objects that are drawn afterwards.
`fill()`	Fills a path with the current color. Call this to fill the path when done.
`stroke()`	Strokes the path with the current color. Call this to stroke the path when done.

Canvas methods used to render paths

A Canvas example

The following code uses several of the methods above to draw different shapes on the same Canvas context. It draws some shapes, text, images and paths, and applies transforms, shadows, clipping and gradients. Compare it to the example shown before in SVG that draws the image (see `Canvas/1-canvas-svg-compare.html`):

```
const canvas = document.getElementById("canvas");
const ctx    = canvas.getContext("2d");

// rectangle
ctx.save(); // save default context

ctx.fillStyle = "#ff0000";
ctx.strokeStyle = "blue";
ctx.lineWidth = 10;

ctx.fillRect(50,50,50,50);

ctx.globalAlpha = 0.5;
ctx.strokeRect(50,50,50,50);

// dashed shape
ctx.restore();
ctx.save();

ctx.strokeStyle = "blue";
ctx.lineWidth = 2;
ctx.shadowBlur = 6;
ctx.shadowColor = "green";
ctx.shadowOffsetX = ctx.shadowOffsetY = 5;
ctx.setLineDash([5,2,1,2]);

ctx.beginPath();
ctx.moveTo(150,200);
ctx.lineTo(150,150);
ctx.lineTo(100,150);
ctx.bezierCurveTo(100,200,150,250,200,250);
ctx.lineTo(200,200);
ctx.closePath();
ctx.stroke();

ctx.restore();
ctx.save();

// quarter-circle
ctx.translate(100,250);
```

```
ctx.scale(0.5, 0.5);
ctx.strokeStyle = "red";
ctx.lineWidth = 4;
ctx.globalAlpha = 0.5;

ctx.beginPath();
ctx.moveTo(0,0);
ctx.lineTo(0,-100);
ctx.arcTo(-100,-100,-100,0,100);
ctx.lineTo(0,0);
ctx.stroke();

ctx.globalAlpha = 0.2;

ctx.beginPath();
ctx.arc(0,0,100,3.14,-1.57,false);
ctx.lineTo(0,0);
ctx.closePath();
ctx.fill();

ctx.restore();
ctx.save();

// text and half-circle
const text = "Canvas"
ctx.translate(250,150);
ctx.font = "24px monospace";
const textWidth = ctx.measureText(text).width;
const gradient = ctx.createLinearGradient(-50,-50,-50 + textWidth,-50);
gradient.addColorStop(0,"magenta");
gradient.addColorStop(1, "yellow");

ctx.fillStyle = gradient;
ctx.shadowColor = "transparent";

ctx.fillText(text, -45, -5);

ctx.scale(1.1, 1.1)
ctx.rotate(3.14);

ctx.beginPath();
ctx.arc(0,0,40,3.14,0,false);
ctx.fill();

ctx.restore();
ctx.save();

// image and clip
```

```
ctx.beginPath();
ctx.arc(175,75,40,0,6.28,false);
ctx.clip();

const image = new Image(100,100);
image.onload = function() {
    ctx.globalAlpha = 0.75;
    ctx.drawImage(this, 125, 25, this.width, this.height);
}
image.src = "../Data/Images/pluto.jpg";
ctx.save();
```

The following screenshot shows the image generated using Canvas (left) and an identical image generated using SVG (right):

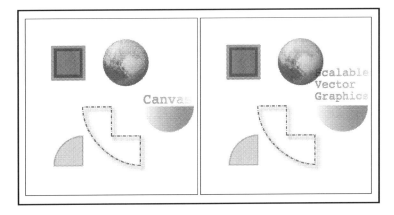

Identical images generated using Canvas (left) and SVG (right). Code: Canvas/1-canvas-svg-compare.html.

Data formats

Data used in visualizations are usually distributed in a standard format that can be shared. Even when the data is served from a database, the data is usually delivered in some standard format. Popular proprietary formats such as Excel spreadsheets are common, but most statistical data is stored or delivered in CSV, XML or JSON formats.

CSV

CSV stands for *Comma-Separated Values*. It's a very popular data format for public data. A CSV file is a text file that emulates a table. It usually contains one header row with names of the columns, and one or more data rows containing value fields. Rows are separated by line breaks, and the comma-separated fields in each row form columns. It maps perfectly to an HTML table. This is a simple CSV file containing the population and land area of seven continents (`Data/continents.csv`):

```
continent,population,areakm2
"North America",579024000,24490000
"Asia",4436224000,43820000
"Europe",738849000,10180000
"Africa",1216130000,30370000
"South America",422535000,17840000
"Oceania",39901000,9008500
"Antarctica",1106,13720000
```

There are no types in CVS. Quotes are used to contain text that might contain the delimiter. They are never necessary if the fields don't contain a comma.

CSV is also used to refer to similar files that don't use a comma as a delimiter. These files are more accurately called DSV files (*Delimiter-Separated Values*). The most common delimiters are *tabs* (TSV), *vertical bars* (|) and *semi-colons*.

CSVs may become corrupt and unreadable, but it's text and you can fix. Missing or unescaped commas are the most common problems.

You can load and parse CSV in D3 using the `d3.csv()` function.

XML

XML – eXtensible Markup Language is a very popular data format. Ajax responses from web services are usually returned as text or XML. It has standard native support in JavaScript via the **DOM (document object model)** APIs and doesn't require additional parsing. Although it is still common to find data in XML format, CSV and JSON alternatives, if available, are usually smaller and easier to work with.

This is an example of an XML file with the same data as the CSV file shown earlier (`Data/continents.xml`).

```
<continents>
    <continent>
        <name>North America</name>
```

```
        <population>579024000</population>
        <area unit="km">24490000</area>
    </continent>
    <continent>
        <name>Asia</name>
        <population>4436224000</population>
        <area unit="km">43820000</area>
    </continent>
...
    <continent>
        <name>Antarctica</name>
        <population>1106</population>
        <area>13720000</area>
    </continent>
</continents>
```

XML files can be validated if a XML Schema is available. You can extract data from a well-formed XML file with DOM, or with XPath (which is easier). There are tools in all languages to manipulate XML. XML is also very easy to generate. Its main disadvantage is verbosity and size.

You can load and parse XML in D3 using the `d3.xml()` function.

JSON

JSON stands for *JavaScript Object Notation*. It looks a lot like a JavaScript Object, but it has stricter formation rules. It's probably the easiest format to work with. It's compact and easy to parse, and it's gradually replacing XML as a preferred data format in Web Services. The data file containing continent data is shown below in JSON format (`Data/continents.json`).

```
[
    {
        "continent": "North America",
        "population": 579024000,
        "areakm2": 24490000
    },{
        "continent": "Asia",
        "population": 4436224000,
        "areakm2": 43820000
    },{
        "continent": "Europe",
        "population": 738849000,
        "areakm2": 10180000
    },{
```

```
            "continent": "Africa",
            "population": 1216130000,
            "areakm2": 30370000
    }, {
            "continent": "South America",
            "population": 422535000,
            "areakm2": 17840000
    }, {
            "continent": "Oceania",
            "population": 39901000,
            "areakm2": 9008500
    }, {
            "continent": "Antarctica",
            "population": 1106,
            "areakm2": 13720000
    }
]
```

JSON is the preferred format for data manipulation in JavaScript. There are many online tools you can use to transform CSV and XML files into JSON.

You can load and parse JSON in D3 using the d3.json() function.

Summary

This chapter covered some technology fundamentals you should know to get the most out of D3: SVG, which is the main standard used by D3 to draw graphics, ES2015 JavaScript used in all code examples (although D3 supports earlier versions as well), HTML Canvas and popular data formats.

In the next chapter, we will finally start diving deeper into D3 and create a bar chart using HTML and SVG, and also a world map, using a bit of most of the features we will cover in this book.

References

- MDN JavaScript reference: `developer.mozilla.org/bm/docs/Web/JavaScript`
- W3C HTML Canvas specification: `www.w3.org/TR/2dcontext/`
- W3C CSS Selectors specification: `www.w3.org/TR/selectors-3/`
- W3C DOM Level 3 specification: `www.w3.org/TR/2004/REC-DOM-Level-3-Core-20040407/`
- ECMA JavaScript specification: `www.ecma-international.org/ecma-262/6.0/`
- W3C SVG 1.1 specification: `www.w3.org/TR/SVG11/`

3
Quick Start

The goal of this chapter is to get you up and running with D3.js. You will learn how to use the most important modules and walk through a collection of examples that demonstrate how D3 maps data to visualizations. We will start by binding data to HTML `<div>` elements and paragraphs to create a simple horizontal bar chart, complete with labels, a color scheme, and dynamic scaling, and then bind the same data to SVG, which offers many more possibilities. You will learn how to add gradients, configure animated transitions, and handle events in this chart. Before the end of the chapter, you will even draw a world map using D3. After finishing this chapter, you should have a general working knowledge of D3 that will enable you to create simple charts with your own data.

To follow the examples in this chapter, you should set up a development environment with D3, which can be as simple as a text editor where you can edit your code, but you should view your files using a web server, since operations that use Ajax won't work with *file:* URIs. You can set up a full NPM environment for D3, as described in `Chapter 1`, *Introduction*, or simply install a Web server to run your files. Most Web development editors automatically run a Web server when you choose to view a file. If you aren't using NPM, make sure that you load the D3.js library in your HTML file. You can download the *.js* file or use CDN, as shown:

```
<script src="https://d3js.org/d3.v5.min.js"></script>
```

This book was written for D3 version 5. If you are using a later version, some examples may not work as expected.

The following topics will be covered in this chapter:

- Selecting and binding data
- Creating a bar chart with HTML
- Creating a bar chart with SVG
- Updating data visualizations
- Drawing a map with SVG

Selecting and binding data

Before we start with a step-by-step example, you should have a basic understanding of how D3 manipulates DOM elements and binds them to data sources. You already had a basic introduction to selections in the previous chapters. This section will provide some more details about selecting, appending, and removing elements.

This section will also provide an introduction to data binding, which will be necessary for the step-by-step example and will be covered in detail in Chapter 4, *Data Binding*. We will investigate what happens to an element when D3's data-driven mechanism is applied. You should try running these examples by using the files available in the GitHub repository for this chapter, or by typing the commands directly in your browser's JavaScript console. The code for this section is in the Selecting/ and Binding/ subfolders.

Selecting and appending

You don't need to use jQuery or the DOM to select and manipulate elements in a web page. If all you want to do is select elements; change styles, attributes, classes, and contents; or add and remove elements from the DOM tree; you just need to create an HTML page and include the *d3-selection* module in your page, using the following script:

```
<script src="https://d3js.org/d3-selection.v1.min.js"></script>
```

This is enough to create an entire chart, and it only takes 13 KB.

The selection methods select() and selectAll() receive a CSS selector expression and return a D3 handle for a node or a set of nodes. You can convert the D3 handle into a DOM object calling node() or nodes().

Add the following HTML to the <body> of your HTML file (or use Selecting/1-select.html):

```
<p>See results in console log.</p>
<div id="section">
    <p>Paragraph 1</p>
    <p>Paragraph 2</p>
</div>
<p>Paragraph 3</p>
```

Now you can use the JavaScript console (or a `<script>` block in your page) to type in the following code, which shows how `select()` and `selectAll()` can be used:

```
const div = d3.select("#section");       // selects element with the
                                         // "section" ID
const domDiv = div.node();               // converts the object into a
                                         // DOM node
const firstP = d3.select("p");           // selects the first <p>
                                         // in the page
const allParagraphs = d3.selectAll("p"); // selects all four <p> nodes
                                         // in the page
const allPDom = allParagraphs.nodes();   // converts selection into
                                         // DOM nodelist

const sectionParagraphs =
        d3.select("div")
                .selectAll("p");         // selects the two <p> nodes
                                         // inside <div>
```

Note that all these methods can be `chained`. A call to `select()` or `selectAll()` returns a `selection` object, which can again call `select()` or `selectAll()` to select descendants in its context.

A selection object serves as a handle to elements in your page. You can use it to change their styles, properties, attributes, classes, and contents, using methods that can receive static or dynamic values (using functions) as parameters. The following examples demonstrate some of these methods (see `Selecting/2-attributes-styles.html`):

```
div.style('border', 'solid blue 2px'); // draws blue border around <div>
firstP.classed('big', true);           // adds class '.big' to
                                            first paragraph
firstP.text('This is paragraph zero'); // replaces contents of
                                            first paragraph
allParagraphs.style('font-weight', 'bold'); // applies style to set
                                                of paragraphs

d3.select('.first') // selects first element of class '.first'
        .attr('title', 'Tooltip')               // adds an attribute
        .style('font-variant', 'small-caps')    // applies a style
        .html('This is a <b>bold</b> paragraph.'); // replaces contents
                                                       with HTML
```

Note that `attr()`, `style()`, `html()`, and `text()` methods can also be chained. They differ from `select()` and `selectAll()`, as they return the current selection without changing the context.

The `select()` method will always return only *one* object (if the selector matches more items, only the first will be returned). The `selectAll()` method returns a collection, which can be iterated with the `each()` method, which receives a callback function, which receives up to three parameters. Inside the function, `this` refers to the current DOM element, and `d3.select(this)` wraps it in a D3 selection object, which can be manipulated with selection methods, as follows:

```
sectionParagraphs.each(function(d, i) {       // i is the index
    d3.select(this).classed('red', true);
    console.log(`Paragraph ${i}: `, this); // this refers to the current
                                                          element
});
```

This code applies the class `.red` to each element of a collection. If you open the JavaScript console, it will print each element and its index (starting in zero).

You can also use selection methods to modify the DOM tree. Calling `remove()` on a D3 selection removes elements in the selection. You can call `append()` on a selection to add an element as its last child, or use `insert()` to add the new element in a position determined by a selector passed as the second argument. These methods are demonstrated as follows (see `Selecting/3-append-remove.html`):

```
d3.select("#section)        // current context is element with id #section
    .insert("p", '.first') // add a <p> before the child of class '.first'
    .append('a')            // context is now <p>; inserts an <a> in <p>
    .attr('href', 'https://d3js.org') // context is now <a>
    .text("D3 website");    // contents of the <a> element

const div = d3.select('div')              // context is first <div> in page
            .select('p:last-of-type') // context is now last <p> in
                                      // <div>
            .remove(); // context is detached <p> (parentNode is null)

div.append("p")                  // adds a new <p> as last child of
                                 // selected <div>
    .text("New paragraph");  // sets the text contents of <p>

d3.select("body")       // selects the <body> element of the page
    .insert("h1", "*")   // adds a new <h1> as the first child (before *)
    .text("New title"); // sets the text contents of <h1>

d3.select("body")
    .append("h2")        // adds a new <h2> as the last child
    .text("Footer");
```

The append() and insert() methods can also be chained, since they return the nodes they added. You just have to pay attention to the current so you don't modify or add data to the wrong elements. The remove() method returns the removed selection (a node or a set of nodes) after it's detached from the DOM (*null* parent).

D3 selections are not limited to HTML. In fact, they are most commonly applied to SVG elements, but can also be used with any embedded XML. This was a brief introduction. In Chapter 4, *Data Binding*, we will explore these methods in detail.

Binding data

D3 makes it almost trivial to bind data to DOM elements. Data binding requires calling at least two of the following four methods in the context of a selection:

- data(array) or datum(object): Receives an array or an object/value that contains data that should be mapped to DOM elements
- join(), enter() or exit(): Binds the data to DOM elements by populating an update array returned as a selection of elements that should be added or removed from the document

The exit() method returns a selection of unbound elements. After an exit(), remove() is usually called, which removes the entire selection. The enter() method returns a selection of placeholders for new elements that need to be created. After an enter(), either append() or insert() is called, which connects the elements to the DOM tree. The join() method is a magic method that replaces enter() and exit(), automatically updating, removing, or adding elements, as necessary.

Once data is connected to an element, the attributes, style, and contents of each element can be modified using the attr(), style(), text(), and html() methods that take a callback function as the second argument. This binding process is illustrated as follows:

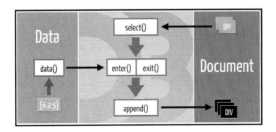

D3.js architecture showing the data-binding mechanism

Let's try an example. Create an HTML page with this code in the <body> and open it in a browser (or use Binding/1-binding.html):

```
<div id="section">
    <p>Paragraph 1</p>
    <p>Paragraph 2</p>
</div>
```

In a <script> block, create this array of numbers (or type it in your JavaScript console):

```
const numbers = [6, 2, 5, 7, 9];
```

The following code will bind each number in the array to a paragraph. The data will be copied to an internal array and can be used to change the attributes, styles, or contents of the existing paragraphs:

```
const selection = d3.select("#section")
                    .selectAll("p")
                    .data(numbers);
```

The data() method returns the current selection. The value of each item in the array is received as the first parameter of a callback function in attr(), style(), text(), and so on. The text() method is used in the following code that replaces the contents of each paragraph with the first two values of the array:

```
selection.text(d => d); // binds to existing paragraphs (update)
```

But we need more paragraphs, since we have five elements of data. By calling enter(), a new selection is created with three more placeholder nodes, containing the remaining data, but not yet mapped to any element:

```
const newSelection =
    selection.enter(); // binds data to a selection of placeholders
```

We can't just call text() on the selection yet. First, we need to append or insert those elements into the DOM tree. You call append() only once, and it will be executed three times. Now, you can use text() to print the paragraph with the data:

```
newSelection.append("p")
            .text(d => d); // binds to new paragraphs (enter)
```

Run the code by loading the page in a browser. You should see the following result:

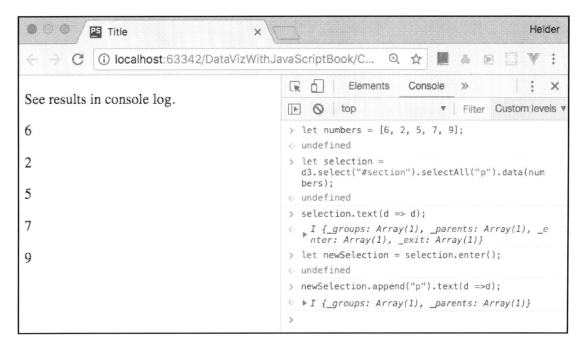

Data binding using d3-selection. Code: *Binding/1-binding.html.*

Try it again, and use the JavaScript inspector to view the structure of the DOM objects that are created in each step. This is a fundamental mechanism in D3, and it's important that you understand it well. Also, see `Binding/2-binding-new-old.html`, which attaches different text to new and existing paragraphs.

Normally, the entire selecting-binding-appending process is written as a chain of commands. The following code achieves the same result, using the same array and paragraphs (see `Binding/3-chain-text.html`):

```
d3.select("bod          // select the body element
  .select("div")        // select the first div element inside <body>
    .selectAll("p"      // select all <p> elements (there are two)
    .data(numbers)      // load the data from the numbers array
      .text(d => d)     // set contents of existing paragraphs
    .enter()            // bind remaining data to array with 3 elements
    .append("p")        // add 3 new <p> elements to end of <div>
      .text(d => d);    // set the contents of the new paragraphs
```

It's simpler (and more common, when using D3) to use JavaScript (and not HTML) to create *all* of the elements you need. After all, data is dynamic and you won't always know how many items you have to display. Most of the time, HTML is just used to provide the basic structure, such as the <body> tag, a container <div>, or <svg>.

The following code achieves the same result starting with an empty <body> tag (and the same data array). The <div> and all the <p> are created using D3 commands (see Binding/4-empty-binding.html):

```
d3.select("body")         // select the body element
    .append("div")        // append a div element inside <body>
        .selectAll("p")   // select all <p> elements (there are none)
        .data(numbers)    // load the data from the numbers array
        .enter()          // bind the data to enter array with
                          //   5 placeholders
        .append("p")      // create 5 new <p> elements and add to end of
                          // <div>
            .text(d => d); // set the contents of the new paragraphs
```

Note that even though there are no <p> elements in the page, the selectAll("p") command is still necessary, since it provides the selection context for the data binding. The selectAll() command can use any CSS selectors to locate its elements, but it should return a selection containing the same type of elements added by the append() command.

As you have seen, once you have data bound to DOM elements, you can use the data to change attributes, styles, classes, and properties, using callbacks. The callback function has a second parameter that contains the index of the data array, which is used in the following example to change the contents and style of list items:

```
d3.select("body")           // select the body element
    .append("ul")           // append an <ul> element inside <body>
        .selectAll("li")    // select all <li> elements (there are none)
        .data(numbers)      // load the data from the numbers array
        .enter()            // create an enter array with 5 objects
        .append("li")       // create 5 new <li> elements and append to <ul>
            .text(function(d, i) {
                return "Item " + (i+1) + ": " + d;
            })
            .style("font-size", function(d, i) {
                return ((i+2) * 5) + "pt";
            });
```

The result is shown in the following screenshot:

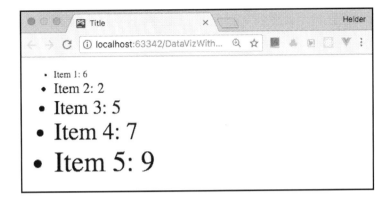

D3 used to create and style new elements from data. Code: *Binding/5-callbacks.html*.

Callback functions also have a third parameter that contains the array of elements in the selection. You might need it if you want to obtain the current element when using arrow functions, since the `this` reference in these functions doesn't refer to the current element:

```
.text( (d, i, nodes) => console.log("Current element: " + nodes[i]) );
```

You can easily reuse the preceding code with different types of data. If you have an array of objects containing values of different types, you don't need to convert it to an array of numbers. You can directly pass the entire object array to the `data()` method, and later select which properties of each object you wish to use. For example, you can use practically the same code that was shown previously to display the contents of the following array:

```
const distances = [
    {name: "Mercury", distance: 0.387},
    {name: "Venus", distance: 0.723},
    {name: "Earth", distance: 1},
    {name: "Mars", distance: 1.52},
    {name: "Jupiter", distance: 5.2},
    {name: "Saturn", distance: 9.54},
    {name: "Uranus", distance: 19.2},
    {name: "Neptune", distance: 30.1},
    {name: "Ceres", distance: 2.765},
    {name: "Pluto", distance: 39.481},
    {name: "Eris", distance: 67.67},
    {name: "Haumea", distance: 43},
    {name: "Makemake", distance: 45.346}
];
```

The object array is received by the `data()` command. Each array item is available as the first parameter of the callback, which can be used to extract the property that contains the data (see `Binding/6-object-array.html`):

```
d3.select("body")      // select the body element
   .append("ul")       // append an <ul> element inside <body>
   .selectAll("li")    // select all <li> elements (there are none)
   .data(distances)    // load the data from the numbers array
   .enter()            // bind the data to enter array with 5 placeholders
   .append("li")       // create <li> from enter selection and append
                          to <ul>
   .text(function(d, i) {
       return d.name + ": " + d.distance;
   });
```

Since D3 Version 5.8, you can replace `enter().append(element)` in simple binding operations, as shown with the `join(element)` method (see `Binding/7-join.html`):

```
d3.select("body")
   .append("ul")
   .selectAll("li")
   .data(distances)
   .join("li")  // obtains enter selection and appends 5 new <li> elements
   .text(function(d, i) {
       return d.name + ": " + d.distance;
   });
```

The preceding code will generate an HTML list with the data.

Creating a bar chart with D3 and HTML

Now that you have had a quick introduction to D3's basic data-binding mechanisms, let's create some full data visualization examples that will demonstrate the power of D3. You should know HTML very well, so we will start with a simple bar chart using HTML and CSS. Later, we will repeat the exact same procedure using SVG, the main standard used by D3 to create visualizations.

All the code for these examples is available in the GitHub repository for this chapter.

Binding data to HTML

In this example, we will draw a horizontal bar chart using HTML <div> elements. The colors and length of each bar are controlled by CSS, which we can configure using the selection.style() command. We will use the object array containing planetary distances from the last example. First, let's create a style sheet with classes for the bar-chart and each individual bar:

```
<style>
    .bar-chart {
        border: solid 1px gray; /* a gray border around the container */
        position: relative;
    }
    .bar {
        height: 20px;
        background-color: orange;
        position: absolute;
    }
</style>
```

The bars are positioned absolutely. Since each bar has an equal height (20px), we need to position each bar slightly below the previous one. This can be achieved by setting the value for the CSS top property (in pixels) so that it contains the sum of the heights of all the previous bars, plus an extra pixel to keep them slightly apart. The top property can be dynamically calculated as proportional to each entry's array index, using a callback in selection.style() (see HTML_Bar/1-bar-chart.html):

```
d3.select("body")
    .append("div").attr("class", "bar-chart")  // container div for
                                               //   the chart
      .style("height", () => distances.length * 21 + "px")  // set chart
                                                           //   height
    .selectAll("div").data(distances) // binds data
        .enter().append("div")            // appends a div for each
                                          //   data element
          .attr("class", "bar")      // these divs are the bars of
                                     //  the chart
          .style("top", (d,i) => i * 21 + "px")    // stacks bars
          .style("width", "100px")                 // fixed width
```

This prints all the bars, one on top of the other, but they all have the same static width! We need to use a callback to change the width of each individual bar. In a bar chart, the actual width should be *proportional* to the distance. A solution would be to multiply each value by 10. This will make the smallest bar three pixels wide, and the largest over 670 pixels:

```
.style("width", d => (d.distance * 10) + "px")
```

Now, the lengths of the bars are proportional to the data values. This code is in `HTML_Bar/2-bar-width.html`. The result is shown as follows:

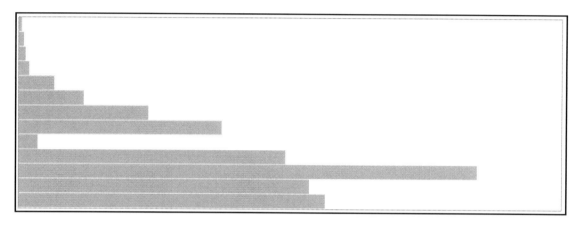

HTML bar chart with D3: Drawing DIVs and using the data to change the CSS width. Code: *HTML_Bar/2-bar-width.html*

Scales

What if a new planet is discovered that is 10 times the largest distance? The bars wouldn't fit and their widths would need to be recalculated! D3 also provides a solution for this: `scales`.

Scales are mappings between different dimensions. In our case, we have to deal with two dimensions: the dimension of the data, called the `domain`, and the dimension of the graphics context where the data will be displayed, called the `range`. Before using a scale, you have to configure its domain and range. There are several different kinds of scales in D3, including linear and logarithmic scales, with many configuration options.

A scale is created with a special generator function available in the *d3-scale* module. To use this module, you need to load several dependencies, so let's replace the `<script>` tag with the default bundle:

```
<script src="https://d3js.org/d3.v5.min.js"></script>
```

To create a scale function, you call a special generator function. A linear scale function can be created using the following:

```
const barScale = d3.scaleLinear();
```

To use the scale function you created, you pass a value as the argument and receive the converted result:

```
const result = barScale(45); // returns 45
```

This will return 45, because the scale hasn't been configured yet (the default scale is 1:1). To configure the scale, you need to call two methods to set up the domain (data dimensions) and range (graphical dimensions). Each method receives an array. For example, we can set up the domain as follows:

```
barScale.domain([0, 100]); // input domain from 0 to 100
```

This fits all the distances in our data. The range is set up in a similar fashion:

```
barScale.range([0, 600]); // output domain from 0 to 600
```

This means that zero is mapped to zero, and 100 **astronomical units** (**AU**) is mapped to 600 (pixels). Intermediate values will be interpolated.

If you now call `barScale(45)`, you will get 270. We can use the scale to convert the distances in AU to pixels, replacing the previous expression with a scale conversion (see `HTML_Bar/3-scales.html`):

```
.style("width", d => barScale(d.distance) + "px");
```

Array utilities

We chose 100 as the upper limit in our scale domain because it's larger than any of the distances in the data, but the choice was rather arbitrary. We could have chosen the largest value in the array. If you have hundreds of lines of data, you can use JavaScript array functions (see `Chapter 1`, *Introduction*) to find out the maximum value.

D3 also includes a collection of array manipulation functions that extend JavaScript's native functions. Some look similar but may be more efficient for data manipulation (for example, by ignoring `null`, `NaN`, and `undefined` values). In order to use them, you need the *d3-array* module (which is also part of the default bundle).

Here, we changed the configuration of our `barScale()` function so that it uses the largest distance from the `distances` object array as the upper value for the domain. This is achieved with by calling the `d3.max()` function, which receives an array and an accessor function for each array element, as follows:

```
const barScale = d3.scaleLinear()
                    .domain([0, d3.max(distances, d => d.distance)])
                    .range([0, 600]);
```

The `d3.max()` function will scan the `distances` array and compare the `distance` property of each object, returning the largest one.

There are many more useful functions in *d3-array*, which we will cover in the next chapter. Two of them, `d3.descending(a,b)` and `d3.ascending(a,b)`, are used to provide a sorting rule for JavaScript's native `sort()` method. We can use it to sort the array by the distance:

```
distances.sort((a,b) => d3.ascending(a.distance, b.distance));
```

See and run the code after these transformations in `HTML_Bar/4-max-sort.html`.

Adding labels

Since the `<div>` elements in HTML can contain text, you can call the `text()` method for each `<div>` and set its contents based on the data:

```
d3.select("body")
        .append("div").attr("class", "bar-chart")
        // ...
        .text(d => d.distance); // display distance in the <div>
```

With CSS, we can right-align the text and adjust the fonts. Since these styles are static and don't change with the data, instead of calling `style()` for each property, you should use a style sheet:

```
<style>
    /* ... */
    .bar {
        height: 20px;
        left: 100px;
        background-color: orange;
        position: absolute;
        text-align: right;
        padding: 0 5px;
        font-family: sans-serif;
```

```
            font-size: 9pt;
        }
    </style>
```

As a result, the labels are placed inside the bars, as follows:

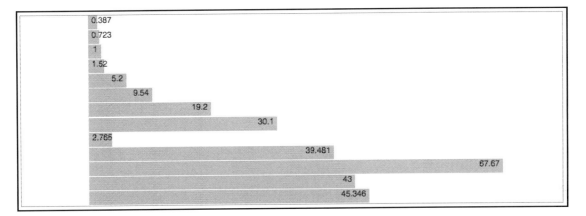

Adding labels to the bars. Code: *HTML_Bar/5-labels.html.*

More labels, formatting, and colors

Each object in our data array also contains a `name` property that can be used to label each bar. To position text outside the bar, we will need to refactor the code so that each data entry contains a container `<div>`, which will be bound to the data values. This entry `<div>` will then contain three other `<div>` elements: a category label (the name of the planet), the bar, and a value label (the distance). Classes will be used to identify each `<div>`. The following style sheet contains the static properties for these elements:

```
    <style>
        .bar-chart {         /* The container <div> for the entire chart /
            border: solid 1px gray;
            position: relative;
            width: 800px;
        }
        .entry {             /* a container <div> for each data entry /
            position: absolute;
            width: 100%;
        }
        .bar {               /* the colored rectangle */
            height: 20px;
            top: 1px;
```

```
        left: 100px;
        background-color: orange;
        position: absolute;
    }
    .label {                  /* a text label */
        padding: 4px 5px;
        font-family: sans-serif;
        font-size: 9pt;
        position: absolute;
        height: 20px;
    }
    .category {               /* the category text label at left (name) */
        text-align: right;
        width: 80px;
    }
    .value {                  /* the value text label at right (distance) */
        text-align: left;
    }
</style>
```

Since each entry <div> has three children, we need to keep a reference to its selection so that the child elements can be appended. The following code saves references for each one of the container <div> elements. The chart constant contains a selection of the root <div> element, and the entries constant contains the selection of all entry <div> elements:

```
// selects the entire chart (one node)
const chart = d3.select("body")
            .append("div").attr("class", "bar-chart")
            .style("height", distances.length * 21 + "px");

// selects each entry (a nodelist)
const entries = chart.selectAll("div").data(distances)
        .enter().append("div")
        .attr("class", "entry")
        .style("top", (d,i) => i * 21 + "px");
```

You can now use the `entries` constant to append the child elements to each entry `<div>` (see `HTML_Bar/6-entries.html`):

```
entries.append("div").attr("class", "label category")
        .text(d => d.name);

entries.append("div").attr("class", "bar")
        .style("width", d => barScale(d.distance) + "px");

entries.append("div").attr("class", "label value")
        .style("left", d => (barScale(d.distance) + 100) + "px")
        .text(d => d.distance + " AU");
```

Each `append()` shown is called once for each entry. The attributes, style, and text are set using the data that was bound to the parent container.

You can add child elements without having to break the selection chain with the `selection.each()` method, which calls a function for each entry. Inside it, you can obtain a selection to the current element using `d3.select(this)`. The following code produces the same result (see `HTML_Bar/7-entries-each.html`):

```
entries.each(function(d) {
    const entry = d3.select(this); // the current entry
    entry.append("div").attr("class", "label category")
        .text(d.name);

    entry.append("div").attr("class", "bar")
        .style("width", barScale(d.distance) + "px");

    entry.append("div").attr("class", "label value")
        .style("left", (barScale(d.distance) + 100) + "px")
        .text(d.distance + " AU");
});
```

We can improve the rendering of the labels by formatting the numbers to display only two decimal places, using the `d3.format()` generator function (from the *d3-format* module). The following code creates a function `fmt()` that can be used to format numbers:

```
const fmt = d3.format(".2f");
```

Now, we can use it to format the distances:

```
.text(d => fmt(d.distance) + " AU");
```

The final result is shown as follows:

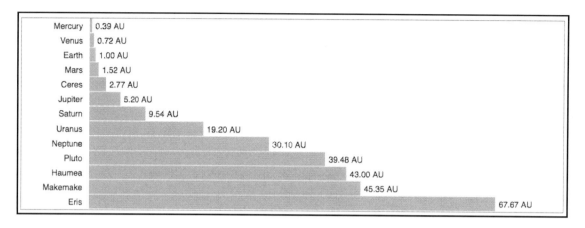

Adding category names and placing the formatted label values outside the bars. Code: *HTML_Bar/7-entries-each.html*

Changing colors

The *d3-colors* module contains functions to generate, convert, and transform colors. Passing any CSS-compatible color representation to d3.color() generates an object with methods that can be used to modify the color. The darker() and brighter() methods receive a value between 0 (no change) and 1 (maximum change) to adjust the lightness component of a color and return a hexadecimal color string.

Let's use this feature to darken the bars when the distance from the sun increases. We will need a scale that maps the distance domain to the [0-1] range, which contains the values accepted by the darker() function:

```
colorScale = d3.scaleLinear()
        .domain([0, d3.max(distances, d => d.distance)])
        .range([0,1])
```

Now, this colorScale can be used to generate different tones for the bars:

```
entry.append("div").attr("class", "bar")
    .style("width", barScale(d.distance) + "px")
    .style("background-color", d3.color('orange')
                            .darker(colorScale(d.distance)))
```

See the code in `HTML_Bar/8-colors.html`. The result is shown as follows:

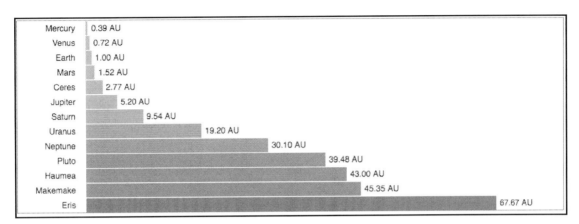

Changing bar colors with the distance. Code: *HTML_Bar/8-colors.html*

Loading external files

Usually, your data will come from external files that need to be loaded with an Ajax request. You can, of course, use jQuery or ECMAScript `fetch()` commands (and promises, if you need to load multiple files). After loading, you will also need to parse the data and convert it into JavaScript arrays and objects. D3 again provides a more efficient solution in the *d3-fetch* module: a set of convenient methods for loading and parsing files in popular formats, such as XML, JSON, or CSV. The *d3-fetch* module is also included in the default bundle.

The planetary data we used in the previous examples is actually part of a larger JSON file containing several properties for planets, asteroids, and satellites. The basic structure of this file (`Data/sol_2016.json`) is shown as follows:

```
{
    "star":{...},
    "planets":[
        {
            "id":"p1",
            "name":"Mercury",
            "diameterKm":4879,
            "semiMajorAxisAU":0.387,
            ...
        },{
            "id":"p2",
```

```
                    "name":"Venus",
                    "diameterKm":12104,
                    "semiMajorAxisAU":0.723,
                        ...
                },  ...
    }
```

You can load the data using the d3.json() function. After it loads and parses the file, it will become available in a callback provided as a parameter to the then() method (which is a JavaScript promise).

We don't need all the loaded data. The distance used in our examples is stored in the property called semiMajorAxisAU. After loading the file, we can filter the dataset to only save the semiMajorAxisAU and name properties. The following code demonstrates this. It loads the file, and it then uses the data obtained in the then() callback to loop through the planets array, adding only the chosen properties to a new object and pushing it into an array. The array is used to create an HTML list with these properties (see Loading/1-loading-json.html):

```
    d3.json("../Data/sol_2016.json")
        .then(function(data) {
            const planets = [];
            data.planets.forEach(function(obj) {
                planets.push({
                    name: obj.name,
                    distance: obj.semiMajorAxisAU
                });
                distances.push(obj.semiMajorAxisAU);
            });
            draw(planets);
        });

    function draw(distances) {
        d3.select("body").append("ol")
          .selectAll("li")
          .data(distances)
          .join("li")
          .text(d => d.name + " (" + d.distance + " AU)");
    }
```

To apply this to our chart, you just need to replace the contents of the `draw()` method shown with the entire code used in the previous examples (except for the distances array). See an example in `HTML_Bar/9-load-json.html`. As an exercise, try feeding the bar chart with a list of Jupiter's moons, instead of the planets (use `data.planets[4].satellites` to obtain the array, and the `semiMajorAxisKm` property as the distance, and `d3.format(",.0f")` to format the distance values).

Creating a bar chart with D3 and SVG

It's easy to create a horizontal bar chart in HTML. It's a bit trickier to make a vertical one, and quite challenging to create other charts, such as line charts, pie charts, and network diagrams, since HTML wasn't intended for vector graphics. While you can create such charts using HTML and CSS, it's not at all simple, nor is it recommended. You can, of course, use Canvas, but there are no graphical DOM elements to bind in Canvas. Canvas is used in D3 charts, but mostly for performance optimization. D3 works best with SVG.

The same bar chart that we created with HTML can be created with SVG. Do you think you can do it? Why not try it as an exercise before proceeding? You already learned how to use D3 and HTML, and you know the basics of SVG rectangles, attributes, and styles. That's all you need!

Most of the code is the same. You can reuse the scales, formatting function, sorting function, and JSON parsing code. The CSS will be simpler, since positioning is done in SVG. You only need to change the selection code, replacing the bar `<div>` element with `<rect>`, text label `<div>` elements with `<text>`, and container `<div>` elements with `<g>`. Remember to use `fill` (and not `background-color`) to fill the bars.

The same step-by-step files that were used in the HTML example are available for the SVG example in the `SVG_Bar/` folder. The following, final code produces exactly the same chart as the HTML version.

This is the CSS style sheet that's used. Since all positioning is done in SVG, it's much smaller:

```
<style>
    * {
        font-family: sans-serif;
    }
    .bar-chart {
        border: solid 1px gray;
        width: 800px;
    }
```

```
      .bar {
          height: 20px;
          fill: orange;
      }
      .label {
          font-size: 9pt;
      }
      .category {
          text-anchor: end;
      }
  </style>
```

The main container is the `<svg>` element, which is appended to the body, as shown in the following code snippet. We renamed the chart object `svg`:

```
// selects the entire chart (one node)
  const svg = d3.select("body")
                .append("svg").attr("class", "bar-chart")
                .style("height", distances.length * 21);
```

The containers used for each entry are `<g>` elements, which group several child elements and can have their own coordinate system configured using a *transform*. Although the `transform` property is supported in both CSS and SVG, you should use the SVG version (selected with the `attr()` method), because it considers pixel values and degrees as the default. You don't have to append `deg` or `px` to any values:

```
// selects each entry (a nodelist)
  const entries = svg.selectAll("g").data(distances)
                     .enter().append("g")
                     .attr("class", "entry")
                     .attr("transform", (d,i) => `translate(0, ${i * 21})`);
```

The `entries` are appended to the container `<g>` in the `each()` method, as follows. Compare this code to the HTML version:

```
entries.each(function(d) {
    const entry = d3.select(this); // the current entry

    entry.append("text").attr("class", "label category")
          .attr("y", 15)
          .attr("x", 90)
          .text(d.name);

    entry.append("rect").attr("class", "bar")
          .attr("x", 100)
          .attr("width", barScale(d.distance) + "px")
          .style("fill", d3.color('orange')
```

```
                              .darker(colorScale(d.distance)))

        entry.append("text").attr("class", "label value")
            .attr("y", 15)
            .attr("x", barScale(d.distance) + 105)
            .text(fmt(d.distance) + " AU");
});
```

Try the full code from `SVG_Bar/9-load-json.html`. If you open it in your browser, you will notice that the result is identical to the one you get with `HTML_Bar/9-load-json.html`. To explore more D3 features, in the next sections, we will use the SVG version of this bar chart.

Updating data visualizations

Once the data is bound to SVG elements, you can change the original data values and reflect the changes in the chart. Values can change immediately or transition smoothly. This section will provide an introduction on how to trigger data updates and configure smooth transitions using D3.

First, we need more data. Let's change the code where we create our data object and include two more values that use the same dimensions: the *aphelium* (the longest distance between a planet and the sun) in the `max` property, and the *perihelium* (the shortest distance) in the `min` property. The distance is now stored in the `avg` property (see `Updating/1-three-charts.html`):

```
const planets = []; // this array will store all the data when loaded

d3.json("../Data/sol_2016.json")
   .then(function(data) {
      data.planets.forEach(function(obj) {
         planets.push({
            name: obj.name,
            avg: obj.semiMajorAxisAU,
            max: obj.apheliumAU,
            min: obj.periheliumAU});
      });
      init();
   });

function init() { /* ... */ }
```

You can create bar charts with any of these three values, or all of them. Let's create an application where the user can choose which chart to display using HTML buttons. The following is the HTML code for the page; it includes an `<svg>` element and some buttons:

```
<body>
<h1><span id="chart">Average</span> distance from the Sun</h1>
<svg class="bar-chart"></svg>
<form>
    <button type="button" id="avg">Average</button>
    <button type="button" id="max">Maximum</button>
    <button type="button" id="min">Minimum</button>
</form>

<script>...</script>
</body>
```

These buttons will be attached to event handlers. They will select the data that should be displayed in the bar charts. The following array relates a key to a title and a color. The key contains the name of a property from each element in the planets array. It's also used for the button IDs:

```
const charts = [
    {key: "avg", title: "Average", color: "orange"},
    {key: "max", title: "Maximum", color: "blue"},
    {key: "min", title: "Minimum", color: "red"},
];
```

The chart object stores the dimensions of the current chart (which may have a variable height) and the chart that is currently displayed:

```
const chart = {
    width: 800,
    height: 0,           // the height is set after data is loaded
    current: charts[0]   // chart to display first
}
```

These other global constants initialize scales, a formatting function, and a selection of the svg object:

```
const barScale = d3.scaleLinear().range([0, 600]);
const colorScale = d3.scaleLinear().range([0, 1]);
const format = d3.format(".2f");

const svg = d3.select("svg.bar-chart"); // the container SVG
```

The `init()` function that is called right after the data is loaded and the planets array is populated performs basic initialization that requires the loaded data. In this case, it sets the height of the chart:

```
function init() {    // runs once
    chart.height = planets.length * 21;
    svg.attr("width", chart.width)
       .attr("height", chart.height);

    setupView(); // sets up scales

    // ...
}
```

The `setupView()` function called inside `init()` configures the current view. It disables the button that refers to the currently displayed view, replaces the `<span>` element in the title with the title of the current chart, sorts the planets array, and initializes the domains of the scales, based on the current data:

```
function setupView() {
    // disable all buttons
    d3.selectAll("button").property("disabled", false);
    // enable only buttons that are not current chart
    d3.select("#" + chart.current.key).property("disabled", true);

    // update page title
    d3.select("#chart").text(chart.current.title);

    // sort the planets using current data
    planets.sort((a,b) => d3.ascending(a[chart.current.key],
                                       b[chart.current.key]));

    // update scale domain with current data
    const maxValue = d3.max(planets, d => d[chart.current.key]);
    barScale.domain([0, maxValue]);
    colorScale.domain([0, maxValue]);
}
```

After setting up the view, the `init()` function uses the `current` data to render the chart. This code is identical to the code we used in the previous examples. The only difference is that it uses a key reference to access the data property: instead of `d.avg`, it uses `d[chart.current.key]`. This will allow the chart to reference other properties when the current key changes:

```
function init() {
    // ...
    setupView();

    svg.selectAll("g")
        .data(planets)
        .enter().append("g").attr("class", "entry")
        .attr("transform", (d,i) => `translate(0,${i * 21})`)
        .each(function(d) {
            const entry = d3.select(this); // the current entry

            entry.append("text").attr("class", "label category")
                .attr("y", 15)
                .attr("x", 90)
                .text(d.name);

            entry.append("rect").attr("class", "bar")
                .attr("x", 100)
                .attr("height", 20)
                .attr("width", barScale(d[chart.current.key]) )
                .style("fill", d3.color(chart.current.color)
                                .darker(colorScale(d[chart.current.key])))
    )

            entry.append("text").attr("class", "label value")
                .attr("y", 15)
                .attr("x", barScale(d[chart.current.key]) + 105)
                .text(format(d[chart.current.key]) + " AU");
        });
}
```

The result is shown as follows. It's the same chart we created before, with a title and some buttons that don't work yet:

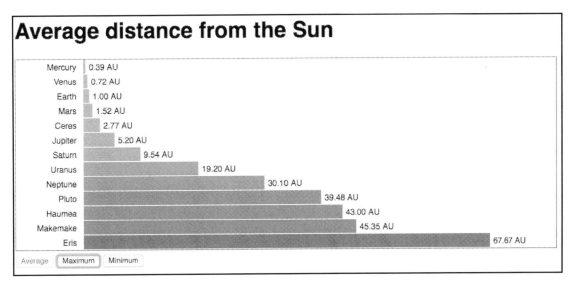

The previous example adapted to show three different charts. Code: *Updating/1-three-charts.html*.

Handling events

The `on()` method is used to handle events, and it can be called from any selection. The first parameter is a standard JavaScript event name string (such as *click* or *mouseover*), and the second parameter is the handler function that will execute when the event happens.

The following code obtains a selection containing all button objects and attaches an event handler to all of them. It obtains the `id` of the button that was clicked and uses it to change the current chart by assigning a corresponding object from the `charts` array. After changing the current chart, it calls the `draw()` function, which will update the chart. This code should be placed in a global context, since it only needs to run once:

```
d3.selectAll("button")
    .on("click", function() {
        chart.current = charts.filter(c => c.key == this.id)[0];
        draw();
    });
```

The `draw` function in this example only prints the current array. You can use it to test whether the buttons are selecting the correct chart, as expected. The call to `setupView()` will disable/enable the buttons and update the chart's title according to the current view (see `Updating/2-events.html`):

```
function draw() {
    console.log(chart.current.key);
    setupView();
}
```

Data updates

To update the data on a selection, you just need to update the styles and attributes. If the data has changed, you should call the `selection.data()` method with the new data, and then update everything that depends on it, such as attributes and styles, and any functions called by them, such as scales.

In our case, the data bound to the container `g.entry` object is the entire `planets` array, which may have been sorted in a different order (in the `setupView()` function). It can be updated simply by reassigning it to the selection:

```
svg.selectAll("g.entry").data(planets)
```

Then, you need to update the attributes and styles, which depend on properties from this array that have changed, but *before* doing that, you need to update the scales' domains, since they are called from the `style()` and `attr()` methods, and their maximum value depends on the new data. The scales were updated in the `setupView()` function. The rest of the `draw()` function contains the data updates:

```
function draw() {
    setupView(); // sorts data and updates scales

    svg.selectAll("g.entry").data(planets)
        .each(function (d) {
            d3.select(this).select(".label.category")
                .text(d.name); // the order may have changed
            d3.select(this).select(".bar")
                .attr("width", barScale(d[chart.current.key]))
                .style("fill", d3.color(chart.current.color)
                        .darker(colorScale(d[chart.current.key])));
            d3.select(this).select(".label.value")
                .attr("x", barScale(d[chart.current.key]) + 105)
                .text(format(d[chart.current.key]) + " AU");
```

```
        });
    }
```

Now, when you click any button, a new bar chart will be displayed. The chart reuses the same graphical elements, changing its colors, dimensions, and text contents. Bars are always sorted in ascending order (see `Updating/3-updates.html`):

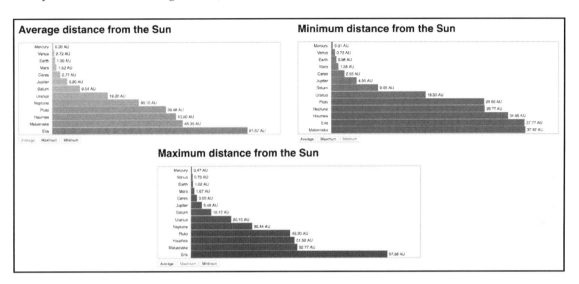

Each button replaces the current chart with a new chart, reusing the same chart elements. Code: *Updating/3-updates.html.*

Smooth transitions

Instead of immediately replacing one chart with another, you can add transitions, so that they occur in smooth animations. Adding a transition is very easy. You just need to call the `transition()` method on a selection before setting the new properties and styles. Instead of changing the old data with the new data, it will interpolate intermediate values during a quarter of a second. Add it to your update selections, and you will notice that when you change the chart, the bars and labels will animate to their new sizes, colors, and positions.

In our examples, transitions were added before changing the color and width of each bar, and before changing the position of each value label (see `Updating/4-transitions.html`):

```
svg.selectAll("g.entry").data(planets)
    .each(function (d) {
        d3.select(this).select(".label.category").text(d.name);
        d3.select(this).select(".bar")
```

```
    .transition()                          // 1) transition fill and width
      .attr("width", barScale(d[chart.current.key]))
      .style("fill", d3.color(chart.current.color)
                      .darker(colorScale(d[chart.current.key])));
d3.select(this).select(".label.value")
  .transition()                          // 2) transition x position
    .attr("x", barScale(d[chart.current.key]) + 105)
    .text(format(d[chart.current.key]) + " AU");
});
```

If you want a slower transition, just add `duration(value)` after the `transition()` command, with a value in milliseconds. The following code will make the animation last one second (see `Updating/5-durations.html`):

```
d3.select(this).select(".bar")
  .transition()
  .duration(1000)                    // animate during a second
    .attr("width", barScale(d[chart.current.key]))
    .style("fill", d3.color(chart.current.color)
                    .darker(colorScale(d[chart.current.key])));
```

You can also configure a delay before the transition starts with the `delay()` method. It can receive a fixed value in milliseconds, or a callback function that will apply a different delay for each object. In the following example, each bar will wait an amount of milliseconds proportional to its array index (the second parameter in the `each()` function), making each bar animate in a sequence:

```
.each(function (d,i) {      // include the i (index) parameter
  // ...
  d3.select(this).select(".bar")
    .transition()
    .duration(1000)              // animate during a second
    .delay(50 * i)               // longer animations for each bar
      .attr("width", barScale(d[chart.current.key]))
      .style("fill", d3.color(chart.current.color)
                      .darker(colorScale(d[chart.current.key])));
  // ...
});
```

The following diagram shows a snapshot of the animation captured in the middle of a transition. Try it out and see the effects for yourself (see the code in `Updating/6-delays.html`):

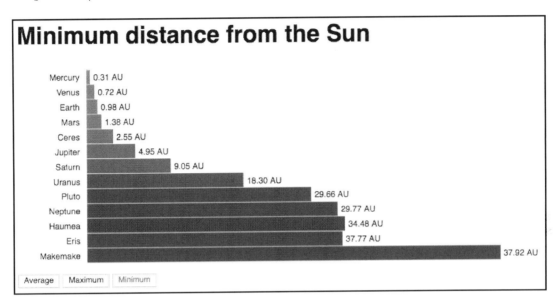

Transition with delay. Code: *Updating/6-delays.html.*

So far, you've used the most common features of D3, rendering charts in HTML and SVG. We will finish this chapter with a D3 visualization of a map of the world, using the same methods you have used in the previous examples.

Displaying a map using D3 and SVG

In this section, you will learn how to load a JSON file that contains geographical data and use it to draw SVG polygons. We will use the `Data/world-lowres.geojson` file (from the repository for this chapter). This is a fragment of this file:

```
{"type":"FeatureCollection","features":[
  {
    "type":"Feature",
    "id":"AFG",
    "properties":{"name":"Afghanistan"},
    "geometry":{
      "type":"Polygon",
      "coordinates":[[[61.210,35.650],[62.230,35.270], …
```

```
  ,[61.210,35.650]]]  }
    },{
      "type":"Feature",
      "id":"AGO",
      "properties":{"name":"Angola"},
      "geometry":{
        "type":"MultiPolygon",
        "coordinates":[[[[16.326,-5.877],[16.573,-6.622],...,[12.436,-5.684]]]]
  }
    },
    ...
  ]}
```

This file contains an array with all countries in the features property. That means that
when you load and parse the file and store it in a variable, data, you can obtain the data
array from data.features. The following code (see Loading/2-loading.html) loads
the file, extracts every properties.name and id property from each object in the
features array, and stores it in a new array. It then displays the data in an HTML list:

```
d3.json("../Data/world-lowres.geojson")
    .then(function(data) {
        const countries = [];

        data.features.forEach(function(obj) {
            countries.push({
                name: obj.properties.name,
                id: obj.id
            });
        });
        draw(countries);
    });

function draw(countries) {
    d3.select("body").append("ol")
      .selectAll("li")
      .data(countries)
      .join("li")          // same as enter().append("li")
      .text(d => d.name + " (" + d.id + ")");
}
```

But to draw the map, the property we need from each feature element is the geometry
property, which contains an object with two other properties: type and coordinates. The
array structure in the coordinates property depends on this type. Both *MultiPolygon* and
Polygon types contain coordinates, but *MultiPolygon* has an additional array dimension.
Countries that don't have islands can be drawn with one polygon, but countries with
islands contain an array of polygons, which contain arrays of coordinate pairs.

In Chapter 1, *Introduction,* you learned that the vertices of an SVG <polygon> are defined by a sequence of *x,y* pairs, separated by commas or spaces, in the points attribute. To transform GeoJSON coordinates into a format that can be used by <polygon>, you need to check geometry.type to know whether it's a *Polygon* or *MultiPolygon,* and then get the coordinates in geometry.coordinates, select the array of coordinates for each polygon, and flatten the array structure. The d3.merge() function from the *d3-array* module can be used for this. If you pass an array such as [[1,2], [3,4]] to d3.merge(), you get [1,2,3,4].

Using d3.merge(), and just the selection and binding tools we explored in this chapter, you can draw a world map binding coordinates to SVG polygon points attributes. Can you do it? Give it a try. Remember that geographical coordinates can be negative (the domain is -180 to 180 for longitudes and -90 to 90 for latitudes). You can use a d3.scale() or adjust the SVG viewport to show negative units, and flip the map over, since the SVG coordinate system grows downward and to the right.

A solution is provided in the code listing, as follows (see the full code in SVG_Map/1-polygon-map.html):

```
d3.json("../Data/world-lowres.geojson")
    .then(function(data) {
        drawMap(data.features);
    });

const rand = d3.randomUniform(256);

function drawMap(countries) {
    d3.select("#world-map")
        .selectAll(".country")
        .data(countries)
        .enter().append("g").attr("class", "country")
        .each(function(d,i) {
            let points = [];

            if(d.geometry.type == 'MultiPolygon') {
                points = d3.merge(d.geometry.coordinates);
            } else if(d.geometry.type == 'Polygon') {
                points = d.geometry.coordinates;
            }

            d3.select(this).selectAll("polygon")
                .data(points)
                .join("polygon")
                .attr("points", d => d)
                .style("fill", d =>
                'rgb('+rand()+','+rand()+','+rand()+')');
```

```
        });
    }
```

The result of the previous code is shown in the following screenshot. Your colors may be different, since they are generated randomly:

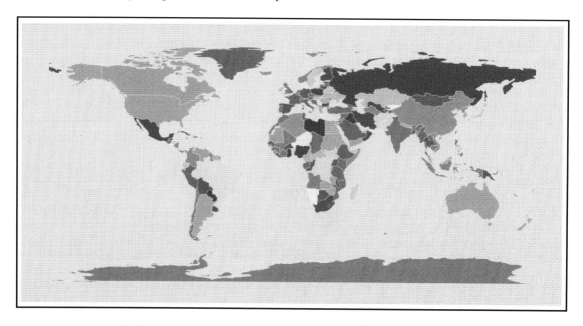

A world map displayed with SVG polygons and D3 using GeoJSON data. Code: *SVG_Map/1-polygon-map.html.*

This code used geographical coordinates directly, without a scale, because it configures the SVG viewport so that the center of coordinates is placed in the middle of the page (using `viewBox`), and the `width` and `height` are slightly larger than the domains for latitudes and longitudes. The coordinates were also flipped upside down (using `transform`), since negative latitudes grow upward:

```
<svg id="world-map"
    width="800"
    viewBox="-200 -100 400 200"
    transform="scale(1,-1)"></svg>
```

You can obtain the same result by using a linear scale (using a simple SVG tag, without any `viewBox` configuration). Try it as an exercise.

Geographical maps are a very important topic in data visualization, and D3 provides specific tools to create and interact efficiently with maps, using different projections and spherical geometry in the *d3-geo* modules. This topic will be covered in detail in `Chapter 10`, *Visualizing Geographical Data*.

Summary

In this chapter, you had a practical introduction to the essential skills needed to create data visualizations with D3.js. This is a little bit of most of what will be explored in greater detail in `Chapters 4`, *Data Binding*, through `Chapter 8`, *Animation and Interactivity*. All examples used the fundamental data-binding mechanism that D3 uses to create data-driven documents, exploring the most common features you will use in most applications.

We created a simple bar chart made of HTML elements, an equivalent bar chart using SVG elements, and a map binding standard geographical data to SVG polygons. We also provided a brief introduction to interactive charts by adding event handling and transitions to the SVG bar chart.

The main goal of this chapter was to make you familiar with the API. Starting in the next chapter, we will revisit the data-binding process and explore it in greater depth, covering several small details that we left out of this introductory chapter.

References

- Let's Make a Bar Chart: HTML, By Mike Bostock (D3 version 3): `bost.ocks.org/mike/bar/`
- Let's Make a Bar Chart II: SVG, by Mike Bostock (D3 version 3): `bost.ocks.org/mike/bar/2/`
- Let's Make a Bar Chart III: Vertical Bars with Axes, by Mike Bostock (D3 version 3): `bost.ocks.org/mike/bar/3/`
- How Selections Work, by Mike Bostock (D3 version 3): `bost.ocks.org/mike/selection/`
- Working with Transitions, by Mike Bostock (D3 version 3): `bost.ocks.org/mike/transition/`
- Planetary data: Data/sol_2016.json. Compiled from Solar System data obtained mainly from NASA (JPL) and other public sources.
- GeoJSON map of the world with 245 countries adapted from map generated from naturalearthdata.com: `Data/world-lowres.geojson`.

4
Data Binding

The *d3-selection* module is a core library in any D3 application. It's hard to find a D3 application that doesn't use most of its methods, which form the vocabulary of a **Domain-Specific Language** (**DSL**) that chains together operations to select, bind, and update data, creating expressions that run as data-driven streams, dynamically transforming **Document Object Model** (**DOM**) components. One of the main goals of this chapter is to introduce you to the methods of this module, demonstrating how to use them for selections, updates, joins, and DOM manipulation.

This chapter will also cover the data-binding strategies used by D3, most of which are based on the *general update pattern*, which is a fundamental paradigm in D3. It was briefly introduced in the previous chapter, but it's important that you understand it very well, since it's used in practically all D3 applications. It's not, however, a trivial concept. This chapter will describe several data-binding strategies used in D3, through short code examples that you can try in your browser's console. You will learn how to bind individual data items to HTML and SVG elements and efficiently use the general update pattern to bind data items to any DOM element, perform data updates, and automatically add and remove elements from a DOM tree.

Most of the data you will use in D3 visualizations will probably be loaded from external files. While standard JavaScript and popular third-party libraries already include tools for loading and parsing data in formats such as CSV and JSON, you might prefer to use D3's optimized native modules for efficiency and simplicity. These tools are part of the *d3-dsv* and *d3-fetch* modules, which you will also learn how to use in this chapter.

We will cover the following topics in this chapter:

- Selections
- The general update pattern
- Loading and parsing data
- A complete step-by-step example

Selections

D3 provides a functional flow-based DSL for connecting data to DOM elements. It's an efficient alternative to the verbose DOM API (or to libraries such as *jQuery*). It's also very compact and easy to read, once you understand its fundamental concepts.

The *d3-selection* module contains not only methods for *selecting* DOM nodes, but also methods for *merging* and *filtering* selections; *joining data* to elements; *modifying* properties, attributes, styles, classes, and contents; *adding* and *removing* elements from a node tree; handling and dispatching *events; sorting* nodes; *calling* arbitrary functions; and *iterating* a node set.

A selection expression consists of a series of chained operations that select and transform a DOM node set, appending or removing sub-nodes; changing attributes, styles, and contents; adding event listeners; and calling custom functions. It starts with a *selector*: a string pattern that matches against elements in a DOM tree and returns a *selection object*, which contains references to a list of elements and its parents. Once you have a selection object, you can use it to read or modify a node's properties, as well as get and set styles, classes, attributes, text contents, and HTML contents. You can also change the structure of a DOM tree by adding, removing, and reordering elements.

W3C selectors

The *Selectors W3C Specification* is one of the standards used to select nodes in HTML and XML documents. Selector strings are used by the CSS specification to apply style properties to HTML and XML elements. They are also used to select nodes in popular JavaScript libraries, such as *jQuery*. In D3, W3C selectors are used to match against existing nodes, but also to create entirely new DOM trees.

Most of your D3 selection expressions will consist of a single simple selector of one of the six types described in the *W3C Level-3 specification*, listed in the following table. Selections always select *elements* and are applied to a *context* (defined by the application). The result of a selection can be an empty set or a set that contains one or more elements.

Type	Examples	Description
Type selector	`div`	Selects elements by type.
Universal selector	`*`	Selects all elements. This selector is optional if used in combination with attribute, class, ID, or pseudo-class selectors (for example, `*[height]` is the same as `[height]`).

		Selects elements that contain the named attribute. Elements can be selected by the exact contents of the attribute's value, expressed as `name="value"` (non-exact value matches are also supported). If preceded by * or *nothing*, the selector applies to any type; otherwise, it restricts the scope to the prefixing selector. Quotes are optional.

Attribute selectors	`[height]` or `*[height]`
	`[height="300"]`
	`div[height=300]`
		Selects elements that contain the named attribute. Elements can be selected by the exact contents of the attribute's value, expressed as `name="value"` (non-exact value matches are also supported). If preceded by * or *nothing*, the selector applies to any type; otherwise, it restricts the scope to the prefixing selector. Quotes are optional.

Class selectors	`.bar`
	`.horiz`
	`.bar.horiz` or
	`.horiz.bar`
	`div.bar`
		Selects elements that are part of the named class. If preceded by * or *nothing*, the selector applies to any type; otherwise, it restricts the scope to the prefixing selector. To match elements that belong to multiple classes, selectors for each class are concatenated (in any order).

ID selectors	`#main-table`	Selects a single element that is tagged with a named ID.

Pseudo-classes	`:enabled`
	`:first-child`
	`div:nth-child(2n+1)`
	`p:nth-of-type(2n)`
	`g:empty`
	`:not(selector)`
		Selects elements based on characteristics such as state, properties, position, and negation. If preceded by * or *nothing*, the selector applies to any type; otherwise, it restricts the scope to the prefixing selector.

W3C selectors used in D3

Combinators are used to make contextual selections of existing nodes. A combinator expression always selects the element represented by the *last simple selector* in the expression. The previous simple selectors are used to build the context. The following table lists combinators supported by CSS and D3:

Type	Example	Description
Descendant	`table td`	Selects elements that descend from the elements represented by the previous selector.
Child	`table > tbody > tr > td`	Selects elements that are child nodes of the elements represented by the previous selector.
Next-sibling	`#sec2 + div + form`	Selects sibling elements that appear after the elements represented by the previous selector.
Subsequent-sibling	`#sec2 ~ form`	Selects sibling elements that immediately follow the elements represented by the previous selector.

W3C combinators (for contextual selections)

In typical D3 applications, where you create your entire DOM tree or most of it, you rarely use complex selection expressions. When you need to select elements in a context, such as the children of a selected node, the typical pattern is to chain a series of selection methods with simple selectors. Each selection provides the context for the next one. Here's an example:

```
const selection = d3.select("body")
                    .select("#main-table")
                    .selectAll("tr")
                    .selectAll("td");
```

Contextual selection allows greater flexibility, since you can apply different pieces of data to each level (such as attributes and styles) and modify an entire DOM tree in one line. Here's an example:

```
d3.select("body")
    .select("#main-table")
        .style("border-collapse", "collapse") // applying style to <table>
    .selectAll("tr")
    .selectAll("td")
        .style("color", "blue");                // applying style to <td>
```

But if you are just selecting an existing node set or one you created previously, and wish to obtain a flat selection of all <td> nodes, it may be simpler to use descendant combinators:

```
const flatSelection = d3.selectAll("body #main-table tr td");
```

In both cases, you get all of the <td> elements in the table, but the first selection returns them grouped by their original context. You can see the difference if you run this code in the JavaScript console (see Selectors/1-w3c-selection.html).

Selecting and filtering elements

The most important functions and methods used to select elements in D3 are listed in the following table. They all return a *selection object* created from a selection string, a DOM node or list, or a function that filters the elements to be included. Each *selection* object provides a context where a second selection method can be applied. Selections are typically chained together.

Method or top-level function	Description
d3.select (*string* | *node*)	If the parameter is a selector string, it returns a selection object with the *first* element that matches the selector. If the parameter is a DOM *node*, it returns a selection object that contains the node.
d3.selectAll (*string* | *nodes*)	If the parameter is a selector string, it returns a selection object with *all* elements that match the selector. If the parameter is a DOM *node list* (or pseudo-array), it returns a selection object that contains the nodes.
selection.select (*string* | *function*)	If the parameter is a selector string, it works like d3.select() in the context of the selection where it is called. If the parameter is a *function*, it is evaluated for each element in the selection. Functions can have up to three parameters: the current *datum* (d), the current *index* (i), or the current *group* (nodes), and must return one element or *null*. The local *this* reference refers to the current object in regular functions, but not arrow functions (which should use nodes[i]).
selection.selectAll (*string* | *function*)	If a selector *string* is provided, this method is like d3.selectAll() in the context of the selection where it is called. If the parameter is a *function*, it is evaluated for each element in the selection. Functions must return an array of elements, which can be empty.
selection.filter (*string* | *function*)	If a selector *string* is provided, this method works like *selection*.selectAll(). It usually receives a filtering function, which should test each element and return *true* or *false*.

Selection functions and methods in *d3-selection*

To experiment with these functions, load a page with the following HTML <body> and use your browser's developer tools (JavaScript console) to type in the code fragments in this section (you can load Selection/1-empty.html):

```
<html>
  <head>
    <script src="https://d3js.org/d3.v5.min.js"></script>
  </head>
  <body>
    <div id="words">
      <p>One</p>
      <p>Two</p>
      <p>Three</p>
    </div>
    <p>Four</p>
    <p>Five</p>
  </body>
</html>
```

Open your browser's JavaScript console and declare the following selection. It will select all five paragraphs:

```
const selection = d3.selectAll("p");
```

The result is stored in the *selection* object, which stores an array with references to the elements. (When coding in a file, use console.log(**selection**) to print its structure in the JavaScript console, but you usually won't need that if you type directly in the JavaScript console.) You can extract the DOM nodes from *selection* objects using the methods listed here:

Method	Description
nodes()	Returns an array of nodes (a DOM node list). If the selection contains a single node, this method will return it inside an array.
node()	Returns a single node. If the selection contains a list of nodes, this method will return the first node.

Methods of a *d3.selection()* object that return the DOM nodes wrapped in selection objects

DOM nodes can be read or modified with methods or properties from the standard DOM API. The following commands will print node information in the JavaScript console:

```
const nodelist = selection.nodes();
console.log(nodelist);                 // shows nodelist with 5 p elements
console.log(nodelist[2]);              // prints <p>Three</p> in console
console.log(nodelist[2].innerText);    // prints 'Three'
```

You rarely need to use the DOM API, since D3 provides equivalent properties and methods that are much easier to use, but sometimes you may need it, and it's very useful for debugging. You can always use `console.log(selection.nodes())` to verify that a selection object includes the nodes you expect.

To select only the paragraphs that are inside the `<div>` element, you can first select the `div`, and then nest a contextual selection for all of the paragraphs:

```
const pInDiv = d3.select("div")      // top-level selection
               .selectAll("p");      // nested contextual selection
```

The following selection selects the same elements in this page:

```
const pInDiv2 = d3.selectAll("div#words p");
```

But it places all `<p>` elements in a single array with the document root as parent. The contextual selection preserves the `<div>` context. If you are just interested in reading the contents of the paragraphs, it makes no difference, but you might prefer the contextual selection if you plan to configure attributes for the parent elements (see `Selection/2-select-no-data.html`).

Functions used in selection operations are called for each element in the current selection and can have up to three parameters: the current datum (`d`), the current index (`i`), and the current group (`nodes`). If you use regular or anonymous functions, the `this` reference is equivalent to `nodes[i]`. The following code prints the values of the current *datum*, the nodes/data array *index*, the *nodes* array, and the `this` reference for each `<p>` element in `div#words`:

```
const selection = d3.select("#words") // selects the div
    .selectAll("p")
    .filter(function(d,i,nodes) { // not filtering anything, just logging
        console.log(d, i, nodes, this); // will print undefined for d
        return true;
    });
```

The current datum is *undefined* for all three elements because no data is yet bound to the elements. When you bind the data, it will be printed. The following code binds a three-element array to the selection and appends each data value to the previous text in each paragraph (see `Selection/3-select-data.html`):

```
selection.data([7,4,8])
    .filter(function(d,i,nodes) { // not filtering anything, just logging
        console.log(d,i,nodes, this); // will print data value for d
        return true;
    })
```

```
.text(function(d) {
    return d3.select(this).text() + " " + d
});
```

You can use arrow functions instead of anonymous functions. Since most browsers today support ES6, using one or the other is a matter of style. Arrow functions are great when you just need to run a single operation. If you need to write multiple lines, an anonymous or regular function might be best for readability. But you must be aware that the `this` reference does not refer to the current element in arrow functions. If you need the current element in an error function, you must declare all three parameters (`d`, `i`, and `nodes`) so you can use `nodes[i]`. The previous code could be rewritten with arrow functions, as follows (see `Selection/4-select-data-arrow.html`):

```
selection.data([7,4,8])
    .filter((d,i,nodes) => console.log(d,i,nodes,nodes[i]) || true)
    .text((d,i,nodes)   => d3.select(nodes[i]).text() + " " + d);
```

Wrapping a DOM node in `d3.select()` turns it into a *selection object*, which allows it to use the D3 API. The following code converts a selection into a DOM node list, filtering elements with odd indexes, creating a new D3 selection from the list, and using it to paint the nodes red:

```
const odd_nodes = d3.selectAll("p") // [p#a1, p#a2, p#a3, p#a4, p#a5]
                  .nodes()
                  .filter((d,i) => i%2 == 0);
d3.selectAll(odd_nodes)             // [p#a1, p#a3, p#a5]
    .style("color", "red");
```

You don't need DOM to filter. The `selection.filter()` method returns the same result:

```
d3.selectAll("p")                 // [p#a1, p#a2, p#a3, p#a4, p#a5]
    .filter((d,i) => i%2 == 0) // [p#a1, p#a3, p#a5]
    .style("color", "red");
```

Although filtering selects elements correctly, their original index is lost. Some operations, such as merging, ordering, and inserting, use the index as default and require that it is preserved (but you can also configure a key function to be used in place of the index). You can preserve indexes if you filter using the `selection.select()` method, providing a function that uses the selection data to decide when to return the current element. An equivalent index-preserving odd-node filter is shown here (`Selection/5-filter-no-data.html`):

```
d3.selectAll("p")
    .select(function(d,i) {
        return i%2 == 0 ? this : null;
```

```
})
    .style("color", "red");
```

You can discover the number of elements in a selection with the methods listed here:

Method	Description
size()	Returns the total number of elements in a selection. Shortcut for selection.nodes().length.
empty()	Returns true if the selection is empty. Shortcut for selection.size() > 0.

Methods of d3.selection() that return size information about selections

The following code uses the size() method to count the number of elements in a selection:

```
const selection = d3.selectAll("div p"); // 3 elements
console.log("Size: ", selection.size()); // 3
```

No data was bound to the selection, so the data in any selection function is *undefined*. The following filter only selects items that have a value (but none do):

```
const empty = selection.filter(d => d); // returns a new selection
console.log("Is it empty: ", empty.empty() ? "Yes" : "No"); // Yes
```

The data() method is used here to bind a five-element array to the selection:

```
selection.data(["Odin","Dva","Tri","Chetire","Pyat"]); // 5 data items
```

Since there are more data items (5) than elements (3), each element will receive an item, and the extra items will not be used. Since index order is used by default, the first three items will be bound in order:

```
const not_empty = selection.filter(d => d); // true for all
console.log("Is it empty: ", not_empty.empty() ? "Yes" : "No"); // No
console.log("Size: ", not_empty.size()); // 3 (first 3 <p> elements)
```

Now the data can be used. The following code will replace the text in each <p> with the data values (see Selection/6-select-bind-data.html):

```
selection.text(d => d);
```

Joining data

The most important methods in the *d3-selection* module are used to bind data values to DOM elements. Some of these methods, which are listed in the following table, were briefly introduced in the last chapter. They will be explored in dedicated sections in this chapter:

Method	Description
datum(*value | function*)	This joins a single value to each element of a selection and returns the current selection. If the *value* attribute is absent, this method works as a getter function that returns the datum bound to a single element (the first non-null element). If the *value* attribute is present, it will be applied to each element in the selection. If *null*, any existing datum is detached from the element. If the attribute is a *function*, it can be used to bind a different value for each element from the parameters passed to the *datum* (*undefined*, if not previously bound to data), *index*, and *nodes* functions.
data(*array, keyFunction*)	This joins a data array to a selection, connecting each datum to an existing element and returning the current selection. Binding uses array index order as default. An optional *keyFunction* may be included as the second parameter to compute a unique key that connects each datum to a specific element. This is important if the positions of your data items change, for example, after insertions, deletions, or sorting. If there are more elements than data, the extra elements are transferred to the _exit array (in the selection object). If there are more data items than elements, the extra items are transferred to the _enter array.
enter()	This returns a selection from the _enter array (in the selection object).
exit()	This returns a selection from the _exit array (in the selection object).
merge(*otherSelection*)	This returns a new selection that merges the current selection with a provided compatible selection. This method should only be used to merge *enter* and *update* selections after a data join (see the *general update pattern*). Despite its name, this method *does not* merge arbitrary selections. For general-purpose merging, use d3.merge() or concat(). See Selection/7-merge-no-data.html.

join (*string*) join (*enter, update, exit*)	A new alternative to the *general update pattern*, which performs *enter*, *update*, and *exit* steps in a single method. If a string is provided as a single argument, it should be the name of the joined element. You can also provide functions as parameters and apply separate operations to *enter*, *update*, and *exit* selections. This method is available in *d3-selection* version 1.4 or later (see *D3 general update pattern*).

Methods for joining data to DOM elements

The datum() method is used for one-to-one data binding (without the *general update pattern*). It's useful when your data is an object (not an array), when the data is applied to a single element, or when your dataset never grows or shrinks. It's also used to bind a data array to graphical elements that aren't represented individually in the DOM (and consequently don't support the *general update pattern*), such as HTML Canvas paths.

The following example uses the datum() method to bind data objects to styled <div> elements and create simple a horizontal bar chart (see Binding/datum-loop.html):

```
// An array of objects used as data for the chart
const diameters = [
    {planet: 'Mercury', diameterKm: 4879},
    {planet: 'Venus',   diameterKm: 12104},
    {planet: 'Earth',   diameterKm: 12756},
    {planet: 'Mars',    diameterKm: 6792},
    {planet: 'Jupiter', diameterKm: 142984},
    {planet: 'Saturn',  diameterKm: 120536},
    {planet: 'Uranus',  diameterKm: 51118},
    {planet: 'Neptune', diameterKm: 49528}
];

// A scale to convert diameters in thousands of km to pixels
const scale = d3.scaleLinear().range([0,800])
                .domain([0, d3.max(diameters, d => d.diameterKm)]);

// Selects the parent <div> container where the bars will be appended
const sel = d3.select("div#list");

// Appends a new child <div> for each data item
diameters.forEach(function(item) {
    sel.append("div").attr("class", "planet")
        .datum(item)                              // binds the item to the <div>
        .style("width", d => scale(d.diameterKm) + "px")  // sets bar size
        .text(d => d.planet);                     // sets the bar label
});
```

The same result can be obtained with the *general update pattern* (see `Binding/5-gup.html`):

```
sel.selectAll("div")   // initial selection (may be empty)
    .data(diameters)   // binds data to existing elements
    .enter()           // if there is more data, creates a selection for it
    .append("div")     // appends a new <div> for each element in _enter
    .attr("class", "planet")
    .style("width", d => scale(d.diameterKm) + "px")
    .text(d => d.planet);
```

Or this result can be obtained with join updates (see `Binding/6-join.html`):

```
sel.selectAll("div")
    .data(diameters)
    .join("div")        // adds or removes elements to match data
    .attr("class", "planet")
    .style("width", d => scale(d.diameterKm) + "px")
    .text(d => d.planet);
```

All of these produce the same practical result, but are slightly different. The last two strategies will be explored in detail in the final sections.

Getting and setting attributes, styles, and content

D3 contains easy-to-use alternatives for common DOM operations, such as `setAttribute()`, and properties, such as `style` or `innerHTML`. These methods are listed in the following table. They all return the same selection that is being modified, so you can chain several of these methods and use a single-chained expression to modify attributes, styles, and content.

These methods can also be used as *getters*. Most have a mandatory *name* parameter to identify a property, style, or attribute, and an optional *value* parameter. If *value* is included, the method sets a value and returns the current selection. When *value* is not present, it returns the current value. A value can be a static string or a function (with the *datum, index,* and *nodes* parameters) that will be applied to each element in the selection:

Method	Description
attr (*name, value* | *function*)	This sets an attribute value for each element in the selection. If *value* is not present, it returns the current attribute value.
style (*name, value* | *function, priority*)	This applies a CSS style property to the elements in the selection. If *value* is not present, it returns the current value for the property. The *priority* is optional. If present, it should be the *important* string.

`property` (*name, value | function*)	This is used for HTML elements that don't have addressable attributes or styles (such as `checked` and `enabled`). You can set a property with a Boolean value or a function that results in *true* or *false*. If a value is not present, it returns the current state.
`classed` (*names, value | function*)	This adds or removes one or more classes from an element. The *value* parameter should be a Boolean value or expression that returns *true* or *false*. This method is not used as a getter.
`text` (*value | function*)	This sets the text contents of the elements in a selection. If *value* is not present, it returns the current contents.
`html` (*value | function*)	This sets the HTML contents of the elements in an HTML selection. If *value* is not present, it returns the current contents.

Methods that get and set node attributes, properties, styles, classes, text, and HTML contents

Selections are *immutable* objects. You can chain commands, manipulate the elements they contain, and return different selections, but you can't modify the selection object. You can, however, change the DOM properties of the elements contained in a selection.

The preceding methods, when used as getters, return a string. When used as setters, they return the same selection object. You can chain several setters together to change many styles and properties at once. For example, the following code sets attributes, styles, and content for all <p> elements in `div#words`, based on their data (see `Selection/8-attr-style.html`):

```
d3.select("#words")      // initial selection: div#words
    .style("border", "solid 1px black")  // style applied to div#words
    .selectAll("p")      // contextual selection: div#words p
        .data([1,4,9])
        .style("font-family", "sans-serif") // style applied to each <p>
        .style("text-decoration", "underline")
        .style("color", d => `hsl(${ Math.sqrt(d) * 120},100%,50%)`)
        .style("transform", d => `rotate(${2 * Math.sqrt(d)}deg)`)
        .attr("class", (d,i) => i%2 == 0 ? "odd" : "even")
        .text((d,i,n) => d3.select(n[i]).text() + " " + d);
```

The generated HTML is shown here (you can inspect the generated tags using your browser's developer tools). Compare how each attribute and style was declared in the generated code:

```
<div id="words" style="border: 1px solid black;">
    <p class="odd"
        style="color: rgb(0,255,0); transform:rotate(2deg);">One 1</p>
    <p class="even"
        style="color: rgb(0,0,255); transform:rotate(4deg);">Two 4</p>
```

```
      <p class="odd"
          style="color: rgb(255,0,0); transform:rotate(6deg);">Three 9</p>
  </div>
```

All of the preceding `data()`, `style()`, `attr()`, and `text()` methods return the same selection, but that is not true for all selection methods. Although a single chained expression was used, styles were applied to two different selections. Methods that filter or modify DOM trees, such as `select()`, `append()`, or `insert()`, always return a *different* selection. Some methods may even return a completely different type of object. Getter methods are one example: they return a string. Another example is the `transition()` method, which returns a transition object (it supports many of the same methods in selections). If you think chaining makes your code confusing, or when you need to access a selection outside the chain, you can declare separate constants. The following code produces the same effect as the preceding code (`Selection/9-attr-style-separate.html`):

```
  const divSelection = d3.select("#words")         // div#words
    divSelection.style("border", "solid 1px black");

  const pSelection = divSelection.selectAll("p"); // div#words p
  pSelection.data([1,4,9]);
  pSelection.style("font-family", "sans-serif")
            .style("text-decoration", "underline")
            .style("color", d => `hsl(${ Math.sqrt(d) * 120},100%,50%)`)
            .style("transform", d => `rotate(${2 * Math.sqrt(d)}deg)`)
  pSelection.attr("class", (d,i) => i%2 == 0 ? "odd" : "even")

  pSelection.text(function(d) {
      const selectedP = d3.select(this);
      const currentText = selectedP.text();
      return currentText + " " + d;
  });
```

It's good practice to only use the `style()` method when strictly necessary, that is, when you need to change styles dynamically. Static style properties should be declared in a CSS style sheet, especially if you apply the same styles to different objects. This removes duplication and keeps your code cleaner and shorter. You can remove two lines from the preceding code by declaring the following:

```
  <style>
      #words p {
          font-family: sans-serif;
          text-decoration: underline;
      }
  <style>
```

Instead of appending to the *class* attribute, you can use the `classed()` method, which adds or removes a class from an element. The following code removes the `odd` class from the selection, and adds a `special` class to the *first* <p> element (see `Selection/10-classed-property.html`):

```
d3.select("#words")
   .selectAll("p")
       .classed("odd", false)                  // remove
       .classed("special", (d,i) => i == 0); // conditionally add/remove
```

The `property()` method is used in a similar way to turn on and off HTML Boolean attributes, such as `disabled`, `checked`, and `readonly`. The following code hides the last <p> element:

```
d3.select("#words")
   .selectAll("p")
       .property("hidden", (d,i,nodes) => i == nodes.length-1);
```

When using SVG, you can use `attr()` or `style()` to apply styles that can be set in XML or CSS, but you should be aware that CSS styles override XML styles, which means that you can only override a CSS property previously declared in a style sheet if you use `style()` instead of `attr()`. The `style()` method is the recommended way to apply fills, strokes, fonts, opacities, and other visual styles, including lengths (units can be omitted in SVG CSS). An exception is transforms: since CSS requires explicit units and XML uses defaults, it's best to use `attr()`.

Modifying the structure of the node tree

The methods listed here alter the structure of a DOM tree, either by adding new elements, changing their position, or detaching them from the tree. Since selections are immutable, these methods always return new selections:

Method	Description
`append(`*tagname* | *function*`)`	If the parameter is a *string*, it must be a tag name. The method will create a new element and append it as the *last child* of each element in the selection, returning a new selection with the appended nodes. If the selection is an *enter* selection (see *general update pattern*), the nodes are added as *siblings* following the selected nodes. If the parameter is a *function*, it must return a *DOM element* to be appended.

insert (*tagname* | *function*, *selector* | *function*)	If the first parameter is a *string*, it must be a *tag name*. If the second parameter is a *string*, it must be a *selector*. The method will create a new element and insert it *before* the nodes matched by the selector. If the first parameter is a *function*, it must return a *DOM element* to be appended. If the second parameter is a *function*, it must return the *DOM element* before which the element should be inserted.
remove ()	This detaches the selected elements from the DOM. It returns the detached elements.
sort (*comparator*)	This returns a new selection with data sorted according to a comparator function. The elements bound to the data are reinserted into the DOM tree according to the ordered data. The comparator function should receive two parameters, *a* and *b*, and return *zero* if *a == b*, a *positive* value if *a > b*, or a *negative* value if *a < b*.
order ()	This reinserts each element in the DOM tree according to the order of the data bound to it (if the data is already sorted, this is equivalent to sort ()).
raise ()	This reinserts each element in the selection as the last child of its parent. This is used to place graphical elements *on top* of others in SVG (*bring to front*).
lower ()	This reinserts each element in the selection as the first child of its parent. This will invert the order of the elements and is used to place graphical elements *under* all others in SVG (*send to back*).

Methods that modify the DOM structure of selected elements

The examples that follow will use the following HTML, which contains a single <div> in its <body> (see Append/1-empty.html):

```
<html>
<head>
    <script src="https://d3js.org/d3.v5.min.js"></script>
    <style>
        div { margin: 2px 25px; padding: 5px; width: 300px;
              border: solid 1px blue; }
        div>div {border: solid 1px red; width: 200px;}
        div>div>div {border: solid 1px green; width: 100px;}
        div>div>div>div {border: solid 1px magenta; width: 50px;}
    </style>
</head>
<body>
    <div>One</div>
```

```
</body>
</html>
```

The following code appends a new `<div>` element as the *last child* of the previous element and returns a new selection which contains the appended element:

```
const sel1 = d3.select("div");
const sel2 = sel1.append("div").text("Two");
```

Chaining several `append()` calls will append each new element *as the last child* of the previous selection. Each call to `append()` returns a new selection:

```
d3.select("div")                   // selection 1 (existing element)
    .append("div").text("Two")     // selection 2 (context: selection 1)
    .append("div").text("Three")   // selection 3 (context: selection 2)
    .append("div").text("Four")    // selection 4 (context: selection 3)
```

Check the results using your browser's developer tools (or inspect the HTML in `Append/2-append.html`). It should look like the following:

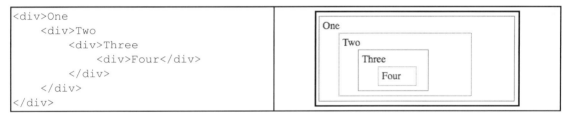

Appending elements places the new element as the last child of the selection. Code: *Append/2-append.html.*

When `append()` is called in an *enter* selection (see *general update pattern*), it is declared only once and called for every element in the `_enter` array of the selection object. In this case, the new elements will be appended as *siblings*. Consider the following code:

```
d3.select("div")                    // selects the single existing <div>
    .selectAll("div")               // empty selection
    .data(["Two","Three","Four"])   // creates _enter array with 3 elements
    .enter()                        // returns enter selection (3 slots)
    .append("div").text(d => d);    // appends each <div> to slot
```

The preceding code (`Append/3-append-enter.html`) will produce the following:

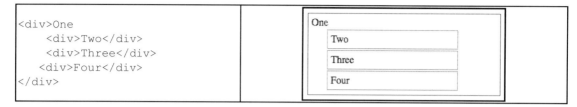

You can insert a child element in any position inside a selection that calls `insert` (*element, selector*). The element will be inserted as a *preceding sibling* of the *first* element that matches the selector. For example, consider a page with the following body contents:

```
<div>
    <div>One</div>
    <div>Two</div>
    <div>Three</div>
    <div>Four</div>
</div>
```

The following code (`Append/4-insert.html`) will insert a `<div>` *before* the *third* child:

```
d3.select("div")
  .insert("div", ":nth-child(3)")
    .text("INSERTED");
```

The result is shown as follows:

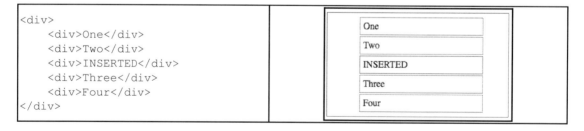

The `remove()` method detaches all of the elements in a `remove()` method detaches all of the elements in a selection. For example, the following code selects all children of `<div>` that have an even index and removes them:

```
d3.select("div").selectAll(":nth-child(2n)").remove();
```

Applied to the previous example, it will remove the *Two* and *Three* nodes (see `Append/5-remove.html`). This method is normally used to remove excess elements from an *exit* selection (see *general update pattern*).

The `join()` method used in data-binding also changes the DOM structure, since it appends and removes elements from a selection. See `Selection/11-append-insert-join.html` for an example that compares the three methods.

Node ordering

Ordering and sorting is very important in data visualizations, which might stack several objects over each other. In HTML, you can use the CSS `z-index` to place an object above the others, but in SVG, you need to change the document order. The `raise()` and `lower()` methods can be used to perform *bring-to-front* and *send-to-back* operations.

For example, this code will place all nodes with an even index after the odd-indexed nodes:

```
d3.select("div").selectAll("p:nth-child(2n)").lower()
```

And this will place the even ones before the odd ones (see `Append/6-raise-lower.html`):

```
d3.select("div").selectAll("p:nth-child(2n)").raise()
```

Elements are bound to data in array index order. If you bind elements and then sort the array, their positions will change. For example, this code binds an unsorted array to a sequence of <p> elements. The first element will be bound to 5, the second to 3, and so on:

```
const selection = d3.select("div")
                 .selectAll("p")
              .data([5,3,2,1,4])
              .text((d,i,n) => d3.select(n[i]).text() + " " + d);
```

Using *selection*`.sort()`, the elements will be rearranged to reflect the new structure of the data array (see `Append/7-sort.html`):

```
const sorted = selection.sort( (a,b) => a - b);
```

You can also change the order of the elements, which will interfere with how elements are updated and appended. Consider the following selection and data. This will print five paragraphs that list the data values and indexes (see `Append/8-key-empty.html`):

```
d3.select("div").selectAll("p")
    .data([1,2,3,4,5]).enter().append("p")
    .text((d,i) => "datum: " + d + ", i:" + i);
```

Now, suppose you select it again, this time passing a smaller array to the `data()` method. This is an *update* operation. The data in the new array will be used to replace the values bound to the first three elements of the selection, because they have the same indexes. This is the default behavior:

```
d3.select("div").selectAll("p")
    .data([2,4,6]) // will update first three indexes (0, 1, 2)
    .style("color", "blue")
    .text((d,i) => "updated: " + d + ",j:" + i);
```

If you pass a larger array, excess items will be transferred to the `_enter` array, preserving their indexes. Calling `append()` on the enter selection will add three new elements after the last element of the original selection. This is also the default behavior (see `Append/9-key-index.html`):

```
d3.select("div").selectAll("p")
    .data([7,7,7,7,7,2,4,6]) // last 3 indexes added to enter selection
    .enter().append("p")
        .style("color", "red")
        .text((d,i) => "appended: " + d + ",j:" + i);
```

The default behavior uses an index-based key function to bind data to DOM elements. You can change that behavior by passing a different function as the second argument to the `data()` method. It should be a unique value. For example, you might use an object's `id` field:

```
selection.data(objects, d => d.id);
```

Now, instead of the array index, the data object's *id* will be used to connect it to the data. You can now insert and remove elements from the array and each other element will continue to be connected to the same datum.

The following selection, which performs an *update* and an *enter-append*, uses the current datum value as the key function, so that elements are uniquely identified by their value. The *update* operation only updates the elements that have values that exist in the original selection, independent of their index, and the enter selection will only contain elements for values that don't yet exist (see `Append/10-key-function.html`):

```
d3.select("div").selectAll("p")
    .data([2,4,6], d => d) // only existing values (2, 4) are updated
    .text((d,i) => "updated: " + d + ",j:" + i)
    .style("color", "blue")
    .enter().append("p") // only new value (6) added to enter selection
        .style("color", "red")
        .text((d,i) => "appended: " + d + ",j:" + i);
```

You can compare the difference when using a key function that returns the current datum to the default behavior that uses the array index in the following screenshot:

Initial data [1,2,3,4,5]	key function: **index** update: [2,4,6] enter: [2,4,6]	key function: **datum** update: [2,4,6] enter: [2,4,6]
datum: 1, i:0 datum: 2, i:1 datum: 3, i:2 datum: 4, i:3 datum: 5, i:4	updated: 2,j:0 updated: 4,j:1 updated: 6,j:2 datum: 4, i:3 datum: 5, i:4 appended: 2,j:5 appended: 4,j:6 appended: 6,j:7	datum: 1, i:0 updated: 2,j:0 datum: 3, i:2 updated: 4,j:1 datum: 5, i:4 appended: 6,j:2

Differences when updating a selection and calling enter().append(). Left: Initial selection. Center: Default behavior. Right: Using a key function to return the datum as the key. Code: *Append/9-key-index.html* and *10-key-function.html*.

Calling functions from a selection

D3 allows arbitrary functions to be called in the middle of a selection chain using the two methods listed in the following table. One is called for *each* element in a selection. The other is called only *once* during the selection.

They both return the current selection:

Method	Description
each (*function*)	This calls a function for each element in the selection. The function receives three parameters: *datum* (d), *index* (i), and *group* (nodes). The this reference is equivalent to nodes[i]. Return values are not used.
call (*function, args*)	This calls a function once with optional arguments. Return values are not used.

Methods for calling functions inside a selection chain

The each() method is useful for adding branches to a node set, without having to break the selection chain. For example, to append three child nodes to a selection of <div> elements, you need to save the selection in a constant, which can be used to append each child (see Selection/12-without-each.html):

```
const parents = d3.select("div.container")   // an existing <div>
                  .selectAll("div.item")
                  .data([1,2,3]).enter()        // three child <divs>
                   .append("div")
                   .attr("class","item");

// each line below will run three times, for each element in selection
parents.append("div").text("header");
parents.append("div").style("width", d=>(d*25) + "px");
parents.append("div").text("footer");
```

Using the each() method, you can run arbitrary code *for each element*. In the following example, a reference to the current selection is obtained in the each() function with d3.select(this) (or d3.select(nodes[i]) if it's an arrow function) and the child elements are added and configured, without breaking the chain. The result is the same (see Selection/13-with-each.html):

```
d3.select("div.container")
  .selectAll("div.item")
  .data([1,2,3]).enter()
  .append("div").attr("class","item")
  .each(function(d) {
     const parent = d3.select(this);
     parent.append("div").text("header");
     parent.append("div").style("width", d=>(d*25) + "px");
     parent.append("div").text("footer");
  });
```

The `call()` method can be used to run a function *once* per selection without leaving the selection chain. It's useful to call functions that receive a selection, as in the example:

```
function addNode(sel) {
    sel.append("div").text("extra node");
}
```

Normally, you would create the selection and pass it as an argument. The following code calls the function before and after adding a collection of nodes (`Selection/14-without-call.html`):

```
const selection = d3.select("div")
    .selectAll("div")
    .data([1,2,3]).enter()
    .append("div");

addNode(selection);
selection.each(function(d) {...});
addNode(selection);
```

With the `call()` method, the function is called from the selection chain (`Selection/15-with-call.html`):

```
d3.select("div")
    .selectAll("div")
    .data([1,2,3]).enter()
    .append("div")
    .call(addNode)
    .each(function(d) {...})
    .call(addNode)
```

Using the `call()` method to execute code from a selection is a very common practice in D3. You will use it to draw axes, apply zooming and dragging behaviors, and configure transitions.

Event handling

The on() method, described here, is used to register event listeners in selections. It replaces the addEventListener() and removeEventListener() standard DOM methods in D3, and supports native and custom events:

Method	Description
on (*names, listener, options*)	This registers a listener for one or more event type *names*. Any standard DOM event type is supported (for example, *click* or *mouseover*) Multiple type names can be specified, separated by spaces. If a *listener* function is not specified, the method returns the currently-assigned listener on the first selected element. If the second parameter is null, the current listener is removed.

Method used to register an event listener to a selection

The following code registers two event listeners. The first one changes the contents of the `<h1>` element when a *mouseover* event occurs on a `<p>` element. The second prints a default text when a *mouseout* or a *click* event occurs on the `<p>` element (Selection/16-events.html):

```
d3.selectAll("div p")
    .data([1,2,3,4,5])
    .on("mouseover", function(d) {
        const text = d3.select(this).text();
        d3.select("h1").text(`Item ${d}: ${text}`);
    })
    .on("mouseout click", () => d3.select("h1").text("Select an item"));
```

The *d3-selection* module also contains methods to dispatch and handle custom events, and obtain details for specific event types. They will be covered in detail in Chapter 8, *Animation and Interactivity*.

Multiple selections

With the *d3-selection-multi* module, you can set attributes, styles, and properties using reusable objects, which can contain static data and functions. If you have many attributes to apply to multiple selections, this can make your code cleaner and more efficient. But this library is not part of the default bundle. To use it, you need to import it separately. If you are using an NPM environment, run the following:

```
npm install d3-selection-multi
```

Otherwise, you can download it or link it directly from d3js.org and include it in your page:

```
<script src="https://d3js.org/d3.v4.min.js"></script>
<script src="https://d3js.org/d3-selection-multi.v1.min.js"></script>
```

This module adds three methods to selections, listed as follows:

Method	Description
attrs (*object*)	This receives an object and allows multiple attributes to be set at once. It's equivalent to calling attr (*key, value*), where each *key* is an object property.
styles (*object*)	This receives an object and allows multiple CSS styles to be set at once. It's equivalent to calling style (*key, value*), where each *key* is an object property.
properties (*object*)	This receives an object and allows multiple HTML properties to be set at once. It's equivalent to calling property (*key, value*), where each *key* is an object property.

Selection methods from the *d3-selection-multi* module

Consider the following SVG and data:

```
<svg width="800" height="600"></svg>
<script>
    const width = 800, height = 600;
    const data = [
        {color: "red", x: 200, y: 150},
        {color: "green", x: 400, y: 300},
        {color: "blue", x: 600, y: 450}
    ];
// ...
</script>
```

The following objects declare styles and attributes that will be shared by different SVG objects:

```
const shapeStyles = {
    fill: d => d.color,
    stroke: "black",
    "stroke-width": () => Math.ceil(Math.random() * 5),
    "fill-opacity": 0.5,
    "stroke-opacity": 1
};

const circleData = {
    cx: d => d.x,
    cy: d => d.y,
    r: 50
};

const rectData = {
    x: d => width - 50 - d.x,
    y: d => height - 50 - d.y,
    width: 100,
    height: 100
};
```

The objects are reused in the following code. This eliminates several lines of duplicated code (see `Selection/17-selection-multi.html`):

```
d3.select("svg")
    .selectAll("circle")
    .data(data).enter()
    .append("circle")
        .styles(shapeStyles)
        .attrs(circleData);

d3.select("svg")
    .selectAll("rect")
    .data(data).enter()
    .append("rect")
        .styles(shapeStyles)
        .attrs(rectData);
```

The result is shown in the following screenshot:

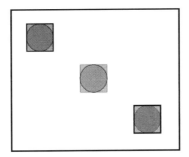

Applying multiple attributes and styles using objects. Code: *Selection/17-selection-multi.html.*

The attrs() and styles() methods are also supported for transition objects.

D3 general update pattern

Data is usually bound to DOM elements in D3 using the *general update pattern*. We used it to create the bar charts in the last chapter, and in several small code fragments in this chapter. In this section, we will demonstrate it using a simple example that focuses on the selection methods and avoids other APIs, such as transitions and scales. You can follow the example by downloading and modifying the GUP/1-template.html file from the GitHub repository for this chapter or running the individual files for each step.

Although most D3 applications use SVG, we will use HTML for this example, since the goal is to understand the binding mechanisms, and the structure of HTML is probably more familiar to most readers. At the end of this chapter, you will have the opportunity to create a full example using SVG.

The best way to understand how D3 works is to use your browser's development tools, which show the structure of the generated DOM elements and a JavaScript console. As in previous sections, you can use the JavaScript console to type in code after loading the template HTML.

The template file contains the following HTML code, which displays nothing in the browser. The CSS is not shown. We will use the <div> container to draw some graphical elements, and the <form> container to store the buttons that will cause updates in the graphical elements:

```
<body>
<div id="container"></div>
```

```
<form></form>
<script>
    const datasets = ["one", "two", "three", "four"];
    const colors = ["red", "blue", "green", "purple"];
    let idx = 0;
</script>
</body>
```

The application will display one of the words from the datasets array, placing each letter in a colored box. Initially, the application will use datasets[idx] and colors[idx], where idx is zero, so the word *one* will be displayed in red. Clicking on buttons will change the idx variable and redraw the page, displaying a different set of letters that correspond to a different word.

We use D3 to generate a set of four buttons in the following code. You should be able to understand what this code is doing, since all of the commands were explored in the previous section:

```
d3.select("form")
  .selectAll("button")
     .data(datasets)
     .enter()
     .append("button")
        .attr("type", "button")
        .attr("id", (d,i) => "b" + i)
        .property("disabled", (d,i) => d == datasets[idx])
        .style("background-color", (d,i) => colors[i])
        .text(d => d.toUpperCase())
        .on("click", function(d,i,nodes) {
            idx = d3.select(nodes[i]).attr("id").substring(1);
            d3.selectAll(nodes)
              .property("disabled", t => t == datasets[idx]);
            redraw();
        });

function redraw() {
    console.log(idx, datasets[idx], colors[idx]);
}
```

The code will generate the following HTML (use your browser's development tools to inspect the DOM).

When you click a button, it will print the current data values to the console:

```
<form>
  <button type="button" id="b0" disabled
          style="background: red;">ONE</button>
  <button type="button" id="b1"
          style="background: blue;">TWO</button>
  <button type="button" id="b2"
          style="background: green;">THREE</button>
  <button type="button" id="b3"
          style="background: purple;">FOUR</button>
</form>
```

Rendering buttons by joining a dataset: Code: *GUP/2-buttons.html*.

Creating elements

Now let's create a `draw()` function to display the first word. The array of letters that is used as a dataset can be created with `dataset[idx].split("")`. Each letter will be contained in a `<div>` element. The following code achieves this:

```
function draw() {
    d3.select("#container")
      .selectAll(".letter")
      .data(datasets[idx].split('')).enter()
      .append("div")
        .attr("class", "letter")
        .style("background-color", d => colors[idx]).text(d => d);
}
```

Call the `draw()` function after running the code that displays the buttons. See `GUP/3-create.html`. The resulting generated HTML is shown here. The `<div>` element uses the `display: inline-block` CSS style so that it displays as shown, without line breaks:

```
<div id="container">
    <div class="letter"
        style="background-color: red;">o</div>
    <div class="letter"
        style="background-color: red;">n</div>
    <div class="letter"
        style="background-color: red;">e</div>
</div>
```

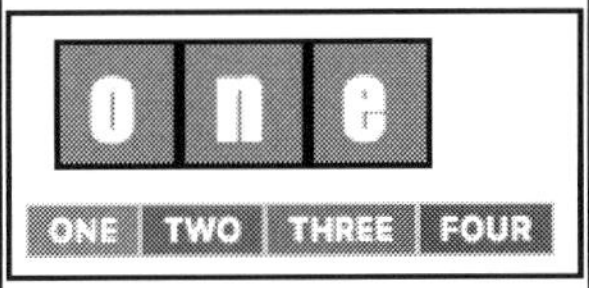

Result of binding the ["o","n","e"] array to a new selection of <div> elements. Code: *GUP/3-create.html*.

Data binding in D3 involves two sets of data and three different operations. This is illustrated in the following diagram:

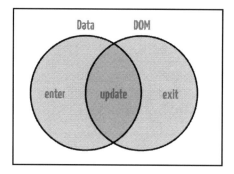

Enter, exit, and *update* sets formed by the intersection of Data and DOM elements

An *update* selection occurs when there is an equal amount of data items and DOM elements. An *enter* selection occurs when there is more data than DOM elements, and an *exit* selection when there are more DOM elements than data. Both selections are set up when the `data()` method is called. Using the `enter()` or `exit()` methods, you can return one or the other.

If you inspect our example in the JavaScript console, you will see that the `data(array)` command creates two arrays, _enter and _exit, besides the _groups and _parent arrays already present in the selection (this structure is used in D3 version 5 and may change in a future version). You can see their contents printing the selection with `console.log()`:

```
console.log(d3.select("#container")
              .selectAll(".letter")
              .data(datasets[idx].split('')));
```

Since there are no elements in the DOM, the contents of the entire data array will be transferred to the _enter array. When you call the `enter()` method, the _enter array will be transferred to the _groups array of the new selection.

The `append()` method is called for *each* element in the selection, creating the new elements. Then, each element is updated with a class attribute, style, and contents. This process is illustrated as follows:

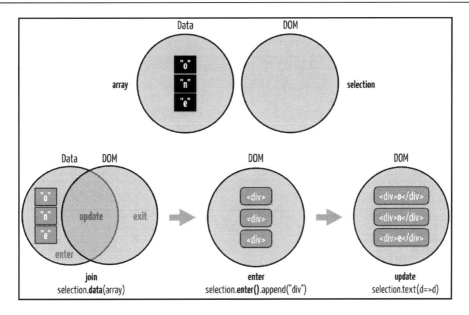

An initial enter/append selection

Updating selections

We can now proceed to the next step, which is to *update* the colors and contents of the letterboxes when a corresponding button is clicked. At each click, the `idx` variable is changed and the `redraw()` function is called. We just need to implement this function.

The code in `redraw()` is similar to the code in `draw()`, but if it doesn't add new elements, it won't call `enter()` or `append()`. All it needs to do is call `data()` to update the selection with the new data and set contents and style, as follows:

```
function redraw() {
    d3.select("#container")
        .selectAll(".letter")              // selects elements to be updated
        .data(datasets[idx].split(""))    // replaces with new data
        .style("background-color", d => colors[idx])  // sets color
        .text(d => d);                                // updates content
}
```

Compare it with the `draw()` function. Now when you click the **TWO** button, the browser will generate the DOM structure and render the result, as follows:

```
<div id="container">
    <div class="letter"
        style="background-color: blue;">t</div>
    <div class="letter"
        style="background-color: blue;">w</div>
    <div class="letter"
        style="background-color: blue;">o</div>
</div>
```

Result of updating the selection with ["t"."w"."o"]. Code: *GUP/4-update.html*.

The process is illustrated as follows:

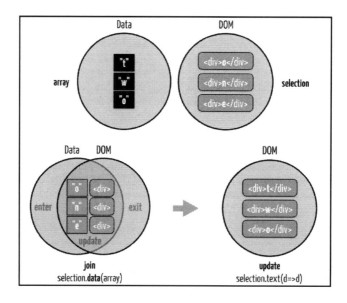

An update selection

Note that we did not call `enter()` or `append()` because both the selection and the data have the same size, so the _enter array is always empty. But what happens if you click on the **THREE** or **FOUR** button?

As shown here, if you click on the **FOUR** button, the existing boxes get correctly updated with the new data, but some data was lost, since there are not enough elements available.

Extra boxes are needed to fit the extra letters:

```
<div id="container">
 <div class="letter"
 style="background-color: purple;">f</div>
 <div class="letter"
 style="background-color: purple;">o</div>
 <div class="letter"
 style="background-color: purple;">u</div>
</div>
```

Elements were updated but the data is larger than the available elements. Code: *GUP/4-update.html.*

Entering new elements

You need to create additional elements for the extra data that is in the _enter array. Calling enter() will return a selection with these elements. Let's try it:

```
function redraw() {
    d3.select("#container")
        .selectAll(".letter")         // selects the existing letters
        .data(datasets[idx].split("")) // sets new data
        .style("background-color", d => colors[idx])
        .text(d => d)
        .enter()        // returns a selection with only the new items
        .append("div")  // appends a div for each new item
        .attr("class", "letter"); // sets the class of the new items
}
```

Look at the results as follows. It's not what we expected. The rendered results don't show the extra letters, but two new elements were actually added to the DOM tree, as you can see from the generated HTML. What's the problem? Take a look:

```
<div id="container">
  <div class="letter"
      style="background-color: green">t</div>
  <div class="letter"
      style="background-color: green">h</div>
  <div class="letter"
      style="background-color: green">r</div>
  <div class="letter"></div>
  <div class="letter"></div>
</div>
```

Elements were appended but the new selection was not updated. Code: *GUP/6-enter-append.html*

Look carefully at the code. It might be easier to understand what's happening if we store each step in a separate constant. The following is another way to write the same code (see `GUP/5-enter-append-step.html`):

```
function redraw() {
  // context selections
    const step_1 = d3.select("#container"); // s1
    const step_2 = step_1.selectAll(".letter"); // s2

    // update selection
    const step_3 = step_2.data(datasets[idx].split("")); // s3
    const step_4 = step_3.style("background", d => colors[idx]); // s3
    const step_5 = step_4.text(d => d); // s3

    // enter selection
    const step_6 = step_5.enter(); // s4
    const step_7 = step_6.append("div"); // s5
    const step_8 = step_7.attr("class", "letter"); // s5
}
```

Remember that some methods return different selections, while others return the same selection object they were called upon. There are *five* different selections in the preceding code: the `step_3`, `step_4`, and `step_5` constants refer to the same selection (*s3*), which is *not* the same selection as `step_7` and `step_8` (*s5*). The `style()` and `text()` methods were called on *s3*, the `old` selection, but only the `attr()` method was called on the new *s5* selection (the old selection already contains this attribute because it was defined in the `draw()` function).

We can fix this quickly by cutting and pasting the `style()` and `text()` commands after the new selection:

```
function redraw() {
    d3.select("#container")
      .selectAll(".letter")
      .data(datasets[idx].split(""))
      .style("background-color", d => colors[idx]) // old elements
      .text(d => d)                                // old elements
      .enter()
      .append("div")
        .attr("class", "letter")
        .style("background-color", d => colors[idx]) // new elements
        .text(d => d);                               // new elements
}
```

The result is shown as follows. Now, the extra elements were correctly added and updated, and all of the data is correctly rendered:

```
<div id="container">
  <div class="letter"
       style="background-color: green">t</div>
  <div class="letter"
       style="background-color: green">h</div>
  <div class="letter"
       style="background-color: green">r</div>
  <div class="letter"
       style="background-color: green">e</div>
  <div class="letter"
       style="background-color: green">e</div>
</div>
```

Result after implementing enter().update(). Code: *GUP/7-enter-append-update-fix.html*.

But this doesn't look so cool, does it? We duplicated code, which is very bad practice. Imagine if you had a dozen lines to update. There is also a lot of duplication in the `draw()` function that we could try to eliminate. There must be a better way to do it.

Merging selections

There is a better way to do it! That's what the `merge()` method is for. If you merge the selections before updating, you can perform the updates once. This eliminates code duplication, and better, you can get rid of the entire `draw()` method, since now `redraw()` can be used to create any new nodes *and* to update existing nodes.

Here is the fixed code without duplication using merge and a single `redraw()` function. The following code lists the entire `<script>` block (omitting some details), showing the places where the `redraw()` function is called (see `GUP/8-enter-append-merge.html`):

```
<script>
    const datasets = ["one", "two", "three", "four"];
    const colors = ["red", "blue", "green", "purple"];
    let idx = 0;

    d3.select("form") // button code omitted...
    .on("click", function(d,i,nodes) { ...
        redraw(); // called at each button click
    });

    redraw();    // called once

    function redraw() {
```

```
        const selection = d3.select("#container")
                            .selectAll(".letter")
                            .data(datasets[idx].split(""));

    selection.enter().append("div")
        .merge(selection) // merges with selection before append
        .attr("class", "letter")
        .style("background-color", d => colors[idx])
        .text(d => d);
    }
</script>
```

The `selection.merge()` method is only used in the *general update pattern*. It should always receive as a parameter a *compatible* selection, which usually is a reference to the selection before the entered elements are appended. The pattern is always as follows:

```
selection // reference to the selection before appending
    .enter() // selection of placeholders from the extra data items
    .append(element)  // returns new modified version of the selection
    .merge(selection) // merges with previous version of the selection
```

The *enter-append-merge* process is illustrated as follows:

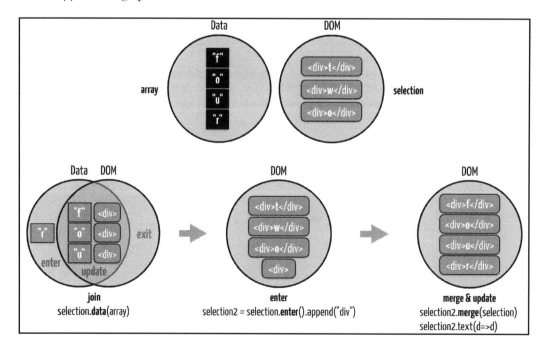

An *enter/append* selection. followed by a *merge* and *update*

But we're not done yet. We still have a problem. If you click on **ONE** after clicking on **FOUR**, the **R** is not removed. This will happen every time you move from a longer text to a shorter one. The old elements don't go away! This problem is shown as follows:

```
<div id="container">
   <div class="letter"
        style="background-color: red">o</div>
   <div class="letter"
        style="background-color: red">n</div>
   <div class="letter"
        style="background-color: red">e</div>
   <div class="letter"
        style="background-color: purple">r</div>
</div>
```

Element is not removed because exit() was not implemented. Code: *GUP/8-enter-append-merge.html*.

Exiting unused elements

Remember that, when there are more elements than needed, these are moved to the `_exit` array. You can obtain a selection of these elements by calling `exit()` and then call `remove()` on that selection. For this, you just need to add one extra line to the `redraw()` function:

```
function redraw() {
    const selection = d3.select("#container") // joins data
                         .selectAll(".letter")
                         .data(datasets[idx].split(""));

    selection.exit().remove(); // removes extra elements

    selection.enter().append("div") // adds elements
      .merge(selection)             // merges selections
      .attr("class", "letter")      // updates merged selection
      .style("background-color", d => colors[idx])
      .text(d => d);
}
```

Now, you can click all four buttons, and the data will be displayed as expected (see GUP/9-exit-remove.html). This process is illustrated in the following screenshot:

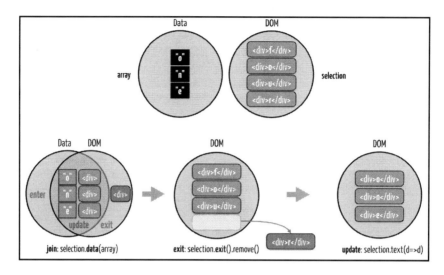

An *exit/remove* selection, followed by an *update*

Now that you've seen how the *general update pattern* works, you have the knowledge and the tools to use D3 to create complex data-driven visualizations. If it still seems confusing, download the code and take some time to review the process before proceeding. Before the end of this chapter, you will have an opportunity to review this process with a full example, using SVG, external files, and scales.

Data joining

A new selection method was introduced with version 1.4 of the *d3-selection module*: join(). It automatically matches data items and elements, appending and removing elements as necessary, and eliminating the need for explicit calls to enter(), exit(), append(), order(), and remove(). It makes data binding much simpler, and methods such as merge() unnecessary and candidates for deprecation in future versions.

That said, it's still important that you understand the *general update pattern* as described in the previous section, since most code examples you will find online and in this book still use it (it was added to D3 when most of this book was already written). It will also be easier to understand how join() works if you are familiar with the *general update pattern*. But you can and should use it whenever possible.

Consider the following HTML used in previous examples in this chapter:

```
<body>
  <div id="words">
    <p id="a1">One</p>
    <p id="a2">Two</p>
    <p id="a3">Three</p>
  </div>
  <p id="a4">Four</p>
  <p id="a5">Five</p>
</body>
```

The following code automatically performs an *enter* operation (because the data is larger than the selection) which binds the first five data items to each selected `<p>`, and appends a new `<p>` element to receive the sixth element. It replaces `enter()` followed by `append(p)` (see `Selection/18-join-enter.html`):

```
d3.select("body") // context where new elements will be created
      .selectAll("p")
      .data([1,2,3,4,5,6]) // one element will be added
      .join("p")
      .text(d => "Joined " + d)
```

This next code automatically performs an *exit* operation (because the data is smaller than the selection) that removes the extra element. It replaces an `exit()` followed by `remove()` (see `Selection/19-join-exit.html`):

```
d3.select("body") // context where new elements will be created
      .selectAll("p")
      .data([1,2,3,4]) // one element will be removed
      .join("p")
      .text(d => "Joined " + d)
```

If the data and selection have the same amount of elements, an automatic update operation is performed. Note that there is no difference in the preceding code fragments. The behavior depends on the relative size of the selection and data array.

If you wish to control what happens in each *enter*, *update*, and *exit* step, you can continue using the *general update pattern*, or call `join()` with the (`Selection/20-join-explicit.html`) function:

```
d3.select("body").selectAll("p").data(data)
    .join(
        function(selection) { // enter
            selection.append("p").text(d => "Joined " + d)
        },
        function(selection) { // update
```

```
                    selection.style("color", "blue");
            },
            function(selection) { // exit
                selection.remove();
            }
        );
```

Let's rewrite the previous example with `join()`. For the buttons, there are no updates. You can simply replace `enter().append("button")` with `join("button")`:

```
d3.select("form")
    .selectAll("button")
        .data(datasets)
        .join("button")
        .attr("type", "button")
//...
```

The `redraw()` function has separate lines for *exit* and *enter/update*. You no longer need the `selection.exit().remove()` line, and `enter().append("div")` `.merge(selection)` can be replaced with `join("div")`:

```
function redraw() {
    const selection = d3.select("#container")
                            .selectAll("div.letter")
                            .data(datasets[idx].split(""));
    selection.join("div")
        .attr("class", "letter")
        .style("background-color", d => colors[idx])
        .text(d => d);
}
```

You also no longer need a reference to the selection, so you can reduce everything to a single selection chain (see GUP/10-join.html):

```
function redraw() {
    d3.select("#container")
        .selectAll("div.letter")
        .data(datasets[idx].split(""))
        .join("div")
        .attr("class", "letter")
        .style("background-color", d => colors[idx])
        .text(d => d);
}
```

Loading and parsing data

D3 provides tools to load files—using Ajax requests—and parse popular data formats. This section explores the microlibraries that contain these tools: *d3-format* and *d3-fetch*. They are both part of the default bundle.

Using delimiter-separated values

Delimiter-Separated Values (**DSV**) is a popular flat, tabular data format that organizes data in rows and columns, separating rows with newlines and data values with a delimiter. **Comma-Separated Values** (**CSV**) is probably the most popular DSV format. D3 applications can use the methods in the *d3-dsv* module (listed here) to parse DSV data structures with any delimiter:

Function or method	Description
d3.dsvFormat (*delimiter*)	This returns a new parser with the specified single-character delimiter.
fmt.parse (*string, function*)	This parses a DSV *string* that treats the first row as the *header* row and converts each item into a key used when parsing all the other rows. Each row is converted into an object, with key-value pairs for each item. It returns an array of objects. An optional row-conversion *function* can be provided to process the contents of each row, returning a value, object, or array.
fmt.parseRows (*string, function*)	This parses a DSV *string* that returns an array of arrays containing the data. This method treats all rows *equally*. An optional row-conversion *function* can be provided to process the contents of each row, returning a value, object, or array. It receives two arguments: the *row* parsed as an array and the *index* of the row.
fmt.format (*array, header*)	This converts an array of objects into a delimiter-separated dataset using the object's keys as the *header* rows. An optional array of headers can also be specified.
fmt.formatRows (*arrayOfRows*)	This converts an array of an array of strings into a delimiter-separated dataset.

General-purpose parsers and formatters for delimiter-separated value datasets

Since the most common separators are tabs and commas, this module contains a set of preconfigured parsers for CSV and TSV datasets. They are listed in the following table:

Function	Description
d3.csvParse (*string,row*)	Shortcut for d3.dsvFormat (",").parse (*string,row*)
d3.csvParseRows (*string,row*)	Shortcut for d3.dsvFormat (",").parseRows (*string,row*)
d3.csvFormat (*rows,columns*)	Shortcut for d3.dsvFormat (",").format (*rows,columns*)
d3.csvFormatRows (*rows*)	Shortcut for d3.dsvFormat (",").formatRows (*rows*)
d3.tsvParse (*string,row*)	Shortcut for d3.dsvFormat ("\t").parse (*string,row*)
d3.tsvParseRows (*string,row*)	Shortcut for d3.dsvFormat ("\t").parseRows (*string,row*)
d3.tsvFormat (*rows,columns*)	Shortcut for d3.dsvFormat ("\t").format (*rows,columns*)
d3.tsvFormatRows (*rows*)	Shortcut for d3.dsvFormat ("\t").formatRows (*rows*)

Parsers and formatters for the CSV (comma-separated) and TSV (tab-separated) datasets

Consider, as an example, the following CSV string (see Parsing/1-parsing.html):

```
const dsv1 = 'PROPERTY,UNIT,JUPITER,SATURN\n'
           +'Diameter,km,142984,120536\n'
           +'Density,kg/m^3,1326,687\n';
```

A call to d3.csvParse (dsv1) will return the structure, shown as follows:

```
[
  {
     PROPERTY: "Diameter",
     UNIT: "km",
     JUPITER: "142984",
     SATURN: "120536"
  },{
     PROPERTY: "Density",
     UNIT: "kg/m^3",
     JUPITER: "1326",
     SATURN: "687"
  },
  columns: ["PROPERTY","UNIT","JUPITER","SATURN"]
]
```

After parsing, you can access the properties using object keys:

```
const res = d3.csvParse(dsv1);
console.log(res[0].PROPERTY + " of Jupiter:" + res[0].JUPITER +" km");
```

Using `parseRows()`, the result is returned as an array of arrays, with contents that you can control with a row-conversion function:

```
d3.csvParseRows(dsv1, function(row, i) {
    return [row[2], row[3], row[4], row[5]]
}).filter((d,i) => i > 0);
```

The preceding code removes the header row and returns only columns with numerical data:

```
[
    ["142984", "120536", "51118", "49528"],
    ["1326", "687", "1271", "1638"],
    ["778.6", "1433.5", "2872.5", "4495.1"]
]
```

Note that the numbers are always returned as strings unless they are explicitly converted. You can convert them automatically by providing `d3.autoType` as a *row accessor function* or writing one yourself if you need more transformations.

For example, consider this DSV string, which contains numbers and dates:

```
const dsv3 = 'vehicle|date|miles\n'
            +'M3C6L2|2012-03-05|66\n'
            +'C9S1X9|2012-03-06|92\n'
            +'M3C6L2|2012-03-12|66\n'
            +'T2P8M5|2012-03-13|36\n'
            +'T2P8M5|2012-03-19|35';
```

The following code will parse it, converting the dates and numbers automatically:

```
const tsvParser = d3.dsvFormat("|");
 const data4 = tsvParser.parse(dsv3, d3.autoType);
```

The result will be the following array of objects:

```
[
    {"vehicle":"M3C6L2","date":"2012-03-05T00:00:00.000Z","miles":66},
    {"vehicle":"C9S1X9","date":"2012-03-06T00:00:00.000Z","miles":92},
    {"vehicle":"M3C6L2","date":"2012-03-12T00:00:00.000Z","miles":66},
    {"vehicle":"T2P8M5","date":"2012-03-13T00:00:00.000Z","miles":36},
    {"vehicle":"T2P8M5","date":"2012-03-19T00:00:00.000Z","miles":35},
    columns: ["vehicle", "date", "miles"]
]

const data5 = tsvParser.parse(dsv3, function(row, i) {
    const date = row.date.split('-');
    return {
        vehicle: row.vehicle,
        month: date[1],
        year:  date[0],
        km:    +row.miles * 1.609}; // '+' coerces to number
});
```

The result is as follows:

```
[
    {vehicle: "M3C6L2", month: "03", year: "2012", km: 106.194},
    {vehicle: "C9S1X9", month: "03", year: "2012", km: 148.028},
    {vehicle: "M3C6L2", month: "03", year: "2012", km: 106.194},
    {vehicle: "T2P8M5", month: "03", year: "2012", km: 57.924},
    {vehicle: "T2P8M5", month: "03", year: "2012", km: 56.315},
    columns: ["vehicle", "date", "miles"]
]
```

If you are loading an external CSV file, you can parse it as soon as you have the data from the Ajax request. For example (see `Parsing/2-dom-fetching.html`):

```
fetch("../Data/SolarSystemData.csv") // EcmaScript fetch() function
    .then(function(response) {
        return response.text();
    })
    .then(function(csvData) {
        const data = d3.csvParse(csvData);
        console.log(data);
        // do something with the data
    });
```

You can further manipulate the structure of the data using JavaScript or tools from the *d3-array* and *d3-collection* modules, which will be covered in Chapter 5, *Manipulating Data and Formatting*.

There are no special parsers for popular formats such as JSON and XML because they can be parsed with native JavaScript tools. You can also fetch and parse any format, as described in the next section.

Loading files

You don't need to first load a file and then parse it. You can do it all at once with a single function from the *d3-fetch* module. Several popular data formats are supported. All functions are *JavaScript promises*, and the data retrieved can be processed in one or more then() steps. They contain at least one mandatory *input* parameter (the URL of the resource to load), and an optional *init* object, that can be used to configure HTTP request details, such as headers and authentication:

Method	Description
d3.dsv (*delim, input, init, row*)	This a DSV with a specified delimiter. An optional row function may be provided for custom row processing as the last parameter (see the *Using delimiter-separated values* section).
d3.csv (*input, init, row*)	This is the same as d3.dsv with a comma (,) as the delimiter.
d3.tsv (*input, init, row*)	This is the same as d3.dsv with a tab character (\t) as the delimiter.
d3.text (*input, init*)	This fetches the IRL provided as *input* and loads as plaintext.
d3.json (*input, init*)	Fetches the URL provided as *input* and parses as JSON.
d3.html (*input, init*)	Fetches the URL provided as *input* and parses as HTML.
d3.xml (*input, init*)	This fetches the URL provided as *input* and parses as XML.
d3.svg (*input, init*)	This fetches the URL provided as *input* and parses as SVG.
d3.image (*input, init*)	This fetches the URL provided as *input* and loads the data as an image.
d3.blob (*input, init*)	Fetches the URL provided as *input* and loads the data as a blob.
d3.buffer (*input, init*)	This fetches the URL provided as *input* and returns the data in an array.

Methods for fetching URLs and parsing data. from the *d3-fetch* module

The following expression will load an URL and parse it as a CSV file. When the parsing is done, the contents of the `then()` step is executed. Compare it with the equivalent expression using standard HTML `fetch()` command shown in the *Using delimiter-separated values section* (see `Parsing/3-csv-fetching.html`):

```
d3.csv("../Data/SolarSystemData.csv")
  .then(function(data) {
      console.log(data);
      // do something with the data
  });
```

You can also use different delimiters and a row function as the *last* parameter. In this case, `d3.autoType` was used as a row function, to convert strings into numbers, when possible (see `Parsing/4-dsv-fetching.html`):

```
d3.dsv(";", "../Data/cities15000.csv", d3.autoType)
  .then(function(data) {
      console.log(data);
  });
```

Fetching JSON is even easier (see `Parsing/5-json-fetching.html`). You will use this in the next section:

```
d3.json("../Data/sol_2016.json")
  .then(function(data) {
      console.log(data);
  });
```

A complete step-by-step example

This section will lead you through a complete SVG data-visualization application with D3. It's a larger example and more complex, but the concepts are the same, and most of the methods used were covered in this chapter. Each step is described briefly with some code examples, but you should download and try running the full listings available in the `StepByStep/` folder from the GitHub repository for this chapter.

What are we going to create?

The following diagram is a sketch of the visualization we plan to create, showing the coordinates, spacing, and margins we will have to consider when drawing the shapes:

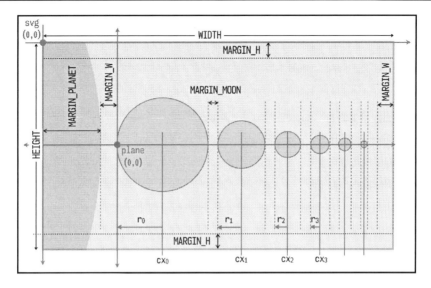

Sketch of the visualization that will be created

The page consists of six views, each showing the relative sizes of the largest moons of planets in the Solar System. We will draw SVG circles that represent planets and moons in scale. These circles should be reused and updated when the view is changed to show a different planet, new circles should be added, and unnecessary circles should be removed. The data is obtained from the `Data/sol_2016.json` file, compiled from data obtained from NASA's *Jet Propulsion Laboratory*.

Setting up the page and view port

We will start with a simple page that contains a minimal CSS style sheet. The HTML body includes static elements that will later be filled with new elements using D3:

```
<!DOCTYPE html>
<html lang="en">
<head>
    <title>Moons</title>
    <script src="https://d3js.org/d3.v5.min.js"></script>
    <!-- Using free Yanone Kaffeesatz fonts:
        https://www.yanone.de/fonts/kaffeesatz/ -->
    <style>
        svg { border: solid 1px gray; }
        * { font-family: 'Yanone Kaffeesatz', sans-serif; }
        text { font-size: 11px; }
    </style>
```

```
</head>
<body>

<h1>The largest moons</h1>
<div id="container" width="500" height="300">
    <svg height="100%" width="100%" id="moons"></svg>
</div>
<form></form>
</body>
</html>
```

Before loading the data files, some constants and global variables need to be set up. Compare these variables to the preceding diagram:

```
<script>
    // This object contains data used for the application
    const app = {
        planets: [],   // data will be loaded from external file
    }

    // This object contains variables that change for each view
    const current = {
        moons: [],          // the moons to be displayed
        id: undefined,      // key to select current object
        planet: {},         // the object used in the current view
        color: "black"      // color of the planet
    }
    current.id = "p5"; // start with Jupiter id = "p5"

    // A function that will scale the diameters in km to pixels
    const scale = d3.scaleLinear();

    // Dimensions and spacing for the SVG graphics context
    const WIDTH = 500, HEIGHT = 300;
    const MARGIN_W = 20, MARGIN_H = 50;
    const MARGIN_MOON = 10;     // space between moons
    const MARGIN_PLANET = 100; // space be reserved for the planet

    // Obtain a handle to the SVG element and set up the view port
    const svg = d3.select("#moons")
            .attr("viewBox", `0 0 ${WIDTH} ${HEIGHT}`);

    // All moons will be anchored on this object (the orbital plane)
    const plane = svg.append("g")
            .attr("transform", `translate(${[MARGIN_PLANET, HEIGHT/2]})`);

    // Next steps
    // 1) Load the data
```

```
        // 2) Select the data for the initial view
        // 3) Bind the data to graphical elements and draw the view
        // 4) Add interactive behavior: change planets and update moons
    </script>
```

Note the last two constants. The first one, svg, selects the SVG object and sets the *view port*, which has an origin at the top-left corner of the SVG graphics context. The second constant, named plane, is the line where the center coordinates for all of the circles will be placed. It's situated horizontally at the middle of the view port and 100 pixels from the left.

This code is in StepByStep/1-page-setup.html.

Loading data

The data file for this example (*Data/sol_2016.json*) is a JSON object that contains entries for several bodies that orbit the sun. It has the following structure:

```
{
    "star":{...},
    "planets":[...], // we only need the data from this array!
    "asteroids":[...],
    "tnos":[...],
    "centaurs":[...],
    "comets":[...]
}
```

We are only interested in the objects inside the planets array that have an id property with one of the following values: p3, p4, p5, p6, p7, p8. This excludes dwarf planets and planets that don't have any moons. We will only use a few properties from each object. They are listed as follows:

```
"planets": [
    {"id",  "name",  "diameterKm",
     "satellites": [
          {"name", "diameterKm"}
     ]
]
```

With this information, you can load the file and filter the planets array so that it only includes the objects that are going to be used. In the following listing, the d3.json() fetch method saves the filtered data in the app.planets array:

```
    // Loads the data file (take a look at it before proceeding)
    d3.json("../Data/sol_2016.json")
        .then(function(data) {
```

```
                    // only include planets with moons (p3 to p8)
                    app.planets = data.planets
                                    .filter(p => +p.id.substring(1) >= 3
                                            && +p.id.substring(1) <= 8);
                configureView(); // sets data and scales for each view
                draw();          // draws and updates moons and planets
            });

        function configureView() {
            console.log(planets); // check if data was correctly filtered
        }
        function draw() {}


        // Next steps
        // 1) Select the data for the initial view: configureView()
        // 2) Bind the data to graphical elements and draw the view
        // 3) Add interactive behavior: change planets and update moons

    </script>
```

This code is in `StepByStep/2-load-data.html`. If you load it in your browser, it will only display the title and an empty SVG graphics context as shown here. Use your browser's JavaScript console to check whether the data was loaded and to inspect the structure of the data array:

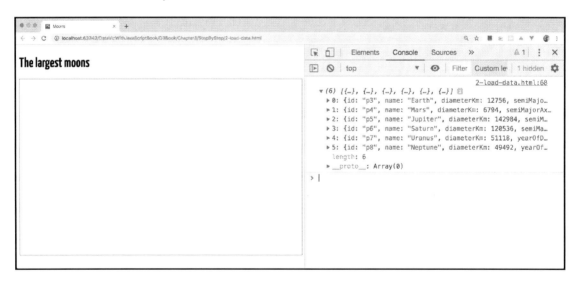

Printing the loaded data in the JavaScript console. Code: *StepByStep/2-load-data.html*.

Configuring scales and filtering data

To adequately fit a graphical representation of the data on the screen, you need to decide on the size of the sample you will use and its *extent* (maximum and minimum values). Based on that information, you may decide to filter the data values, limiting the amount of data shown. The extent is also necessary to configure a scale that will translate from kilometers into pixels, so that the chart will fit in the view port. These tasks can be performed with data manipulation methods and *scales* (the topics of the next two chapters). Since these operations need to be called every time the data changes (when a different planet is selected), we will place it in a function:

```javascript
function configureView() {
    // 1) Set the current data object
    current.planet =
        app.planets.filter(p => p.id == current.id)[0];

    // 2) Configure scales for this view
    // a) obtain the diameter of the largest moon
    const maxDiameter =
        d3.max(current.planet.satellites, d => d.diameterKm);

    // b) include moons with 1/50 of the largest moon or larger
    current.moons = current.planet.satellites
                .filter(s => s.diameterKm > maxDiameter/50);

    // c) add diameters (they will be drawn side by side)
    const sumDiameters =
        d3.sum(current.moons,d => d.diameterKm);

    // d) calculate space occupied by the circles
    const horizSpace = WIDTH - (MARGIN_PLANET + MARGIN_W*2 +
                    current.moons.length * MARGIN_MOON);
    const vertSpace  = HEIGHT - MARGIN_H*2;

    // e) configure the scale
    scale.range([0, d3.min([vertSpace, horizSpace])])
        .domain([0, sumDiameters]);

    // Inspect results
    console.log("Planet", current.planet);
    console.log("Largest moon diameter", maxDiameter);
    console.log("Selected moons", current.moons);
}
```

Compare the preceding values with the diagram. The code is in `StepByStep/3-config-scales.html`.

Drawing the planet

Now that the scales are set up, you can start drawing the circles. Recall that the `plane` object is a `<g>` element that had its (0,0) coordinates translated into the `x=MARGIN_PLANET`, `y=HEIGHT/2` position. If you want to view this guide line, include the following code in your `draw()` function. It will draw a red line that shows where the centers of the circles will be placed:

```
function draw() {
    // 1) Draw a guide line showing the orbital plane
    plane.append("line")
            .attr("x1",0)
            .attr("x2",WIDTH)
            .style("stroke","red");
    // ...
}
```

The line is only a guide. You can remove it later.

If a circle has a `cy` attribute equal to zero, it will be placed on that line and centered vertically. The scale was calculated so that all of the circles that represent moons could be placed side by side and fit in the viewport, but the planet was not included in that calculation. Its scaled radius won't fit in the view port, however, the visible curvature will still be in the same scale as the moons. Using a scaled negative radius as `cx`, part of the planet will be visible on the left side.

The following code can be used to draw the planet:

```
function draw() {
    // ...
    plane.append("circle").attr("class", "planet")
        .datum(current.planet)
        .attr("r", d => scale(d.diameterKm)/2)
        .attr("cx", d => -(MARGIN_W + scale(d.diameterKm)/2));
}
```

The *general update pattern* isn't necessary in this case, since there is only one object (not an array) and it's only added once, so we used `datum()`, which takes a single object, instead of `data()`, which requires an array.

A margin was added (MARGIN_W) so that there is some space between the planet and the first moon. If you open the page in a browser now, you should see a slightly curved black margin on the left, which is the visible part of the planet:

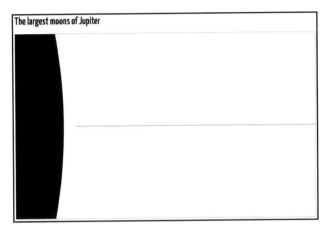

Positioning the planet and the orbital plane where the moons will be placed. Code: *StepByStep/4-draw-planet.html.*

Since each page will show a different planet, the page title should display its name. Add a `<span>` placeholder element with the corresponding ID in the HTML:

```
<h1>The largest moons of <span id="planetName"></span></h1>
```

Then, you can insert the planet's name, obtained from the data object, into the `<span>` element. Place the following line at the beginning of the `configureView()` function, after the data object is loaded:

```
// 2) Change page title
d3.select('#planetName').text(() => current.planet.name)
```

The full code section so far is in the `StepByStep/4-draw-planet.html` file.

Calculating the position of each moon

The position of each moon depends on where the center of the SVG circle is placed, represented by the `cx` and `cy` attributes. Appending the circles to the plane object will place them in the vertical middle and only require the calculation of `cx`. The `cy` attribute can be omitted, since zero is the default.

The cx coordinate for the first moon is its *radius,* or half its diameter. The cx attribute for the next circle is the diameter of the *previous* circle, plus the (MARGIN_MOON) spacing, plus the radius of the *current* circle. We can calculate the cx attribute for each moon and store it in a property of the data object, so it can be retrieved later when drawing the circle. You can select any valid identifier that is not yet used in the object as a property name. We named it cx in the following code. A good place for this code is at the end of the configureView() function (or any place after the scale has been configured):

```
function configureView() {
    // ...
    // 4) Compute cx center coordinates to position each moon
    current.moons.forEach(function(moon, i) {
        let space = 0;
        if(i > 0) {
            let previous = current.moons[i-1]
            space = previous.cx
                    + scale(previous.diameterKm)/2
                    + MARGIN_MOON;
        }
        moon.cx = space + scale(moon.diameterKm)/2;
        console.log(moon.name, moon.cx); // inspect results
    });
}
```

You can inspect the computed results in the JavaScript console, and check whether they fit in the available space. The preceding code prints the following *x* pixel values for the centers of each circle:

```
Amalthea 0.6427486268552063
Io 32.49620193993222
Europa 81.94928129017178
Ganymede 140.93841299520858
Callisto 209.84924623115575
Himalia 249.00666121304192
```

The code so far is in StepByStep/5-compute-moon-positions.html.

Entering the moons

The r attribute for each circle is obtained by scaling the diameterKm property and dividing it by two. Since cy is zero, it doesn't need to be set. The cx attribute uses the property calculated in the previous section, which is already scaled.

Since no circles of the `moon` class exist in the plane, the initial *enter* selection will contain the same number of elements in the `current.moons` array:

```
function draw() {
    // ...
    // 3) draw the moons
    plane.selectAll("circle.moon")
        .data(current.moons)
        .enter()
        .append("circle").attr("class", "moon")
        .attr("cx", d => d.cx)
        .attr("r", d => scale(d.diameterKm)/2);
}
```

If you comment or remove the red guideline, you should see a representation of the planet and its largest moons to scale, as shown in the following screenshot:

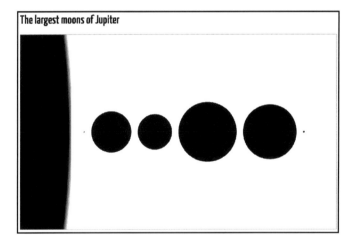

The largest moons of Jupiter

The moons of Jupiter to scale. sorted by relative position. Code: *StepByStep/6-enter-moons.html*.

The circles were ordered according to their data array indexes (the array was sorted by the ascending relative distance of each satellite to its planet). Since this chart only displays a selection of the planet's moons (they are filtered by size), and ignores the actual distance between them, you might prefer to follow the diagram and order the moons by size. This can be achieved by sorting the array *before* calculating `cx`.

Insert the following line in `configureView()` *after* the moons array is filtered but *before* the `cx` attributes are calculated, to sort moons by their diameter:

```
// 4) Sort the moons by their diameter
current.moons.sort((a,b) => d3.descending(a.diameterKm, b.diameterKm));
```

The result will be the circles displayed from largest to smallest. This code including the preceding line is in StepByStep/7-sort-moons.html.

Adding text labels

If you are interested in the largest moons of Jupiter, you probably want to know their names. That information is available in the data object, but we need to place it somewhere in the chart and relate it to the corresponding moon. One solution is to assign a color to each moon and add a legend that relates the color to each name. Try that as an exercise! An alternative is to place the label beside the moon. In this section, we will demonstrate the second solution.

Unlike HTML, you can't just add text inside an SVG element. You have to create a <text> element and use its attributes to place the object in a coordinate system. Since the text is related to the circle, it's best to refactor our code and place each circle and label in an SVG group using the <g> element, and then position the text and circle relatively to the group.

If the group is positioned where the circles were, you don't need to define cx or cy for each circle, since 0 is the default. But <g> elements don't have any x and y attributes. You will need to position it using a transform attribute. The following code (StepByStep/8-text-labels.html) is a refactored version that moves the <circle> elements inside the <g> elements and uses the moon class to label each <g> element, and no longer the circle:

```
// 3) draw the moons
// a) create moon groups positioned at cx,0 relative to plane
const moons = plane.selectAll("g.moon")
                   .data(current.moons)
                   .enter()
                   .append("g").attr("class", "moon")
                   .attr("transform", d => `translate(${[d.cx,0]})`);
```

A moons reference was saved for the selection because we need to add two elements to it. The following code adds the *circle*:

```
// b) add circle to each moon group positioned at cx=0,cy=0
//    relative to group
moons.append("circle")
     .attr("r", d => scale(d.diameterKm)/2);
```

If you load the page now, you will notice that the visual result is exactly the same as the previous example. Nothing changed, just the internal structure.

The next step is to place the *text* label. A good fit is to rotate it 90 degrees counterclockwise and place it in a central position few pixels from the edges of each moon. This can be done with a `transform` applied to the text element:

```
// c) add a text label positioned relatively to the group
moons.append("text")
    .text(d => d.name)
    .attr("transform", function(d) {    // updates text position
        const x = scale(d.diameterKm/2) + MARGIN_MOON;
        const y = this.getBBox().height/4;
        return `rotate(-90) translate(${[x,y]})`;
    });
```

The `getBBox()` method is part of the SVG DOM. It returns the bounding box of the text element, which has four properties (x, y, `height`, and `width`). The height was used to center the middle of the text with the circle (instead of the baseline, which is default).

You can add the circle and the text label to the moon group without breaking the selection chain by using the `each()` method, and selecting the `this` (or `nodes[i]`) reference inside the function to access the current element (see `StepByStep/9-text-labels-each.html`):

```
// 3) draw the moons
plane.selectAll("g.moon")
    .data(current.moons)
    .enter()
    .append("g").attr("class", "moon")
    .attr("transform", d => `translate(${[d.cx,0]})`)
    .each(function() {   // each g object contains a circle and text
        const moon = d3.select(this); // current group

        moon.append("circle")
            .attr("r", d => scale(d.diameterKm)/2);

        moon.append("text")
            .text(d => d.name)
            .attr("transform", function(d) {
                const x = scale(d.diameterKm/2) + MARGIN_MOON;
                const y = this.getBBox().height/4;
                return `rotate(-90) translate(${[x,y]})`;
            });
    });
```

The result is shown in the following screenshot:

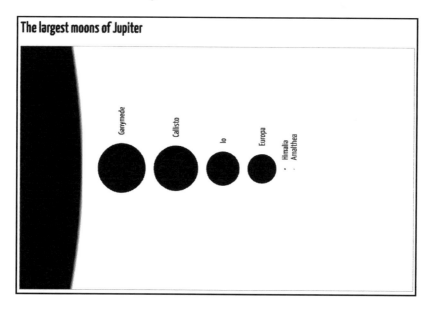

Moons sorted by size and labeled. Code: *StepByStep/9-text-labels-each.html.*

Changing views

Now that we have successfully displayed one complete view, we can demonstrate the power of D3 by automatically updating the view with new datasets. First, we need an interface to trigger the changes, such as a panel with a button for each view. The buttons can also be generated using D3's data-binding mechanism. Since buttons are only created and configured once, we will set them up inside a new `init()` function, called inside the JSON fetch promise:

```
d3.json("../Data/sol_2016.json")
    .then(function(data) {
        // only include planets with moons (p3 to p8)
        app.planets = data.planets
                        .filter(p => +p.id.substring(1) >= 3
                                && +p.id.substring(1) <= 8);
        init(); // add this line
        configureView();
        draw();
    });

function init() {}
```

The init() function uses the app.planets array as a data source, extracting each planet's name for the label and the planet's id for the button's id attribute. It also adds an event listener for the click event, which uses the button's id to set the new value for current.id, calling configureView() and draw() after the change. The buttons are added in the HTML <form> element, which is already in place after the <svg> element:

```
function init() {
    d3.select("form")
        .selectAll("button")
        .data(app.planets)
        .enter()
        .append("button")
        .attr("type", "button") // disables default submission event
        .attr("id", d => d.id)
        .text(d => d.name)
        .on("click", function(d) {
            current.id = d.id;
            configureView();
            draw();
        });
}
```

If you load the page in your browser, it should look like the following screenshot. You can click the different buttons and see the changes in the title, but the chart is not yet being updated correctly.

The code for this section is in `StepByStep/10-change-views.html`. Check out the moons now:

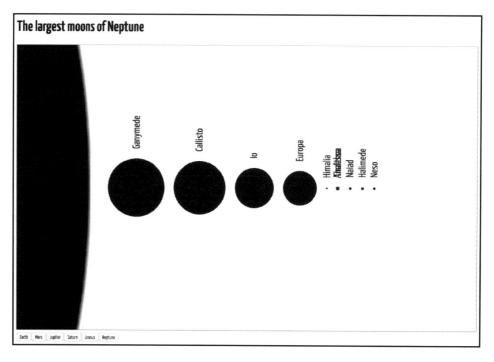

Multiple views, but still not updating correctly (the first six are moons of Jupiter). Code: *StepByStep/10-change-views.html.*

Updating views

Now we need to *update* the data every time the view changes. Let's start by making some improvements in the graphical interface, such as disabling a button when its ID is equal to `current.id` and enabling all buttons that have a different ID. These commands need to be placed in one of the functions called when the button is clicked. It can be anywhere in `configureView()`, as in the example:

```
function configureView() {
    // ...
    // 3) Disable button for currently displayed planet
    d3.selectAll("button").property("disabled", false);
    d3.select("button#"+current.id).property("disabled", true);
}
```

When changing views, you will notice that new planets are being drawn over the previous ones. If you inspect the circle in your browser's development tools, you will notice that a new <circle> element is being appended every time a button is clicked. This happens because draw(), where the circle is created, is called on every click. We can fix this by moving the code that appends the circle to the end of the init() function, which is called only once:

```
function init() {
    // ...
    // 2) Add circle for the planets
    plane.append("circle")
         .attr("class", "planet")
}
```

In init(), you only need to append the circle and set its class, so it can be selected. The datum and attributes should be set in the draw() function, because they need to be updated every time the data changes. To obtain a reference to the circle, just select it by its class:

```
function draw() {
    // ...
    // 2) update the planet
    plane.select(".planet")
        .datum(current.planet)
        .attr("r", d => scale(d.diameterKm)/2)
        .attr("cx", d => -(MARGIN_W + scale(d.diameterKm)/2))
        .style("fill", d => current.color);
    // ...
}
```

Click on the buttons now. You should see the curvature change for each planet.

It would be nice to display each planet in a different color. Add the following colors array to the global app object. The colors are similar to each planet's color:

```
const app = {
    planets: [],
    colors: ['#4169e1','#cc8530','#d4a450','#dab520','7fffd4','1e90ff']
}
```

Also, add a `color` property to the current global object:

```
const current = {
    moons: [],          // the moons to be displayed
    id: undefined,      // key to select current object
    planet: {},         // the object used in the current view
    color: "black"      // color of the planet
}
```

The array's index can be calculated from its `id` by removing the *p* prefix and subtracting 3 (since the IDs start with *p3*). This code should be included in `configureView()`:

```
current.color  = app.colors[(+current.id.substring(1) - 3)];
```

Finally, use the CSS `fill` property to update the planet's color in `draw()`:

```
// 2) update the planet
plane.select(".planet") // ...
    .style("fill", d => current.color);
```

The results so far are in `StepByStep/11-update.html`.

Adding new elements and merging selections

The moons are still not being updated correctly. They are only added once, when the circle is created, and appended to the DOM tree. When all of the elements already exist, the `_enter` array is empty, so nothing after `enter()` ever gets called (this is the expected behavior). To fix this, you need to update two selections: the *enter selection*, if it exists, appending new circles and setting initial properties (this is already working), and the *update selection*, selecting elements previously updated and applying new values to their properties (this is what needs to be done). You can reuse the same code for the updates if you *merge* the selections.

You need to save a reference to the *original selection*, so it can be later merged with the *enter selection*. The following code breaks the selection stream into three parts: the first selects the elements to be appended or updated and binds it with the data, the second appends new elements to an *enter selection* (which may be empty, if there are no new elements to be added), and the third merges both selections, updating the attributes, style, and contents to the merged selection:

```
function draw() {
    // ...
    // 3) Moons: general update pattern
    // a) the update selection (bind new data to each existing element)
    const updateMoons = plane.selectAll("g.moon").data(current.moons)

    // b) the enter selection (adds elements) - may be initially empty
    const enterMoons =
            updateMoons.enter()
                .append("g").attr("class", "moon")
                .each(function() {
                    const moon = d3.select(this);
                    moon.append("circle");
                    moon.append("text")
                });

    // c) the merged selection (updates data values)
    enterMoons.merge(updateMoons)
        .attr("transform", d => `translate(${[d.cx,0]})`)
        .each(function() {
            const moon = d3.select(this);
            moon.select("circle").attr("r", d => scale(d.diameterKm)/2);
            moon.select("text").text(d => d.name)
            .attr("transform", function(d) {
                const x = scale(d.diameterKm/2) + MARGIN_MOON;
                const y = this.getBBox().height/4;
                return `rotate(-90) translate(${[x,y]})`;
            });
        });
}
```

Note that all of the appended elements (circle and text) should be included in the *enter* selection. Their attributes will only be set when the selection is merged.

The result is in `StepByStep/12-enter-append-merge.html`. The following screenshot shows one of the views with extra moons:

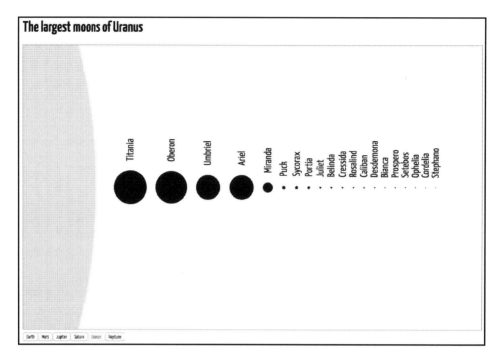

One of the views showing moons appended after an enter selection. Code: *StepByStep/12-enter-append-merge.html*

Removing extra elements

It's almost done, but we still have one problem. The extra elements don't go away. Try clicking on Earth or Mars, or look at the following screenshot to see what happens! We have to deal with the exit selection:

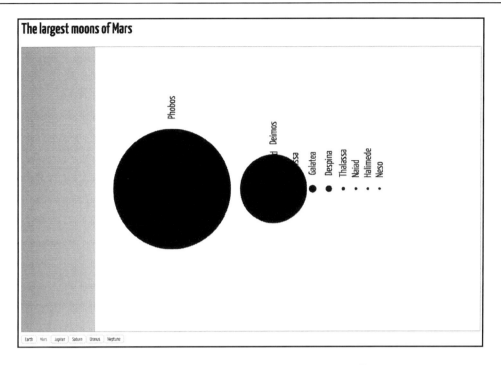

Extra elements not removed (Mars's moons were updated, but Neptune's moons still appear).
Code: *StepByStep/12-enter-append-merge.html*

The *exit selection* contains elements every time you change to a view that displays *fewer* moons than the previous ones (the size of the selection is larger than the dataset). These elements need to be removed. All you have to do is to add the following code to the draw() function:

```
updateMoons.exit().remove();
```

And that's it. Try it out! The final result is in StepByStep/13-exit-remove.html.

Using join() for updates

In this example, we can't just replace enter-append-merge for `join()`, since the enter selection appends two child elements, so an enter function is passed as the first argument. It's no longer necessary to save references for intermediate selections, and everything fits in a single selection chain:

```
// 3) Moons: general update pattern with join
plane.selectAll("g.moon")
    .data(current.moons)
    .join(enter => enter.append("g")
                        .each(function() {
                            d3.select(this).append("circle");
                            d3.select(this).append("text");
                        })
    )
    .attr("class", "moon")
    .attr("transform", d => `translate(${[d.cx,0]})`)
    .each(function() {
        const moon = d3.select(this);
        moon.select("circle").attr("r", d => scale(d.diameterKm)/2);
        moon.select("text").text(d => d.name)
        .attr("transform", function(d) {
            const x = scale(d.diameterKm/2) + MARGIN_MOON;
            const y = this.getBBox().height/4;
            return `rotate(-90) translate(${[x,y]})`;
        });
    });
```

This change improves the code, but the result is the same. The code is in `StepByStep/14-join.html`.

Other improvements

There are still several small improvements you can make in this chart, such as adding colors and tooltips. They will be left as exercises for you. A solution using tooltips, shown in the following screenshot, is provided in `StepByStep/15-tooltips.html`:

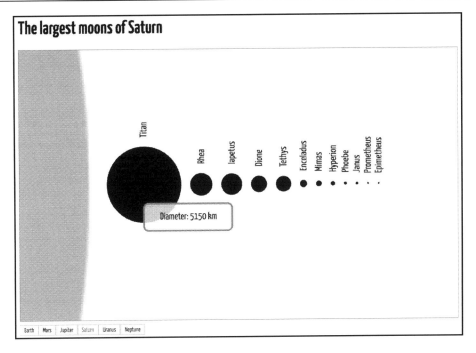

The final application with colors and tooltips. Code: *StepByStep/15-tooltips.html*.

Summary

This chapter covered the most important module in the D3 library: *d3-selection*, which provides a flow-based DSL for selecting DOM elements, binding them to data, and updating their properties after the data changes. Most of the methods in this library were used in examples that explored the *general update pattern*, which is a fundamental concept used in practically all D3 applications that should be very well understood. This chapter also introduced the `selection.join()` method, which is a modern and simpler alternative to the *general update pattern*.

You also learned how to load external files and parse popular data formats, such as CSV and JSON, using methods from the *d3-dsv* and *d3-fetch* modules.

There's still a lot to learn before mastering D3. In the next chapter, you will continue to use most of the methods from this chapter, and learn how to use some new tools that will help you to transform and generate data.

References

- Module documentation, D3.js: `github.com/d3/d3-selection`, `github.com/d3/d3-dsv`, `github.com/d3/d3-fetch`.
- General Update Pattern I, by Mike Bostock: `bl.ocks.org/mbostock/3808218`
- General Update Pattern II: Key Functions, by Mike Bostock: `bl.ocks.org/mbostock/3808221`
- General Update Pattern III: Update Transitions, by Mike Bostock: `bl.ocks.org/mbostock/3808234`
- Planetary data. Compiled from Solar System data obtained mainly from NASA (JPL) and other public sources: `Data/sol_2016.json`
- Geographical database: `Data/cities15000.csv` from `GeoNames` geographical database: `www.geonames.org`

5
Manipulating Data and Formatting

Unless you create your datasets yourself, it's usually necessary to prepare the data so that it can be used in your visualization. This might involve changing its structure; filtering unwanted fields; sorting, merging and splitting values; and deriving new fields, or even generating data values. You don't need much more than the standard ES6 methods and functions for manipulating arrays, objects, and collections, but D3 extends that set with extra tools that have been optimized for transforming datasets.

The *d3-array* module contains most of the data manipulation tools that you will need. It includes functions for sorting and transforming data, generating sequences, obtaining statistical information, grouping, and nesting. You can use these functions with standard JavaScript arrays, objects, maps, and sets, combined with native functions and operators.

The *d3-collection* module also contains functions for working with maps, sets, and nesting data, but most of its functions are deprecated, since they can be replaced by standard ES6 equivalents. We still use it for grouping operations because it offers a simpler approach than the suggested replacements that are available in the *d3-array*.

The *d3-random* module extends JavaScript's `Math.random()` with number generators based on normal, exponential, and other random distributions. They also support sequence generation and bin quantization for histograms. In this chapter, you will use the most important methods in these modules.

Interpolation is a method that's used for *tweening*: obtaining intermediate values between two data points. D3 supports interpolation between different kinds of data, transitions, and behaviors. The basic functions are in the *d3-interpolate* module, which will be introduced in this chapter.

This chapter also covers the *d3-format* and *d3-time-format* modules, which are used to parse date strings and format dates and numbers according to a specific locale.

Here is what will be covered in this chapter:

- Manipulating arrays, collections, and objects
- Grouping data
- Histograms
- Random numbers
- Interpolation
- Text formatting and internationalization

Manipulating arrays, collections, and objects

The *d3-array* module contains functions and methods for obtaining information about data in arrays (statistics), searching, sorting, and transforming arrays. It also supports JavaScript's iterable collections and nesting/grouping. In this section, you will learn about most of the methods in this module and have the opportunity to try them out in simple code examples.

Searching and statistics

Unlike equivalent native JavaScript methods, most of the *d3-array* functions in the following table are optimized for data manipulation, since they ignore missing data (the exception is `d3.quantile()`). This means you don't have to preprocess the data to deal with `undefined`, `null`, and `NaN` values. These functions can be applied to arrays of numbers or arrays of objects. Arrays of objects require the use of an `accessor` function, which is used to select the object property to be used:

Function	Description
d3.min (*array, accessor*)	Returns the smallest element of the array in natural order.
d3.max (*array, accessor*)	Returns the largest value of the array in natural order.
d3.extent (*array, accessor*)	Returns an array with minimum and maximum values. This is equivalent to [d3.min (*array, accessor*), d3.max (*array, accessor*)].
d3.sum (*array, accessor*)	Returns the sum of all the elements in the array.
d3.mean (*array, accessor*)	Returns the mean of all the elements in the array.

d3.median (*array, accessor*)	Returns the median of the elements in the array.
d3.quantile (*array, p, accessor*)	Returns the *p*-quantile of the sorted array, where *p* is a value between 0 and 1.
d3.variance (*array, accessor*)	Returns an unbiased estimator of populator variance.
d3.deviation (*array, accessor*)	Returns the standard deviation.

Functions from d3-array that return information about data in arrays

Try typing the following examples into the JavaScript console of your browser. The following arrays are used in the examples that follow (you can also run the code from `Arrays/1-statistics.html`):

```
const array = [4,2,9,12,6,23, NaN, 9,71,55, undefined, 49];
const objects = [{label: 'label1', value: 5},
                 {label: 'label2', value: 3},
                 {label: 'label3', value: 9}]
```

The following code examples should be self-explanatory. The comments contain the expected results:

```
const min = d3.min(array);                     // 2
const min2 = d3.min(objects, d => d.value);    // 3
const min3 = Math.min(array);                  // NaN
const max = d3.max(array);                     // 71
const max2 = d3.max(objects.map(d => d.value)); // 9
const extent = d3.extent(array);               // [2, 71]
const sum = d3.sum(array);                      // 240
const mean = d3.mean(array);                    // 24
const median = d3.median(array);                // 10.5
const variance = d3.variance(array);            // 622
const sqrtVariance = Math.sqrt(variance);       // 24.939927826679853
const deviation = d3.deviation(array);          // 24.939927826679853
```

Quantiles divide a dataset into equal-sized groups. The `d3.quantile()` function is used to compute the cut points and take two arguments. The resulting datasets can be used to chart a histogram. The first argument is an array that must be sorted and should contain numeric values and no `null`, `undefined`, or `NaN` values. A number between 0 and 1 should be provided as the second argument, informing the desired quantile. For example, to obtain the *quartiles* for a dataset, you need to compute three cut points (25%, 50%, and 75%):

```
const array2 = [4,2,9,12,6,23,9,71,55,49];
array2.sort((a,b) => a-b);
const quartile25 = d3.quantile(array2, .25);   // 6.75
const quartile50 = d3.quantile(array2, .5);    // 10.5
const quartile75 = d3.quantile(array2, .75);   // 42.5
```

Sorting

For simple ascending and descending sorting order, you can use the native JavaScript `sort()` method to sort arrays without having to write a comparator function, thus returning one of the two built-in comparators provided in *d3-array*:

Comparator	Description
`d3.ascending`(*a,b*)	Comparator to sort an array in ascending order.
`d3.descending`(*a,b*)	Comparator to sort an array in descending order.

Built-in sort comparator functions

The following code examples demonstrate the use of these comparators and the expected results (see `Arrays/2-sort.html`):

```
const array = [4,2,9,12,6,23,9,71,55,49];
const objects = [{value: 5},{value: 3},{value: 9}]
array.sort((a,b) => d3.descending(a,b));  // [71,55,49,23,12,9,9,6,4,2]
objects.sort((a,b) => d3.ascending(a.value, b.value));
                                // [{value: 3},{value: 5},{value: 9}]
```

Transforming data

Most of the *d3-array* functions that are listed in the following table are used to create new arrays by transforming or extracting data from one or more existing arrays. All except `shuffle()` return new arrays:

Function	Description
`d3.merge`(*arrayOfArrays*)	Merges a provided array of arrays into a single array. This method can be used to flatten bi-dimensional arrays. It is similar to the JavaScript `concat()` method, but requires an array.
`d3.permute`(*array, indexes*)	Returns a new array containing the elements of the provided array according to an array of indexes that's provided as a second argument.
`d3.permute`(*object, keys*)	Returns an array containing the values of the provided object according to an array of keys that's provided as the second argument.

d3.cross (*a, b, reducer*)	Computes the Cartesian product of two arrays, a and b, and returns a two-element array for each pair unless an optional *reducer* function is provided to compute a result for each tuple.
d3.pairs (*array, reducer*)	Returns an array of adjacent pairs of the provided array, unless an optional *reducer* function is provided to compute a value for each adjacent pair.
d3.zip (*arrays*)	Receives a list of arrays and creates an array of arrays, where the sub-arrays group the items of the same index in each array. If any array is larger than the other, the items in excess are truncated.
d3.transpose (*matrix*)	Receives a matrix (array of arrays) and applies the d3.zip() function to its sub-arrays, resulting in a transposed matrix.
d3.shuffle (*array, start, stop*)	Randomizes the order of the elements in an array. This method does not return a *new* array. It alters the existing array and returns it. The optional *start* and *stop* indexes can be used to shuffle a part of the array.

Functions from *d3-array* for transforming data in arrays

The following code example demonstrates the use of these methods and their expected results (see Arrays/4-transforms.html):

```
const merge = d3.merge([[3,4], [5,6]]); // [3,4,5,6]
const concat = [3,4].concat([5,6]);       // [3,4,5,6]
const permuted = d3.permute([1,2,3,4], [0,3,0,3,0,3]); // [1,4,1,4,1,4]
const cross  = d3.cross([3,4], [5,6]); // [[3,5], [3,6], [4,5], [4,6]]
const cross2 = d3.cross([3,4], [5,6], (a,b) => a*b);// [15, 18, 20, 24]
const pairs = d3.pairs([3,4,5,6]);   // [[3,4], [4,5], [5,6]]
const pairs2 = d3.pairs([3,4,5,6], (a,b) => a+b);   // [7, 9, 11]
const zip = d3.zip([1,2,3],[4,5,6],[9,8,7,6]);
const transpose = d3.transpose([[1,2,3],[4,5,6],[9,8,7]]);
  // Same result for zip and transpose: [[1,4,9],[2,5,8],[3,6,7]]
const array = [1,2,3,4,5,6,7,8,9];
d3.shuffle(array);  // [6,8,5,9,4,3,2,1,7]
```

Generating data

The *d3-array* functions that are listed as follows are used to generate numerical sequences:

Function	Description
d3.range (*start, stop, step*)	Generates an array containing an arithmetic progression. If *stop* is provided, the sequence will be from *0* to *stop -1*. If *start* is provided, it will be from *start* to *stop* -1. If *step* is provided, the sequence will be generated, skipping *step* numbers.
d3.ticks (*start, stop, count*)	Similar to range() but generates rounded values that are powers of 10 multiplied by 1, 2, or 5. All arguments are mandatory. It includes both start and stop values if they are exact.
d3.tickStep(*start, stop, count*)	Returns the rounded difference between adjacent tick values using the same parameters that are passed to d3.ticks().
d3.tickIncrement(*start, stop, count*)	Similar to tickStep() but returns $-step^{-1}$ if step is less than 1.

Functions from *d3-array* for generating numerical data sequences

The following example demonstrates the use of these methods and shows the expected results in the comments (see `Arrays/5-sequence.html`):

```
const range  = d3.range(10);       // [0,1,2,3,4,5,6,7,8,9]
const range2 = d3.range(-5, 5); // [-5,-4,-3,-2,-1,0,1,2,3,4]
const range3 = d3.range(-25, 75, 10); // [-25,-15,-5,5,15,25,35,45,55,65]
const ticks2 = d3.ticks(-25, 75, 10); // [-20,-10,0,10,20,30,40,50,60,70]
const ticks3 = d3.ticks(5, 7.5, 5);   // [5, 5.5, 6, 6.5, 7, 7.5]
const tickStep = d3.tickStep(5, 7.5, 5);      // 0.5
const tickInc  = d3.tickIncrement(5, 7.5, 5); // -2
```

Grouping operations

With grouping, you can convert a **flat tree structure** (common in CSV data files) into a **hierarchical tree**, grouped by selected keys. You can also group by multiple keys, therby creating multi-level hierarchies. Each object is preserved as a leaf in the hierarchy, but a `rollup` function can be used to reduce the leaf object to a single value.

There are grouping functions in *d3-collection* and *d3-array*, starting with version 2. This function will cover the two newer functions that are available in *d3-array*. To use them in the current distribution, you need to import `d3-array.v2.js` using NPM or using the script tag:

```
<script src="https://d3js.org/d3-array.v2.min.js"></script>
```

There are two functions listed in the following table:

Method	Description
d3.group (*iterable, ...keys*)	Receives an iterable dataset (*array, Map, Set*), one or more key functions, and returns an ES6 *Map* with objects grouped by key. If multiple keys are provided, they will produce nested maps.
d3.rollup (*iterable, reduce, ...keys*)	Receives an iterable dataset (*array, Map, Set*), a reduction function, one or more key functions, and returns an ES6 *Map* with the result of the reduction function grouped by key. If multiple keys are provided, they will produce nested maps.

Functions from *d3-array* for grouping by keys

Consider the following dataset with a list of movies (see `Arrays/6-grouping.html`):

```
const movies = [
    {title: 'Arrival', director: 'Denis Villeneuve', year: 2016},
    {title: 'Interstellar', director: 'Christopher Nolan', year: 2014},
    {title: 'Rogue One', director: 'Gareth Edwards', year: 2016},
    {title: 'The Shining', director: 'Stanley Kubrick', year: 1980},
    {title: 'A Clockwork Orange', director: 'Stanley Kubrick', year:
     1972},
    {title: 'Dunkirk', director: 'Christopher Nolan', year: 2017},
    {title: 'Solyaris', director: 'Andrei Tarkovsky', year: 1972},
    {title: 'Stalker', director: 'Andrei Tarkovsky', year: 1979},
    {title: 'Wonder Woman', director: 'Patty Jenkins', year: 2017},
];
```

With the `d3.group()` function, you can group objects by selected keys. The following code groups the movies by the `director` key (see `Arrays/7-grouping-sort.html`):

```
const groupByDirector = d3.group(movies, d => d.director);
```

This code example groups by the `year` key, sorting the dataset before grouping:

```
const sortedMovies = movies.sort((a,b) => d3.ascending(a.year, b.year))
const groupByYear = d3.group(sortedMovies, d => d.year);

Map(6) {
    key:1972 => value:[{title:'A Clockwork...',...},{title:
    'Solyaris',...}]
    key:1979 => value:[{title:'Stalker', ...}],
    key:1980 => value:[{title:'The Shining', ...}],
    key:2014 => value:[{title:'Interstellar', ...}],
    key:2016 => value:[{title:'Arrival',...},{ title:'Rogue One', ...}],
    key:2017 => value:[{title:'Dunkirk',...},{title: 'Wonder Woman', ...}]
}
```

You can also group by multiple keys, in order. The following code groups first by `year`, and then by `director`:

```
const byYearAndDirector = d3.group(movies, d => d.year, d => d.director);
```

This will result in nested maps.

If you don't want to store the entire object in each value, you can reduce it to any format you wish using `d3.rollup()`, which takes a reduction function as the second parameter. The following code groups movies by year and saves each leaf as a single string containing the title and the director (see `Arrays/8-rollup.html`):

```
const groupByYear =
        d3.rollup(movies,
                v => v.map(d => d.title + ` (${d.director})`),
                d => d.year)
```

The `d3.group()` and `d3.rollup()` functions return ES6 *Maps*. To use the data from a map in a selection, you first need to turn it into an array. This can be done with the *spread operator* or the `Array.from()` function (see `Arrays/9-grouping-array.html`):

```
const array1 = Array.from(groupByYear);
const array2 = [...groupByYear]; // ES6 spread operator
```

This works for the first level. If you use the `byYearAndDirector` object, which groups the data in *two* levels, only the outer *Map* will be converted into an array. You may also need to perform additional transformations before using the data as the source of a layout or shape generator.

ES2015 replacements for d3-collection

The *d3-collection* module contains functions for creating maps and sets, manipulating the data stored in them, and extracting properties from objects. These functions were created before ES6 (ES2015) was widely supported, but are no longer necessary. You might still find them in older D3 code or in code that contains functions that use these structures. In a few cases, there is no difference between using a D3 function or an ES6 function, but if you are creating new code, you should use the ES6 standards whenever possible, since D3 sets and maps are not iterable and don't work with operators that assume iterable collections (such as *spread operator*).

The following table compares standard ES2015 functions with deprecated *d3-collection* functions that you may find in older D3 code, or that is returned by operations using `d3.nest()`:

Function	Replace with	Differences
`d3.keys`(*object*)	`Object.keys`(*object*)	None
`d3.values`(*object*)	`Object.values`(*object*)	None

`d3.entries`(*object*)	`Object.entries`(*object*)	`d3.entries()` returns a `{key,value}` object. `Object.entries()` returns an array of `[key,value]` arrays. You can convert D3 entries into ES6 using the following code:
		``const entriesArray =
		  entriesObject.map(d =>
		                   [d.key,d.value]);```

`d3.map`(*entriesObject*)	`new Map()` or
	`new Map`(*entriesArray*)
		Incompatible implementations. You can convert a D3 map into an ES6 map using the following code:
		``const entriesArray =
		  d3map.entries()
		       .map(d => [d.key,d.value]);
		const esMap = new Map(entriesArray);```

`d3.set`(*array*)	`new Set()` or
	`new Set`(*array*)
		Incompatible implementations. You can convert a D3 set into an ES6 set using the following code:
		``const array =
		  d3Set.values().map(d => +d);
		const esSet = new Set(array);```

ES2015 replacements for deprecated *d3-collection* functions. See code examples in the *Collections/* folder.

See `Collections/1-d3-collection-objects.html`, `2-d3-collection-maps.html`, and `3-d3-collection-sets-objects.html` for examples of using both ES2015 and deprecated *d3-collection* structures.

Grouping data with d3.nest()

The *d3-collection* module contains the `d3.nest()` function, which is widely used for grouping. It can be replaced by the `d3.group` and `d3.rollup()` functions from the *d3-array* module, but, at the time of writing, it's not a ready-to-use replacement yet, for the following reasons:

- You still need to convert the resulting map or set into an array before using it, since the current version of `selection.data()` only supports arrays
- With one level of grouping, the spread operator or the `Array.from()` function can be used to obtain an array, but it's harder if you need to group and sort multiple levels
- Generator functions in other D3 modules and plugins that require nested structures frequently assume the nested object structure that's produced by `d3.nest()` as the default

Mike Bostock suggests creating reusable functions for nesting and rollup using the `d3.group()` and `d3.rollup()` functions (see `observablehq.com/@mbostock/nested-groups`), and it's likely that such functions will be part of a future D3 release, but since they aren't yet part of D3, we will stick to `d3.nest()` from the *d3-collection* module for most of the examples in this book that require nesting.

Nesting configuration

A grouping operation starts with a call to `d3.nest()` and is followed by operations to set the keys and the data that will be processed. These functions and methods are listed in the following table:

Function or method	Description
d3.`nest()`	Creates a nest operator with an empty set of keys.
nest.`key` (*function*)	Registers a function that returns a key to be used in grouping.
nest.`sortKeys` (*comparator*)	Sorts keys using a provided *comparator* function.
nest.`sortValues` (*comparator*)	Sorts leaf elements using a provided *comparator* function.
nest.`rollup` (*function*)	Registers a *rollup* function that returns a collapsed value. The result will also replace the *entry*.`values` key with the *entry*.`value` key.
nest.`map` (*array*)	Applies the grouping operator to an array and returns the result as a D3 map. This structure is incompatible with an ES2015 map, but you can convert it, as shown in the previous table.
nest.`object` (*array*)	Applies the grouping operator to an array and returns the result as an object.
nest.`entries` (*array*)	Applies the grouping operator to an array and returns the result as an array of `{key,value}` objects.

Functions and methods for grouping operations using d3.nest().

Consider the following object array. It's identical to the one we used in the `d3.group()` examples (see `Collections/4-nesting.html`):

```
const movies = [
  {title:'The Shining', director:'Stanley Kubrick', year:1980},
  {title:'A Clockwork Orange', director:'Stanley Kubrick', year:1972},
  {title:'The Shape of Water', director:'Guillermo del Toro', year:2017},
  {title:'Laberinto del Fauno', director:'Guillermo del Toro', year:2006},
  {title:'2001:A Space Odyssey', director:'Stanley Kubrick', year:1968},
  {title:'Wonder Woman', director:'Patty Jenkins', year: 2017},
];
```

The objects can be grouped using one or more *keys*. For example, the following code will group the objects by director:

```
const groupByDirector =
    d3.nest()
        .key(d => d.director)
        .entries(movies);
```

Unlike `d3.group()`, which returns an ES6 map, `d3.nest().entries()` returns the result as an array of objects. This is the output of the preceding line (see `Collections/5-nesting-entries.html`):

```
[
 {
  key: "Stanley Kubrick", values: [
   {title:"2001:A Space Odyssey", director:"Stanley Kubrick", year:1968},
   {title:"A Clockwork Orange", director:"Stanley Kubrick", year:1972},
   {title:"The Shining", director: "Stanley Kubrick", year: 1980},
  ]
 },{
  key: "Guillermo del Toro", values: [
   {title:"Laberinto del Fauno", director:"Guillermo del Toro", year:
    2006},
   {title:"The Shape of Water", director:"Guillermo del Toro", year:2017}
  ]
 },{
  key: "Patty Jenkins", values: [
   {title: "Wonder Woman", director: "Patty Jenkins", year: 2017}
  ]
 }
]
```

Sorting

You can sort the objects (the leaves) inside each group using `sortValues()`. For example, this code will sort the movies by `year` (see `Collections/6-nesting-sort.html`):

```
const groupByDirector =
    d3.nest()
        .key(d => d.director)
        .sortValues((a,b) => d3.ascending(a.year, b.year))
        .entries(movies);
```

You can also sort by `keys` using `sortKeys()`:

```
const groupByDirector =
    d3.nest()
      .key(d => d.director)
      .sortKeys((a,b) => d3.ascending(a, b))
      .sortValues((a,b) => d3.ascending(a.year, b.year))
      .entries(movies);
```

Multiple `key()` methods can be called in order with different keys for multi-level nesting (see `Collections/5-nesting-entries.html`).

Rollup

Finally, you can transform each leaf object and replace it with derived or filtered data using the `rollup()` method with a reduction function based on the `values` array. For example, this code will replace each leaf object with a string in a `value` key (see `Collections/7-nesting-rollup.html`):

```
const groupByDirector =
        d3.nest()
          .key(d => d.director)
          .sortKeys((a,b) => d3.ascending(a, b))
          .sortValues((a,b) => d3.ascending(a.year, b.year))
          .rollup(values => values.map(d => `${d.title} (${d.year})`))
          .entries(movies);
```

The result of running the preceding code is as follows:

```
[
  {
     key: "Guillermo del Toro",
     value: ["El Laberinto del Fauno (2006)",
             "The Shape of Water (2017)"]
  },{
     key: "Patty Jenkins",
     value: ["Wonder Woman (2017)"]
  },{
     key: "Stanley Kubrick",
     value: ["2001: A Space Odyssey (1968)",
             "A Clockwork Orange (1972)",
             "The Shining (1980)"]
  }
]
```

A step-by-step grouping example

To demonstrate nesting with multiple keys, we will use a complete step-by-step example using `d3.nest()`. The code is available in the `StepByStepNest/` folder.

Consider the following CSV file (`Data/rain_sao_paulo.csv`), which contains the average amount of rain in millimeters measured monthly in the city of São Paulo, Brazil, from 1984 to 2017:

```
Month,Year,Rain_mm
01,1984,259.3
02,1984,32.5
03,1984,54
04,1984,96.8
05,1984,113
... +400 lines
0,2017,149.4
11,2017,159.8
12,2017,151.3
```

The data can be loaded using `d3.csv()`, which makes it available as a JavaScript object when it has finished loading. This process is illustrated as follows:

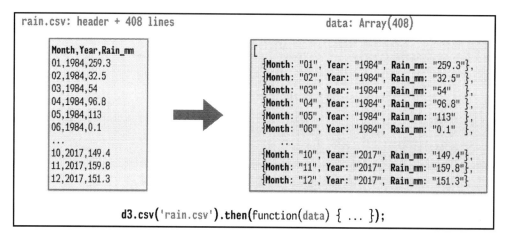

Loading a CSV and converting it into an object

Now, you need to display that data in an HTML table, with one row for each month and one column for each year. How can you achieve this?

Since HTML tables are nested structures, it will be easier if you nest the data in the same way. In a table, the `<td>` data cell is part of a `<tr>` row, which is part of `<table>`. You need to reorganize the data so that years are grouped in months, and then the data can be located by finding the month, followed by the year. You can also use `rollup()` to reduce the leaf object to just the value that's needed (amount of rain in millimeters). This process, using the `d3.nest()` function, is illustrated as follows:

Converting a flat tabular structure into a two-level-deep nested tree using d3.nest(). Code: *StepByStepNest/1-nest.html*.

Now that the data is in the expected format, you can use it to populate an HTML table and display it. The nested data can be directly bound to nested `<tr>` and `<td>` selections. The `entries` array (with 12 elements/months) is bound to the `<tr>` elements, and for each `<tr>`, the `entry.values` array (with 34 elements/years) is bound to a `<td>` element.

This is illustrated as follows:

Mapping the nested data to a nested HTML table selection. Code: *StepByStepNest/2-html-table.html*.

Assuming you have a `<table></table>` element in your `<body>`, the following code will select it and populate the table with the nested data (see `StepByStepNest/2-html-table.html`):

```
const table = d3.select("table");
const tr = table.selectAll("tr.month")  // binds entries to <tr> rows
    .data(entries)  // list of 12 month objects
    .enter()
    .append("tr").attr("class", "month")
    .attr("title", d => d.key);  // the month number
tr.selectAll("td.year") // binds entry.values to <td>
    .data(d => d.values) // list of 34 year objects per month
    .enter()
    .append("td").attr("class", "year")
    .attr("title", d => d.key)  // the year in each month
    .text(d => d.value); // the data-value (amount of rain in mm)
```

This will generate a table with all the results, as follows:

259.3	190.1	250.7	442.3	293.4	359.2	280.7	270.7	203.4	248.7	231.9	379	354.9	313.3	200.6	319.1	328.3	144.2	284.8	317.2	284.5	312.1	348	213.5	318.5	351.8	480.5	493.7	332.6	169.2	237.9	156.2	175.9	454
32.5	281.4	268.4	177.5	284.7	326.5	152.8	358	184	265.6	170.8	445.5	305.6	181.1	394.2	369.8	246.6	290.1	172.5	109.4	335.6	99.9	166	285.9	236.3	200.2	296.5	311.5	224.2	278	197.6	273	275.1	127.3
54	166.9	230.6	178.5	203.6	185.1	228.8	451.3	273.7	92.5	252.3	304.1	396.8	76	252.9	187.3	100.1	138.5	326.5	126.5	130.7	286.6	607.9	185.4	180.8	125.7	184.5	164	187.6	174.5	226.9	332.7	256.6	160.4
96.8	31.4	84.9	91.5	173.4	96.2	77.1	169	59.3	118.4	99.9	64.9	81.7	71.6	92.8	35.8	6.3	32.9	53.5	45.6	123.4	133.2	51.1	124.8	96.6	69.6	124.5	133	155.9	70.7	79.7	108.1	2.4	143.1
113	107.2	84.6	241.2	210.8	30.4	52.8	34.2	71.4	101.2	40.7	74.4	33.1	75	130	355	9.3	86.1	93	33.1	60.1	199	15	59	80.3	50	65.2	30.4	82.7	42.5	46	50.7	105.7	153.4
0.1	14.2	2.4	195.9	58.8	44.4	39.2	85.8	18.6	57.5	31.9	58.7	54.1	122.5	16.1	84.3	12.7	74.5	1.3	16	66.8	30.4	24.2	30.7	78.2	49.8	13.1	81.6	233.7	143.2	9.7	20.3	206.8	102.9
26.7	0.6	28.1	10.7	7.2	144.7	121	26.2	39.1	15.2	26.1	47.1	7.2	10	10.1	25.6	65.6	41	22.9	19	97.4	13.7	71	148.3	0	179.7	93.5	4.5	74.7	90.9	21.4	65.1	6.4	0.8
110.6	21.6	97.2	17.4	2.6	32.3	49.6	39.3	25.8	52.1	3.1	16.7	31.6	22.3	42.5	1.4	86.3	32.8	46.4	25.3	2.7	9.5	5.8	0	78.5	102.8	0.4	46.3	0.3	7.7	29.6	31.6	82.4	60.5
162.5	110.1	34.7	59.2	34.7	82.2	96.1	65.6	180.6	206.7	1.3	41.5	178.9	140.9	95	80.1	111.1	88.5	54.8	34.5	9.3	138.8	77.7	15.7	43.9	192.2	104.8	7.4	19.2	81.3	58.7	201.7	22.2	11.1
31.1	11.2	43.9	89.9	170.1	65.4	117.6	153.9	177.5	148.5	126.8	229.3	154	96.1	216.4	62	59	204.3	124.9	126.7	97.4	172.1	100.4	109.3	161.4	154.5	70.1	149.6	128.3	126.6	25.2	92.1	104.1	149.4
140	86	155.6	96.1	85.7	82.4	76	48	213.8	96.2	122.8	97.7	93.3	220.1	38.6	101.4	186	185.2	226.5	99.3	173.6	106.1	230.7	219.9	165.1	177.3	109.6	141.3	91.6	123.6	117.5	247.2	166.8	159.8
139.6	176.3	383.2	146.3	279.6	121.7	124.7	220.6	201	180.3	311.1	202	331.4	255.4	241.2	74.6	249.7	187	235.3	139.8	262.9	228.2	311.5	230.9	220.2	363.7	343.1	136.8	401.9	83.1	203.1	318.1	165.4	151.3

An HTML table displaying nested data. Code: *StepByStepNest/2-html-table.html*.

To add headers, we need to insert an extra row and column. The following code adds a column with months, a row with years, and an extra cell at the beginning of the table so that the years start on the second column (see `StepByStepNest/3-headers.html`):

```
// insert a column before first column for month labels
tr.insert("th", "td:first-of-type").attr("class", "month-label")
    .text(function(d) {
        // this converts the number into a month
        const format = d3.timeFormat("%b");
        return format(new Date(2000, d.key-1, 1));
    });
// insert a row above first row for year labels
const header = table.insert("tr", "tr:first-of-type")
                    .attr("class", "header-row");
header.selectAll("th.year-label")
    .data(entries[0].values) // the year objects of any month
    .enter()
    .append("th").attr("class", "year-label")
    .text(d => return d.key); // the year
// insert empty cell at table position 0,0
header.insert("td", "th:first-of-type");
```

Finally, we can convert the table into a heatmap visualization by mapping a color scale to display the drier and wetter months. The following code creates an array containing all the values so that we can use them to compute the maximum and minimum values (extent) in order to create the color scale:

```
const color = d3.scalePow().exponent(.75);
const numbers = d3.merge(entries.map((v,k)=> v.values.map(d=>d.value)));
color.domain(d3.extent(numbers));
```

Now, you can add color to each table cell. The following code uses a color scheme interpolator from the *d3-scales-chromatic* module (which you will explore in the next chapter). The text is displayed in black or white, depending on the background color, so that it will have enough contrast:

```
d3.selectAll("td.year")
    .style("background-color",d => d3.interpolateYlGnBu(color(d.value)));
    .style("color", d => color(d.value) > .5 ? 'white' : 'black');
```

A fragment of the HTML, generated as a result is listed as follows (see `StepByStepNest/4-rain-heatmap.html`):

```
<table>
  <tr class="header-row">
    <td></td> <!-- empty cell -->
    <th class="year-label">1984</th>
    <th class="year-label">1985</th>
     . . .
    <th class="year-label">2016</th>
    <th class="year-label">2017</th>
  </tr>
  <tr class="month" title="1">
    <th class="month-label">Jan</th>
      <td class="year" title="1984" ... >259.3</td>
      <td class="year" title="1985" ... >190.1</td>
      . . .
      <td class="year" title="2017" ... >454</td>
  </tr>
  <tr class="month" title="2"> ... </tr>
   . . .
  <tr class="month" title="12"> ... </tr>
</table>
```

The result is as follows (with CSS styling, titles, and a footnote added in static HTML):

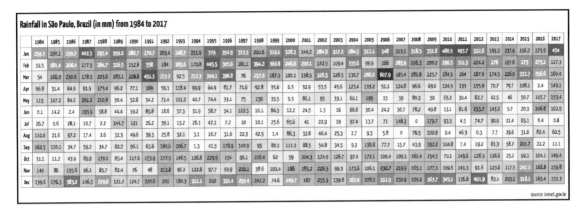

Heatmap visualization created in HTML by grouping data in table format. Code: *StepByStepNest/4-rain-heatmap.html*.

You can also see an example of using the new `d3.rollup()` function (from the *d3-array* module) instead of `d3.nest()` (from the *d3-collection* module) in `StepByStepNest/5-rain-heatmap-d3-rollup.html`.

Histograms

Histograms are bar charts that are used to visualize distributions of numerical data. You can create a histogram if you have a dataset consisting of discrete samples of data in *bins*, or *buckets*, representing data intervals. The number of items in each bin represents the *frequency*, and is used for the bar height. The bar width is a fraction of the number of *intervals*.

The following diagram contains 26 buckets, each one representing a letter of the English alphabet. The height of each bar represents the frequency of each letter in a sample of 26 million characters from the top 50 books published by *Project Gutemberg* in September 2018:

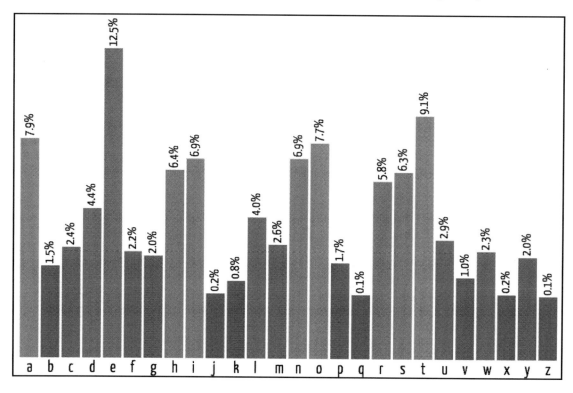

A diagram showing the relative frequency of the letters in the English language. Code: *Examples/1-letter-histogram.html*

The *d3-array* module also includes the `d3.histogram()` function, which is a histogram data generator. Calling this function will return a new function that can be applied to a dataset, returning an array of bins. Each bin contains an array of elements (the `length` property is the size of the bin), and two properties, `x0`, which is the lower bound of the bin, and `x1`, which is the upper bound (not included in the bin).

The following methods can be used to configure the histogram function:

d3.histogram() method	Description
value (*accessor*)	If the data provided to the function is not numeric, an accessor must be provided to point to the numeric data. The default is d => d.
domain (*domain*)	An array [*max, min*] with the *domain* for the histogram. If ommitted, the entire extent of the data will be used as the domain.
thresholds (*array*)	The array should contain data from the domain that will be used to split the domain into bins.
thresholds (*number*)	The number provided will be used to divide the domain into number bins of equal size.

Configuration methods for *d3.histogram()*

If thresholds() is not informed, *Sturges' formula* is used by default to estimate the number of bins. You can also use other formulas (they are provided in *g* functions) to compute the number of bins, or choose a static number yourself.

The following code generates a uniform distribution of 1 million random numbers between 0 and 160 and uses it to create 100 bins:

```
const values = []
for(let i = 0; i < 1000000; i++) {
    values.push(Math.random() * 160);
}
const histogram = d3.histogram().thresholds(100);
const bins = histogram(values); // 100-element array
```

The following code renders the chart as a histogram:

```
const width =  500 / bins.length;
const color  = d3.scaleSqrt()
                    .range(["darkgreen", "brown"])
                    .domain(scaleY.domain());
const scaleX = d3.scaleLinear()
                    .range([50, 450])
                    .domain(d3.extent(values));;
const scaleY = d3.scaleLinear()
                    .range([300, 0])
                    .domain(d3.extent(bins, d => d.length));
d3.select("svg").selectAll("rect.bar")
        .data(bins).enter().append("rect").attr("class", "bar")
        .attr("x", d => scaleX(d.x0))
```

```
.attr("width", width)
.attr("y", d => scaleY(d.length))
.attr("height", d => 300 - scaleY(d.length))
.style("fill", d => color(d.length))
```

The result is as follows (see `Histogram/1-histogram.html`):

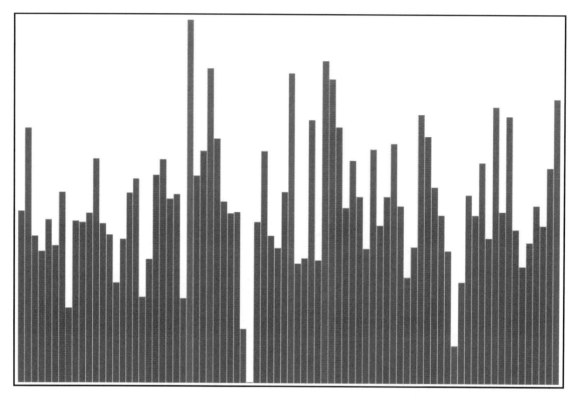

A histogram with 100 bins of random data. Code: *Histogram/1-histogram.html.*

Random numbers

The *d3-random* module, which is also part of the default bundle, provides generator functions with algorithms to create random sequences with different distributions. These functions are listed as follows:

Function	Description
d3.randomUniform(*min, max*)	Returns a function that generates random numbers using a uniform distribution (same as `Math.random()`), between the optional arguments *min* (default 0) and *max* (default 1).
d3.randomNormal(*mu, sigma*)	Returns a random number generator for a normal distribution with the expected value *mu* (default 0) and the deviation *sigma* (default 1).
d3.randomLogNormal(mu, sigma)	Returns a random number generator for a natural logarithmic normal distribution with an expected value *mu* (default 0) and the deviation *sigma* (default 1).
d3.randomBates(*n*)	Returns a random number generator for a *Bates* distribution with *n* independent variables.
d3.randomIrwinHall(*n*)	Returns a random number generator for an *Irwin-Hall* distribution with *n* independent variables.
d3.randomExponential(*lambda*)	Returns a random number generator for an exponential distribution with a *lambda* rate.

Methods for generating random data sequences of different distributions

The following example creates a random number generator function for a uniform distribution (see code in `Random/1-random.html`). Each time it is called, it will return a random number between 1 and 10. The following results are random and should be different if you run these commands:

```
const uniform = d3.randomUniform(1, 10);
console.log(uniform());  // 6.221558528510091
console.log(uniform());  // 4.758234458579456
console.log(uniform());  // 3.8534405981966366
```

Of course, you can always use JavaScript's native `Math.random()` function to obtain random numbers from a uniform distribution:

```
console.log(Math.random() * 10);            // 4.936373044819254
console.log(Math.random() * 10 | 1);        // 9
console.log(Math.ceil(Math.random() * 10)); // 6
```

The following code generates 1 million random numbers using a normal distribution:

```
const random = d3.randomNormal(1,.5);

const values = []
for(let i = 0; i < 1000000; i++) {
    values.push(random() * 160);
}
```

The following diagram shows a histogram that was created using the data in the `values` array:

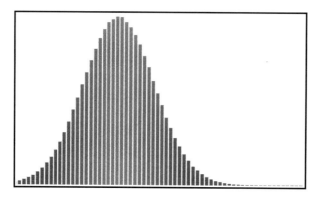

A histogram that was created with data generated by the d3.randomNormal() function. Code: *Random/3-normal.html*

Try using the other generators and experiment with different parameters. Four data distributions that were created with functions from the *d3-random* module are shown in the following screenshots. The code is available in the `Random/` folder:

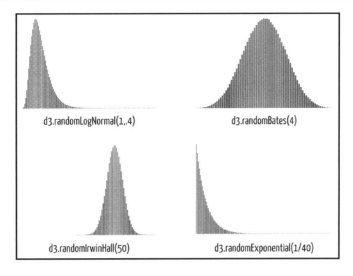

Histograms created with different random distributions. Code: *Random/4-lognormal.html, 5-bates.html, 6-irwin-hall.html* and *7-exponential.*

Interpolation

With interpolation, you can obtain intermediate values between a pair of values. The *d3-interpolate* module contains functions that create interpolator functions for colors, numbers, strings, arrays, and objects. The main functions are listed as follows:

Function	Description
d3.interpolateNumber (*a,b*)	Returns a numeric interpolator between numeric values *a* and *b*. Avoid using zero (use 1e-6 instead, whenever possible).
d3.interpolateRound (*a,b*)	Similar to d3.interpolateNumber(), but rounds the value to the nearest integer.
d3.interpolateString (*a,b*)	Returns an interpolator that finds numbers embedded in *b* and looks for a corresponding number in *a*, then creates a numeric interpolator for each one, using static parts of the string and unmatched numbers as a template.
d3.interpolateDate (*a,b*)	Returns a date interpolator between dates *a* and *b*.

d3.interpolateArray (*a,b*)	Returns an interpolator that, for each element in the *b* array, searches for corresponding elements in *a*, creating the appropriate interpolator for each match, treating unmatched elements as a static template.
d3.interpolateObject (*a,b*)	Returns an interpolator that, for each property in the *b* object, searches for corresponding properties in a, creating the appropriate interpolator for each match, treating unmatched properties as a static template.
d3.interpolateRgb (*a,b*)	Returns an RGB color space interpolator between two color strings *a* and *b*. The interpolator returns an RGB string.
d3.interpolate (*a,b*)	Returns an interpolator between arbitrary values *a* and *b*. The type of *b* selects which type-specific interpolator will be used (d3.interpolateNumber, d3.interpolateRgb, d3.interpolateDate, d3.interpolateString, d3.interpolateArray, or d3.interpolateObject). After the selection, *a* is converted into a compatible type.
d3.interpolateDiscrete (*array*)	Returns a discrete interpolator, dividing the interval between 0 and 1 in an equal number of segments and mapping each value in the array to a segment.

Main interpolation functions available in the *d3-interpolate* module.

The following code uses d3.interpolate(a,b) on pairs of numbers, strings, dates, colors, and objects:

```
const parseTime = d3.timeParse("%Y-%m-%d");
const data = [
    [25, 123],
    ["Part 0 of 100","Part 100 of 100"],
    [new Date(), parseTime("2020-03-07")],
    [[3,10,100],[30,100,0]],
    ["red", "blue"],
    [{a: -30, b: "red"}, {a: 50, b: "blue"}],
]

data.forEach(function(d) {
    const interpolate = d3.interpolate(d[0], d[1]);
    console.log( interpolate(0) );
    console.log( interpolate(.25) );
    console.log( interpolate(.5) );
```

```
      console.log( interpolate(.75) );
      console.log( interpolate(1) );
})
```

The initial and intermediate interpolated values are shown in the following table, and are obtained by running the preceding code (see `Interpolate/1-interpolate.html`):

t = 0 (a)	t = 0.25	t = 0.5	t = 0.75	t = 1 (b)
25	49.5	74	98.5	123
Part 0 of 100	Part 25 of 100	Part 50 of 100	Part 75 of 100	Part 100 of 100
2019-03-07	2019-06-07	2019-09-06	2019-12-06	2020-03-07
[3,10,100]	[9.75,32.5,75]	[16.5,55,50]	[23.25,77.5,25]	[30,100,0]
rgb(255, 0, 0)	rgb(191, 0, 64)	rgb(128, 0, 128)	rgb(64, 0, 191)	rgb(0, 0, 255)
`{ a:-30, b:"rgb (255,0,0)" }`	`{ a:-10, b:"rgb (191,0,64)" }`	`{ a:10, b:"rgb (128,0,128)" }`	`{ a:30, b:"rgb (64,0,191)" }`	`{ a:50, b:"rgb (0,0,255)" }`

Interpolation of different types of data with functions created with d3.interpolate(a.b). Code: *Interpolation/1-interpolate.html*.

Other interpolators

Color interpolators will be explored in Chapter 5, *Scales, Axes, and Colors,* and zoom interpolation will be introduced in Chapter 7, *Animation and Interactivity.* Other functions included in the *d3-interpolate* module are not covered in this book. These include spline interpolators, interpolators for CSS, and SVG transforms and composite interpolators, but some examples are available in the Interpolate/ folder of the GitHub repository for this chapter. Also, check out the references to online interactive samples at the end of this chapter.

Text formatting and internationalization

The way numbers are represented internally is seldom useful for human consumption. Large numbers are hard to read, currency is limited to two digits after the decimal point, and simple operations can easily result in undisplayable numbers such as 0.7000000000000001.

Formatting tools allow numbers to be displayed as strings, formatted according to a template. But culture also influences how dates and numbers are represented. Many countries use commas as decimal points, and dots as thousands separators. A date represented as *3/6/2019* may refer to *March 6, 2019* or to *June 3, 2019,* depending on the country where you read it. The *d3-format* and *d3-time-format* modules, which are both part of the default bundle, deal with these issues with functions that format and parse dates and numbers by using string templates based on a locale.

Number formatting

The *d3-format* module creates string representations of numbers. Its main function is d3.format(), which returns a function that can be used to format numbers. Other functions configure locales and provide additional configuration.

The main functions are listed as follows:

Function or method	Description
d3.format (*specifier*)	Creates a formatting function that formats a number according to the provided *specifier* template and default locale.
d3.formatLocale (*definition*)	Returns a locale object for the specified locale *definition* object. The object must include the properties decimal, thousands, grouping, and currency, respectively, contain a decimal point, grouping separator, grouping size, and a currency symbol for a locale. Ready-to-use objects are available from unpkg.com/d3-format/locale/<LCID>.json, where LCID is a locale code ID such as en-US, ru-RU, fr-CA, pt-BR, and so on.
locale.format (*specifier*)	Creates a formatting function that formats a number according to the provided *specifier* template and the caller's locale.
d3.formatDefaultLocale (*definition*)	Sets the *default* locale according to the provided *definition* object.

Main number-formatting functions available in the *d3-format* module.

Also included in this module are methods for parsing the format specifier, configuring the default precision, and rounding and setting metric prefixes. These methods are not described in this book.

A formatting function is generated from d3.format() and a specifier template. The code that follows creates three formatting functions:

```
const formatPercent = d3.format(".2%"),
      formatUnit    = d3.format(".3s"),
      formatMoney   = d3.format("$,.2f ");
```

Now, they can be applied to numbers and generate strings:

```
const string1 = formatPercent(0.23478) );        // 23.48%
const string2 = formatUnit (0.0000045367) );     // 4.537μ
const string3 = formatMoney (123456789.9876) );  // $123,456,789.99
```

The results will be different if you use a different locale. You can create a definition object with at least four properties, as follows:

```
const pt_BR = {
    decimal: ",",
    thousands: ".",
    grouping: [3],
    currency: ["R$ ", ""]
};
```

Then, you create a locale object and generate formatting functions from it:

```
const localeBR = d3.formatLocale(pt_BR);
const formatMoney = localeBR.format("$,.2f ");
console.log(formatMoney (123456789.9876) );   // R$ 123.456.789,99
```

You can also change the *default* locale:

```
d3.formatDefaultLocale(pt_BR);
```

Now, any calls to `d3.format()` will use the new locale.

Several ready-to-use locales are also from `unpkg`; for example, this code uses a German locale:

```
d3.json("https://unpkg.com/d3-format@1.3.2/locale/de-DE.json")
  .then(function(locale) {
      d3.formatDefaultLocale(locale);
      const formatMoney = d3.format("$,.2f ");
      console.log(formatMoney (123456789.9876) ); // 123.456.789,99 €
});
```

Most of the time, you will use simple format specifier templates such as the ones that are just shown, but you can control many more formatting parameters if you need to. The general structure of a specifier template is described as follows:

```
[[fill[align][sign][symbol][0][witdh][,][.precision][~][type]
```

All template components are optional. The following table presents a summary describing each one in the order they can appear in the template string:

Symbol or character	Component	Description
Any character	*fill*	A character for fill padding. It will be aligned according to the *align* component and fit in the space according to the *width* component.
> or < or ^	*align*	Aligns the fill to the right, left, or center, respectively.

=	*align*	Aligns the fill to the left, placing any symbol to the left of the padding.
−	*sign*	Shows nothing if the number is positive. Shows - if negative.
+	*sign*	Shows + if the number is positive. Shows - if negative.
(	*sign*	Adds nothing if the number is positive. Places it within parentheses if negative.
space	*sign*	Adds a space if the number is positive. Shows - if negative.
$	*symbol*	Applies currency symbols as a prefix or suffix (or both), depending on the current locale.
#	*symbol*	Applies binary, octal, and hexadecimal notation. The specifier should also contain the appropriate type component (*b*, *o*, d, *x*, *X*).
0	*zero*	Applies zero padding if necessary.
number	*width*	Minimum field width (will apply padding if less).
,	*comma*	Enables group separator (locale dependent).
.number	*precision*	Number of digits that follow the decimal point (if type is *f* or %), or number of significant digits (if type is *none*, *e*, *g*, *r*, *s*, or *p*). The default is 6 for all types except *none* and ignored for types *b*, *o*, d, *x*, *X*, and c.
~	*trim*	Trims insignificant trailing zeros.
e	*type*	Exponent notation, for example: 1.2e-3.
f	*type*	Fixed point notation.
g	*type*	Decimal or exponent notation rounded to significant digits.
r	*type*	Decimal notation rounded to significant digits.
s	*type*	Decimal notation with an SI (metric) prefix, rounded to significant digits. Prefixes are applied to multiples or divisors of 1,000, such as *m* (milli 10^{-3}), *μ* (micro 10^{-6}), *k* (kilo 10^{3}), *M* (mega 10^{6}), and so on.
%	*type*	Multiplies value by 100 and shows in decimal notation with a % sign.
p	*type*	Multiplies value by 100, rounds to significant digits and shows in decimal notation with a % sign.
b, o, d, x, X	*type*	Numbers rounded to an integer, in binary, octal, decimal, hexadecimal, and uppercase hexadecimal notations, respectively.
c	*type*	Converts the integer into the corresponding Unicode character.

Components of the *d3.format( )* specifier template.

The following table shows the results of applying a d3.format() function in different locales. See the code examples in the Format/ folder:

Format configuration	Raw number	Locale: en-US (default)	Locale: de-DE
d3.format('.2%')	0.23478	23.48%	23,48%
d3.format('.0%')	0.23478	23%	23%
d3.format('$,.2f')	123456789.9876	$123,456,789.99	123.456.789,99 €
d3.format('$,.3r')	123456789.9876	$123,000,000	123.000.000 €
d3.format('$,.2d')	123456789.9876	$123,456,790	123.456.790 €
d3.format('.4e')	123456789.9876	1.2346e+8	1,2346e+8
d3.format(',.3s')	123456789.9876	123M	123M
d3.format(',.3s')	0.0000045367	4.54µ	4,54µ
d3.format('#x')	65432	0xff98	0xff98
d3.format('#>12')	123456	#####123456	#####123456
d3.format('$<12')	123456	123456$$$$$$	123456$$$$$$
d3.format('*^12')	123456	***123456***	***123456***
d3.format('#016b')	56	0b00000000111000	0b00000000111000
d3.format('d')	123.0001	123	123
d3.format('(')	-123456	(123456)	(123456)

Examples using *d3.format()*. Code: *Format/2-format-*.html*

Date and time parsing and formatting

The *d3-format-time* module contains functions to format and parse dates, based on specifier templates and locales. The main methods are d3.timeFormat() and d3.timeParse(), and are described as follows:

Function	Description
d3.timeFormat(*specifier*)	Creates a formatting function that formats a date according to the provided specifier template and default locale.
d3.timeParse(*specifier*)	Creates a parsing function that parses a data string that's compatible with the provided specifier template and default locale.

d3.timeFormatLocale(*definition*)	Returns a locale object for the specified locale *definition* object. The object must include the properties *dateTime*, *date*, and *time*, contain specifier strings, and *periods*, *days*, *shortDays*, *months*, *shortMonths*, and contain arrays with locale-specific names. Ready-to-use objects are available from `unpkg.com/d3-time-format@2/locale/<LCID>.json`, where LCID is a locale code ID such as *en-US, ru-RU, fr-CA, pt-BR*, and so on.
locale.format(*specifier*)	Creates a formatting function that formats a date according to the provided *specifier* template and the caller's locale.
locale.parse(*specifier*)	Creates a parsing function that parses a data string that's compatible with the provided *specifier* template and the caller's locale.
d3.timeFormatDefaultLocale(*definition*)	Sets the *default* locale according to the provided *definition* object.

Main date and time formatting and parsing functions available in the *d3-time-format* module.

Additional functions (not included in this book) are available to format and parse using **Coordinated Universal Time (UTC)** and ISO8601 formats.

The following code creates new JavaScript data and uses a time format to display the day of the week, day of the month, and month using a specific locale:

```
d3.json("https://unpkg.com/d3-time-format@2.1.3/locale/fr-CA.json")
  .then(function(locale) {
      d3.timeFormatDefaultLocale(locale);
      const format = d3.timeFormat("%A %d %B %Y");
      console.log(format(new Date())) ; // jeudi 07 mars 2019
});
```

This code parses a date string in a specific format and converts it into a JavaScript date:

```
const parser = d3.timeParse("%Y-%m-%d")  ;
console.log( parser("2019-06-28") ) // Fri Jun 28 2019 00:00:00 GMT-0300
```

The following table illustrates the common date, time, and date-time formats, and the result that's applied to data in different locales. See the code examples in the `Format/` folder:

Directive	Locale en-US (default)	Locale ca-ES
`d3.timeFormat('%c')`	3/6/2019, 9:58:27 PM	dimecres, 6 de març de 2019, 22:01:18
`d3.timeFormat('%x')`	3/6/2019	06/03/2019
`d3.timeFormat('%X')`	9:58:27 PM	22:01:18

Common long and short locale-dependent formats for dates and times. Code: *Format/time-format-*.html*.

You can build any kind of date and time string by combining directives in a specifier template. The main directives are listed as follows:

Directive	Description and examples (using, *2019-03-07T13:23:03.991-0300*)
`%c`	Locale-dependent representation of date and time, for example, *3/7/2019, 1:23:03 PM*.
`%x`	Locale-dependent date, for example, *3/7/2019*.
`%X`	Locale-dependent time, for example, *1:23:03 PM*.
`%A`	Day of week (locale-dependent name), for example, *Thursday*.
`%a`	Day of week (abbreviated, locale-dependent name), for example, *Thu*.
`%d`	Day of month with zero-padding [01,31], for example, *07*.
`%e`	Day of month with space-padding [1,31], for example, *7*.
`%j`	Day of the year with space-padding [001,366], for example, *066*.
`%B`	Month (locale-dependent name), for example: *March*.
`%b`	Month (abbreviated, locale-dependent name), for example: *Mar*.
`%m`	Month number [01,12], for example, *03*.
`%Y`	Year, for example, *2019*.
`%y`	Year without century [00,99], for example, *19*.
`%u`	Monday-based day of the week as a number [1,7], for example, *4*.
`%w`	Sunday-based day of the week as a number [0,6], for example, *4*.
`%H`	Hour in 24-hour notation [00,23], for example, *13*.
`%I`	Hour in 12-hour notation [01,12], for example, *01*.
`%M`	Minute [00,59], for example, *23*.
`%S`	Second [00,61], for example, *03*.
`%L`	Millisecond [000, 999], for example, *991*.
`%f`	Microsecond (depends on clock precision) [000000, 999999], for example, *991000*.

| %p | AM or PM (locale-dependent), for example, *PM*. |
| %Z | Time zone offset, for example, *-0300*. |

Main directives used in a date string specifier template

Since the percent sign is a special character, to print a literal percent sign, it must be doubled: %%.

A padding modifier may be used between the % and the letter, and can be any of the following:

- 0 : Pad with zero
- _ : Pad with space
- – : No padding

The default is 0 for all directives except %e.

Summary

In this chapter, you learned how to use most of the methods of the *d3-array* module, which extend JavaScript with several tools for data manipulation, making it easier to prepare data for use in selections, and in layout and shape generators.

You learned about two strategies for grouping data. The d3.nest() function from *d3-collection* is the most popular and the simplest one to use, but it may be replaced in the near future with functions derived from d3.group() and d3.rollup(), which are used in recent versions of the *d3-array* module. A full example using multi-level grouping was explored in this chapter using d3.nest(). You might want to try and repeat the example using d3.group() or d3.rollup() as an exercise.

We also introduced four other modules: *d3-random*, which is used to generate random distributions that we displayed as histograms, *d3-interpolate*, for interpolation of all kinds of objects, and the locale-sensitive modules, d3-*format* and *d3-time-format*, which are used to format numbers and dates.

In the next chapter, we will explore scales in detail. You will learn how to add axes to your Cartesian grids and configure colors for your data visualizations

References

- Module documentation, D3.js: `github.com/d3/d3-array`, `github.com/d3/d3-collection`, `github.com/d3/d3-random`, `github.com/d3/d3-interpolate`, `github.com/d3/d3-format`, `github.com/d3/d3-time-format`, `github.com/d3/d3-time`.
- Nested Selections, by Mike Bostock: `bost.ocks.org/mike/nest/`
- Thinking with Joins, by Mike Bostock: `bost.ocks.org/mike/join/`
- Pluviometry in the city of São Paulo from 1984 to 2017. Dataset compiled from INMET (Instituto Nacional de Meteorologia): `Data/rain_sao_paulo.csv`
- Frequency of letters in the english language. Generated from top 50 books in Project Gutemberg in Sept 2018: `Data/common-letters.json`

6
Scales, Axes, and Colors

Quantitative data visualizations that employ dots, lines, and other shapes to represent values usually need to situate those values within the context of a domain. The most common way to provide this context is using axes. Each axis represents a data domain, providing lines, tick marks, and labels that are rendered in the same scale as the data points. One axis represents one dimension. The Cartesian system, which used in most bar, line, area, and scatter charts, employs two perpendicular axes that provide context for a two-dimensional space. Other visualizations may use three or more axes.

The *d3-axis* module contains ready-to-use one-dimensional SVG axes that you can attach to a scale, configure, and use to assemble linear, Cartesian, and radial grids. In this chapter, you will learn how to use it to create axes for your charts, configure position, ticks, paddings, and other visual aspects using selections, axis styling methods, and CSS.

A typical visualization is a scaled representation of data. To encode data values in visual artifacts, you need to map data values to graphical aspects, such as pixel dimensions, areas, and colors. This is achieved with reusable transformation functions called **scales**. The *d3-scale* module contains a collection of generators that create different types of scale functions that can be used to expand or shrink a domain so that it fits in the output range of a viewport, or convert values into dates and colors using interpolation, quantizing, or discrete mapping. You will use all these different types of scales in this chapter.

This chapter also covers the *d3-color* module, which contains generators for popular color spaces and several color manipulation tools, color interpolators from the *d3-interpolate* module that was introduced in the last chapter, and the *d3-scale-chromatic* module, which provides a huge collection of interpolators and color palettes that you use with sequential and ordinal scales.

Finally, you will have the opportunity to practice all that you learned so far by following the complete step-by-step scatter and bubble chart example at the end of this chapter.

We will cover the following topics in this chapter:

- Axes
- Scales
- Color palettes, schemes, and spaces
- Creating a scatterplot

Axes

Axes are lines containing units of measure in a specified scale. Every axis is connected to a scale, which should be the same scale that's used for the data points it represents. D3 generates SVG for horizontal and vertical axes using the methods in the *d3-axis* module. Each axis consists of an SVG `<path>` element (of the domain class), followed by several `<g>` elements (of the `tick` class), each containing a small `<line>` (perpendicular to the path line) and a `<text>` element. There are methods to configure the positions, size, and padding of the tick marks, and you can change any position and style using D3 selection operations or CSS to create any axis-based system you like.

An axis is created using one of the four generator functions listed in the following table, which require a scale (that can also be provided later using the `scale()` configuration method). All ticks are created with a size of 6 and a padding of 3. All axes are located at the (0,0) position:

Function	Description
d3.axisTop (*scale*)	Creates a top-oriented axis generator function for the given *scale*. Ticks are drawn *above* the horizontal domain path.
d3.axisRight (*scale*)	Creates a right-oriented axis generator function for the given *scale*. Ticks are drawn to the *right* of the vertical domain path.
d3.axisBottom (*scale*)	Creates a bottom-oriented axis generator function for the given *scale*. Ticks are drawn *below* the horizontal domain path.
d3.axisLeft (*scale*)	Creates a left-oriented axis generator function for the given *scale*. Ticks are drawn to the *left* of the horizontal domain path.

Functions from the *d3-axis* module for creating SVG axes.

Once an axis function is created, it must be called with a selection that returns an SVG context (usually a `<g>`) element so that it can be appended to the DOM tree and rendered. The following code generates a simple 250-pixel wide horizontal bottom-oriented axis inside a 500 x 50 pixel SVG viewport, using the default domain for a linear scale, which is [0,1] (see `Axes/1-axis.html`):

```
const scale = d3.scaleLinear().range([0,250]);
const axis1 = d3.axisBottom(scale);

const svg = d3.select("body").append("svg")
            .attr("width", 500).attr("height",50);

axis1(svg.append("g"));
```

Normally, you won't call the axis function with a selection parameter, as shown in the following code, but in the *context* of a selection chain using the `call()` method, this has the same effect (see `Axes/2-axis-call.html`):

```
svg.append("g").call(axis1);
```

Any one of the preceding code fragments will generate the following SVG code inside `<body>` (use your browser's developer tools to inspect the generated code). Pay attention to the SVG structure, default style properties, and classes. You can retrieve these elements with selectors and transform them:

```
<svg width="500" height="50">
    <g fill="none" font-size="10" font-family="sans-serif"
       text-anchor="middle">
       <path class="domain" stroke="currentColor"
           d="M0.5,6V0.5H250.5V6"></path>
       <g class="tick" opacity="1" transform="translate(0.5,0)">
           <line stroke="currentColor" y2="6"></line>
           <text fill="currentColor" y="9" dy="0.71em">0.0</text>
       </g>
       <g class="tick" opacity="1" transform="translate(25.5,0)">
           <line stroke="currentColor" y2="6"></line>
           <text fill="currentColor" y="9" dy="0.71em">0.1</text>
       </g>
             <!-- eight more lines not shown ... -->
       <g class="tick" opacity="1" transform="translate(250.5,0)">
           <line stroke="currentColor" y2="6"></line>
           <text fill="currentColor" y="9" dy="0.71em">1.0</text>
       </g>
    </g>
</svg>
```

The rendered axis is shown in the following diagram. (A gray border was drawn around the SVG viewport.) Note that the text label of the first tick was clipped out, since the axis is positioned exactly at (0,0).

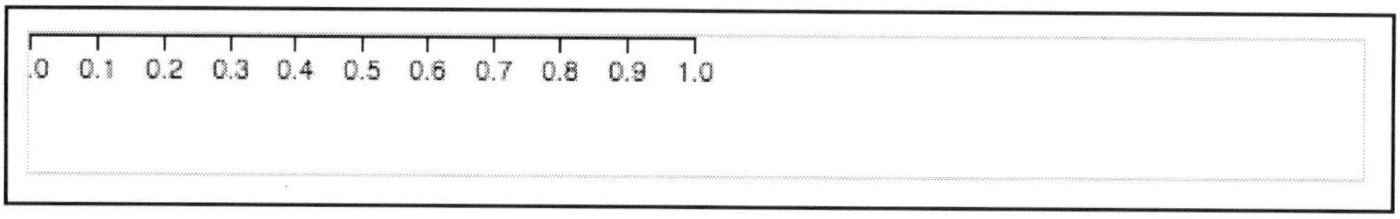

A bottom-oriented axis that was created for a linear scale with a domain [0,1] and range of [0,250] inside a 500 x 50 SVG viewport
(a border is drawn around the viewport). Code: *Axes/1-axis.html or 2-axis-call.html*.

Each generator function creates an axis function with a different orientation, but it is always located at the origin. You can move an axis anywhere by placing it in a container and translating its origin. The following code snippet creates all four types of axes inside `<g>` containers and then moves them to different parts of the view port using transform/translate (see `Axes/3-axes-all.html`):

```
const scale = d3.scaleLinear().range([0,250]);

const axis1 = d3.axisBottom(scale);
const axis2 = d3.axisTop(scale);
const axis3 = d3.axisLeft(scale);
const axis4 = d3.axisRight(scale);

const svg = d3.select("body").append("svg")
              .attr("width", 500).attr("height",350);

svg.append("g").attr("transform", "translate(10,100)")
              .call(axis1);
svg.append("g").attr("transform", "translate(10,250)")
              .call(axis2);
svg.append("g").attr("transform", "translate(350,50)")
              .call(axis3);
svg.append("g").attr("transform", "translate(400,50)")
              .call(axis4);
```

The result, with added labels (see `Axes/4-axes-all-labelled.html`), is as follows:

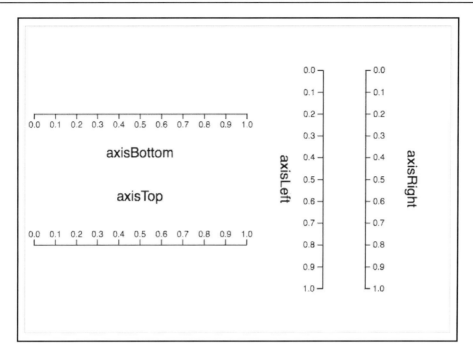

Four types of axes. Code: *Axes/4-axes-all-labelled.html.*

The scale doesn't have to be set when the axis function is created. You can use the scale() method to set it or replace it later. There are also several other methods that can be used to configure ticks. The most important methods are listed in the following table. All return the current axis so that they can be chained together:

Method	Description
scale (*scale*)	Sets the scale for the axis or replaces the existing scale. This is useful for dynamically changing the axis's domain during zooming operations.
ticks (*count, format*)	The arguments for this method depend on the scale type. Most commonly, the first argument is the desired number of ticks to generate, and the second, if present, is a format specifier string (see the *d3-format* module).
tickValues (*array*)	Overrides tick generation and uses the array as a source for the ticks to be displayed. The values must be within the scale's domain.
tickPadding (*number*)	Sets the padding between tick lines and text. The default is 3.

tickSizeInner (*number*)	Sets the size of the inner tick line, preserving padding values and moving the text label. Inner ticks are groups of the *tick* class that contains a line and a text element. Tick lines grow following the orientation of the axis.
tickSizeOuter (*number*)	Sets the outer tick-line size only, but doesn't preserve padding or text position. There are two outer ticks in each axis. Outer ticks are not lines but are part of the domain path. They have no text elements and are drawn for the first and last inner tick lines.
tickSize (*number*)	Sets both the inner and outer tick-line sizes with the same value. The default is 6.

Main methods for axis configuration.

Configuring ticks

A tick is a `<g>` object of the `tick` class that contains a `<line>` element and a `<text>` element. You can use D3 to select these elements and configure them any way you wish. For example, one way to change the tick size is to select the line and change its `y2` attribute:

```
d3.selectAll(".tick line").attr("y2", 25);
```

But then you need to do the same with the text labels, set adequate margins, and deal with the outer ticks, since they are actually part of the axis's domain path. A simpler way to do this is by using the `tickSize()` method:

```
d3.axisBottom(scaleX).tickSize(25);
```

This will make all ticks the same size and move the labels, while preserving the margins, as shown in the following screenshot:

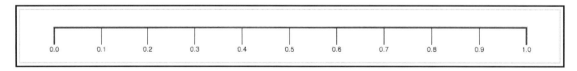

Applying the tickSize() method to make inner and outer tick lines longer. Code: *Axes/5-tick-size.html*.

You can control the outer and inner ticks separately using `tickSizeInner()` and `tickSizeOuter()`, but only `tickSizeInner()` preserves padding and the relative position of the text labels. Actually, the first and last tick lines are rendered on top of the domain path ticks' lines, which are controlled by `tickSizeOuter()`.

The following code sets different sizes for inner and outer ticks:

```
d3.axisBottom(scaleX)
  .tickSizeOuter(25)
  .tickSizeInner(10)
  .tickPadding(5);
```

To keep the first and last tick labels at the same relative distance from all tick lines, you need to move them, as shown in the following code snippet:

```
d3.select(".tick:first-of-type text")
  .attr("transform", `translate(0, 15)`);
d3.select(".tick:last-of-type text")
  .attr("transform", `translate(0, 15)`);
```

The result of the preceding transformations is as follows:

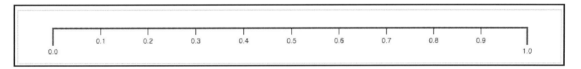

Using tickSizeInner() and tickSizeOuter() to set different tick sizes for inner and outer ticks. Code: *Axes/6-tick-size-inner-outer.html*.

It's actually more common to eliminate the outer ticks, since inner ticks provide the same lines:

```
axis.tickSizeOuter(0);
```

There are many ways to produce ticks lines that appear inside the chart or cross the domain line. One way is by using negative values for y1 in each tick line. This will draw lines inside the domain (see `Axes/7-tick-bleed-inside.html`):

```
d3.selectAll(".tick line").attr("y1", -10).attr("y2", 0);
```

But you also need to move the text labels. A simpler way is to translate the tick lines up, relative to the domain line, or translate the domain down. The following code uses this technique to draw tick lines crossing the domain:

```
d3.axisBottom(scaleX)
    .tickSize(25)
    .tickSizeOuter(0); // eliminate outer ticks
 // ...
d3.select(".domain")
    .attr("transform", "translate(0, 12) "); // moves domain down
```

The result is as follows:

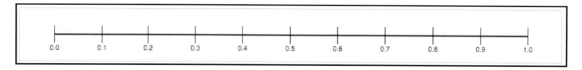

Changing the relative positions of tick lines and the domain line. Code: *Axes/8-tick-bleed-cross.html.*

The number and format of ticks is calculated automatically and depends on the scale that is used by an axis, but you can suggest a different number of ticks and use a specific format using the `ticks()` method. For example, to show approximately five ticks, you can use the following code:

```
axis.ticks(5);
```

The following code suggests 20 ticks and formats the label values so that they preserve three digits after the decimal point:

```
d3.axisBottom(scaleX).ticks(20, ".3f");
```

It will result in the following axis:

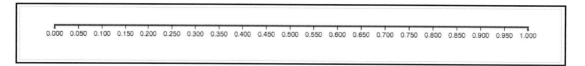

Increasing the number of ticks and formatting the labels. Code: *Axes/9-ticks.html.*

This other example reduces the suggested amount of ticks and displays them as percentages:

```
d3.axisBottom(scaleX).ticks(5, ',%');
```

Note that although five ticks were suggested, six ticks were displayed, as follows:

Tick labels formatted as percentages. Code: *Axes/10-tick-formatting.html.*

You can also specify exactly which values you want the axis to display, passing them as an array to the `tickValues()` method:

```
d3.axisBottom(scaleX)
    .tickValues([0, .05, .1, .15, .2, .5, .8, .85, .9, .95, 1]);
```

The preceding code will produce the following result:

Choosing which values to display. Code: *Axes/11-tick-values.html.*

Styling

In the previous example, the domain line didn't appear because it was removed:

```
d3.select(".domain").remove();
```

But you could have also simply hidden it using the `opacity` property in CSS:

```
.domain { opacity: 0 }
```

You can apply any property you wish to style the domain. Some of the preceding examples showed a thicker domain line and were created by changing the `stroke-width` property, such as in the axis shown in the following screenshot, which also removed the outer ticks with the `tickSizeOuter(0)` axis configuration method:

Styling a domain using CSS and tick configuration methods. Code: *Axes/12-domain-styling.html.*

Ticks can be selected and styled using the `.tick` CSS selector. You can also apply styles to the text labels and lines contained in a tick element using descendant combinators and pseudo-classes. The following CSS code applies different styles to the domain path, different tick groups, and its descendants:

```css
.domain {
    stroke-width: 15;
    stroke: #67b6ba;
}
.tick line {
    stroke: white;
    stroke-width: 2;
}
.tick text {
    fill: #62b6e6;
}
.tick:nth-child(2n) line {
    stroke: #345434;
    stroke-width: 0.5;
}
.tick:nth-child(2n-1) text {
    fill: #4b7880;
    font-weight: 100;
    font-size: 150%;
}
```

The effect is as follows:

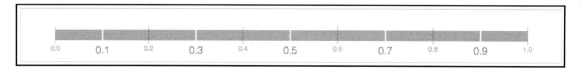

Styling tick lines and text labels. Code: *Axes/13-tick-styling.html*.

The same selectors can be used by D3 selections to append, remove, and apply other transformations to tick lines and labels.

Cartesian axes

To build a pair of standard Cartesian axes, you need to move an `axisBottom()` near the bottom of the viewport and place an `axisLeft()` far enough from the left margin to fit the ticks and labels. The best way to do this is by declaring constants (or properties of a global configuration object) with the dimensions of the viewport and margins, as shown in the following screenshot:

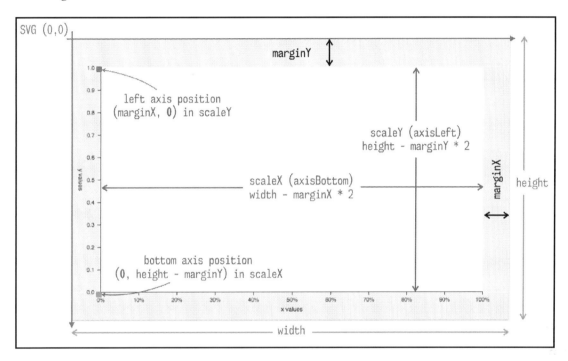

Dimensions and margins for Cartesian axes. Code: *Axes/14-cartesian.html*.

You also need to invert the direction of the *y* axis, since the default origin of the viewport is located in the top-left corner, and grows downward. This can be done by swapping the minimum and maximum values in the scale's `range()` method. For example, the preceding chart maps the input value **0** to the output value `height – margin`, and the input domain value **1** to `margin`. This is configured in the scale, as shown in the following code snippet:

```
const scaleY = d3.scaleLinear().range([height – marginY, marginY]);
```

The following code (see `Axes/14-cartesian.html`) creates the Cartesian that was shown in the preceding code snippet:

```
const height=500, width=800, marginX=50, marginY=50;

const scaleX = d3.scaleLinear().range([marginX, width - marginX]),
      scaleY = d3.scaleLinear().range([height - marginY, marginY]);

const axisX = d3.axisBottom(scaleX),
      axisY = d3.axisLeft(scaleY);

const svg = d3.select("body")
              .append("svg")
              .attr("width", width)
              .attr("height",height);

svg.append("g").attr("class", "x-axis")
              .attr("transform", `translate(0,${height - marginY})`)
              .call(axisX);

svg.append("g").attr("class", "y-axis")
              .attr("transform", `translate(${marginX},0)`)
              .call(axisY);
```

Cartesian grids

You can create a **Cartesian grid** by drawing long tick lines that cross the chart area. One way to do this is to reposition the *x1/x2* or *y1/y2* coordinates of the grid lines and the *x* or *y* positions of each text label. It's simpler to use `tickSize()`, but you will still need to move the lines or axis in the opposite direction because ticks grow in the same direction as the axis's orientation. If you move the entire axis, you should at least move the domain lines back to their original position.

It's also good practice to label each Cartesian axis with a class name so that you can select the correct domain and tick objects. A standard is to use `x-axis` and `y-axis`, as follows:

```
svg.append("g").attr("class", "x-axis").call(axisX);
```

The following CSS will display dashed tick lines for horizontal axes of the x-axis class:

```
.x-axis .tick line {
    stroke-dasharray: 5 5;
}
```

The following code uses tickSize() to create long tick lines and configures their position so that they cross the entire chart:

```
// ...
const axisX = d3.axisBottom(scaleX)
                .tickSize(height - marginY*2 + 10)
                .tickPadding(5)
                .tickSizeOuter(5)
                .ticks(10, ',%');
const axisY = d3.axisLeft(scaleY)
                .tickSize(width - marginX*2 + 10)
                .tickPadding(5)
                .tickSizeOuter(5);

// move each axis to the opposite side of the chart
svg.append("g").attr("class", "x-axis")
   .attr("transform", `translate(0,${marginY})`)
   .call(axisX);

svg.append("g").attr("class", "y-axis")
   .attr("transform", `translate(${width - marginX},0)`)
   .call(axisY);

// move domain lines back to their original places
d3.select(".y-axis .domain")
  .attr("transform", `translate(${-width + marginX*2},0)`);
d3.select(".x-axis .domain")
  .attr("transform", `translate(0,${height - marginY*2})`);
```

The final result is shown in the following diagram. See the full code in `Axes/15-cartesian-grid.html`:

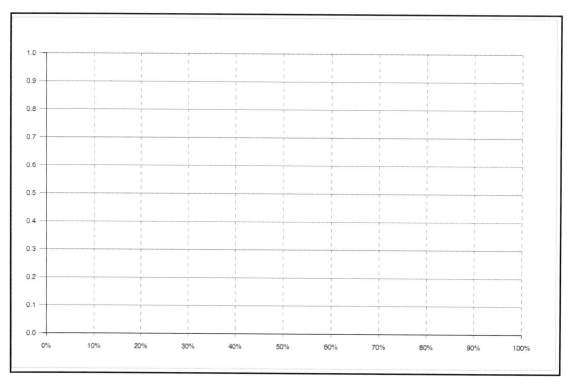

Cartesian grid. Code: *Axes/15-cartesian-grid.html*.

Axis labels can be added by appending `<text>` elements relative to each axis. The CSS for the labels should also configure the text-anchor so that the text is centered:

```
.label { text-anchor: middle; }
```

You then need to rotate the labels for the *y* axis. The following code fragment shows how to append text labels for a Cartesian chart:

```
const xG = svg.append("g").attr("class", "x-axis").call(axisX)
              .attr("transform", "translate(0,"+(height - marginY)+")")

const yG = svg.append("g").attr("class", "y-axis").call(axisY)
              .attr("transform", "translate("+(marginX)+",0)")

xG.append("text").attr("class","label").text("x values")
   .attr("transform",
```

```
        `translate(${[(width/2),(marginY - labelPaddingY)]})`)

yG.append("text").attr("class","label").text("y values")
   .attr("transform",
        `translate(${[-(marginX - labelPaddingX),(height/2)]}) rotate(90)`)
```

The result is shown in the following diagram. See the full code in `Axes/17-cartesian-labels.html`:

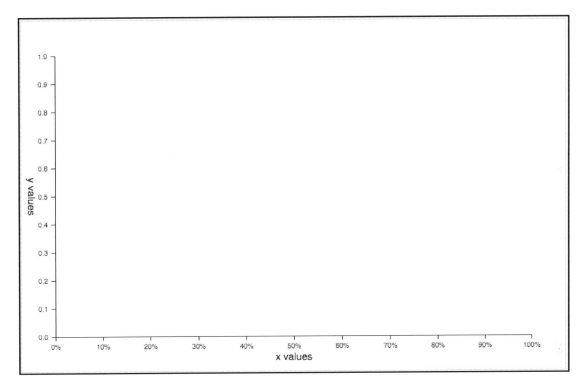

Cartesian axes with domain labels and tick lines crossing the domain line. Code: *Axes/17-cartesian-labels.html*.

Radial axes

Radial axes are used in charts that display two dimensions with an angle and a radius. Examples are radar (radial line or area charts) or polar area charts. To create a radial chart, you can use any axis function and call it from a data selection, rotating the axis on its origin.

The following example creates a simple radial coordinate system with an `axisBottom()` axis, rotated twelve times (the size of its angular dataset):

```
const width  = 800, height = 600, margin = 150;

// A radial scale with 12 angular axes
const angularData = d3.range(0,12,1);    // angular domain
const radialData  = d3.range(0,101,10); // radial domain

const scaleRadius = d3.scaleLinear()
       .domain(d3.extent(radialData))
       .range([0, width/2 - margin]);

const axis = d3.axisBottom(scaleRadius)
       .ticks(5).tickSize(4).tickPadding(2)
       .tickSizeOuter(0); // removes edge lines from domain

const svg = d3.select("body").append("svg")
       .attr("height",height).attr("width",width);

const g = svg.append("g")
       .attr("transform", `translate(${[width/2,height/2]})`);

g.selectAll("g.axis")
    .data(angularData).join("g").attr("class", "axis")
    .classed("blank",(d,i) => i != 0) // blank labels in all except first
    .call(axis)
    .attr("transform", (d,i) => `rotate(${(i * 360/12)})`);

d3.selectAll(".tick line").attr("y1", -3).attr("y2", 4);
```

The axes of the `blank` class are all except the first one. Their text labels, as well as the first tick in all axes, are hidden using CSS:

```
.blank text, .tick:first-of-type {display: none}
```

The result is as follows:

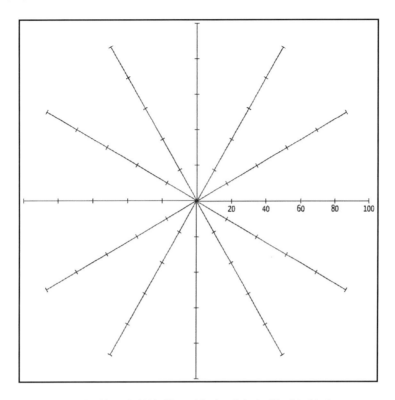

A radial grid created with 12 axisBottom() functions. Code: *Axes/20-radial-axis.html*.

This other implementation places the text labels over the vertical gridline using a small white rectangle as a backdrop and draws dashed circles to create a radial grid. These are the CSS styles:

```
.tick rect {
    fill: white;
}
.grid {
    fill: transparent;
    stroke: gray;
    stroke-width: .5;
    stroke-dasharray: 5 5;
}
```

This time, `axisTop()` was used, and rotated 90 degrees counterclockwise, so that the labels appear vertically. The `radialData` array was used to create the grid of circles, and some small configurations were necessary to put the text labels in place:

```
//...
const axis = d3.axisTop(scaleRadius)
                .ticks(10)
                .tickSize(0)         // will be controlled in SVG and CSS
                .tickPadding(0)
                .tickSizeOuter(0); // removes edge lines from domain

// place in middle of viewport and rotate
const g = svg.append("g")
    .attr("transform", `translate(${[width/2,height/2]}) rotate(-90)`);

// renders the radial grid
g.selectAll("circle.grid")
  .data(radialData).join("circle").attr("class", "grid")
  .attr("r", scaleRadius);

// renders the angular axes
g.selectAll("g.axis")
  .data(angularData).join("g").attr("class", "axis")
  .classed("blank",(d,i) => i != 0) // blank labels in all except first
  .call(axis)
  .attr("transform", (d,i) => `rotate(${(i * 360/12)})`);

// moves tick lines to center of domain
d3.selectAll(".tick line").attr("y1", -3).attr("y2", 4);

// backdrop
d3.select(".axis") // selects only first axis
  .selectAll(".tick")
  .insert("rect", ".tick text")
  .attr("x", -8)
  .attr("width", 16).attr("height", 16);

// moves tick lines to center of domain
d3.selectAll(".tick text").attr("y", 4)
  .attr("transform", "rotate(90)");
d3.selectAll(".tick rect").attr("y", -8);
```

The result is shown in the following screenshot. You can see the full code in `Axes/22-radial-axis-grid.html`:

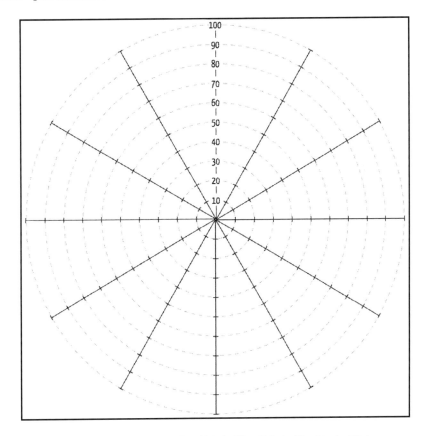

A radial grid with labels placed vertically and dashed grid lines. Code: *Axes/22-radial-axis-grid.html.*

Scales

Scales map abstract dimensions to visual representations. They are functions that receive a value in one dimension (usually a dimension that fits the input data) and return a corresponding value in another dimension (usually a dimension that represents output variables that are used in the visualization, such as positions, lengths, or colors).

For example, if your data consists of a list of 20 values (between 0 and 1,000) and you wish to plot them on a 700 x 500 Cartesian grid using all the space available, you need to multiply each value so that its position is proportional to the space available. To fit the 20 items on the *x* axis, for example, you might divide 700 by 20 and multiply it by the index of each data item. Multiplying each value by 0.5 will squish the [0,1000] domain proportionally on the *y* axis.

If you add more values, you have to recalculate everything again. Scales simplify this process by making all the calculations for you. In D3 Version 5, you can choose from a list of more than 20 generator functions for different scale types that support continuous and discrete inputs and outputs. They are all part of the *d3-scale* module, which is included in the default bundle.

Most of the examples we've seen so far in this book use linear scales. The following code creates a linear scale function with a default domain and range:

```
const scaleFunction = d3.scaleLinear();
```

Once you create a scale function, you can pass a value from its **input domain** as a parameter and receive a converted value that will be within its **output range**. Domain and range are usually defined on initialization or with configuration methods (that can be chained together).

The following code creates a scale and sets the interval [0,1000] as its domain of input values, and the interval [0,500] as the output range:

```
const scaleA = d3.scaleLinear().domain([0,1000]).range([0,500]); // a
```

In some cases, you may also wish to invert the scales, for example, when rendering the *y* axis for a Cartesian chart so that the values grow upward instead of downward:

```
const scaleB = d3.scaleLinear().domain([0,1000]).range([500,0]); // b
```

Once you have the function set up, you can use the scale by passing a value within the domain and obtain the result. Depending on how you set up range and domain, you will get different values:

```
const pixel1 = scaleA(250); // returns 200
const pixel2 = scaleB(250); // returns 400
```

The following diagram shows how scales map domains to ranges:

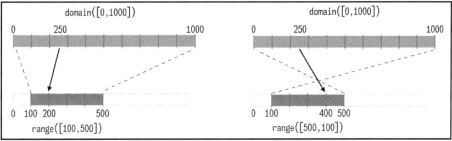

Scales mapping input domains to output ranges

Scales automatically use `d3.interpolate()` to calculate intermediate values. You can also define non-numeric ranges, as follows:

```
const colors = d3.scaleLinear().domain([0,100]).range(["red","green"]);
const middleColor = colors(50); // returns rgb(128, 64, 0)
```

Linear scales are a type of **continuous** scale, which map a continuous domain to a continuous range. Other continuous scales include **logarithmic** and **exponential** scales. The *d3-scale* module also includes generator functions for **interpolated** scales, which map a continuous domain to an output range, which is used by an interpolator to produce the output, and **discrete** scales, such as **quantize** and **ordinal** scales, which map continuous or discrete domains to discrete ranges.

Continuous scales

The following table lists and describes the scale generator functions that are available in *d3-scale* (version 3), which map a continuous input domain to a continuous output range. Output ranges are [0,1] by default:

Generator function	Domain (input)	Description
d3.scaleLinear	Continuous *Default*: [0,1]	Maps a continuous domain to a continuous range using a linear function, $f = ax + b$.
d3.scalePow	Continuous *Default*: [0,1]	Maps a continuous domain to a continuous range using a power function, $f = ax^k + b$, where k can be set with the `exponent(k)` method. The default is $k =1$ (linear scale).

d3.scaleSqrt	Continuous *Default*: [0,1]	The same as d3.scalePow() with exponent(0.5).
d3.scaleLog	Continuous, *value* ≠ 0 *Default*: [1,10]	Maps a continuous domain to a continuous range using a logarithmic function, $f = a \log_k(x) + b$, where $x \neq 0$. k can be set with the base(k) method. The default is $k = 10$ (base 10 logarithm).
d3.scaleSymlog	Continuous *Default*: [0,1]	A bi-symmetric log transformation with a linear interval that includes zero. The linear interval $(-k,k)$ can be configured with constant(k). The default is $k = 1$.
d3.scaleIdentity	Continuous *Default*: [0,1]	Maps a continuous domain to an identical range. This is useful for building axes with pixel coordinates.
d3.scaleTime	Continuous [2000-01-01, 2000-01-02]	A linear scale where domain values are dates and ticks are calendar intervals. Uses local system time.
d3.scaleUtc	Continuous [2000-01-01, 2000-01-02]	A time scale that uses UTC instead of local time.

Continuous scale generator functions from the d3-scale module.

Before using a scale, you will probably need to configure at least its range and domain, by using the range() and domain() methods. The exact syntax varies and depends on each scale and the types of data that's used. The following table lists these and methods that can be used in continuous scales. All methods return the current scale and can be chained together:

Method	Description
domain(array)	Sets the numeric input domain for the scale. In most continuous scales, the domain is a set that contains all possible input data values. If not, setting the scale will use its default domain ([0,1] or [1,10] depending on the scale type).
range(array)	Sets the output range for the scale. It contains the range of values that should be mapped to the domain. It usually consists of numeric pixel values (to scale a dataset so that it fits the screen) or interpolated data such as dates, colors, and so on.

`rangeRound(array)`	Sets a numeric output range for the scale that rounds each number to the nearest integer. This can be used to avoid anti-aliasing.
`invert(value)`	Receives a value from the range (must be numeric) and returns the corresponding value from the domain.
`nice()`	Extends the domain so that it starts and ends in round values. This is useful for generating rounded ticks for axes. For example, if a domain is [-3.76, 7.22], `nice()` will return [-4, 8].
`clamp(boolean)`	If the scale receives a value that is outside the domain, `clamp()` will return the upper or lower limits of the range. For example, if the domain is [0,10] and the range is [0,100], `scale(5)`, which is in range, it will return 50, but `scale(15)` will return 100 and `scale(-20)` will return 0. Without `clamp()`, these limits are not respected.
`interpolate(function)`	Sets the interpolator factory for the scale's range. The default factory is `d3.interpolate(a, b)`, which transparently interpolates numbers, strings, and colors. This is typically used in color scales to change the color space.
`unknown(value)`	Sets the output value for `undefined` or `NaN` input values. The default is `undefined`.

Common methods for continuous scales.

Scales also support functions and methods (not listed in the preceding table) to compute arrays of ticks and that format tick values. These methods are used by axis functions, which is the best place to configure them.

Linear scale

A **linear scale**, created with `d3.scaleLinear()`, preserves proportional differences. Its range is a linear function of the domain.

The following code builds a linear scale and uses it to plot values from 0 to 32 on a 1,000 pixel-wide axis line (see the full code for each of these examples in the `Scales/` folder):

```
const data = d3.range(0,33);
const scale = d3.scaleLinear().domain([0,32]).range([0,1000]);

d3.select("svg").selectAll("circle").data(data)
                .join("circle").attr("r", 5)
                .attr("cx", d => scale(d) )
                .attr("cy", 25);
```

The result, as shown in the following diagram, places the circles uniformly spaced on the axis:

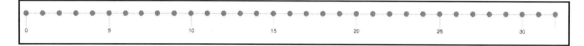

A linear scale created with d3.scaleLinear(). Code: *Scales/1.1-linear.html*.

You can create linear scales with multiple segments. The values between each pair of domain values are mapped to the corresponding pair in the range. The following example creates a scale with two segments:

```
const data = d3.range(-33,33);
const scale = d3.scaleLinear()
                .domain([-32,5,32])    // each pair is a domain segment
                .range([0,300,1000]); // each pair is a range segment
```

The result is as follows:

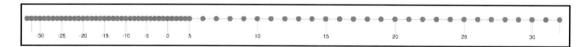

A linear scale with two segments. Code: *Scales/1.2-linear-segmented.html*.

If a scale function receives a value outside its domain, it will return a proportional value outside its range unless the `clamp()` method is used to limit the result:

```
const scale = d3.scaleLinear()
                .domain([0,32])
                .range([0,1000]);
const result1 = scale(64);   // returns 2000
scale.clamp(true);
const result2 = scale(64);   // returns 1000
const result3 = scale(-10);  // returns 0
```

The `invert()` method can be used if you have a value from the range and wish to discover the corresponding value from the domain (`Scales/1.3-invert-clamp.html`):

```
const invert = scale.invert(500);   // returns 16
```

Exponential scale

An exponential scale, which is created with `d3.scalePow()`, applies an exponential transform to each value in the domain, before mapping it to the range. The default exponent is 1, which is identical to the linear scale. An exponent should be provided with the `exponent()` method:

```
const data = d3.range(0,33);
const scale = d3.scalePow()
                .exponent(2)
                .domain([0,32])
                .range([0,1000]);
```

The preceding scale (applied to the same code as the previous examples) will produce the following result:

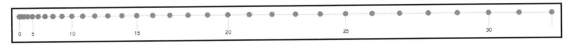

A square power scale created with d3.scalePow().exponent(2). Code: *Scales/2.1-pow-2.html*.

Exponents with a value less than 1 are root functions. A square root scale can be created using `exponent(0.5)`, but you can also use the `d3.scaleSqrt()` shortcut, which has the same effect as `d3.scalePow().exponent(0.5)`:

```
const data = d3.range(0,33);
const scale = d3.scaleSqrt()
                .domain([0,32])
                .range([0,1000]);
```

The result is as follows:

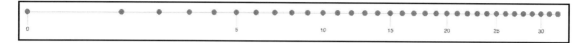

A square root scale created with d3.scaleSqrt or d3.scalePow().exponent(0.5). Code: *Scales/3.1-sqrt.html*.

Applying an exponential scale to an identity function ($y = x$) will produce a curve, which can be viewed in a Cartesian system, as shown in the following diagram:

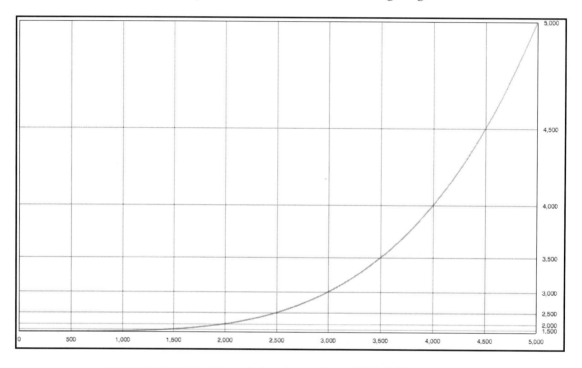

An exponential scale with exponent=4 was used in the y axis to render this curve. Code: *Scales/2.4-pow-4-cartesian.html*.

Logarithmic scale

A logarithmic scale, which is created with d3.scaleLog(), applies a logarithmic transform to each value in the domain, before mapping it to the range. The domain of a logarithmic function doesn't include zero (it can only be strictly positive or strictly negative). The default base is 10:

```
const data = d3.range(1,33);
const scale = d3.scaleLog()
                .domain([1,32])
                .range([0,1000]);
```

The preceding code, when applied to the same axis that was used in previous examples, generates the following visualization:

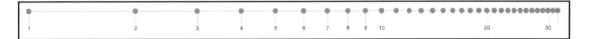

Logarithmic scale with base 10 created with d3.scaleLog().Code: *Scales/4.1-log.html*

You can configure logarithmic scales with other bases with the base() method. The following example uses a base-2 logarithm:

```
const data = d3.range(1,33);
const scale = d3.scaleLog()
                .base(2)
                .domain([1,32])
                .range([0,1000]);
```

The result is shown in the following screenshot. Each equally spaced tick represents twice the value of the previous one:

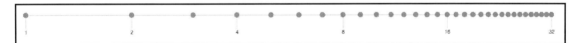

Logarithmic scale with base 2 created with d3.scaleLog().base(2). Code: *Scales/4.3-log-2.html*.

The following Cartesian chart uses a base-10 logarithmic scale for the *y* axis. Each equally spaced tick is 10 times the dimension of the previous one:

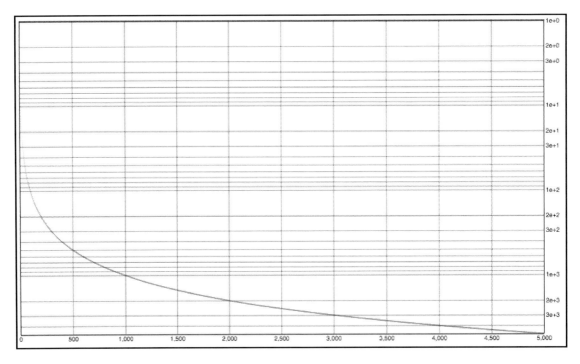

A base-10 log scale is used for the y axis to plot an identity function. Code: *Scales/4.2-log-cartesian.html.*

See `Examples/planetary-density.html`, which uses a log scale to plot a bubble chart to compare planetary volume, density, and diameter.

Symlog scale

A symlog (symmetrical log) scale, which is created with `d3.scaleSymlog()`, is actually a mixture of three functions. In the middle is a linear function that includes zero inside a small interval, and a pair of symmetric logarithmics from the interval to infinity. The default linear interval is (-1,1), and the domain of the logarithmic functions is (-∞,-1] and [1,∞).

The following code creates a symlog scale with a symmetrical domain:

```
const data = d3.range(-32,33);
const scale = d3.scaleSymlog()
                .domain([-32,32])
                .range([0,1000]);
```

The result is as follows:

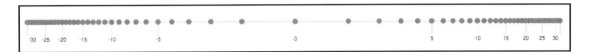

Symlog scale with two logarithmic scales between (-∞,-1] and [1,∞) and a linear scale in (-1,1). Code: *Scales/5.1-symlog.html*.

You can configure the interval where the symlog is linear with the `constant()` method:

```
d3.scaleSymlog()
  .constant(10); // linear interval is now [-10,10]
```

The following Cartesian chart, which plots an identity function, uses a symlog scale for the *y axis*:

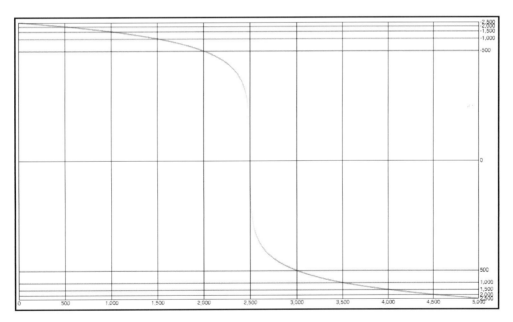

A Cartesian chart with a symlog scale for the y axis. Code: *Scales/5.2-symlog-cartesian.html*.

Identity scale

In an identity scale, which is created with `d3.scaleIdentity()`, the domain and range are identical. These scales are useful when you need to call an axis function (which requires a scale function) that uses pixel coordinates. In the following example, values are used to set the circle radii, along a width of 1,000 pixels:

```
const data = d3.range(0,1001,25);
const scale = d3.scaleIdentity()
                .range(d3.extent(data));
d3.select("svg")
   .attr("cx", d => scale(d));
```

The result is as follows:

Identity scale created with d3.scaleIdentity(). Code: *Scales/6.1-identity.html.*

Time scale

A time scale, which is created with `d3.scaleTime()` or `d3.scaleUtc()` is like a linear scale with a temporal domain. The domain takes an interval of `Date` objects. The following code places dates on an axis:

```
const data = [
        new Date(2017,10,1),
        new Date(2017,11,26),
        new Date(2018,3,15)
    ];
const scale = d3.scaleTime()
            .domain([new Date(2017,9,1),new Date(2018,9,1)])
            .range([0,1000]);
```

The dates are distributed according to their position in the time domain, as follows:

Dates in a time scale created with d3.scaleTime(). Code: *Scales/7.1-time.html.*

This other example displays intervals within a day:

```
const data = [
    new Date(2018,9,15,6,30,0),
    new Date(2018,9,15,12,45,0),
    new Date(2018,9,15,18,55,0)
];

const scale = d3.scaleTime()
        .domain([new Date(2018,9,15,0,0,0),new Date(2018,9,15,23,59,59)])
        .range([0,1000]);
```

The result is as follows:

Instants within a day in a time scale in local time using d3.scaleTime(). Code: *Scales/7.2-time-hours.html*.

Ticks are generated automatically, but you can control and format them using tools from the *d3-format* and *d3-time-format* modules.

Using the same data and `d3.scaleUtc()`, the instants are shifted to match *Greenwich Mean Time*:

```
const scale = d3.scaleUtc()
        .domain([new Date(2018,9,15,0,0,0),new Date(2018,9,15,23,59,59)])
        .range([0,1000]);
```

The result is as follows:

Instants within a day in a time scale in UCT using d3.scaleUtc(). Code: *Scales/7.3-time-utc.html*.

Interpolated scales

Interpolated scales map a continuous domain to a fixed range that's used by an interpolator to produce the output. There are two types: sequential scales, which have unidirectional domains, and diverging scales, which are used with symmetrical domains.

Sequential scale

A sequential scale maps a two-value domain to an interpolator, which is invoked with a value in the range [0,1]. The following scale generators produce sequential generator functions:

Generator function	Domain (input)	Description
`d3.scaleSequential`	Continuous Default: [0,1]	Sequential scale that performs linear interpolation.
`d3.scaleSequentialPow`	Continuous Default: [0,1]	Sequential scale with exponential interpolation. The `exponent(k)` method can be used to set the exponent. The default is $k = 1$ (linear interpolation).
`d3.scaleSequentialSqrt`	Continuous Default: [0,1]	Same as `d3.scaleSequentialPow()` with `exponent(0.5)`.
`d3.scaleSequentialLog`	Continuous, value ≠ 0 Default: [1,10]	Sequential scale with logarithmic interpolation. The base can be set with the `base(k)` method. The default is $k = 10$ (base-10 logarithm).
`d3.scaleSequentialSymlog`	Continuous Default: [0,1]	Sequential scale with symlog interpolation. The linear interval $(-k,k)$ can be configured with the `constant(k)` method. The default is $k = 1$.

Sequential scale generator functions from the *d3-scale* module.

The following example creates a sequential scale that maps a domain to an interpolator. The scale is used to generate tick values for display in an axis. The linear scale is necessary to map the domain to the pixel range that's used by the axis so the values can be displayed:

```
const [a,b] = [-300, 150];
const interpolator = d3.interpolate(a,b);

const scale = d3.scaleSequential(interpolator).domain([a,b]);

const axisScale = d3.scaleLinear() // used by the axis
        .domain([a,b])
        .range([0, 500]); // pixel range
// tick values generated by the sequential scale
const tickValues = scale.ticks(10).map(d => scale(d));
```

```
const axis = d3.axisBottom()
        .scale(axisScale)
        .tickValues(tickValues);

d3.select("body").append("svg").attr("height", 50).attr("width", 550)
        .append("g").attr("transform","translate(25,25)")
        .call(axis);
```

The result is as follows:

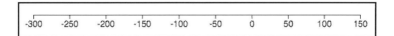

Scale created with d3.scaleSequential() to generate tick values. *Scales/8.1-sequential.html.*

Sequential scales are frequently used to generate colors. In the following code fragment, a linear sequential scale uses an interpolator factory from the *d3-scale-chromatic* module, which generates a rainbow interpolator:

```
const scale = d3.scaleSequential(d3.interpolateRainbow)
                .domain([0,600]);

d3.select("svg").selectAll("rect")
  .data(d3.range(0,601,5)).join("rect")
  .attr("height", 20).attr("width", 4)
  .attr("y", 0).attr("x", d => d)
  .style("fill", d => scale(d));
```

This is the output from the preceding code:

A rainbow generated with a linear sequential scale. Code: *Scales/8.2-sequential-rainbow.html.*

You can obtain different results using a non-linear scale, such as scaleSequentialPow:

A rainbow generated with a non-linear sequential scale. Code: *Scales/8.4-sequential-pow-rainbow.html.*

Diverging scale

A diverging scale is a sequential interpolated scale for symmetric domains. It is usually configured with a three-value segmented domain, where the central value represents the neutral value; the first is the extreme, and the last value is the extreme positive. The interpolator is called with a value in the range [0,1], where 0.5 represents the neutral value.

The following scale generators create diverging scale functions:

Generator function	Domain (input)	Description
`d3.scaleDiverging`	Continuous *Default*: [0, 0.5, 1]	Diverging scale that performs linear interpolation.
`d3.scaleDivergingPow`	Continuous *Default*: [0, 0.5, 1]	Diverging scale with exponential interpolation. The `exponent(k)` method can be used to set the exponent. The default is *k =1* (linear interpolation).
`d3.scaleDivergingSqrt`	Continuous *Default*: [0, 0.5, 1]	Same as `d3.scaleDivergingPow()` with `exponent(0.5)`.
`d3.scaleDivergingLog`	Continuous, *value ≠ 0* *Default*: [0.1,1,10]	Diverging scale with logarithmic interpolation. The base can be set with the `base(k)` method. The default is *k = 10* (base-10 logarithm).
`d3.scaleDivergingSymlog`	Continuous *Default*: [0, 0.5, 1]	Diverging scale with symlog interpolation. The linear interval (*-k,k*) can be configured with the `constant(k)` method. The default is *k = 1*.

Diverging scale generator functions from the *d3-scale* module

In the following example, a `Diverging` scale is used to generate tick values for display in an axis:

```
const [a,b] = [-300, 150];
const interpolator = d3.interpolate(a,b);

const scale = d3.scaleDiverging(interpolator)
          .domain([a,0,b]);  // [a,-75,b] is center

const axisScale = d3.scaleLinear()
```

```
                    .domain([a,b])
                    .range([0, 500]);

const tickValues = scale.ticks(10).map(d => scale(d));
const axis = d3.axisBottom()
                .scale(axisScale)
                .tickValues(tickValues);

d3.select("body").append("svg").attr("height", 50).attr("width", 550)
    .append("g").attr("transform","translate(25,25)")
    .call(axis);
```

The result is shown in the following screenshot. Compare the preceding code and the result with the previous example using a sequential scale:

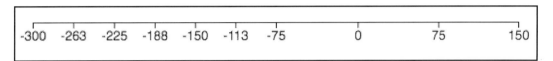

Scale created with d3.scaleDiverging to generate tick values. Code: *Scales/9.1-diverging.html.*

Diverging scales are best to use with diverging color schemes. There are many of them in the *d3-scale-chromatic* module. The following example uses the d3.interpolateBrBG factory, which is a diverging scheme between brown and green:

```
const scale = d3.scaleDiverging(d3.interpolateBrBG)
                .domain([-300,0,300]);
```

The result is as follows:

Colors generated with a diverging scale. Code: *Scales/9.2-diverging-rainbow.html.*

There are also non-linear versions of the diverging scales. The following colors use the same code but replace the scale with d3.scaleDivergingSymlog:

Colors generated with a non-linear diverging scale. Code: *Scales/9.4-diverging-symlog-rainbow.html.*

Discrete scales

Discrete scales map a domain, which can have discrete or continuous input, to a discrete range. This includes scales that map segments based on samples, subsets divided equally or using threshold values, one-to-one mappings, and mappings to spaces and points.

The following table lists the generator functions that create discrete scales:

Generator function	Domain (input)	Range (output)	Description
d3.scaleQuantize	Continuous *Default*: [0,1]	Discrete *Default*: [0,1]	Maps the values of a continous domain to a discrete range by dividing the domain into equal parts, according to the amount of items in the range.
d3.scaleQuantile	Discrete sample and continuous input *Default*: []	Discrete *Default*: []	Maps a sampled input (set of discrete values) to a discrete range, dividing the sample into equal sized sets, according to the amount of items in the range. Once the quantiles are set, the scale can receive continuous input.
d3.scaleThreshold	Discrete list of thresholds and continuous input. [0,1]	Discrete *Default*: [0,1]	A quantize scale where the domain is divided into subsets (based on a list of *n* threshold values) and mapped to a discrete range of size *n+1*.
d3.scaleOrdinal	Discrete *Default*: []	Discrete *Default*: []	A one-to-one mapping between discrete values in the input domain and output range. If the domain is larger than the range, the range will repeat.
d3.scaleBand	Discrete *Default*: []	Discrete bands in continuous range. *Default*: [0,1]	Divides an output range into discrete bands of equal width and padding based on a list of discrete input categories.

d3.scalePoint	Discrete *Default*: []	Discrete points in continuous range. *Default*: [0,1]	Maps a list of discrete input categories to equally spaced positions in an output range.

Discrete scale generator functions from the d3-scale module.

Quantize scale

A quantize scale maps the values of a *continuous domain* to a discrete range by *dividing the domain into equal parts*, according to the number of items in the range.

In the following example, a value in the [0,900] domain is mapped to one of three colors, so the range is divided into three equal parts. Items less than 300 (1/3) are mapped to the 'blue' segment, items between 300 and 600 (2/3) are mapped to the 'green' segment, and items greater or equal to 600 are mapped to the 'red' segment:

```
const scaleBuckets = d3.scaleQuantize()
                      .domain([0,900])
                      .range(['blue','green','red']);

const data = [0,50,100,200,250,290,300,310,400,550,590,650,700,900];

const axisScale = d3.scaleIdentity().domain(d3.extent(data));
const axis = d3.axisBottom().scale(axisScale);

d3.select("body").append("svg").attr("height", 650).attr("width", 1050)
                .append("g").attr("transform","translate(25,25)")
                .call(axis);

d3.select("svg").append("g")
  .selectAll("ellipse")
  .data(data).join("ellipse")
  .attr("rx", 3).attr("ry",6)
  .attr("cx", d => d + 25).attr("cy", 25)
  .style("fill", d => scaleBuckets(d));
```

The data array contains values within the domain that will fall into one of the three categories. The scale is used to obtain the fill color for the ellipses. The result is shown in the following screenshot:

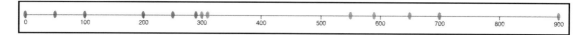

Continuous input mapped to a three-segment discrete range using d3.scaleQuantize().Code: *Scales/10.1-quantize.html.*

Quantize, quantile, and threshold scales support the `invertExtent()` method, which returns the domain, given the range. If you want to know the range that is mapped to the `'red'` sector in the preceding example, you can call the following:

```
const segment = scaleBuckets.invertExtent("red"); // returns [600, 900]
```

Quantile scale

A quantile scale maps a *sampled set of discrete input values* to a discrete range, *dividing the sample into equal sized sets*, according to the number of items in the range. Once the quantiles are set, the scale can receive continuous input that will place output values in each segment according to the quantiles that were computed from the sample.

In the following example, a 12-item sample is mapped to a 3-item range, computing segments that equally distribute the sample (placing 4 items in each). This computes quantile thresholds that will determine in which segment new values will be placed:

```
const sample = [0,8,19,25,65,98,120,170,320,440,800,910];
const colors = ['blue','green','red'];

const scaleBuckets = d3.scaleQuantile()
                        .domain(sample)
                        .range(colors);

const data = d3.range(0,910,16); // 57 items
// ...
d3.select("svg").append("g")
  .selectAll("ellipse").data(data).join("ellipse")
  .attr("rx", 3).attr("ry",6).attr("cx", d => d + 25).attr("cy", 25)
  .style("fill", d => scaleBuckets(d));
```

In the preceding example, a new dataset with 57 items was used to draw a chart with the quantile scale, and each item was placed in its segment. The result is as follows:

A discrete sample mapped to a three-segment discrete range using d3.scaleQuantile(). Code: *Scales/10.3-quantile.html*.

The computed quantile thresholds that separate the segments can be obtained with the `quantiles()` method:

```
const quantiles = scaleBuckets.quantiles();  // [51.666666, 219.999999]
```

Threshold scale

In a threshold scale, *the domain is divided into subsets* based on a list of *n* threshold values, which are mapped to a discrete range of size *n+1*.

The following example uses a threshold scale to map wind speeds to categories of the Saffir–Simpson storm scale. Each adjacent pair of values in the categories array corresponds to the minimum and maximum wind speeds of a storm category (0 = tropical storm; 1 to 5 = hurricane). An ordinal scale is used to map hurricane categories to colors. A linear scale is used for the *x* axis, which represents wind speeds:

```
const speeds = [0,119,154,178,209,252,310];
const categories = [0,1,2,3,4,5];
const colors = ['#62b6e6','blue','green','gold','orange','red'];

const scaleHurricane = d3.scaleThreshold()
            .domain(speeds)      // max wind speeds
            .range(categories); // hurricane categories

const scaleColor = d3.scaleOrdinal()
            .domain(scaleHurricane.range()) // each color is a category
            .range(colors);

const scaleX = d3.scaleLinear()
            .domain(d3.extent(speeds))
            .range([0,1000]);

 const axisX = d3.axisBottom().scale(scaleX);

 d3.select("body").append("svg").attr("height", 650).attr("width", 1050)
    .append("g").attr("transform","translate(25,575)")
    .call(axisX)
```

```
        .append("text").text("Maximum wind speed in km/h")
        .attr("y", 40).attr("x", 500);
```

The data is an array of objects that contains the maximum speeds of Atlantic storms in 2005. A linear scale is used for the the *y* axis, which simply places the storms in chronological order (which is also alphabetical):

```
const storms = [
        {name: 'Arlene', maxSpeed: 110},
        {name: 'Bret', maxSpeed: 65},
        ... 17 more ...
        {name: 'Vince', maxSpeed: 120},
        {name: 'Wilma', maxSpeed: 295}
];

const scaleY = d3.scaleLinear()
                    .domain([0,storms.length])
                    .range([0,550]);
const axisY = d3.axisRight()
                    .scale(scaleY)
                    .tickSize(1000).ticks(20,'s').tickFormat(d=>'');

d3.select("svg").append("g").attr("transform","translate(25,20)")
  .call(axisY)
  .select('.domain').remove();

d3.select("svg").append("g").selectAll("text")
  .data(storms).join("text").text(d=>d.name)
  .attr("x", d => scaleX(d.maxSpeed) + 25)
  .attr("y", (d,i) => 50 + i * 25)
  .style("fill", d => scaleColor(scaleHurricane(d.maxSpeed)));
```

Note that the text-fill color is obtained by calling `scaleHurricane()` on the wind speed, which returns a category number, and then calling `scaleColor()` on this number, to obtain the color. The result is shown in the following screenshot:

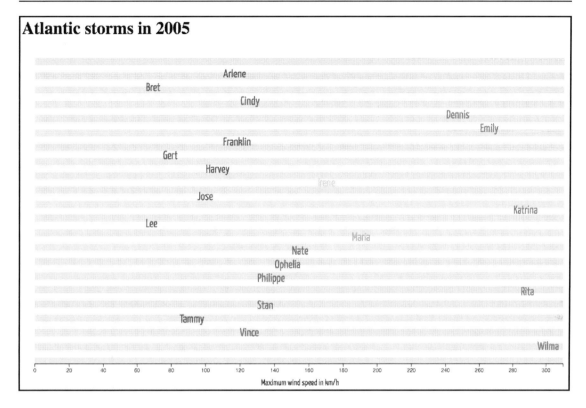

Atlantic storms and hurricanes in 2005. Colors are storm categories in the Saffir–Simpson scale. Wind speeds used as thresholds were mapped to continuous input values using d3.scaleThreshold().Code: *Scales/10.4-threshold.html.*

Ordinal scale

An ordinal scale has a discrete domain and range. You can use `d3.scaleOrdinal()` to establish a one-to-one mapping between discrete values in the input domain and the output range. If the domain is larger than the range, the range will repeat.

In the following example, three ordinal scales were created to map a dataset containing 41 values to 4 colors, 4 sizes, and 2 font weights. Since the dataset is larger than the ranges, they will all repeat:

```
const data = d3.range(0, 10.1, 0.25); // 41 values

const colorScale = d3.scaleOrdinal()
    .domain(data).range(['#000','#00d','#d00','#0a0']); // 4 colors
const sizeScale  = d3.scaleOrdinal()
    .domain(data).range([12,8,10,8]);                    // 4 font sizes
```

```
const boldScale  = d3.scaleOrdinal()
    .domain(data).range(['bold','normal']);               // 2 font styles

// these will be displayed when the value is unknown
colorScale.unknown('gray');
sizeScale.unknown('16');
boldScale.unknown('bold');
d3.select("svg").append("g").selectAll("text")
        .data(data).join("text")
        .attr("x", d => axisScale(d)).attr("y",22)
        .style("font-weight", d => boldScale(d))
        .style("font-size", d => sizeScale(d))
        .style("fill", d => colorScale(d))
        .text(d => d);
```

The result is as follows:

0   0.25 **0.5** 0.75 **1**   1.25 **1.5** 1.75 **2**   2.25 **2.5** 2.75 **3**   3.25 **3.5** 3.75 **4**   4.25 **4.5** 4.75 **5**

Three ordinal scales. created with d3.scaleOrdinal(). controlling color. font-weight and font-size of a sequence of numbers.
Code: *Scales/11.1-ordinal.html.*

Band scale

A scale that's created with `d3.scaleBand()` divides an output range into discrete bands of equal width and padding based on a list of discrete input categories. It's mainly used to create vertical bar charts. The following table lists the configuration methods that are used in band scales:

Method	Description
step()	The distance between the starts of adjacent bands.
bandwidth()	The width of each band.
padding (*value*)	Sets the inner and outer paddings with the same value.
paddingInner (*value*)	A value between 0 and 1 that specifies the proportion of the range used by blank space. A value of 0 places bands side by side without any space in-between. A value of 1 means zero bandwidth. Overrides any value declared for padding().
paddingOuter (*value*)	Padding for the space before the first band, and after the last band, in multiples of step(). Overrides any value declared for padding().

align (*value*)	Aligns the chart within its range and outer padding. A value of zero removes initial padding and doubles padding after. A value of 1 does the opposite.

Methods used for d3.scaleBand scales

The width of each band, which is obtained from the `bandwidth()` method, can be used to create a bar chart, as in the following example. The `padding()` method determines the space between bands, and `step()` returns bandwidth plus padding:

```
const data = d3.range(0,100,5);
const bandScale  = d3.scaleBand().domain(data).range([0,800])
                    .padding(.1);
const colorScale = d3.scaleSequential(d3.interpolatePlasma)
                    .domain([0,200]);
d3.select("svg").append("g").selectAll("rect")
    .data(data).join("rect")
    .attr("x", bandScale).attr("y",22) // position of each band
    .attr("width", d => bandScale.bandwidth())
    .attr("height", d => Math.random() * 200)
    .attr("fill", (d,i,n) => colorScale(d3.select(n[i]).attr("height")));
```

The result is as follows:

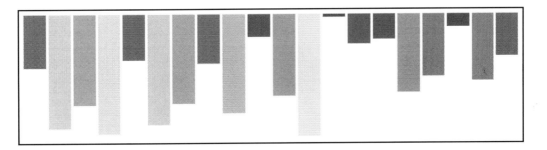

A vertical bar chart created with rectangles positioned with d3.scaleBand(). Code: *Scales/11.2-band.html.*

You can see examples of vertical bar charts being created with `d3.scaleBand` in `Examples/giss-bar-scale-band.html` and `giss-bar-full.html`.

Point scale

The `d3.scalePoint()` generator creates a scale function that fits a number of points that are equally spaced within an interval.

Method	Description
`padding(value)`	Sets the space before the first point and after the last point. The default is zero.
`align(value)`	If there is padding, it moves the points inside the available margins. Points are centered by default (*value* = 0.5), leaving equal space before and after the chart. A value of zero will remove space before and double space after. A value of 1 does the opposite.
`step()`	Returns the distance between the starts of adjacent points.

Methods used for d3.scalePoint scales

A point scale can be used to map a list of discrete input categories to positions in the output range. In the following example, it is used to place several circles on a horizontal grid. A sequential scale was used for the colors:

```
const data = d3.range(0,100,2);
const pointScale = d3.scalePoint().domain(data).range([0,800]);
const colorScale = d3.scaleSequential(d3.interpolateRainbow)
        .domain([0,100]);
d3.select("svg").append("g").selectAll("circle")
        .data(data).enter().append("circle")
        .attr("cx", d => pointScale(d)).attr("cy",22).attr("r", 5)
        .style("fill", d => colorScale(d));
```

The result is shown as follows:

A sequence of circles with radii positioned with d3.scalePoint(). Code: *Scales/11.3-point.html.*

See `Examples/giss-scale-point.html` for a scatter chart that uses `d3.scalePoint` for the horizontal axis.

Color palettes, schemes, and spaces

Choosing an effective color scheme for data visualization is no easy task. Colors aren't simply used to make a chart look nicer. Besides distinguishing and suggesting associations between sets of data, they also communicate information through aspects such as hue, contrast, saturation, or lightness. They can even influence the mood of the viewer. The choice of colors is never neutral. It may attract or repeal the viewer from relevant information.

Colors that vary in lightness and saturation suggest a sequential relationship (stronger/weaker, hotter/colder). Opposing data can be better represented using divergent color palettes, where extremes are represented by complementary colors. If your data represents different categories, it will be better visualized with a qualitative color scheme. Depending on your audience and the purpose of your chart, you may also need to consider accessibility issues such as color blindness or rendering in color-limited devices when selecting colors. All these tasks are facilitated by the use of a specially designed color palette or scheme.

Color palettes

A color *palette* is a fixed-size sequence of colors and is usually represented as an array in JavaScript. A color *scheme* represents a collection of color palettes and is usually represented as an object or function. You can use a scheme to generate a palette containing an arbitrary sequence of colors.

Online services, such as the popular **ColorBrewer** by Cynthia Brewer (*colorbrewer2.org*), can help you choose a color palette by considering the *type of data* to be colored (qualitative, diverging, or sequential) and *accessibility* (color blindness, display/print, and gray scale). You can select and view the effects in real-time, configure accessibility and data properties, and generate a color string in different formats, including JavaScript arrays and CSS.

You can also use the categorical color schemes that are available in D3, which are derived from Cynthia Brewer's *ColorBrewer*, and return arrays of discrete hexadecimal color strings.

Categorical color schemes

A color palette can be created with an ordinal scale, which maps color schemes to categories. There are 37 color schemes in the *d3-scale-chromatic* module (version 1). All schemes are functions that are prefixed with d3.scheme*. The following diagram lists the nine categorical schemes:

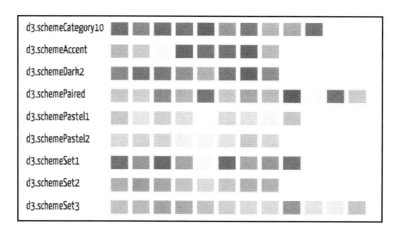

Categorical color schemes. Code: *Scale-Chromatic/1-categorical.html.*

The following code sets up an ordinal scale with a categorical color scheme, using it to paint the bars from a previous example (see Scales/11.4-category-colors.html). Since there are more data items (20) than colors (10), the colors will repeat:

```
const colorScale = d3.scaleOrdinal(d3.schemeCategory10);

d3.select("svg").append("g").selectAll("rect")
  .attr("fill", (d,i) => colorScale(i));
```

The result is as follows:

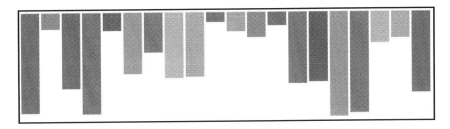

A bar chart using a categorical color scale that was created with d3.scaleOrdinal(). Code: *Scales/11.4-category-colors.html*.

The *d3-scale-chromatic* module also contains diverging, single-hue, and multi-hue schemes. They can be used with ordinal scales, but you have to inform the number of colors to include in your palette.

For example, if you wish to use the colors from `d3.interpolateBlues` in an ordinal scale, use `d3.schemeBlues[k]`, where *k* is the number of colors in the palette. You can choose from 3 to 11 for diverging schemes, or 3 to 9 for multi-hue and single-hue schemes. If you replace the color scale that was used in the previous example with the following code, which uses a four-color diverging scheme, the colors will change and repeat every four bars (see `Scales/11.5-scheme-colors.html`):

```
const colorScale = d3.scaleOrdinal(d3.schemeBrBG[4]).domain([0,600]);
```

There are nine diverging color schemes, listed as follows:

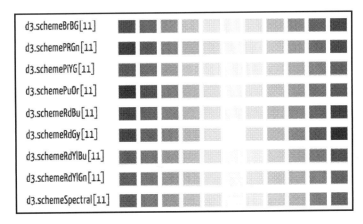

Diverging color palettes for ordinal scales (minimum 3 colors: maximum 11 colors). Code: *Scale-Chromatic/2-categorical-diverging.html*.

There are six single-hue and twelve multi-hue color schemes:

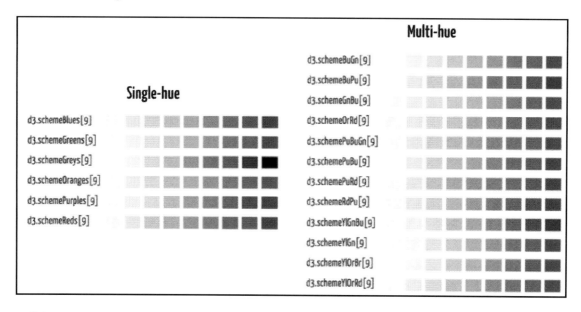

Single and multi-hue color palettes for ordinal scales (min: 3 colors. max: 9 colors). Code: *Scale-Chromatic/3*-categorical-single-hue.html and *4-categorical-multi-hue.html*.

Color spaces

The *d3-color* module contains several methods for color manipulation and representations for color spaces. You can use it to extract different color components or convert colors into different representations so that you can manipulate hue, lightness, and other aspects.

The main function is d3.color(specifier), which takes a color specifier string, which can be a named color, such as aquamarine, a hexadecimal string representation (for example, #f3a, #fe921d) or a CSS color specified with a functional notation the (rgb, rgba, hsl, or hsla function).

The following table lists the methods and properties that are supported by color objects that are created with the `d3.color()` function:

Method or property	Description
`opacity`	Read-write property that contains a value between 0 (transparent) and 1 (opaque), representing the color's opacity.
`rgb()`	Returns an RGB representation of this color: an object with properties r, g, b, and opacity. For example, `d3.color("red").rgb()` returns `{r: 255, g: 0, b: 0, opacity: 1}`.
`brighter` (k)	Returns a brighter copy of the color. K is in the range [0,1]. The default is 1.
`darker` (k)	Returns a darker copy of the color. K is in the range [0,1]. The default is 1.
`hex()`	Returns a hexadecimal representation of the color. For example, `d3.color("red").hex()` returns *#ff0000*.
`toString()`	Returns a CCC string representation of the color. For example, `d3.color("red").toString()` returns *rgb(255,0,0)*.

Methods and properties that modify d3.color() objects

You can use `color.brighter()` and `color.darker()` to apply slightly brighter or darker versions of a color. If no parameter is provided, the default value of 1 will be used. Intermediate values provide a weaker effect, as follows:

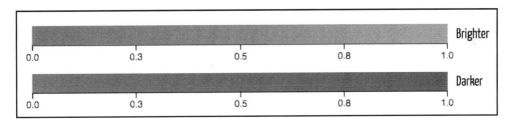

Effect of applying different values for color.brighter() and color.darker(). Code: *Color/1-brighter-darker.html.*

Besides `d3.color()`, which creates a color object from a string specifier, the functions listed in the table that follows create color objects from string specifiers, other color objects, or their color-space components. The resulting objects are representations of the color in a specific color space and contain properties that allow for the selection and modification of individual color components:

Function	Properties	Description
`d3.rgb()`	r, g, b	Creates an RGB color (standard cubic representation of *red, green,* and *blue* components). The range for each component is [0,255].
`d3.hsl()`	h, s, l	Creates an HSL color (cylindrical representation that allows the hue to be controlled separately from saturation and lightness). The ranges are H: [0,360], S: [0,1], L: [0,1]. Typical defaults are S=1 and L = 0.5.
`d3.lab()`	l, a, b	Creates a CIELAB color (designed as a device-independent color reference). Ranges exceed the amount of colors in RGB. Typical L: [0-100], A (green-red): [-100,+100], B (blue-yellow): [-100,+100].
`d3.gray()`		Creates a LAB color with a = b = 0 (only grayscale).
`d3.hcl()`	h, c, l	Creates an HCL color (designed for optimal human perception). HCL is a variation of CIELAB with a single hue channel [0,360], a luminance channel, and a chroma (saturation) channel. Using [0,100] for L and C produces values that exist in RGB.
`d3.lch()`	l, c, h	Creates an HCL color with components in a different order.
`d3.cubehelix()`	h, s, l	Creates a CubeHelix color (an HSL color-space designed to be perceived as increasing in intensity).

Functions that create color representations in different color spaces.

RGB color space

You can create a new RGB color using its *red, green,* and *blue* components:

```
const color = d3.rgb(200,200,100);
```

You can also use any string specifier (or another color object):

```
const color = d3.rgb("#fe9c1a");
```

You can then modify the color's components using the r, g, and b properties:

```
color.r = 196;
color.b = 127;
```

The following diagram shows the individual axes of the RGB color space. You can try an interactive online color picker at bl.ocks.org/mbostock/78d64ca7ef013b4dcf8f:

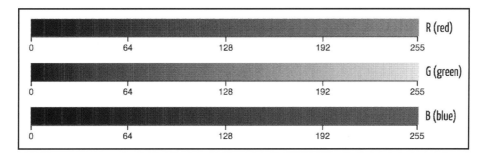

RGB color space created with *d3.rgb( )*. Code: *Color/2-rgb-color.html.*

HSL color space

Using the HSL (Hue, Saturation, Lightness) color space to represent a color, you can manipulate the hue as an angle (0 = red, 120 = green, 240 = blue) and control saturation (0 = grayscale, 1 = full color) and lightness (0 = black, 0.5 full color, 1 = white) using separate components. With d3.hsl(), you can create a new color with hue, saturation, and lightness components, or convert any color into an HSL representation and obtain its components from the h, s, and l properties: lor space designed so that

```
const rgb = d3.rgb("#fe9c1a"); // creates an RGB color
const hsl = d3.hsl(rgb).h; // gets the HSL representation
const hue = hsl.h; // gets the hue
hsl.h = hsl.h + 180; // changes current hue to complementary hue
```

The following diagram shows the individual axes of the HSL color space. You can try an online color picker at `bl.ocks.org/mbostock/debaad4fcce9bcee14cf`:

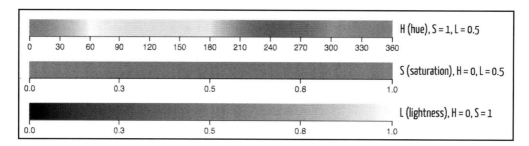

HSL color space created with d3.hsl(). Code: Color/3-hsl-color.html.

CIELAB color space

The CIELAB color space is an **International Commission on Illumination** (**CIE**) standard. It expresses color as lightness (L), a green-red component (A), and a blue-yellow component (B). It's a device-independent color space that was designed so that numerical changes in component values correspond to the same amount of perceived changes in color. It is frequently used to convert RGB into CMYK for printing.

Use the `d3.lab()` function to create a CIELAB color from its components, from another color, or a from color string, and then use the `l`, `a`, and `b` properties to read or modify individual color components. The following diagram shows the axes of the CIELAB color space. You can experiment with this color space using the online color picker at `bl.ocks.org/mbostock/9f37cc207c0cb166921b`:

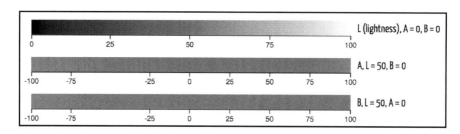

CIELAB color space created with *d3.lab()*. Code: *Color/4-lab-color.html* and *5-gray.html*.

The d3.gray(c) function is a shortcut for d3.lab(c,0,0). It returns a gray tone in the [0,100] range.

HCL color space

The HCL (Hue, Chroma, Luminance) color space is based on CIELAB. It preserves the **Luminance (L)** axis, but transforms the A and B axes into polar coordinates, where the saturation is the **Chroma (C)**, and a single axis is used for the **Hue (H)**. This color space is probably the easiest to manipulate, since variations in each of the axes are easier to perceive.

Use the d3.hcl() or d3.lch() functions to create a HCL color from its components, from another color, or from a color string, and then use h, c, and l properties to read or modify individual color components. The following diagram shows the axes of the HCL color space. You can experiment with this color space using the online color picker at bl.ocks.org/mbostock/3e115519a1b495e0bd95:

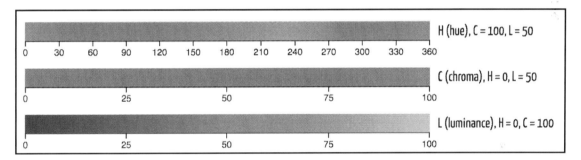

HCL color space created with *d3.hcl()* or *d3.lch()*. Code: *Color/6-hcl-color.html*.

The d3.lch() and the d3.hcl() functions are equivalent. The only difference is the argument order.

Cubehelix

The **Cubehelix** color space is an HSL scale designed so that colors are perceived in an increasing scale of intensity. The reds at the end of the scale seem more intense than the greens. This color space was created to display astronomical images.

Use the `d3.cubehelix()` function to create a Cubehelix color from its components, from another color, or a from a color string, and then use the `h`, `s`, and `l` properties to read or modify individual color components. The following diagram shows the axes of the Cubehelix color space. You can experiment with this color space using the online color picker at `bl.ocks.org/mbostock/ba8d75e45794c27168b5`:

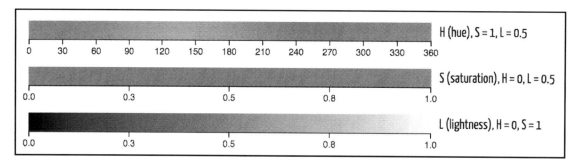

Cubehelix color space created with *d3.cubehelix( )*. Code: *Color/7-cubehelix-color.html.*

Other color spaces

D3 provides several other color spaces (not covered in this book) as separate modules that are not part of the default bundle: *d3-cam16, d3-cam02, d3-hsv, d3-hcg*. See the *d3-color* documentation for details and examples.

Color interpolation

In the last chapter, we introduced the *d3-interpolate* module, which contains factories that generate interpolation functions for several types of data values. Color interpolation is one of the most common applications of its interpolation functions. The following table lists several color interpolator factories from *d3-interpolate*, and are used for colors and color spaces:

Function	Description
d3.interpolateHsl (*a, b*) d3.interpolateLab (*a, b*) d3.interpolateHcl (*a, b*) d3.interpolateCubehelix (*a, b*)	These functions return a color space interpolator between two colors, a and b, using the shortest path between hues, for the HSL, CIELAB, HCL, and Cubehelix color spaces.

`d3.interpolateHslLong`(*a,b*) `d3.interpolateHclLong`(*a,b*) `d3.interpolateCubehelixLong`(*a,b*)	These functions return a color space interpolator between two colors, a and b, using the longest path between hues, for the HSL, HCL, and Cubehelix color spaces.
`d3.interpolateRgb`(*a,b*)	Returns an RGB color space interpolator between two colors, a and b. The interpolator returns an RGB string.
`d3.interpolateRgbBasis`(*colors*)	Receives an array of colors, which are converted to RGB, and returns an interpolator through the array of colors.
`d3.interpolateRgbBasisClosed`(*colors*)	Similar to `d3.interpolateRgbBasis` but also interpolates between the last and first colors, closing the cycle (the initial color is the same as the final color).
`d3.interpolateHue`(*ang1,ang2*)	Returns an interpolator between two angles, *ang1* and *ang2*, returning an angle in the range [0,360).

Interpolator factories from *d3-interpolate* for color interpolation.

To use an interpolator **factory**, you provide two colors, and it returns an interpolation function that gives you an intermediate color for a value between 0 (the initial color) and 1 (the final color):

```
const interHsl = d3.interpolateHsl("red", "navy");
console.log(interHsl(0.5)); // prints rgb(192, 0, 192) (middle of spectrum)
```

Some methods receive interpolator **factories**, for example, the `interpolator()` method of continuous scales, which uses it to interpolate the range:

```
const color = d3.scaleLinear()
                .domain([50, 450])
                .range(["red", "navy"])
                .interpolate(d3. interpolateHsl); // a = red, b = navy
```

Others, such as the initializer function for a sequential or diverging scale, receive interpolator *functions*:

```
const colorScale = d3.scaleSequential(interHsl); // default domain [0,1]
```

The following diagram compares interpolator factories from the *d3-interpolate*, which is used to create interpolators between red and blue (or red and green, for the Cubehelix space), revealing the differences between long- and short-path interpolators:

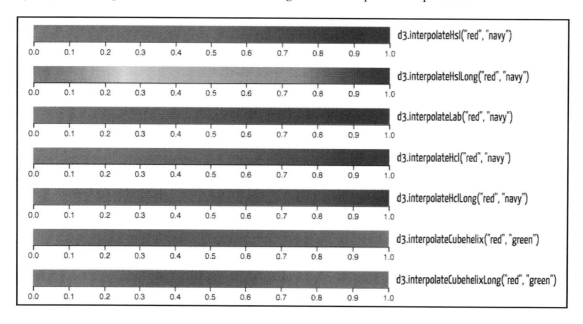

Color space interpolators. from *d3-interpolate*. generating colors between read and blue or red and green.
Code: *Color/8-interpolate.html*.

A d3.interpolateHue interpolator returns a hue angle between 0 and 360 degrees. To create a color, you can use the angle in a d3.hsl function:

```
const interHue = d3.interpolateHue(0,120);
const middleColor = d3.hsl(interHue(0.5), 1, 0.5))
```

The following screenshot shows the colors that were created from the angles that were generated by different d3.interpolateHue interpolators, receiving values from 0 to 1:

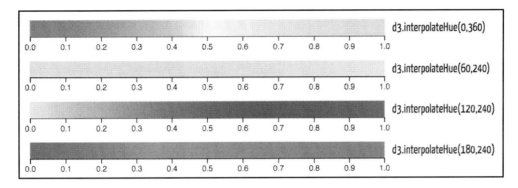

Hue interpolators. from *d3-interpolate*. These functions generate angles between 0 and 360 that can be used to generate hues. Code: *Color/9-interpolate-hue.html*.

The `d3.interpolateRgbBasis` interpolator factory generates intermediate colors from an array of colors. A cyclic color scheme interpolator can be created with `d3.interpolateRgbBasisClosed`, which adds one extra interpolation step to interpolate back to the first color. The following screenshot compares interpolators that were created with these factories (see `Color/10-interpolate-rgb-basis.html`):

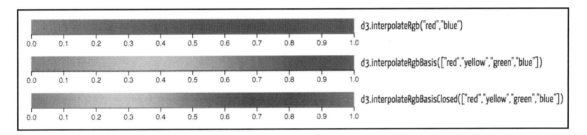

RGB interpolators. from *d3-interpolate*. The last one generates cyclic color schemes.
Code: *Color/10-interpolate-rgb-basis.html*.

Before creating your own color interpolators, take a look at the *d3-scale-chromatic* module (included in the default bundle), which contains a large collection of ready-to-use interpolators for popular color schemes.

Interpolated color schemes

Sequential and diverging scales are commonly used to interpolate colors, which can be mapped to values for use in charts with interpolated scales. There are four groups of interpolated color schemes in the *d3-scale-chromatic* module: *diverging, single-hue, multi-hue,* and *cyclic.*

The most common way to use a color scheme is to use its interpolator to initialize a sequential or diverging scale, which has a default fixed range of [0,1]. For example, the following code draws a sequence of colored rectangles, which is used to generate a rainbow sequence by initializing a d3.scaleSequential() scale with a d3.interpolateRainbow interpolator function:

```
const scale = d3.scaleSequential(d3.interpolateRainbow)
                .domain([0,600]);

d3.selectAll("rect")
    .data(d3.range(0,601,5))
    .enter().append("rect")
        .attr("height", 20).attr("width", 4)
        .attr("y", 0).attr("x", d => d)
        .style("fill", d => scale(d));
```

This code (see Scale-Chromatic/interpolate-*.html) was used to generate the following diagrams, which compare all the interpolators that are available in the *d3-scale-chromatic* module:

The interpolators for single hue sequential color schemes would be as follows:

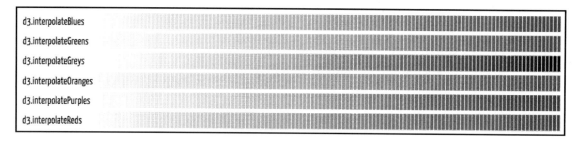

single hue sequential color schemes. Code: Scale-Chromatic/5-interpolate-single-hue.html.

Interpolators for multi-hue sequential color schemes are as follows:

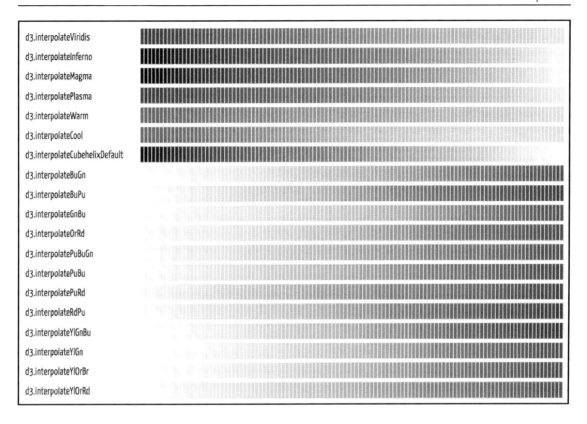

multi-hue sequential color schemes. Code: `Scale-Chromatic/6-interpolate-multi-hue.html`.

Interpolators for cyclic color schemes are as follows:

cyclic color schemes. Code: `Scale-Chromatic/7-interpolate-cyclic.html`.

Interpolators for diverging color schemes are as follows:

diverging color schemes. Code: Scale-Chromatic/8-interpolate-diverging.html.

Of course, you can also call an interpolator directly by passing a value between 0 and 1 as an argument:

```
const purple = d3.interpolatePRGn(0); // the first color in the scale
const green = d3.interpolatePRGn(1); // the last color in the scale
```

Creating a scatterplot

In this final section, you will use the features that you learned about in this chapter to create a scatterplot and compared the **Gross Domestic Product (GDP)** per capital and the **Human Development Index (HDI)** of several countries. This is a step-by-step tutorial. We will start with a simple chart and add axes, labels, and interactive features. You can code as you go or download the files that are available from the StepByStep/ folder, in the GitHub repository for this chapter.

The CSV data file that's used for this visualization (Data/un_regions_gdp.csv) contains data that was obtained from several sources, such as the United Nations and the World Bank. Both the HDI and GDP are from 2017, so they can be compared. The following is a fragment of this file, showing the headers and some rows of data:

```
Country,Continent,Area_km2,Pop_2016,HDI_2017,Code,GDP_2017
Kazakhstan,Asia,2724902,17794055,0.800,KAZ,9030.383889
China,Asia,9562911,1378665000,0.752,CHN,8826.994096
Bolivia,South America,1098580,10887882,0.693,BOL,3393.955818
Canada,North America,9984670,36264604,0.926,CAN,45032.11991
Mozambique,Africa,799380,28829476,0.437,MOZ,426.2219619
```

```
New Zealand,Oceania, 267710,4693200,0.917,NZL,42940.57829
...
```

Our goal is to create a visualization of this data in a scatter chart so that the HDI of each country can be compared to its GDP per capital.

Drawing dots on a Cartesian grid

We will start by setting up a web page, loading the D3.js library, including an SVG canvas and setting the viewport's width, height, and margins:

```
<!DOCTYPE html>
<html lang="en">
<head>
    <meta charset="UTF-8">
    <title>Annual GDP compared to HDI (2017)</title>
    <script src="https://d3js.org/d3.v5.min.js"></script>
</head>
<body>
<svg width="100%" height="100%" viewBox="0 0 500 300"/>
<script>
    const w = 500, h = 300, marginH = 40, marginW = 50;
    // more code here
</script>
</body>
</html>
```

The GDP will run along the vertical y axis, while the HDI will grow horizontally on the x axis. Since the file hasn't yet loaded, we don't know the domain, but we can already create the scales as global functions, and set the output range, which is based on the viewport's dimensions and margins. Note that, since this will be a classical Cartesian grid, the direction of the y axis will be inverted (to grow upward). This is done when defining the range for the y axis:

```
const scaleX = d3.scaleLinear().range([marginW, w-marginW]);
const scaleY = d3.scaleLinear().range([h-marginH, marginH]);
```

The data will also be stored in a global object:

```
const data = {}
```

We don't need all the fields in the CSV, so we will use a row function to return data fields we might use, replace the names of the fields for simpler ones, and convert the numerical fields into numbers. It also guarantees that only entries that have valid values for the HDI and the GDP are included:

```
d3.csv("../Data/un_regions_gdp.csv", function(row) {
    if(row.HDI_2017 >0 && row.GDP_2017 >0) {
        return {
            name: row.Country,
            code: row.Code,
            continent: row.Continent,
            population: +row.Pop_2016,
            hdi: +row.HDI_2017,
            gdp: +row.GDP_2017
        }
    }
})
.then(function(dataset) {...});
```

The resulting dataset will be stored in the global `data.countries` property so that it can be used by any function in the page. Now, we can finally compute the domain for each scale, which will be the full extent of each variable set of data. The `draw()` function is called next, to render the dots:

```
d3.csv("../Data/un_regions_gdp.csv", function(row) {...})
.then(function(dataset) {
    data.countries = dataset;
    scaleY.domain(d3.extent(dataset, d => d.gdp));
    scaleX.domain(d3.extent(dataset, d => d.hdi));

    draw();
});
```

The `draw()` function will draw three pixel-wide circles, using each pair of values as the coordinates of the circle's center. The following code uses the *general update pattern* (with the `join()` method) to bind the circles to the data, and the corresponding scales to convert the raw values into pixel coordinates that will fit the viewport:

```
function draw() {
    d3.select("svg").selectAll("circle.dot")
        .data(data.countries)
        .join("circle").attr("class", "dot")
        .attr("r", 1.5)
        .attr("cx", d => scaleX(d.hdi))
        .attr("cy", d => scaleY(d.gdp))
}
```

The result of this code is shown in the following screenshot (see `StepByStep/1-scatter.html`):

A simple scatterplot comparing GDP per capita (*y* axis) with HDI (*x* axis) among 194 countries in 2017.
Code: StepByStep/1-scatter.html.

The chart shows an exponential relationship between HDI and GDP, but we don't know which countries are represented, which axis is HDI, which is GDP, nor any values. Some context is necessary, which will be provided by axes and labels.

Adding axes and labels

A typical Cartesian chart has a horizontal *x* axis with tick labels at the bottom, and a vertical *y* axis with tick labels at the left. Since we already declared the scales globally, each axis function can be connected to its scale on creation, as shown here (you can also use the `scale()` method, if you need to redefine the scale later):

```
const axisX = d3.axisBottom(scaleX);
const axisY = d3.axisLeft(scaleY);
```

The axis functions require a selection so that they can be appended to the chart. We will create a new function to draw the axes and labels and then call it after the data is loaded, before the `draw()` function:

```
.then(function(dataset) {
    //...
    drawAxes();
    draw();
});
```

The usual way to add an axis to the viewport is with the `call()` method in a selection chain. This is done with in the `drawAxes()` function, which also translates each axis (which is originally at the viewport's origin), to the classical Cartesian positions. It's also good practice to add a descriptive class to each axis, such as *x axis* and *y axis*:

```
function drawAxes() {
    // axes
    const xG = d3.select("svg").append("g").attr("class", "x-axis")
            .attr("transform", `translate(${[0,h-marginH]})`)
            .call(axisX);

    const yG = d3.select("svg").append("g").attr("class", "y-axis")
            .attr("transform", `translate(${[marginW,0]})`)
            .call(axisY);

    // labels
    d3.select("svg").append("text").attr("class","label")
            .text("Human Development Index (HDI)")
            .attr("transform", `translate(${[w/2,h-3]})`)
    d3.select("svg").append("text").attr("class","label")
            .text("Annual GDP per capita (USD)")
            .attr("transform", `translate(${[3,h/2]}) rotate(90)`)
}
```

The preceding code also adds axis labels to the left of the *y* axis and below the *x* axis. The vertical label was rotated 90 degrees after centering. The CSS `text-anchor:middle` property guarantees that it will be rotated along its center. The following is the CSS style sheet that's used for this page:

```
<style>
    text {
        font-family: 'Yanone Kaffeesatz', 'Arial Narrow', sans-serif;
        font-size: 7pt;
    }
    .label {
        font-size: 9pt;
        text-anchor: middle;
    }
</style>
```

The result is shown in the following screenshot. Now, we have some context and can see that high GDP values are somewhat related to high HDI values, that the growth is exponential, and that it seems that most countries have a GDP per capita below 10 thousand dollars.

See the full code in `StepByStep/2-scatter-gdp_hdi.html`:

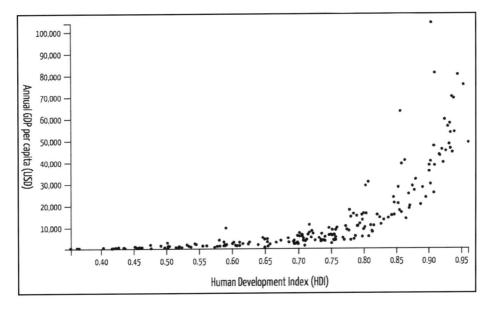

Adding a simple Cartesian grid and labels. Code: *StepByStep/2-scatter-gdp_hdi.html.*

Note that we didn't need to configure the tick formats. The vertical axis, for example, displays large numbers using a comma to separate thousands. If you don't want that, you can use the `ticks()` method to format it differently. The following code will remove the separators:

```
d3.axisLeft(scaleY).ticks(8,"d");
```

Configuring axis styles

Let's configure some styles to make the chart easier to read. Perhaps we don't need those thick domain lines, since there are so many dots that appear right on top of them. You can remove them with D3:

```
d3.select(".domain").remove();
```

But perhaps just hiding them with CSS will be enough:

```
.domain {
    opacity: 0;
}
```

It's hard to read the dots that are far away from the axes. We can create a visible grid by increasing the size of the tick lines so that they fill the entire chart area, adding tick configuration methods to each axis function:

```
const axisX = d3.axisBottom(scaleX)
        .tickSize(h - marginH*2 + 10)
        .tickPadding(2);
const axisY = d3.axisLeft(scaleY)
        .tickSize(w - marginW*2 + 10)
        .tickPadding(2);
```

But since the ticks of our axes grow to the left and to the bottom, they need to be moved in the other direction. The vertical position of the *x*-axis ticks was `h - marginH`. Changing it to `marginH` will move it up to the margin, revealing the tick labels. The *y*-axis ticks need to be pushed left, thus changing its horizontal position from `marginW` to `w - marginW`:

```
xG.attr("transform", `translate(${[0,marginH]})`)
 yG.attr("transform", `translate(${[w-marginW,0]})`);
```

The lines are too dark and thick. Let's make them thinner and lighter with CSS styles:

```
.y-axis line, .x-axis line {
    stroke-width: .25;
    stroke: rgba(114, 138, 74, 0.5);
}
```

The result is shown in the following screenshot. Now, it's much easier to relate the position of a dot to its values:

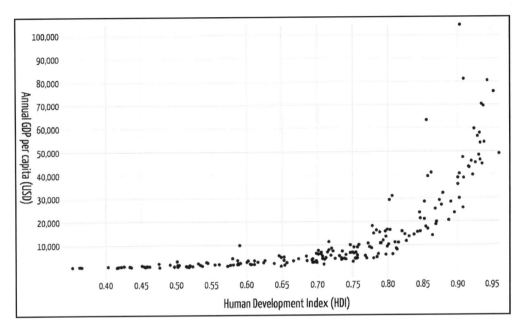

Configuring the style and size of grid lines in the chart area. Code: *StepByStep/3-scatter-gdp_hdi.html.*

Using a logarithmic scale

Since the GDP per capita grows exponentially, and most data points use the first 10% of the scale, a logarithmic scale may improve readability. Since no GDP values are zero, a logarithmic scale can be used. All you have to do is replace `scaleLinear()` with `scaleLog()`:

```
const scaleY = d3.scaleLog().range([h-marginH, marginH]);
```

This change made the vertical scale appear in scientific notation, which is the default when an axis uses a log scale. You can change it back to how it was displayed in the linear scale with the `ticks()` method:

```
axisY.ticks(8, ',');
```

That's it; now, you can finally distinguish most points, as shown in the following screenshot:

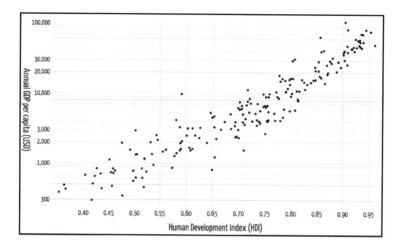

An improved chart using a logarithmic scale for the GDP per capita. Code: *StepByStep/4-scatter-gdp_hdi.html*.

Grouping dots by category

Each data point object contains the continent to which each country belongs in the d.continent property. We can use it as a category to group several countries and identify them with a color code.

First, we need a set containing the names of the available continents. These names can be extracted from the data file and added to Set, which will only add each continent once. Let's create a new Set in our global data object:

```
const data = { continents: new Set() }
```

The set will be populated while loading the CSV in the row function, as shown in the following code snippet:

```
d3.csv("../Data/un_regions_gdp.csv", function(row) {
    if(row.HDI_2017 >0 && row.GDP_2017 >0) {
        data.continents.add(row.Continent);
        // ...
    }
})
```

But since D3 requires an array, not a set, we also need to convert it into an array. This can be done using the `Array.from()` or the *spread* operator, as shown in the following code, before calling `draw()`. The continents were also sorted in ascending (alphabetical) order:

```
.then(function(dataset) {
    data.continents =
        [...data.continents].sort((a,b) => d3.ascending(a,b));
    // ...
    drawAxes();
    draw();
});
```

Since we have a small number of categories, a categorical color scheme can be used. It can be any array of colors, or one of the color schemes that's available in D3. The following code creates an ordinal color scale that outputs a color from the `d3.schemeDark2` color scheme for each different category:

```
const color  = d3.scaleOrdinal(d3.schemeDark2);
```

Since all continent names are different, calling the color function with a continent name will return a unique color for each continent. The following code will paint each dot according to its continent:

```
d3.selectAll(".dot")
    .style("fill", d => color(d.continent)) // uses the continent's name
```

The legend box is an SVG group: a `<g lass="legend">` element placed in an empty part of the chart. It contains one `<g class="item">` element for each continent, which contains a rectangle, filled with the continent's color, and a `<text>` element, with the continent's name. To draw the legend box over the chart, it must be placed after drawing the other objects. In the following code, we placed it at the end of the `draw()` function:

```
function draw() {
    // ...
    const legend = d3.select("svg")
        .append("g").attr("class", "legend")
        .attr("transform", `translate(${[85, 50]})`);

    legend.selectAll("g.item")
        .data(data.continents) // the data is an array of continent names
        .join("g")
        .attr("class", "item")
        .each(function(d, i) {
            d3.select(this)
                .append("rect")
                .attr("y", i * 10)
```

```
                    .attr("height", 8)
                    .attr("width", 20)
                    .style("fill", color(d)); // uses the continent's name

            d3.select(this)
                .append("text")
                .attr("y", i * 10)
                .attr("x", 24)
                .text(d);
        });
    }
```

By default, the *y* coordinate for text is the position of its baseline, but you can change that with CSS. The following style configuration will treat the *y* coordinate as the top-left corner and will keep it aligned with the rectangle:

```
.legend text {
    alignment-baseline: hanging;
}
```

The result is shown in the following screenshot. The chart now reveals which continents have a higher or lower GDP per capita and the HDI:

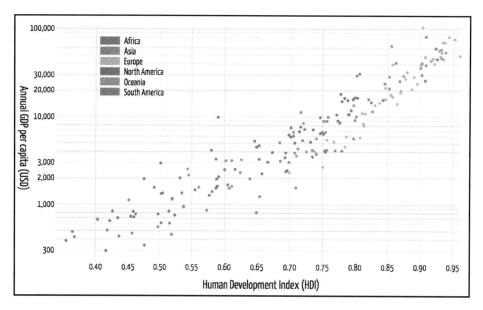

Using color to group dots by continent. Code: *StepByStep/5-scatter-gdp_hdi.html*.

Adding interactivity

You are probably curious to know which European country is indicated by that dot at the top right of the chart, or which African country has nearly 10,000 GDP per capita but lags behind many poorer countries in the HDI. We can't place static labels beside each dot, since that would make the chart unreadable, but we can add interactive tooltips to display the country's name, and perhaps other information, such as the HDI and the GDP values as well.

Let's create a function for that. The following function creates a tooltip as an initially hidden (opacity: 0) SVG <g> object, which contains one <rect> element with rounded corners and three lines of text, all of which are initially empty:

```
function drawTooltips() {
    const tooltip = d3.select("svg")
            .append("g")
            .attr("class", "tooltip")
            .attr("opacity", 0);

    tooltip.append("rect")
            .attr("width", 80)
            .attr("height", 45)
            .attr("rx", 3).attr("ry", 3)
            .attr("x", -3).attr("y", -10);
    tooltip.append("text").attr("class", "name");
    tooltip.append("text").attr("class", "hdi").attr("y", 15);
    tooltip.append("text").attr("class", "gdp").attr("y", 30);
}
```

Since it's hidden, we can render the tooltip invisible after drawing the chart:

```
drawAxes();
draw();
drawTooltips();
```

Other styles can be configured in CSS. The pointer-events: none property is important so that the tooltip doesn't capture mouse events (otherwise, you won't be able to click on any point that appears under a tooltip box). The rectangle is styled with a semi-transparent light-gray background:

```
.tooltip {
    pointer-events: none;
}
.tooltip rect {
    fill: #eee;
    fill-opacity: 0.7;
```

```
        stroke: gray;
        stroke-opacity: .5;
    }
```

Unlike the axes' tick labels, the text in the tooltips won't be formatted automatically. The HDI never has more than three decimal digits, so it doesn't need any formatting, but the GDP may have up to seven decimal digits. The following formatting function will display the GDP per capita with a dollar sign, a thousands separator, and no decimal digits:

```
    const format = d3.format("$,.0f");
```

To show the tooltips, we need to add event handlers to each circle, so when the mouse hovers, the dot above the tooltip is displayed. Add event handlers for the dots:

```
    d3.select("svg")
        .selectAll("circle.dot")
        .on("mouseenter", showDetails)
        .on("mouseleave", clearDetails);
```

The showDetails() function needs to move the tooltip to a position near the dot and make it visible. It also needs to update the contents of the text elements with the data that's currently bound to the dot. The text may be wider than the tooltip box, so after the text elements are updated, we can use the getComputedTextLength() DOM method to discover the width of each text line, select the longest one, and redefine the tooltip rectangle's width so that it's a bit wider to fit the text. The following method also increases the size of the selected dot:

```
    function showDetails(d) {
        d3.select(this).attr("r", 4);
        d3.select(".tooltip").attr("opacity", 1)
            .attr("transform",
                    `translate(${[10 + scaleX(d.hdi), scaleY(d.gdp) - 12]})`)

        const text1 = d3.select(".tooltip .name").text(d.name);
        const text2 = d3.select(".tooltip .gdp").text("GDP: " + format(d.gdp));
        const text3 = d3.select(".tooltip .hdi").text("HDI: " + d.hdi);

        const boxWidth = 6 + d3.max([text1.node().getComputedTextLength(),
                            text2.node().getComputedTextLength(),
                            text3.node().getComputedTextLength()]);

        d3.select(".tooltip rect").attr("width", boxWidth);
    }
```

When the mouse leaves a dot, its radius returns to a normal size and the tooltip is hidden:

```
function clearDetails(d) {
    d3.select(this).attr("r", 1.5);
    d3.select(".tooltip").attr("opacity", 0)
}
```

The result is as follows. Now, you can move the mouse over a dot and discover which country it represents and see the actual values for the GDP and the HDI:

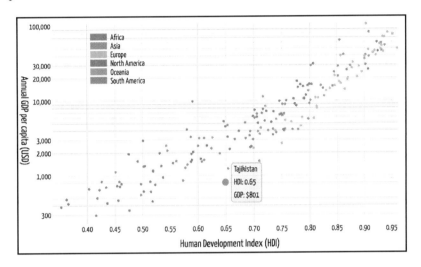

By hovering a dot, it doubles in size and a tooltip is displayed. Code: *StepByStep/6-scatter-gdp_hdi.html.*

We could also make the legends interactive. It would be nice to quickly see where all the African or European countries are, for example. We could do that by highlighting the dots that belong to each continent when hovering over a legend label.

First, we will need to add two CSS classes. The show class will be added to dots when its continent is selected. The fade class will be added to legend items that are not currently selected:

```
.show {
    stroke: black;
    stroke-width: 4;
}
.fade {
    opacity: .5;
}
```

The following code adds the handlers to all legend items:

```
d3.select(".legend").selectAll(".item")
    .on("mouseenter", showContinents)
    .on("mouseleave", clearContinents)
```

The `showContinents()` event handler conditionally adds or removes a class using the `classed()` method, by matching data bound to the current element with selections of legend items and dots. The `clearContinents()` handler simply removes the classes from all elements:

```
function showContinents(d) {
    d3.selectAll(".item").classed("fade", k => k != d)
    d3.selectAll(".dot").classed("show", k => k.continent == d);
}

function clearContinents() {
    d3.selectAll(".item").classed("fade", false)
    d3.selectAll(".dot").classed("show", false);
}
```

The final result is as follows:

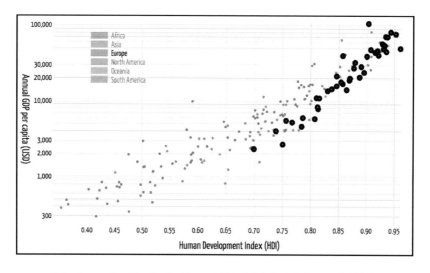

By hovering over a legend item. the related dots are highlighted. Code: *StepByStep/6-scatter-gdp_hdi.html.*

Creating a bubble chart

You can represent a third dimension in a two-dimensional scatter chart using the area of each circle. This turns it into a bubble chart, and will require a new scale. Since it's an area-based scale, a square-root scale is best. The following scale will allow circles with diameters from 2 to 30 pixels wide:

```
const scaleR = d3.scaleSqrt().range([1,15]);
```

This bubble chart will use circles of different areas to show population. After loading the data, configure the domain:

```
scaleR.domain(d3.extent(dataset, d => d.population));
```

Replace the r attribute of the dots with a scaled population, as shown in the following code snippet:

```
d3.selectAll(".dot")
    .attr("r", d => scaleR(d.population));
```

You also need to remove the lines that update the r attribute in the showDetails() and clearDetails() tooltip event handlers (if you don't do that, the dot may shrink after you move the mouse over it).

Increase the height of the tooltip box so that a line for the population can be added:

```
d3.select(".tooltip rect") .attr("height", 60)
```

Then, append a new line of text for the population:

```
d3.select(".tooltip ")
    .append("text").attr("class", "pop").attr("y", 45);
```

Let's use standard SI units to format the population. The following code creates a formatter that will append a *k*, *M*, or *G* after the population, with up to three digits after the decimal point:

```
const formatSI = d3.format(",.3s");
```

The changes in the `showDetails()` and `clearDetails()` event handlers are as follows:

```
function showDetails(d) {
    // d3.select(this).attr("r", 4); // remove this line
    d3.select(".tooltip").attr("opacity", 1)
    // ...
    const text4 = d3.select(".tooltip .pop")
                    .text("Population: " + formatSI(d.population)); // add
    const boxWidth =
        6 + d3.max([/*...*/, text4.node().getComputedTextLength()]); // add
    // ...
}

function clearDetails(d) {
    // d3.select(this).attr("r", 1.5); // remove this line
    d3.select(".tooltip").attr("opacity", 0)
}
```

The final result is as follows:

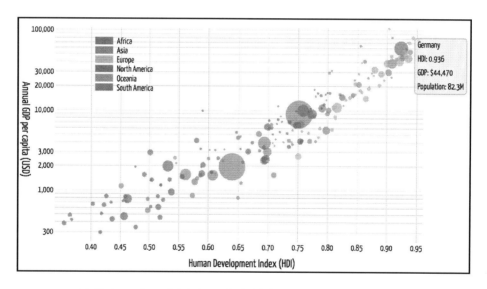

A bubble chart encoding population in the area of each circle. Code: *StepByStep/7-bubble-pop-gdp_hdi.html*.

We will come back to this chart in `Chapter 8`, *Animation and Interactivity,* to implement zooming behavior.

Summary

This chapter covered several tools that you will use to render your visualizations: axes, which provide contextual information for charts; scales, which map abstract and quantitative domain data to pixel dimensions and other visual aspects; and colors, which are also used to encode information in a data visualization. These tools are part of five modules: *d3-interpolate* (introduced in the last chapter), *d3-axis*, *d3-scale*, *d3-scale-chromatic*, and *d3-color*.

We finished this chapter with a complete scatter and bubble chart example that used functions, methods, and properties from practically all of these modules.

Now that you know how to configure scales, axes, and colors, you are ready to explore shape and layout generator functions in D3 so that you can create classic line charts, stacked area charts, pie charts, doughnut charts, and any kind of visualization you can imagine with arbitrary shapes. These are the topics we will explore in the next chapter.

References

- Module documentation, D3.js: `github.com/d3/d3-axis`, `github.com/d3/d3-scale`, `github.com/d3/d3-scale-chromatic`, github.com/d3/d3-color, github.com/d3/d3-interpolate.
- Introducing d3-scale, by Mike Bostock: `medium.com/@mbostock/introducing-d3-scale-61980c51545f`
- Color Brewer, by Cynthia Brewer: `colorbrewer2.org`
- RGB Color Picker, by Mike Bostock: `bl.ocks.org/mbostock/78d64ca7ef013b4dcf8f`
- HSL Color Picker, by Mike Bostock: `bl.ocks.org/mbostock/debaad4fcce9bcee14cf`
- Lab Color Picker, by Mike Bostock: `bl.ocks.org/mbostock/9f37cc207c0cb166921b`
- HCL Color Picker, by Mike Bostock: `bl.ocks.org/mbostock/3e115519a1b495e0bd95`
- Cubehelix Color Picker, by Mike Bostock: `bl.ocks.org/mbostock/ba8d75e45794c27168b5`
- GDP and HDI dataset: `Data/un_regions_gdp.csv`. Compiled from several sources, including United Nations (World Population Prospects 2017: www.un.org) and World Bank (World bank public data. data.worldbank.org)

7
Shape and Layout Generators

D3 is a data-driven data visualization library, but not a charting library. It contains no predefined chart types, but it helps you apply standards such as SVG and Canvas to create absolutely any chart that you can find in a popular charting library, without being limited in any way.

Classic chart types are created in SVG or Canvas with the *d3-shape* module; this is a complete library for drawing geometric shapes that are commonly used in data visualizations. This is the module you need if you want to create line charts, area charts, pie and doughnut charts, and radial charts.

Eight *shape generators* are provided for shapes such as lines, arcs, and areas. They return functions that receive structured data and generate SVG path strings or Canvas path commands, which can be bound to graphical elements in your page. This includes preconfigured symbol shapes that can be used in scatterplots, and smooth Bezier curves for hierarchical linked structures.

There are two *layout generators* to build structures for pies and stacks. A layout generator doesn't generate any shape data but returns functions that transform a dataset, altering its structure and adding properties so that it can be more easily used by a shape generator.

Besides generator functions and their configuration methods, this module also includes different algorithms for ordering datasets, a collection of curve factories for line rendering, and offset strategies for stacked data.

In this chapter, we will explore most of the generator functions in *d3-shape*, using them to create Cartesian and radial line charts, pie and doughnut charts, and stacked bar and steam charts. The charts will be rendered using SVG, which is the default, but a short introduction to Canvas rendering is also included at the end of the chapter.

We will cover the following topics in this chapter:

- Shapes and layouts
- Lines
- Symbols
- Curve functions
- Areas
- Stacked layouts
- Radial charts
- Arcs
- Pie layout
- Canvas rendering

Shapes and layouts

Shape generator functions return data strings for the `<path>` SVG element, which can be used to draw straight lines, Bezier curves, symbols, and arcs. Shapes are described in SVG by a path language expressed as a compact string containing letters and numbers. The letters represent commands, such as M: *moveTo*, L: *lineTo*, A: *arc*, and C: *cubic Bezier curve*. In complex shapes, a path data string can be very long.

Two examples of path data strings drawing arbitrary shapes are shown here (spaces are optional and are usually not present in generated code):

```
M50,20 L200,200 V140 h70 Z
M100,200 C100,100 250,100 250,200 S400,300 400,200
```

Path data strings are used in the **d** (data) attribute of `<path>` elements, as in the following SVG code:

```
<svg width="800" height="300">
    <path d="M50,20L200,200V140h70Z"
        fill="yellow" stroke="red" stroke-width="3" />

    <path d="M100,200C100,100,250,100,250,200S400,300,400,200"
        fill="white" stroke="blue" stroke-width="4"
        transform="translate(200,-80)"/>
</svg>
```

The preceding code will produce the two shapes shown here:

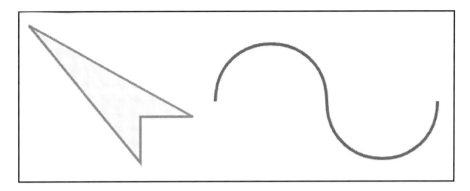

Two SVG shapes created with <path> elements Code: *SVG/1-svg-path.html*

To render a `<path>` element in D3, you need to create or select the element and set its `d` attribute. The following code uses D3 to render the same shapes as the preceding diagram (see `SVG/2-svg-path-d3.html`):

```
const svg = d3.select("body")
            .append("svg")
            .attr("width", "800")
            .attr("height", "300");

svg.append("path")
        .attr("d", "M50,20L200,200V140h70Z")
        .attr("fill","yellow")
        .attr("stroke","red")
        .attr("stroke-width","3");

svg.append("path")
        .attr("d", "M100,200C100,100,250,100,250,200S400,300,400,200")
        .attr("fill","white")
        .attr("stroke","blue")
        .attr("stroke-width","4")
        .attr("transform","translate(200, -80)");
```

Recall that axis generator functions also create `<path>` elements, but their `d` attributes are generated automatically when the function is called in the context of a selection and a scale.

The eight shape generator functions from the *d3-shape* module are listed in the following table. They usually require some configuration parameters and return a function that generates an SVG path data strings that draw straight lines, curves, pie slices, and other shapes:

Function	Description
d3.line	This creates a function that receives an array of coordinates and generates path data that draws a line in cartesian coordinates. The path draws straight lines by default, but it can also be configured to draw curves.
d3.area	Similar to d3.line(), but it generates a closed shape instead of a line, and contains additional methods that allow for the configuration of the baseline.
d3.symbol	This creates a function that generates path data for an arbitrary symbol. D3 comes with seven preconfigured layouts for symbols (such as a circle, star, cross, diamond, square, triangle, and wye), but custom symbols can also be created.
d3.radialLine	Similar to d3.line(), but it generates path data for a line rendered in angular coordinates (that is, the angle and radius).
d3.radialArea	Similar to d3.radialLine(), generating a closed shape instead of a line, with additional methods to configure the inner radius.
d3.arc	This creates a function that receives a pair of angles and radii and returns path data that draws an arc as a closed shape.
d3.link	This creates a link generator function that generates path data for curves between two points. This will be covered in Chapter 9, *Visualizing Hierarchical Data.*
d3.linkRadial	This creates a link generator function with radial tangents. This will be covered in Chapter 9, *Visualizing Hierarchical Data.*

Shape generator functions that return SVG <path> data strings or Canvas path commands

These functions generate <path> SVG data strings as default, but also support a context() method, which takes a Canvas graphics context and, instead of the path string, will return a sequence of Canvas path method calls. An introduction to Canvas rendering with D3 is provided at the end of this chapter, and includes examples using the shape generators listed previously.

Two other generator functions in the *d3-shape* module don't generate path data, but instead return data structures in a format that can be fed into path generator functions; they are listed here:

Function	Description
d3.stack	This creates a function that generates stacked data. When called on an array, the function returns an array of arrays that contain each data series.
d3.pie	This transforms a data array into an array of objects containing *start* and *end* angles for each slice, which can be fed into an arc function to generate SVG slices. Inner and outer radii can be configured to generate pie or doughnut charts.

Layout generator functions that return data structures used in visualizations

Most of these functions will be explored in the remaining sections of this chapter.

Lines

The d3.line() function creates a function that generates the data string of an SVG path element:

```
const line = d3.line();
```

Calling the function with an array of [*x,y*] coordinates creates the path data string:

```
const data = [ [0,0],[100,200],[200,400],[300,150],[400,50],
                [500,350],[600,500],[700,100],[800,250]  ];
const pathData = line(data);
```

The preceding code will store the following string in pathData:

```
M0,0L100,200L200,400L300,150L400,50L500,350L600,500L700,100L800,250
```

You can render the line obtaining a selection for an SVG <path> element and set its d attribute with this value to render the line:

```
d3.select("body").append("svg")
        .append("path")
        .attr("d", pathData)     // the path data string
        .style("stroke", "red")
        .style("fill", "none");
```

The expected result is as follows:

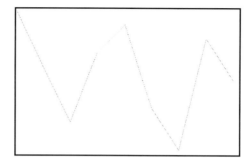

A line created with *d3.line()*. Code: *Lines/1-line.html*.

Another (more flexible and recommended) way to write the same expression is as follows:

```
d3.select("body").append("svg")
        .append("path")
        .datum(data)                // binds the array to <path>
        .attr("d", line)            // calls line(data)
        .style("stroke", "red")
        .style("fill", "none");
```

Binding allows the data to be used in attributes and nested selections. For example, to display the coordinates for each data point, you could bind the data to a parent <g> element, use the array to generate the line, and reuse the data with the *general update pattern* to bind each coordinate to a text element, positioned near the point. This may be easier to understand by looking at the following code:

```
const g = d3.select("body").append("svg")
        .append("g").datum(data);       // binds entire array to <g>

g.append("path")
    .attr("d", line)                // calls line(data) from path
    .style("stroke", "red")
    .style("fill", "none");

g.selectAll("text")
    .data(d => d)       // binds each [x,y] to a <text> element
    .join("text")       // same as enter().append("text")
    .text(d => d)
    .attr("x", d => d[0] + 10)   // positions the text near (x,y)
    .attr("y", d => d[1] + 10)
```

The result is shown in the following screenshot:

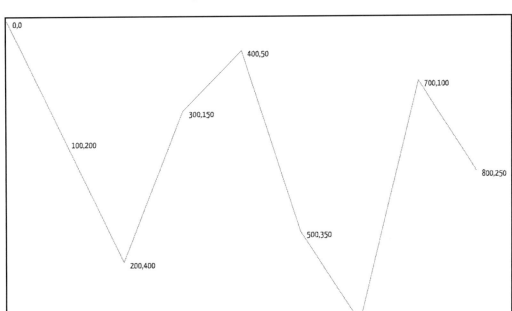

A line chart with value labels. Code: *Lines/2-line-labels.html*.

Instead of printing the values for each point, you can, of course, use axes (see `Lines/3-line-axes.html`).

Unless your data is already transformed to fit the screen, you will need to scale it before rendering the line (see `Lines/4-line-scales.html`). You may also need to retrieve the coordinates from object properties, if your data is not an array of coordinates (see `Lines/5-line-objects.html`). This can be configured with accessor functions provided as parameters to the `x()` and `y()` methods. These and other configuration methods for lines are listed in the following table. All methods also work as getters when called without any parameters:

Method	Description
x (*function*)	This receives an accessor function that returns the value to be used for the x coordinate. This default is `d => d[0]`.
y (*function*)	This receives an accessor function that returns the value to be used for the y coordinate. The default is `d => d[1]`.

defined (*function*)	This receives an accessor function that returns true if the corresponding line segment should be rendered. The default returns true for all segments.
curve (*curveType*)	This returns the curve factory to be used when generating the lines. The default is d3.curveLinear, which generates straight lines between points; see the *Curves* section.
context (*ctx*)	If a non-null Canvas context is specified, instead of an SVG path string, the function will generate a series of Canvas path method calls; see the *Canvas rendering* section.

The main configuration methods for lines

Let's see a complete example. The following code renders a complete line chart with three datasets using scales and axes (see Lines/6-line-multiple.html). The scales are used to stretch the small data values so that they fit the screen. A color scale is also used to generate different colors for each line. Since there are three datasets, we can create the lines using the *general update pattern*, which binds a <path> element for each datum:

```
const width  = 800;
const height = 400;
const margin = 50;

const data = [
   [[0,0],[1,.2],[2,.4],[3,.15],[4,.05],[5,.35],[6,.5],[7,.1],[8,.25]],
   [[0,0],[1,.077],[2,.13],[3,.27],[4,.33],[5,.29],[6,.09],[7,.03],[8,.11]],
   [[0,0],[1,.3],[2,.5],[3,.56],[4,.43],[5,.33],[6,.21],[7,.11],[8,.02]],
];
const scaleX = d3.scaleLinear()
        .domain(d3.extent(d3.merge(data), d => d[0]))
        .range([margin,width - margin]);

 const scaleY = d3.scaleLinear()
        .domain(d3.extent(d3.merge(data), d => d[1]))
        .range([height - margin,margin])
        .nice();

const colorScale = d3.scaleOrdinal(d3.schemeCategory10)
                .domain([0,data.length]);

const line = d3.line()
              .x(d => scaleX(d[0]))
              .y(d => scaleY(d[1]));

const xAxis = d3.axisBottom(scaleX);
const yAxis = d3.axisLeft(scaleY);
```

```
const svg = d3.select("body").append("svg")
            .attr("height",height)
            .attr("width",width);
const axes = svg.append("g").attr("class", "axes");

axes.append("g").call(xAxis)
        .attr("transform", `translate(${[0, height - margin]})`);
axes.append("g").call(yAxis)
        .attr("transform", `translate(${[margin, 0]})`);

svg.selectAll("path.dataset")
    .data(data).join("path")   // same as
.data(data).enter().append("path")
    .attr("class", "dataset")
    .attr("d", line)
    .style("stroke", colorScale);
```

The resulting chart is as follows:

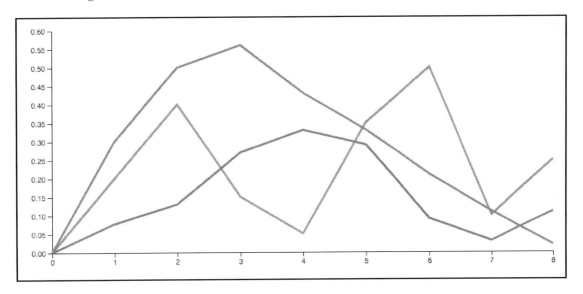

A line chart with three datasets. Code: *Lines/6-line-multiple.html*.

Additional examples are available in the Lines/ folder from the GitHub repository for this chapter.

Symbols

Symbols are preconfigured shapes that are commonly used to identify value points in line charts and scatterplots. For example, instead of using colors, you can use different symbols to distinguish categories (see `Symbol/3-scatter.html`).

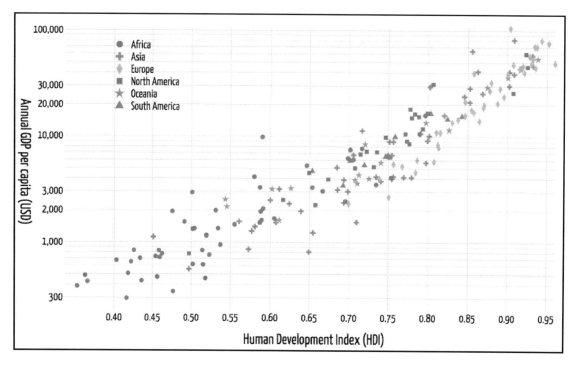

A scatterplot using different symbols for each cagtegory. Code: *Symbol/3-scatter.html*.

A symbol generator function is created with `d3.symbol()`, which returns an SVG path data string representing a 64x64 pixel circle as default:

```
const circle = d3.symbol();
```

To render the symbol, the string should be assigned to the `<path>` element's `d` attribute, and its center coordinates translated to a visible position, since the default center coordinates are (0,0).

The following table lists two methods that can be used to configure symbols:

Method	Description
type (*function*)	This receives a function that draws the symbol. It can be a custom function or one of the seven built-in factory functions listed in the following diagram. The default is d3.symbolCircle.
size (*value*)	The value or function that sets the pixel size of the symbol. The default is 64.

Methods for configuration of symbols

The result is as follows:

The factory functions for built-in symbols Code: *Symbol/1-symbols.html*

The following code generates a data string for a 50x50 star (see Symbol/2-symbol.html):

```
const star = d3.symbol().type(d3.symbolStar).size(50);
```

You can place a star on each data point of the line chart created in previous examples, binding each point to a symbol, as shown in the following code:

```
svg.selectAll("g.line")
svg.selectAll("g.line")
   .data(data).join("g")          // binds each line (data[d]) to g
   .attr("class", "line")
   .each(function(d,i) {
       d3.select(this)
         .append("path")
          .attr("d", line)  // calls line(d) to draw line path
          .style("stroke", colorScale); // colorScale(d)
       d3.select(this)
         .selectAll("path.point")
         .data(d).join("path")  // binds each point (data[d][k]) to path
          .attr("class", "point")
          .attr("d", star)  // calls star(k) to draw star path
          .style("fill", colorScale(d))   // use line's color
               .attr("transform",
                     k => `translate(${[scaleX(k[0]),
scaleY(k[1])]})`);
   });
```

The last transform moves the symbols to the positions $k = [x,y]$ where the points are located. The result is shown in the following screenshot:

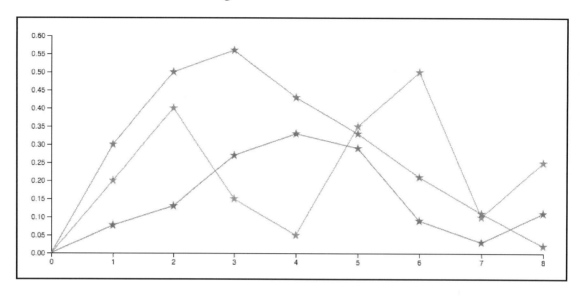

A line chart with symbols on data points. Code: *Lines/8-line-symbol.html*

Curve functions

Curve factory functions change the way a line is interpolated between data points. The default factory for new lines and areas is d3.curveLinear, but that can be overridden by calling the .curve() method with one of the factories illustrated and listed in the diagram that follows:

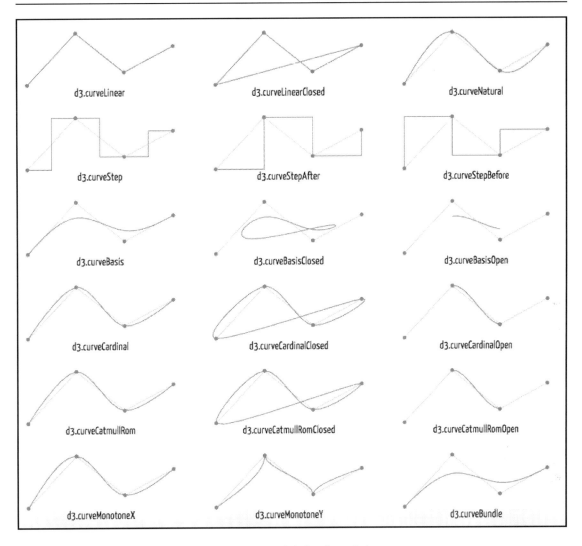

Built-in curve types Code: *Curves/1-curves.html*

For example, the following code will replace the straight line segments with a monotonic curve in relation to the *x* axis:

```
const line = d3.line()
            .x(d => scaleX(d[0]))
            .y(d => scaleY(d[1]))
            .curve(d3.curveMonotoneX);
```

Three types of curve can be fine-tuned with additional methods:

- `d3.curveCardinal`, which produces a cubic cardinal spline, can be tensioned from 0 (default) to 1 (straight line segments, such as `d3.curveLinear`) using the `tension()` method.
- *d3*.`curveCatmullRom`, which produces a cubic Catmull-*Rom* spline, has an `alpha()` parameter that can be adjusted from 0 to 1. The default value is 0.5.
- `d3.curveBundle`, which produces a basis spline, has a `beta()` parameter that can be adjusted from 0 (a straight line from the beginning to end) to 1. The default value is 0.85.

These configurations are illustrated as follows. The result depends on the curve shape. The same configuration may render subtle differences in one curve shape, and pronounced differences in another.

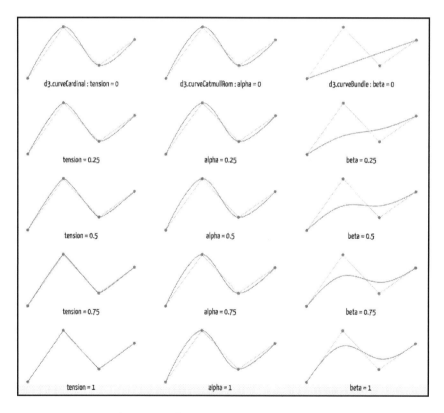

Tensioning parameters for cubic curves. Code: *Curves/2-curves-tension.html*

Applying a monotone curve to the line chart in the previous example will make it look like the one shown here:

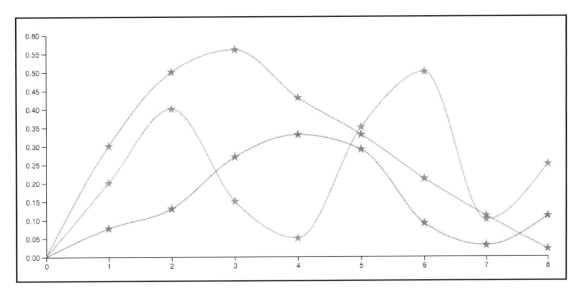

Line chart with curve interpolation Code: *Lines/9-line-curve.html*

Areas

An area is a closed polygon. Area charts are typically created using two bounding lines that share the same x values, but may have different y values. A simple area chart has a constant baseline ($y0$) in zero, and a topline ($y1$), which interpolates the data points. In stacked charts, the baseline of one area corresponds to the topline of the preceding area.

The `d3.area()` function creates a function that generates the data string of an SVG path element:

```
const area = d3.area();
```

Calling the function with an array of data creates the path data string:

```
const data = [ [0,0],[100,200],[200,400],[300,150],[400,50],
                [500,350],[600,500],[700,100],[800,250]  ];
const pathData = area(data);
```

The preceding code stores the following string in `pathData`:

```
M0,0L100,200L200,400L300,150L400,50L500,350L600,500L700,100L800,250
    L800,0L700,0L600,0L500,0L400,0L300,0L200,0L100,0L0,0Z
```

This is almost the same shape that we previously created as a line chart, but now it's a closed polygon with a zero baseline. Using exactly the same code to render `pathData` (with an empty fill) will generate the following shape:

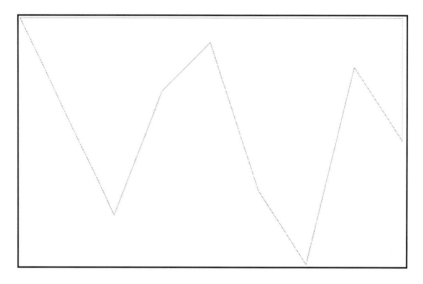

A polygon created with d3.area(). Code: *Areas/1-area.html*

You can use a scale to invert the chart. The baseline is configured with the `y0()` method, which in a simple non-stacked chart will be zero or the minimum *y* value (see `Area/3-area-axes.html`):

```
const scaleX = d3.scaleLinear()
                .domain(d3.extent(data, d => d[0]))
                .range([0, width]);

const scaleY = d3.scaleLinear()
                .domain(d3.extent(data, d => d[1]))
                .range([height, 0]);

const area = d3.area()
                .x(d => scaleX(d[0]))
                .y1(d => scaleY(d[1]))
                .y0(scaleY(0)); // zero as baseline
```

The baseline can change for each point. The following dataset contains three points. The first is used for the *x* values, the others for `y0` and `y1`:

```
const data = [
    [0,0,0],[1,.2,.25],[2,.4,.49],[3,.15,.33],[4,.05,.25],
    [5,.35,.7],[6,.5,.4],[7,.1,.15],[8,.25,.15],
];
```

Using the following scales and configuration, you can fill the area between the two lines:

```
const scaleY = d3.scaleLinear()
        .domain(d3.extent(d3.merge(data).filter((d,i) => i%3 != 0)))
        .range([height - margin, margin]);

const area = d3.area()
                .x(d => scaleX(d[0]))
                .y1(d => scaleY(d[1]))
                .y0(d => scaleY(d[2]));
```

The result is as follows:

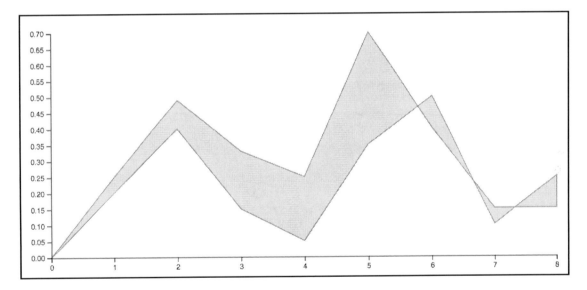

An area chart with a variable baseline

Area functions support the d3.line() methods—x(), y(), curve(), and defined(). Additional configuration methods and line generators are listed in the following table. These methods work as getters when called without parameters:

Method	Description
x0 (*function*)	This receives an accessor function that returns the value to be used for the *x* coordinate of the bounding line, 0. The default is d => d[0].
x1 (*function*)	This receives an accessor function that returns the value to be used for the *x* coordinate of the bounding line, 1. The default returns *null*.
y0 (*function*)	This receives an accessor function that returns the value to be used for the *y* coordinate of the bottomline. The default returns *0*.
y1 (*function*)	This receives an accessor function that returns the value to be used for the *y* coordinate of the topline. The default is d => d[1].
lineX0(), lineX1() lineY0(), lineY1()	The return line generators for each bounding line.
context (*ctx*)	If a non-null Canvas context is specified, instead of an SVG path string, the function will generate a series of Canvas path method calls; see the *Canvas rendering* section.

Configuration methods and line generators for *d3.area()* functions

A line generator creates a line from an area function. You can use it to treat lines and areas separately. You can obtain the topline from an area with the lineX0() method:

```
const line = area.lineX0();
```

Multiple areas are overlapped by default. The line chart from Lines/9-line-curve.html can be rendered as an area chart replacing d3.line with d3.area and configuring a baseline:

```
d3.area().x(d => scaleX(d[0]))
        .y(d => scaleY(d[1]))
        .y1(scaleY(0)) // scale is necessary because chart is inverted
        .curve(d3.curveMonotoneX);
```

The result is as follows (with a color fill added for each dataset):

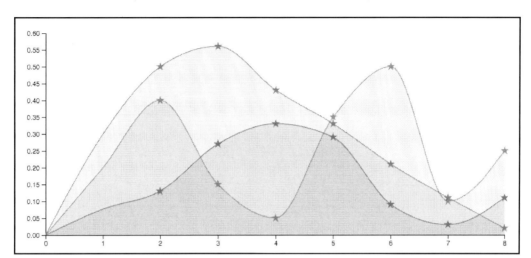

An area chart created with *d3.area( )*. Code: *Areas/7-area-curve.html*.

Stacked layouts

Stacked bar charts stack comparable quantities together for a given category, allowing the viewer to compare the totals and how each quantity contributes to each total. Stacked area charts and steamgraphs are frequently used to display cumulative data over time.

To create a stack, it's necessary to move bars or areas so that one shape is rendered on top of the other. The stack layout generator in D3 takes a dataset and returns a new data structure containing computed positions that can be used to stack bars or to set the top ($y1$) or bottom ($y0$) lines in an area function.

A stack layout generator is created with `d3.stack()`:

```
const stack = d3.stack();
```

Configure the function with keys (or array indexes) that select the series that should be stacked, and then call it with the data:

```
const data = [ [190, 90,  150],
               [330, 160, 275],
               [390, 207, 310] ];
stack.keys([0, 1, 2]);
const stackedData1 = stack(data);
```

Calling the preceding function will return the following stacked data array (see `Stacks/1-array.html`):

```
[
    [ [0,190],   [0,330],   [0,390]    ],
    [ [190,280],[330,490],[390,597] ],
    [ [280,430],[490,765],[597,907] ]
]
```

Each one of the stacked items also contains a data property, containing the original array from which the data was extracted. For example:

```
const data_0_0 = stackedData[0][0].data; // contains [190, 90, 150]
const data_0_1 = stackedData[0][1].data; // contains [330, 160, 275]
```

You can modify the structure of a stacked array by configuring the stack generator function with the methods listed in the following table:

Method	Description
`keys` (*array*)	An array of keys that identify the series of values that will be stacked. The default will return an empty array.
`value` (*function*)	If the content of each key is not a number, this method should provide an accessor function that returns a number.
`order` (*orderType*)	This receives an ordering function that modifies the order of the stacked data. There are five built-in functions. The default is `d3.stackOrderNone`.
`offset` (*offsetType*)	This receives an offsetting function that modifies the baseline of the stacked data. There are five built-in functions. The default is `d3.stackOffsetNone`.

The methods for the configuration of stack generators

If your data is structured as an array of objects that contain keys with the values to be stacked, the `keys()` method should receive an array containing these keys, as here:

```
const data = [
    {name: "Dataset 1", a: 190, b: 90,  c: 150},
    {name: "Dataset 2", a: 330, b: 160, c: 275},
    {name: "Dataset 3", a: 390, b: 207, c: 310}
];

const stack = d3.stack().keys(['a', 'b', 'c']);
const stackedData = stack(data);
```

This will return the same stacked data array as shown previously (see `Stacks/2-object.html`).

If you are loading external data from a CSV, you can obtain the `keys()` array by filtering the headers from the first row; for example, consider the following CSV:

```
dataset,a,b,c
"Dataset 1",190,90,150,
"Dataset 2",330,160,275,
"Dataset 3",390,207,310
```

The stack generator for this data can be set up as follows (see `Stacks/3-csv.html`):

```
d3.csv("../Data/test.csv")
    .then(function(data) {
        const stack = d3.stack()
                .keys(Object.keys(data[0])
                            .filter(d => d != "dataset"));
        const stackedData = stack(data);
        // use the stackedData
    });
```

If your data is structured differently, then you need to reorganize your data *before* using it. You can do that by using D3's data manipulation functions, such as `d3.group()`, `d3.nest()`, `d3.transpose()`, `d3.permute()`, and standard JavaScript functions, or you can prepare your data before loading it.

For example, suppose your data has the following structure (see `Stacks/4-object-flatdata.html`):

```
const data = [
    {
      name: "Dataset 1",
      series: [{key: 'a', value: 190},
               {key: 'b', value: 90},
               {key: 'c', value: 150}]
    },
    {
      name: "Dataset 2",
      series: [{key: 'a', value: 330},
               {key: 'b', value: 160},
               {key: 'c', value: 275}]
    },
    {
      name: "Dataset 3",
      series: [{key: 'a', value: 390},
               {key: 'b', value: 207},
```

```
                    {key: 'c', value: 310}]
        }
    ];
```

The stack generator can't use this structure, but it can be converted into an array of objects, where each value is assigned to a key that can be passed to the `keys()` method. The following code will transform it into the flat structure that is required by the function and generate a stacked data array:

```
const keys = data[0].series.map(k => k.key);

const flatData = data.map(function(d) {
    const obj = {};
    obj.dataset = d.name;
    keys.forEach(function(k) {
        obj[k] = d.series
                    .filter(f => f.key == k)
                    .map(m => m.value)[0]
    });
    return obj;
});
const stack = d3.stack().keys(keys);
const stackedData = stack(flatData);
```

Once you have a stacked data array, you can draw a stacked chart using each pair to compute its position and size. The following code uses the preceding stacked data to render a simple stacked bar chart:

```
svg.selectAll("g")
    .data(stackedData).join("g") // binds stackedData to g
    .each(function(d) {
        d3.select(this)
            .selectAll("rect")
            .data(d).join("rect")   // binds stackedData[d] to rect
                .attr('width', d => d[1] - d[0])   // use stacked data
                .attr('height', 18)
                .attr('x', d => d[0] + 65)          // use stacked data
                .attr('y', (d,i) => i * 20)
    }).append("text").text((d,i) => flatData[i].dataset)
                .attr("y", (d,i) => i * 20 + 14).attr("x", 10);
```

The result is as follows:

A stacked bar chart created with a stacked array generated with d3.stack(). Code: *Stacks/5-simple-bar.html*. See also *Stacks/9-bar-na.html*.

The following chart illustrates the effects of applying different ordering algorithms on a stacked bar chart. Most of these are self-explanatory, except perhaps d3.stackOrderInsideOut, which places the larger series on the inside, and the smaller series on the outside (this is recommended for steamgraphs):

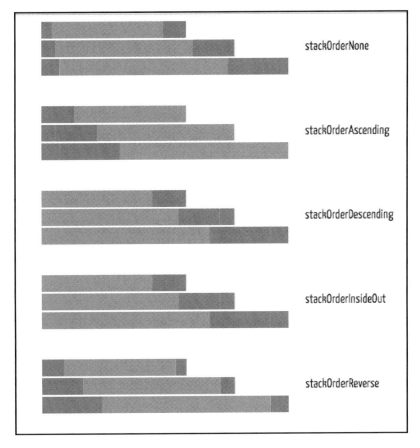

Stack ordering functions. Code: *Stacks/6-orders-bar.html*

The offset algorithms are illustrated in the following stacked area charts, using positive and negative values for the data:

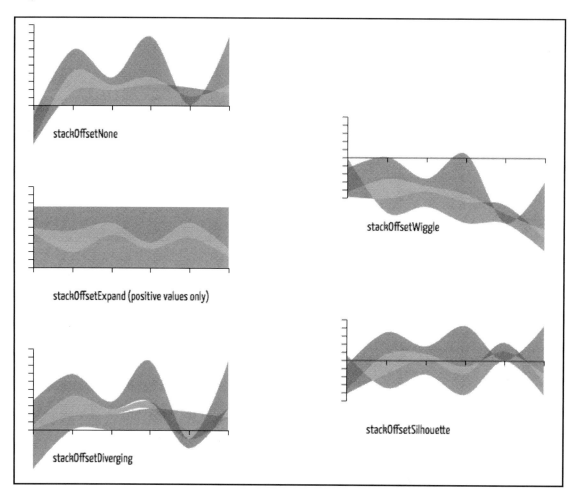

Stack offset functions. Code: *Stacks/7-offsets-area.html.*

The following code (`Stacks/10-area-sa.html`) creates a stacked area chart that compares the population growth of the countries in South America over six decades.

The original data is presented as an array of objects. The following code extracts the entries (key/value pairs) from the first sample (1950), sorts them by value, and then extracts the keys, saving them in the *keys* array. The years are extracted from the data, since they will be used for the horizontal axis:

```
const width  = 800;
const height = 600;
const margin = 50;

const populations = [
    {"year":1950,"Argentina":17150,"Bolivia":3090...},
    {"year":1960,"Argentina":20619,"Bolivia":3693...},
    {"year":1970,"Argentina":23973,"Bolivia":4506...},
    {"year":1980,"Argentina":28106,"Bolivia":5590...},
    {"year":1990,"Argentina":32730,"Bolivia":6856...},
    {"year":2000,"Argentina":37057,"Bolivia":8340...}
];

// Selecting the keys pairs (from the first element)
const keys = Object.entries(populations[0])
                   .sort((a,b) => d3.descending(a[1],b[1]))
                   .filter(d => d[0] != 'year')
                   .map(d => d[0]);

// Selecting data for the horizontal axis
const years = populations.map(d => new Date(d.year,1,1));
```

The stack is configured in the following code snippet, sorting areas in descending order and using the default offset:

```
const stack = d3.stack()
                .keys(keys)
                .order(d3.stackOrderDescending);
const stackedData = stack(populations); // stacks the data
```

Colors, scales, and axes are configured as follows:

```
const scaleTime = d3.scaleTime()
        .domain([new Date(1949,12,1),new Date(2000,1,1)])
        .range([margin, width - margin])

const colorScale = d3.scaleOrdinal(d3.schemeSpectral[11])
        .domain([0,stack.keys().length]);

const scaleY = d3.scaleLinear()
        .domain([0, d3.max(d3.merge(d3.merge(stackedData)))])
        .range([height - margin, 10])
        .nice();
const timeAxis = d3.axisBottom(scaleTime).ticks(6);
const yAxis = d3.axisLeft(scaleY);
```

The `area` function will use each stacked data element. The first value of the array provides the baseline `y0()` value as the first element of each array, and the topline *y* value as the second element:

```
const area = d3.area()
                .x((d,i) => scaleTime(years[i]))
                .y0(d => scaleY(d[0]))
                .y1(d => scaleY(d[1]))
                .curve(d3.curveMonotoneX);
```

Finally, the following code binds the stacked data, using the `area` function to render each path:

```
const svg = d3.select("body").append("svg")
                .attr("height",height).attr("width",width);
svg.selectAll("path")
    .data(stackedData).enter()
    .append("path")
    .attr("d", area)
    .style("fill", (d,i) => colorScale(stack.keys().length - i - 1));
```

The rest of the code renders the axes and creates a legend. You can see and run the full code in `Stacks/10-area-sa.html`. The result is as follows:

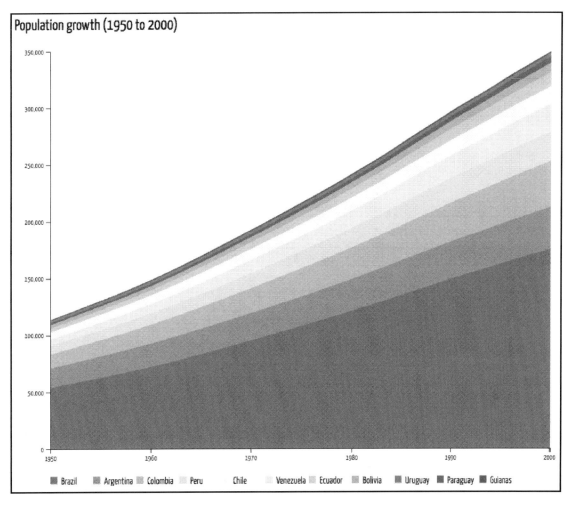

A stacked area chart comparing population growth between the countries of South America

Configuring the stack with the `d3.stackOffsetExpand` offset strategy will render a normalized chart that may be more efficient to visualize proportional contributions to the total.

```
stack.offset(d3.stackOffsetExpand);
```

This is shown as follows:

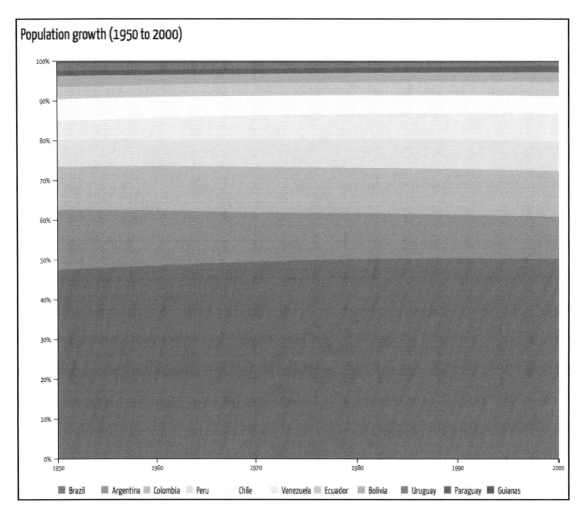

A stacked area chart showing proportional total population in South America from 1950 to 2000. Code: *Stacks/11-area-sa-expand.html*.

Radial charts

In radial charts, values are represented as a distance from the center and an angle from a reference meridian (the 12 o'clock position). You can create any kind of radial chart in D3, but function generators are provided for radial line and radial area charts. They are similar to their Cartesian correlates, with data points expressed in terms of radius and angle, instead of *x* and *y*.

Radial line

A radial line function can be created with `d3.lineRadial()`. The coordinates of each data point are specified by the methods listed in the following table. Radial lines also inherit other line methods, such as `defined()` and `curve()`, which function in the same way.

Method	Description
angle (*function*)	This returns an angle in radians. The reference meridian (0) is located at –*y* (12 o'clock).
radius (*function*)	This returns the distance from the center (0,0).

The point coordinate methods for radial lines

There is a very cool real-world example we can create to demonstrate radial line charts. It uses a JSON file that you can download from the NASA GISS (Goddard Institute for Space Studies) website (`data.giss.nasa.gov/gistemp`), which includes monthly global temperature measurements for each year between 1880 and 2016. It will be very interesting to plot the numbers for all months in a single chart; the following is a fragment of this file:

```
[
    {"Date": "2016-12-27", "Mean": 0.7895,  "Source": "GCAG"},
    {"Date": "2016-12-27", "Mean": 0.81, "Source": "GISTEMP"},
    {"Date": "2016-11-27", "Mean": 0.7504,  "Source": "GCAG"},
    {"Date": "2016-11-27", "Mean": 0.93, "Source": "GISTEMP"},
    {"Date": "2016-10-27", "Mean": 0.7292,  "Source": "GCAG"},
    {"Date": "2016-10-27", "Mean": 0.89, "Source": "GISTEMP"},
    /* ... many, many more lines ... */
    {"Date": "1880-02-27", "Mean": -0.1229,  "Source": "GCAG"},
    {"Date": "1880-02-27", "Mean": -0.21, "Source": "GISTEMP"},
    {"Date": "1880-01-27", "Mean": 0.0009,  "Source": "GCAG"},
    {"Date": "1880-01-27", "Mean": -0.3, "Source": "GISTEMP"}
]
```

In `Radial/1-radial-line.html`, we used the data to draw a line for each year, with data points at each month. The result is a spiral that grows outward since global temperatures are increasing. Each data point is placed within a -2 and 1 °C domain, where -2 °C is the center, and in 12 angular increments of 30 degrees. In the following code (`Radial/2-radial-line.html`), we filtered every fifth year, reducing the clutter and making the spiral easier to perceive:

```
d3.json('../Data/monthly_json.json').then(function(result) {
        data = result.filter(d => d.Source == 'GISTEMP')
                .map(d => {d.year = +d.Date.split("-")[0]; return d})
                .filter(d => d.year % 5 == 0);

        const scaleRadius = d3.scaleLinear()
                .domain([-2, d3.max(data, d => d.Mean)])
                .range([0, width/2 - margin]);

        const spiral = d3.lineRadial()
                .angle((d,i) => ((i % 12)/12) * Math.PI * 2)
                .radius(d => scaleRadius(d.Mean));

        const svg = d3.select("body")
                .append("svg").attr("height",600).attr("width",800);

        const g = svg.append("g")
                    .attr("transform","translate("+[400,300]+")");

        g.append("path")
                .datum(data)
                .attr("d", spiral)
                .style("stroke", "red")
                .style("fill", "none");
});
```

The result is as follows:

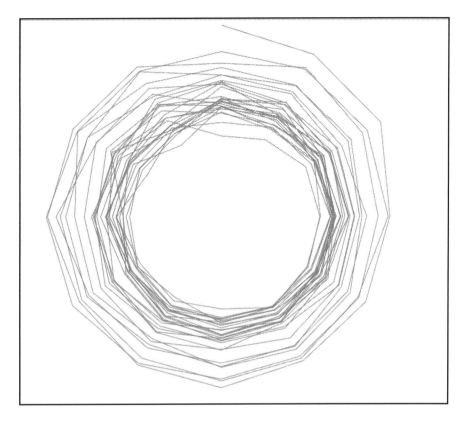

A radial line chart showing increasing relative global temperatures. Code: *Radial/2-radial-line.html*

Grouping the datasets per year, applying a different color to each one, adding a radial axis (by rotating 12 `axisBottom()` objects), and interpolating the lines as curves (with `d3.curveNatural`) resulted in an improved version of the same chart, shown in the following screenshot.

The code for this chart is available in `Radial/4-radial-line-axis.html`:

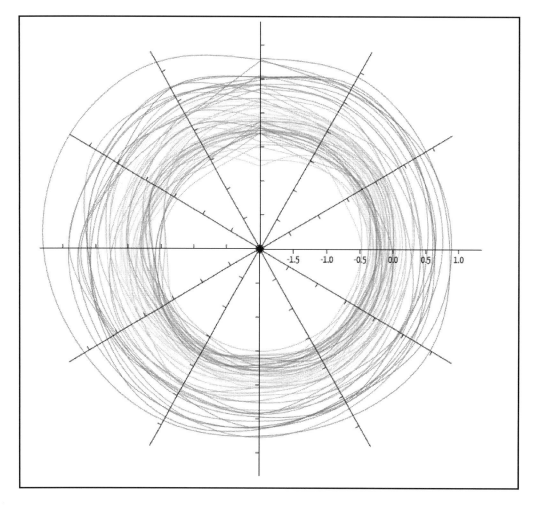

An improved radial line chart showing increasing relative global temperatures. Code: *Radial/4-radial-line-axis.html*

Radial area

A radial area function can be created with `d3.areaRadial()`. The coordinates of each data point are specified by the methods listed in the following table. Radial areas also inherit line methods, such as `defined()` and `curve()`, and radial line methods, such as `angle()`:

Method	Description
innerRadius (*function*)	This is equivalent to `y0()` in Cartesian areas, but returns a distance from the origin.
outerRadius (*function*)	This is equivalent to `y1()` in Cartesian areas, but returns a distance from the origin.
startAngle (*function*) angle (*function*)	This is equivalent to `x1()` in Cartesian areas, but returns an angle in radians. Typically, only the inherited `angle()` method is used.
endAngle (*function*) angle (*function*)	This is equivalent to `x0()` in Cartesian areas, but returns an angle in radians. Typically, only the inherited `angle()` method is used.
lineStartAngle() lineInnerRadius() lineEndAngle() lineOuterRadius()	The return line generators for each bounding line.

Configuration methods and line generators for d3.areaRadial()

The code in `Radial/7-radial-area-axis.html` creates a radial area chart using the same data as the radial line chart created in the previous section. The main parts are listed in the following code snippet. The only difference between the `lineRadial()` configuration is that `radius()` was replaced by `outerRadius()`:

```
const spiral = d3.areaRadial()  // this is the area generator
            .angle((d,i) => i/12 * Math.PI * 2)
            .outerRadius(d => scaleRadius(d))
            .curve(d3.curveNatural); const axis =
d3.axisBottom(scaleRadius).ticks(6).tickSize(0);
const svg = d3.select("body").append("svg")
            .attr("height",height).attr("width",width);
const g = svg.append("g")
            .attr("transform","translate("+[width/2,height/2]+")");
```

The nested array contains the data grouped by year. This code applies a warmer color to each year; calling the axis generator 12 times, in different angles, created the radial axis:

```
g.selectAll("path").data(nested).enter().append("path")
                 .attr("d", d => spiral(d.value))
                 .style("fill", (d,i) => colorScale(i));
```

The result is as follows:

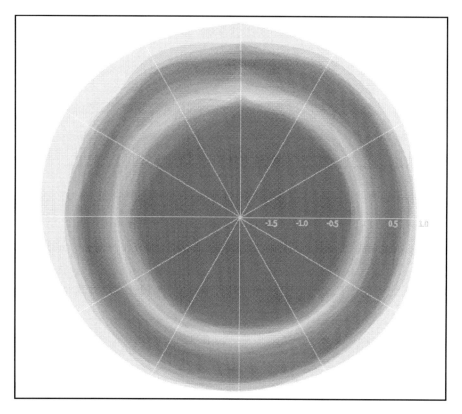

A radial area chart showing increasing relative global temperatures. Code: *Radial/7-radial-area-axis.html*.

Arcs

The d3.arc() function creates an arc generator, which given an *inner* and *outer* radius, and a *start* and *end* angle, generates an SVG path data string (or Canvas path commands) that draws a circular or annular sector, such as the ones used in pie and doughnut charts. Besides these charts, arcs can also be used to create radial area charts.

The following code creates a generator function for a 90-degree arc starting at 45 degrees (the origin is at 12 o'clock), with an outer radius of 100 pixels and no inner radius (the arc will be drawn as a slice starting at the origin):

```
const arc = d3.arc()
        .innerRadius(0)
        .outerRadius(100)
        .startAngle(Math.PI * 45/180)
        .endAngle(Math.PI * 135/180);
  const slice = arc();
  console.log(slice);
```

The resulting SVG path data string is shown as follows:

```
M70.71,-70.71A100,100,0,0,1,70.71,70.71L0,0Z
```

To render the arc, the data string should be assigned to the d attribute of an SVG path selection, and translated to a visible part of the viewport:

```
const svg = d3.select("body").append("svg");
  svg.append("path")
        .datum(slice)
        .attr("d", d => d)
        .attr("transform", "translate(120,120)");
```

The result is as follows:

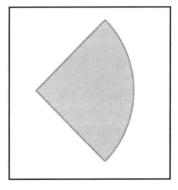

An arc created with d3.arc. Code: *Arcs/1-arc.html*

The following table lists the methods that can be used to configure arc generator functions:

Method	Description
innerRadius (*value*)	If zero, the arc will be drawn as a circular sector. A positive value will render an annular sector. A function can be used to provide computed values (used in stacked radial area charts).
outerRadius (*value*)	This defines the outer radius of the arc. It must be greater than *innerRadius*. A function can be used to provide computed values (used in radial area charts).
startAngle (*angle*)	The angle (relative to the 12 o'clock position, clockwise) where the arc begins in radians.
endAngle (*angle*)	The angle in radians where the arc ends.
centroid (*args*)	This computes the midpoint of the center line of the arc, defined by *(startAngle + endAngle)/2* and *(innerRadius + outerRadius/2)*.
cornerRadius (*value*)	The radius of the circle that rounds the outer corners of the arc. If *innerRadius* is non-zero, the corner radius is also applied to the inner corners.
padAngle () and padRadius ()	The padAngle * padRadius product adds parallel space between segments if the inner diameter is larger than the space. If the inner radius is small or zero, the spacing between segments may not be parallel.
context (*ctx*)	If a non-null Canvas context is specified, instead of an SVG path string, the function will generate a series of Canvas path method calls; see the *Canvas rendering* section.

Configuration methods for the d3.arc() function

Configuration parameters can also be passed to the generator function as an object. The same arc shown previously can be created with the following code (Arcs/2-arc-object.html):

```
const arc = d3.arc().innerRadius(0).outerRadius(100);
const s1 = {
    startAngle: Math.PI * 45/180,
    endAngle: Math.PI * 135/180
};
const slice = arc(s1);
```

This makes it easier to create several arcs with similar properties. The following code generates a doughnut chart from an arc generator function with a 50-pixel inner radius and a100-pixel outer radius. The start and end angles of each sector are obtained from an object array:

```
const arc = d3.arc()
                .innerRadius(50)
                .outerRadius(100)
                .cornerRadius(10);
  const arcData = [
      {startAngle: 0,                        endAngle: Math.PI * 90/180},
      {startAngle: Math.PI * 90/180,  endAngle: Math.PI * 240/180},
      {startAngle: Math.PI * 240/180, endAngle: Math.PI * 2}
  ];
  const slices = arcData.map(d => arc(d));
```

The result is an array of SVG path data strings, which can be bound to shapes using the general update pattern (see `Arcs/3-arc-doughnut.html`):

```
d3.select("body").append("svg").selectAll("path.arc")
        .data(slices).enter()
        .append("path").attr("class", "arc")
        .attr("d", d => d)
        .style("fill", (d,i) => colorScale(i))
        .attr("transform", "translate(120,120)");
```

The preceding code used a CSS style sheet configuring *stroke-width* and a white *stroke* to add visual space between sectors:

```
<style>
    .arc {
        stroke: white;
        stroke-width: 5;
        fill-opacity: .5;
    }
</style>
```

But a similar effect can be obtained for this chart by configuring `padAngle()` and `padRadius()` (see `Arcs/4-arc-padAngle.html`):

```
const arc = d3.arc().innerRadius(4).outerRadius(100).cornerRadius(10)
                .padAngle(4)
                .padRadius(4);
```

The centroid is useful to add slice labels. The following code (`Arcs/5-arc-centroid.html`) draws a small black circle at each centroid:

```
const g = svg.selectAll("g").data(slices).enter().append("g")
        .attr("transform", "translate(120,120)");
g.append("path")
        .attr("d", d => d).style("fill", (d,i) => colorScale(i));
g.append('circle')
        .attr("cx",(d,i) => arc.centroid(arcData[i])[0] )
        .attr("cy",(d,i) => arc.centroid(arcData[i])[1] )
        .attr("r",5);
```

All the arcs created with the preceding code are as follows:

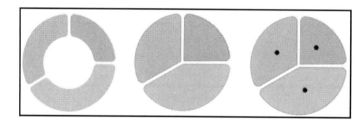

Arcs using different configurations of inner/outer radius, corner radius, and padding.Code: *Arcs/3-arc-doughnut.html, 4-arc-padAngle.html* and *5-arc-centroid.html*.

Pie layout

The layout function created by the `d3.pie()` generator takes an array of data and returns an object array containing the original data plus computed start and end angles that can be used to render arcs. It's perfect for creating pie and doughnut charts. The function can be configured with the methods listed in the following table:

Method	Description
`startAngle(angle)`	This method changes the angle, in radians, where the pie starts. The default is 0 (12 o'clock).
`endAngle(angle)`	This method changes the angle, in radians, where the pie ends. The default is Math.PI * 2.
`value(function)`	This method receives an accessor function that returns the (numerical) value for each datum, when necessary. The default is `d => d`.
`padAngle()`	This method returns an angular separation in radians between adjacent arcs.

`sort(comparator)`	This method sorts the arcs according to a given comparator function that operates on the data (for example, it can be used to sort by angle). This function overrides other comparators.
`sortValues(comparator)`	This method sorts the arcs according to a given comparator function that operates on the data values (obtained from the *value* accessor). This function overrides other comparators. The default order is *descending*.

Configuration methods for pie and doughnut charts

In the following code, a pie layout generator is used on a six-element array.

```
const data = [12, 45, 99, 22, 10, 76];
 const pie = d3.pie();        // creates the generator function
 const arcData = pie(data);  // generates layout array
 console.log(arcData);
```

This is the array returned by the generator function. Note that the original array order is not preserved. The resulting array is sorted by value in descending order:

```
[
    {data:12, index:4, value:12, startAngle:5.75, endAngle:6.04,
padAngle:0},
    {data:45, index:2, value:45, startAngle:4.16, endAngle:5.23,
padAngle:0},
    {data:99, index:0, value:99, startAngle:0,     endAngle:2.35,
padAngle:0},
    {data:22, index:3, value:22, startAngle:5.23, endAngle:5.75,
padAngle:0},
    {data:10, index:5, value:10, startAngle:6.04, endAngle:6.28,
padAngle:0},
    {data:76, index:1, value:76, startAngle:2.35, endAngle:4.16, padAngle:0}
 ]
```

The generated data can be used as the input for an arc function:

```
const arc = d3.arc().innerRadius(0).outerRadius(100);
 console.log(arcData.map(d => arc(d)));
```

The preceding code generates the following array of SVG path data strings:

```
["M-49.9999,-86.6025A100,100,0,0,1,-23.5758,-97.1811L0,0Z",
 "M-85.3881,52.0467A100,100,0,0,1,-86.6025,-50.000014L0,0Z",
 "M6.1232e-15,-100A100,100,0,0,1,70.7106,70.7106L0,0Z",
 "M-86.6025,-50.0000A100,100,0,0,1,-49.9999,-86.6025L0,0Z",
 "M-23.5758,-97.1811A100,100,0,0,1,-1.8369e-14,-100L0,0Z",
 "M70.7106,70.7106A100,100,0,0,1,-85.38812,52.0467L0,0Z"]
```

To draw the pie, this data should be bound to a selection, wherethe arc generator function for each datum will return an SVG path data string:

```
const colorScale = d3.scaleOrdinal(d3.schemeCategory10);
  d3.select("body").append("svg").selectAll("path.slice")
          .data(arcData).enter()
          .append("path").attr("class", "slice")
          .attr("d", arc)
          .style("fill", (d,i) => colorScale(i))
          .attr("transform", "translate(120,120)");
```

The result is as follows:

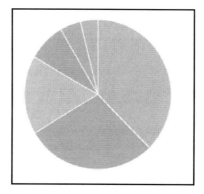

A pie chart created with the d3.pie() layout generator. Code: *Pies/1-pie.html.*

You can change the start or end angles to rotate the pie, or to produce pie charts with a circumference smaller than 360 degrees. The angles should be expressed in radians. This code will produce a half-pie (`Pies/2-pie-half.html`):

```
const pie = d3.pie().startAngle(0).endAngle(Math.PI);
```

The following example uses arc and pie generator functions to produce a chart comparing the populations of countries in North America (in 2000):

```
const data = [
    {"country": "Mexico", "population": 101720},
    {"country": "Canada", "population": 30736},
    {"country": "United States", "population": 281983},
  ];

  const pie = d3.pie()
          .value(d => d.population)
          .sort((a,b) => d3.ascending(a.population, b.population))
          .startAngle(Math.PI/2).endAngle(2.5 * Math.PI);
```

```
const arc = d3.arc().innerRadius(25).outerRadius(100)
                    .padAngle(4).padRadius(4);

const colorScale = d3.scaleOrdinal(d3.schemeCategory10);

const g = d3.select("body").append("svg")
        .selectAll("g")
        .data( pie(data) ).enter()
        .append("g")
        .attr("transform", "translate(120,120)");

g.append("path").attr("class", "slice")
        .attr("d", arc)
        .attr("fill", (d,i) => colorScale(i));

g.append('text')
        .attr("x",(d,i) => arc.centroid(d)[0] + 5)
        .attr("y",(d,i) => arc.centroid(d)[1] + 5)
        .attr("text-anchor", "middle")
        .text(d => d.data.country);
```

The result is as follows:

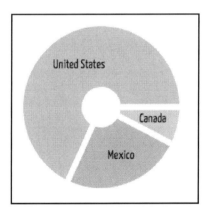

A pie chart with labels placed on the centroid. Code: *Pies/3-pie-labels.html*

Canvas rendering

All shape generators that create SVG path strings by default can be configured with a Canvas context. This will change the return type for the shape, which will no longer be a string, but a sequence of method calls on the context object.

The following D3 and Canvas code will produce the first diagram shown in this chapter (which was also generated in pure SVG and D3). This code is in `Canvas/2-canvas-path-d3.html`:

```
<script>
    const canvas = d3.select("body")
                    .append("canvas")
                    .attr("width", "800")
                    .attr("height", "300");

    const ctx = canvas.node().getContext("2d");

    ctx.fillStyle = "yellow";
    ctx.strokeStyle = "red";
    ctx.lineWidth = 3;

    ctx.beginPath();
    ctx.moveTo(50,20);
    ctx.lineTo(200,200);
    ctx.lineTo(200,140);
    ctx.lineTo(270,140);
    ctx.closePath(200,210);
    ctx.fill();
    ctx.stroke();

    ctx.fillStyle = "white";
    ctx.strokeStyle = "blue";
    ctx.lineWidth = 4;

    ctx.translate(200, -80);
    ctx.beginPath();
    ctx.moveTo(100,200);
    ctx.bezierCurveTo(100,100,250,100,250,200);
    ctx.bezierCurveTo(250,300,400,300,400,200);
    ctx.fill();
    ctx.stroke();

</script>
```

Let's render some of the charts we created in this chapter using HTML Canvas. We will start with a line chart (see `Canvas/3-canvas-line.html`). Since we still need axes, which are generated in SVG, we will stack the Canvas and the SVG viewports one on top of the other, using CSS:

```
<style>
    svg, canvas {
        position: absolute;
```

```
            top: 5px;
            left: 5px;
        }
    </style>
```

The next step is to append the viewports to the DOM tree. The order is important, since the object added last will be drawn over the previously rendered objects.

The following code places the SVG (where the axes will be rendered) under the Canvas (where the lines will be rendered). They both have exactly the same size. The Canvas context is obtained through the `getContext()` method, which is called on the DOM object (with `node()`):

```
const svg = d3.select("body").append("svg")
            .attr("height",height).attr("width",width);
const canvas = d3.select("body").append("canvas")
            .attr("height",height).attr("width",width);
const ctx = canvas.node().getContext("2d");
```

The line is created as before, but including the `context()` method, which makes all calls to the `line()` function generate a sequence of Canvas path methods on the provided context (instead of returning an SVG path string):

```
const line = d3.line()
            .x(d => scaleX(d[0]))
            .y(d => scaleY(d[1]))
            .context(ctx);
```

Before drawing a path, `fillStyle`, `strokeStyle`, `globalAlpha` (opacity) and other properties must be set on the context. You might also need to apply a `scale` or `translate`. The `line()` function can be called after *context*.`beginPath()` method is called, since it contains path commands. Finally, you will need to call *context*.`stroke()` to draw the lines, and *context*.`fill()` if you need to fill shapes.

```
data.forEach(dataset => {
    ctx.fillStyle = "transparent";
    ctx.strokeStyle = colorScale(dataset);
    ctx.lineWidth = 3;

    ctx.beginPath();
    line(dataset); // calls to moveTo(), lineTo(), etc.
    ctx.fill();
    ctx.stroke();
});
```

Note that since there are no individual objects, there is also no *general update pattern*. You have to loop through your data array calling the line function for each element.

Canvas can be used in any shape generator that has a `context()` method. Let's render the global warming radial area chart using Canvas (see `Canvas/4-canvas-radial-area.html`). Use the same CSS but this time place the SVG *in front* of the Canvas, since the axes are white and are rendered *over* the data, in the center of the screen:

```
const canvas = d3.select("body").append("canvas")
        .attr("height",height).attr("width",width);

const svg = d3.select("body").append("svg")
        .attr("height",height).attr("width",width);

const ctx = canvas.node().getContext("2d");

const g = svg.append("g")
        .attr("transform","translate("+[width/2,height/2]+")");
```

The radial area function is configured with the Canvas context. When the function is called, it will call Canvas path methods on the current context:

```
const spiral = d3.areaRadial()
        .angle((d,i) => i/12 * Math.PI * 2)
        .outerRadius(d => scaleRadius(d))
        .curve(d3.curveNatural)
        .context(ctx);
```

Before drawing the chart, translate the context to the center of the viewport. The context's globalAlpha (opacity) also needs to be set, since Canvas doesn't read CSS styles. A different color is applied to each area:

```
ctx.translate(width/2,height/2);
  nested.forEach((d, i) => {
        ctx.globalAlpha = 0.1;
        ctx.fillStyle = colorScale(i);
        ctx.beginPath();
        spiral(d.value);  // calls to moveTo(), lineTo(), etc.
        ctx.fill();
    });
```

See examples in the `Canvas/` folder.

Using Canvas makes it harder to select individual objects, since you can't use `d3.selection`, but it also reduces the amount of objects in memory, which may significantly improve performance if you create tens of thousands of SVG objects.

SVG to Canvas and back

Optimization techniques that use Canvas, frequently convert objects from Canvas to SVG and vice-versa. Canvas is used in static parts or during expensive operations. When the user needs to interact with an object, the objects are converted back to SVG. The *d3-path* module includes the `d3.path()` function, which contains methods that have the same names as Canvas path methods, but generate SVG path strings. You can use them to write code that works the same in Canvas and SVG.

The following example (see `Canvas/6-canvas-to-svg.html`) uses `d3.path()` methods to draw the SVG shapes used in an example at the beginning of this chapter in Canvas or in SVG.

This example uses the *d3-selection-multi* module, which must be imported separately:

```
<script src="https://d3js.org/d3-selection-multi.v1.min.js"></script>
```

First, both Canvas and SVG viewports are created (and positioned one over the other in CSS):

```
const width  = 800, height = 400;
 const svg     = d3.select("body").append("svg")
                    .attr("height",height).attr("width",width);
 const canvas = d3.select("body").append("canvas")
                    .attr("height",height).attr("width",width);
```

The two shapes are represented below as functions, which contain Canvas context methods to draw the shape, its styles and transforms:

```
function shape1() {
     function draw(ctx) {
         ctx.moveTo(50,20);
         ctx.lineTo(200,200);
         ctx.lineTo(200,140);
         ctx.lineTo(270,140);
         ctx.closePath(200,210);
     }
    draw.styles = {
         fill: "yellow",
         stroke: "red",
         "stroke-width": 3
    };
    return draw;
 }

 function shape2() {
```

```
            function draw(ctx) {
                ctx.moveTo(100, 200);
                ctx.bezierCurveTo(100, 100, 250, 100, 250, 200);
                ctx.bezierCurveTo(250, 300, 400, 300, 400, 200);
            }
            draw.styles = { fill: "white", stroke: "blue", "stroke-width": 4 };
            draw.transforms = { translate: [200, -80] };
            return draw;
        }
```

These abstractions can be used with a *context* object, which can be an HTML Canvas or a **d3.path()** object. Both have the same methods:

```
    const context = ... // HTML Canvas context or d3.path
     const shape = shape2(context);
```

This is used in the following function, which receives one of the shape functions above and a *context* object. It first creates the object function f, then checks if the context is a Canvas context. If so, it will use the styles and transform properties to configure Canvas properties, translate if necessary, call beginPath() and f(context). Then it will apply *context*.stroke() and *context*.fill(). If the object is not a Canvas, it will append a <path> element to the DOM tree, and use the result from f(context) as the path string, applying styles and transforms with selection methods:

```
    function drawShape(func, context) {
        const f = func();

        if(context.canvas) {
            context.fillStyle = f.styles.fill;
            context.strokeStyle = f.styles.stroke;
            context.lineWidth = f.styles["stroke-width"];

            if(f.transforms && f.transforms.translate) {
                context.translate(f.transforms.translate[0],
                                   f.transforms.translate[1]);
            }
            context.beginPath();

            f(context); // calls path rendering commands

            context.fill();
            context.stroke();
        } else { // object is SVG d3.path
            f(context); // generates path string in context

            const path = svg.append("path")
                            .styles(f.styles)
```

```
                      .attr("d", context);
          if(f.transforms && f.transforms.translate) {
              path.attr("transform",
  `translate(${f.transforms.translate})`);
          }
      }
  }
```

The following code uses the functions above and draws the same shapes either in Canvas or SVG, depending on the value of the `useCanvas` constant:

```
const useCanvas = true; // change to false to see result in SVG

if(useCanvas) {
    // Using Canvas
    drawShape(shape1, canvas.node().getContext("2d"));
    drawShape(shape2, canvas.node().getContext("2d"));
} else {
    // Using SVG
    drawShape(shape1, d3.path());
    drawShape(shape2, d3.path());
}
```

As an exercise, try applying this to one of the charts you created in this chapter.

Summary

In this chapter, you explored most of the generator functions available in the d3-shape module, which provide the tools you need to create classic pie and doughnut charts, line and area charts, radial charts, stacked charts, and preconfigured symbols that can be used to represent points in scatterplots, line, and area charts.

All the shapes created in this chapter were rendered as SVG path elements. The generator functions either create SVG path strings or generate data structures that can be used by other functions to generate path strings. In the last section, we had a brief introduction to Canvas rendering, which is an important technique that you may need to use when facing performance problems due to excessive memory use.

But D3 is has much more to offer than static bar, pie, and line charts. In the next chapter, we will explore several ways to make your charts more interactive, responding to events, and reacting with animated transitions.

References

- Module documentation, D3.js: `github.com/d3/d3-shape`, `github.com/d3/d3-path`.
- Populations of North and South America dataset: `Data/Americas_population.json`. Compiled from United Nations data (`www.un.org`).
- Ocean temperatures: `Data/monthly_json.json`. GISTEMP Team, 2019: GISS Surface Temperature Analysis (GISTEMP). NASA Goddard Institute for Space Studies. Dataset accessed 2019-02-01 at `data.giss.nasa.gov/gistemp/`. Hansen, J., R.

8
Animation and Interactivity

D3 extends JavaScript's native event handling and dispatching mechanisms with objects, functions, and methods that facilitate integration with selections, transitions, and interactive behaviors. It provides container-scoped event objects for mouse and touch gestures, handler methods that can be attached to selections and transitions, and dispatchers for custom events that can be used to create notification mechanisms where any object can emit events to arbitrary listeners. This chapter explores the main tools you need to make any visualization interactive.

Transitions automatically animate changes to DOM elements, smoothly interpolating colors, positions, lengths, and other dimensions during a given duration. In this chapter, you will learn how to configure transitions and control aspects of the animation, such as easing algorithms, timing, scheduling, interrupting, and flow control, using methods from the *d3-transition* and *d3-ease* modules. You will also learn the basic functions of the *d3-timer* module, which is used by transitions.

Zoom, *drag*, and *brush* are complex interactive behaviors that require the management of the responses to several different native events in a multiple-stage operation. Zooming requires keeping track of current translate and scale parameters so that SVG, Canvas, or CSS transforms can be applied. Brushing involves the selection of an area or segment of a chart to obtain the coordinates of the selected space, which are inverted to redefine a new domain used to update scales. During a dragging operation, you keep track of an object's coordinates while the user moves it around. This chapter will introduce modules provided by D3 that encapsulate each one of these behaviors: *d3-zoom*, *d3-brush*, and *d3-drag*. They are all included in the default bundle.

This chapter will cover the following topics:

- Events
- Transitions
- Timers
- Drag behavior
- Brush behavior
- Zoom behavior

Events

The objects that represent events in D3 are extensions of DOM event objects. They inherit methods and properties from DOM's `Event` interface. Events can originate from any DOM source and can be captured by any DOM targets. When using a library such as D3, you can frequently ignore the details of event handling and dispatching, but when things don't work out as expected, the solution may require some low-level tuning.

This section describes some common event configurations you can apply using DOM and CSS, and introduces methods and objects from the D3 library that make DOM events easier to use in SVG selections. Since event handling in D3 is an extension of native event handling, a brief overview of native DOM events is provided in the following section.

Native DOM events

DOM events are asynchronous notifications issued by the operating system and propagated by the browser. Events are commonly triggered by an action performed by the user (for example, a mouse click), but they can also be called programmatically (for example, calling the `click()` method from any DOM target) or dispatched as a configurable synchronous operation (for example, calling `dispatchEvent()` on a DOM target).

DOM targets usually register as *event listeners* using their `addEventListener()` method. The following code registers a `click` listener for all the `<rect>` elements in a page (see `Events/1-element-handler.html`):

```
const rects = [...document.getElementsByTagName("rect")];
rects.forEach(d => d.addEventListener('click', handler));
```

You can also capture DOM events using D3 with `selection.on()`, as seen in Chapter 4, *Data Binding*. This is shown in the following code :

```
d3.selectAll("rect").on("click", handler);
```

Inside an event-handler function, you can obtain the object that *registered* the event listener with the `this` reference. You can also obtain the current event object using the `event` reference. Its `target` property contains the element that *caught* the event (the element that was clicked in a *click* event), which may or may not be the same object that registered the listener, as shown in the following code:

```
function handler() {
    console.log("Handler", this);        // which element handled event
    console.log("Target", event.target)  // which element caught event
}
```

A generic event is represented by the `Event` interface, which defines properties and methods that are common to all events. DOM includes several other specialized *event interfaces* that extend the main `Event` interface, inherit `Event`'s properties and methods, and add their own event-specific methods and properties. The `MouseEvent`, for example, adds the `clientX` and the `clientY` properties, which store the pixel coordinates of the mouse on the screen. In modern browsers, you can also use the `x` and `y` properties.

An event interface may represent several different *event types*. When multiple listeners handle different events, you can use `event.type` to discover which event occurred.

A `MouseEvent` represents event types such as *click*, *dblclick*, and *mouseenter*. If you handle any of these events, you can access `MouseEvent` properties from the `event` object, as shown in the following code:

```
function handler() {
    // ...
    console.log("Target", event.target);
    if(event.type == 'click') { // prints coords only
on 'click' event
        console.log("Coords", [event.clientX,
event.clientY]);
    }
}
```

A listener is not always attached to a target. Most events are configured to support *event bubbling*, which means that the event will be propagated to all ancestors of the target element, and any one or all of them can handle it. You could register a listener for a page's root element, for example:

```
window.addEventListener('click', handler);
```

With this configuration, the `handler()` function will print different values for `this` and `event.target`, unless you click on the root element itself (see `Events/2-root-handler.html`).

Normally, if an event handler is not added to the target itself, it's placed in a nearby ancestor. For example, suppose you have the following SVG structure:

```
<svg>
    <g class="datapoint">
        <rect class="symbol"> ...
```

Clicking on `<rect>` causes this element and all its ancestors to receive the click event. You can place a listener in any of the three objects. But if any other ancestor elements are also registered as listeners for this event, clicking `<rect>` will run all of them (see `Events/3-bubbling.html`).

You can use this behavior to treat the event differently in each handler, or you can avoid it by calling `event.stopPropagation()` after capturing the event so it will no longer bubble up and run other listeners (see `Events/4-stop-bubbling.html`), as shown in the following code:

```
function handler() {
    event.stopPropagation(); // event won't propagate to ancestors
    // ...
}
```

Not all events behave in the same way. For example, *mouseenter* and *mouseleave* don't bubble, but instead fire separate events on all descendants. There are also simple events that are emitted as part of a composite gesture. For example, a click also emits *mousedown* and *mouseup* events.

You might also wish to cancel a default event. For example, an `<input type="submit">` button will automatically submit form data when clicked, but calling `event.preventDefault()` cancels this behavior (see `Events/5-prevent-default.html`), as shown in the following code:

```
d3.select("input[type=submit]").on("click", function() {
    event.preventDefault(); // don't submit the form!
    // ...
});
```

Calling `preventDefault()` is effective only if the `cancellable` property of the event is true.

You can disable certain types of events using CSS. The `pointer-events` property allows you to control which parts of an SVG element are considered targets of pointer events (clicking, hovering, dragging).

The following code example (see `Events/6-pointer-events.html`) contains a transparent `<g>` with circles that appear behind rectangles:

```
<svg style="position:absolute; left:100px; top:100px"
    height="400" width="800">
    <g class="container">
        <rect class="back" width="800" height="400" x="0" y="0"/>
        <circle r="50" cx="120" cy="120"/>
        <circle r="50" cx="280" cy="120"/>
        <circle r="50" cx="120" cy="280"/>
        <circle r="50" cx="280" cy="280"/>
        <circle r="50" cx="520" cy="120"/>
        <circle r="50" cx="680" cy="120"/>
        <circle r="50" cx="520" cy="280"/>
        <circle r="50" cx="680" cy="280"/>
        <rect class="red"  width="300" height="300" x="50" y="50"/>
        <rect class="blue" width="300" height="300" x="450" y="50"/>
    </g>
</svg>
```

Event listeners are registered for circles and rectangles, but if you move the mouse over the circles, their opacity doesn't change as expected. The rectangles capture the event first, and since the circles are behind them, they never get selected, as shown in the following code:

```
<script>
    const circles = [...document.getElementsByTagName("circle")];
    const rects   = [...document.getElementsByTagName("rect")];

    rects.map(d=> d.addEventListener("mouseover",
```

```
                function() { this.style.strokeWidth = 5}));
        rects.map(d=> d.addEventListener("mouseout",
                function()  { this.style.strokeWidth = 1}));

        circles.map(d=> d.addEventListener('mouseover',
                   function() { this.style.opacity = 1 }));
        circles.map(d=> d.addEventListener('mouseout',
        function() { this.style.opacity = .3}));
        </script>
```

One solution would be to declare the handler for the `<g>` element and rely on bubbling to capture events of any child element (circles or rectangles). But then you would need to write code to detect whether the mouse is over a circle.

If you don't need to capture events for the rectangle, you can turn off its handling of mouse events. This will allow the circles to be selected. The following code turns pointer events off for the blue rectangle only (see `Events/7-pointer-events-none.html`):

```
rect.blue { pointer-events: none; }
```

Now you can move the mouse over each circle and see the circles' opacity changing, but the rectangle no longer reacts to *mouseover*, as shown in the following screenshot. This is a common and useful configuration for objects that you usually don't want as event targets, such as tooltips, text labels, lines, and so on:

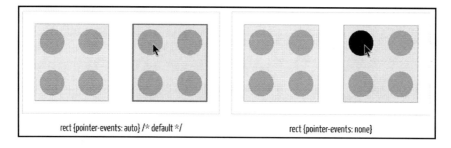

Using CSS pointer-events: none to turn off event handling for an object so that other objects can capture the event. Code: *Events/7-pointer-events-none.html*

The transparent `<rect class="back"/>` doesn't capture any mouse events because transparent objects don't capture pointer events by default. That behavior can also be changed with the `pointer-events` property, as shown in the following code, which affects all descendants of the `<g>` object that didn't set this property explicitly (see `Events/8-pointer-events-all.html`):

```
g.container { pointer-events: all; }
```

Most of the code examples in this section only use pure CSS and JavaScript, but the code would be much simpler using D3 (see `Events/9-d3-pointer-events-all.html`).

Mouse events in D3

The global `d3.event` object is a generic event wrapper that contains the current event during the execution of a listener. You can use it to access standard `Event` fields, such as the `defaultPrevented`, `type`, or `target`; fields of the specific interface type (for example, `clientX` if `MouseEvent`); and methods, such as `preventDefault()` and `stopPropagation()`.

In a listener that captures `MouseEvents`, for example, you can capture the mouse pointer's coordinates, (relative to the browser's viewport) using the `d3.event` object, as shown in the following code (see `Events/10-d3-event.html`):

```
const point = [d3.event.x, d3.event.y];
```

The browser's viewport is usually *not the same* as the SVG viewport (unless you position the SVG element absolutely at 0,0 and make its height and width occupy all the available space), but clicking a container element in a translated coordinate space will still return absolute coordinates, which will need to be translated to local coordinates. A better option is to use one of the functions listed in the following table, which returns coordinates that are relative to the parent container:

Function or object	Description
`d3.clientPoint` (*container, event*)	Returns an [x,y] array with the coordinates of the provided event relative to the coordinates of the user space of the selected component. The user space is usually defined by a parent container element, such as `<svg>` or `<g>`. It can also be defined by a shape (for example, a `<rect>`) if positioned with a `transform` attribute (instead of its x and y attributes).
`d3.mouse` (*container*)	Same as `d3.clientPoint` (*container, event*); *event* is the current *mouse* event.
`d3.touch` (*container, id*)	Same as `d3.clientPoint` (*container, event*); *event* is the current *touch* event.
`d3.touches` (*container*)	Returns an array of [x,y] coordinates related to the current *touch* event.

Event functions that return relative coordinates.

If you have an SVG that configures a user space with a left margin of 100 pixels, using the d3.event.x coordinate to draw an element inside the SVG will place it 100 pixels left of the point where the mouse was clicked. You can either compensate, adding 100 pixels to d3.event.x, or use d3.mouse(this), which does this for you, returning the coordinates of the nearest container (see Events/11-d3.mouse.html).

The following code example illustrates the differences between d3.event and d3.mouse when using different coordinate systems. Consider the following document structure, which contains three different coordinate systems: the *browser's viewport*, the *SVG viewport* and a *group coordinate space:*

```
<html>
 <body>
  <svg style="position:absolute; left:100px; top:100px"
       height="500" width="800">
    <g transform="translate(100,400)">
        <rect class="red"  width="600" height="300" y="-300"/>
        <rect class="blue" width="400" height="100" x="100" y="-200"/>
    </g>
  </svg>
 </body>
</html>
```

The browser's viewport is platform dependent. It may start at the top-left corner without any padding, but the <body> element usually has a small amount of padding (about three pixels).

The SVG viewport's origin was set in CSS, since <svg> is an HTML element, placing it in absolute coordinates at (100,100).

The position of the <g> group element is relative to its parent <svg> container. Its transform attribute establishes a new coordinate space at (100,100) in relative <svg> coordinates, which is (200,200) in absolute coordinates. Since both <rect> objects were created inside this group, their x and y positions are relative to the group's coordinate system. The following screenshot shows this hierarchy:

> document root, origin at (0,0) browser viewport coordinates
>   body
>   svg: 800x500 px, svg origin at (100,100) browser viewport coordinates
>   g: group, group origin at (100,100) svg coordinates
>   rect: 600x300 px, at (0,0) group coordinates
>   rect: 400x100 px, at (100,100) group coordinates

Document structure showing coordinate spaces

Now, suppose you want to make a tooltip appear when the user clicks somewhere on the bar, anchored at a position near the place where the user clicked. You will need to get the coordinates of the clicked point. You have three options:

- `[d3.event.x, d3.event.y]` will give you the root coordinates (for example, [313, 313]), which is the distance from the top-left corner of the viewport plus browser padding.
- `d3.mouse(d3.select("svg").node())` will give you the SVG coordinates (for example, [210, 210]).
- `d3.mouse(d3.select("g").node())` will give you the group's coordinates (for example, [110, 110]).
- `d3.mouse(this)` will give you the group's coordinates too. Since the group is the rectangle's container, the rectangle is inside the group's coordinate system.

You can have coordinates relative to the rectangle, but *only if* the rectangle is positioned with a `transform` attribute instead of `x` and `y` attributes (see `Events/13-cartesian.html`).

The following diagram shows the three coordinate systems and the point where the mouse was clicked inside the blue rectangle (in black). The dot was placed using `d3.mouse(this)` coordinates. The green and red points show the wrong positions where the point will be drawn if you position the point using `d3.event` coordinates (you can run this code from `Events/12-d3-mouse-coords.html`):

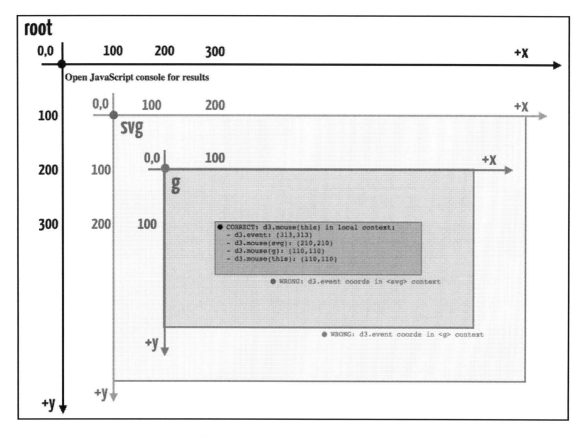

Three different coordinate systems. Code: *Events/12-d3.mouse-coords.html.*

It's usually best to always choose `d3.mouse` over `d3.event`, especially when you have multiple containers with inverted coordinate systems (common in Cartesian charts—see `Events/13-cartesian.html`). Besides keeping the coordinates relative to a container, `d3.mouse` also guarantees that the mouse positions don't depend on the HTML placement of the SVG canvas, which may have different defaults among browser platforms.

Custom events and dispatching

An **event dispatch** can be used to directly invoke listeners for an event. This is useful if your application uses custom events, or if for some reason you need to call another object's event handler. Custom events can be used for communication between parts of your application—for example, to display multiple charts and have them update at the same time in response to data changes or user interaction, or to compose many native events to perform a complex behavior.

The following table lists methods from the *d3-selection* and *d3-dispatch* modules that are to be used for event dispatching and custom events:

Function or method	Description
`selection.dispatch`(*type, options*)	A `d3.selection` method that dispatches a custom event for each element in a selection. Optional parameters can be used to configure event properties (the `bubbling` and `cancellation` properties) or include custom data in the event (using the `detail` property).
`d3.customEvent` (*event, listener, context, args*)	A function from the *d3-selection* module that can be used to invoke an event listener. The context is *this* by default. Arguments are passed as an array (and can be recovered from the *args* array in the listener).
`d3.dispatch` (*names...*)	A function from the *d3-dispatch* module. Creates a new dispatch for a list of event types, which can be used to register listeners that don't have to be linked to a selection.
dispatch.`on` (*names, listener*)	Registers a listener for one or more event types. The *names* parameter is a string with one or more event types separated by spaces, and must be previously declared in `d3.dispatch()`.
dispatch.`call` (*type, context, args...*) *dispatch*.`apply` (*type, context, args*)	Calls all registered listeners for the specified type. The *context* is typically set as `this`. Listeners are called using JavaScript's `call()` or `apply()` methods that differ only in how they receive arguments (*array* in `apply`, or *argument list* in `call`).

Functions and methods used to dispatch and handle custom events

The following code (`Events/14-selection-dispatch.html`) contains a `<g>` element selection that registers an arbitrary event name, *dots*. It will add a child `<circle>` to the selection when it receives a *dots* event, using data obtained from the `d3.event.detail` object to set the circle's properties:

```
const target = svg.append("g").attr("class", "target")
                    .attr("transform", `translate(500,50)`)
                    .on("dots", function() {
                        d3.select(this)
                            .append("circle").attr("class","dot")
                            .attr("r",  d3.event.detail.r)
                            .attr("cx", d3.event.detail.x)
                            .attr("cy", d3.event.detail.y);
                    });
target.append("rect").attr("height", 200).attr("width", 200);
```

The event is triggered by any action or event that calls the `placeDots()` function. In this example, clicking on a circle will make the program wait half a second and call `placeDots()` periodically, using `d3.timer()`:

```
let timer;
svg.append("circle").attr("class", "source")
    .attr("r", 100)
    .attr("cx", 200)
    .attr("cy", 150)
    .on("click", () => timer = d3.timer(placeDots,500));
```

The `placeDots()` function computes random positions and radii for circles and dispatches a *dots* event to the target selection if there are fewer than 250 dots; otherwise, it stops the timer. The first parameter in the dispatch method is the event type name. The second parameter is a standard *options* object, which can have up to three properties. The `detail` property is the only one that can be used to send event data. Look at the following code:

```
let dots = 0;

function placeDots() {
    ++dots;
    const randW = d3.randomUniform(0,200);
    const randH = d3.randomUniform(0,200);
    const randR = d3.randomUniform(0.5,10);
    if(dots < 250) {
        d3.select(".target")
            .dispatch("dots", {detail:{x: randW(), y: randH(), r: randR()}})
    } else {
        timer.stop();
```

```
        }
    }
```

The following screenshot shows circles being appended to the target at each *dots* event:

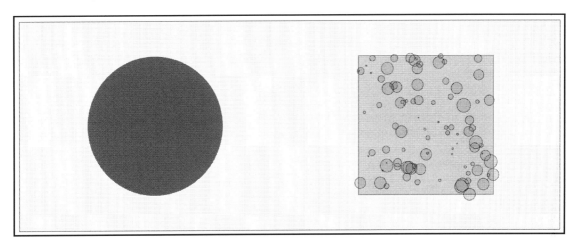

Using selection.dispatch() to dispatch custom events. Code: Events/14-selection-dispatch.html.

You don't need a selection to create a dispatch. Using `d3.dispatch()`, you can register a dispatch for a list of events and then connect them to listeners without having to link them to any selections.

The following example code declares a dispatch for two types of events, which we called *dots* and *squares*:

```
const dispatch = d3.dispatch("dots", "squares");
```

Now you can register callbacks for each event. Each callback that follows is registered for one type of event, and appends circles or squares to a selection depending on the event received. The properties for the shapes are obtained from a data object (d) received by the callback, as shown in the following code:

```
dispatch.on("dots",
            d => d3.select(".b")
                    .append("circle").attr("class","dot")
                    .attr("r", d.r)
                    .attr("cx", d.x)
                    .attr("cy", d.y))
        .on("squares",
            d => d3.select(".a")
                    .append("rect").attr("class","sqr")
```

```
                        .attr("x", d.x)
                        .attr("y", d.y)
                        .attr("width", d.s)
                        .attr("height", d.s));
```

Unlike `selection.dispatch()`, you don't need a selection and the data doesn't need to be placed in a `detail` property. Use either `dispatch.apply()` to send the data as an *array* of arguments or `dispatch.call()` to send the data as a *list* of one or more arguments (they are equivalent).

In the `placeDots()` and `placeSquares()` functions in the following code, properties for randomly positioned circles or squares were generated and included in the notification objects sent to each event handler:

```
function placeDots() {
    ++dots;
    const randW = d3.randomUniform(0,200);
    const randH = d3.randomUniform(0,200);
    const randR = d3.randomUniform(0.5,10);
    if(dots < 250) {
        dispatch.call("dots", this, {x: randW(), y: randH(), r: randR()})
    } else {
        timerDots.stop();
    }
}

function placeSquares() {
    ++squares;
    const angle  = d3.randomUniform(0,Math.PI * 2)();
    const radius = d3.randomUniform(1,100)();
    const randS = d3.randomUniform(1,15);

    const x = radius * Math.cos(angle)  - randS()/2;
    const y = radius * Math.sin(angle)  - randS()/2;

    if(squares < 250) {
        dispatch.call("squares", this, {x: x, y: y, s: randS()})
    } else {
        timerSquares.stop();
    }
}
```

To trigger the events, we attached *click* listeners to a circle and a square. Clicking any one of them once will make several calls to `placeDots()` and `placeSquares()`, after a short delay of half a second:

```
let timerDots, timerSquares;
let dots = squares = 0;

svg.append("g").attr("class", "a")
        .attr("transform", `translate(200,150)`)
        .append("circle").attr("r", 100)
        .on("click", () => timerDots = d3.timer(placeDots,500));

svg.append("g").attr("class", "b")
        .attr("transform", `translate(500,50)`)
        .append("rect").attr("height", 200).attr("width", 200)
        .on("click", () => timerSquares = d3.timer(placeSquares,500));
```

You can run the code from `Events/15-d3-dispatch.html`, as shown in the following screenshot:

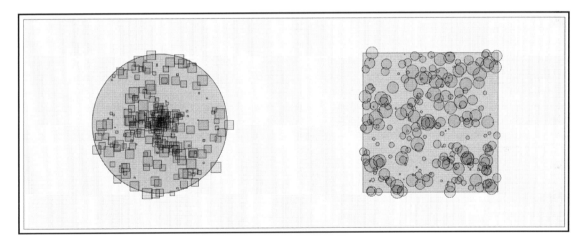

Using d3.dispatch() to dispatch custom events. Code: *Events/15-d3-dispatch.html*.

Transitions

A **transition** operates on a selection of elements, animating changes in the DOM structure, attributes, or styles after updates. Transitions use interpolation to smoothly change from one state to another. You can configure durations and delays and choose up to 28 easing algorithms. Transitions use the browser's native display refresh rate (usually 60 frames per second), which guarantees fluid animations.

The *d3-transition* module contains all the functions used for transitions except for the easing algorithms, which are stored in *d3-ease*. Both are included in the default bundle.

Transitions can be created for any element. For example, you can create a new transition for the DOM root (`document.documentElement`) with `d3.transition()`, as shown in the following code (see `Transitions/1-transition.html`):

```
const transition = d3.transition();
```

A default transition starts immediately and lasts a quarter of a second, but you can configure the following parameters:

```
transition.delay(1000);      // wait 1 second before starting
transition.duration(2000);   // the transition will last 2 seconds
```

You can then select the elements that will participate in the transition using `select()` or `selectAll()` methods and set the final values of the styles or attributes that will be changed. The following code selects all <h1> elements in a document and changes their color to red when the transition ends:

```
transition.selectAll("h1")   // obtain selection to apply transition
        .style("color", "red"); // set final styles and attributes
```

Normally, you obtain a transition object from an existing selection with the `transition()` method and chain the configuration parameters followed by the final styles and attributes, as shown in the following code:

```
d3.selectAll("h1")   // select all <h1>
  .transition()      // obtain a transition object from selection
   .delay(3000)      // configure transition
   .duration(2000)
   .style("color", "blue");   // set final styles and attributes
```

The following table lists functions and methods from the *d3-selection* and *d3-transition* modules that create a transition or obtain an active transition:

Function or method	Description
d3.transition (*name* | *ref*)	Returns a new transition created on the DOM root. An optional *name* can be provided, which will allow multiple simultaneous transitions. If a transition object *reference* is provided, it may return it, if it refers to a transition that exists for the selected element, or inherit the timing of the transition, if it refers to an existing transition on the nearest ancestor of the selected element.
transition.transition (*name* | *ref*)	Returns a new transition that will be scheduled to start when the current transition ends. It can also receive a *name* or transition object *reference*.
selection.transition (*name* | *ref*)	Returns a new transition created on the current selection. It can also receive a *name* or transition object *reference*.
d3.active (*node*)	Returns the active transition on the specified *node*.

Functions and methods that are used to create or obtain a transition

Transitions extend selections and support most of their methods, but not all of them. Appending and binding operations are not supported. You need to perform them on a selection *before* chaining the transition (Transitions/2-selection.html), as shown in the following code:

```
d3.selectAll("g").transition().append("rect") // this won't work
```

But you can obtain the selection corresponding to a transition using transition.selection(), as follows:

```
d3.selectAll("g").transition().selhection().append("rect");
```

The following table lists the `selection()` methods and several methods supported by transitions that are equivalent to the `d3.selection` methods of the same name:

Method	Description
`selection()`	Returns the selection corresponding to this transition
`select`(*selector*), `selectAll`(*selector*), `filter`(*filter*), `merge`(*other*)	Equivalent to `transition.selection().`*method*`.transition`(*transition*), where *method* is one of the methods listed in the first column
`each`(*function*), `call`(*function*), `empty()`, `nodes()`, `node()`, `size()`	Equivalent to the corresponding `d3.selection` methods

Methods from d3.transition that are equivalent to d3.selection methods

Transition dynamics

You can configure the delay, duration, and easing of a transition using the methods described in the following table:

Method	Description
`delay`(*value*)	The transition will start after a specified *value* in milliseconds. The default is zero. The value can also be provided as a function per element (receiving *datum* d, and *index* i).
`duration`(*value*)	After starting, the transition will last the specified *value* in milliseconds. The default is 250. The value can also be provided as a function per element (receiving *datum* d, and *index*, i).
`ease`(*function*)	The easing function that will be invoked at each animation frame. The function can be any interpolator that receives a value in the range [0,1] and returns values (usually within that range, but not necessarily) that start in 0 and end in 1. The default is `d3.easeCubic`.

Timing methods for a d3-transition

You can create sequential effects with `delay()` using a function instead of a static value. In the bar chart that you created in `Chapter 3`, *Quick Start*, the `delay()` function was applied to the selection with a data-based function that caused the transition to start in each bar following a sequential order, as shown in the following code (see `Chapter3/Updating/6-delays.html`):

```
.each(function (d, i) {
    d3.select(this)
        .select(".bar")
        .transition()
        .duration(1000)
        .delay(50 * i) // delay depends on index i
        // ...
```

You can also configure `duration()` as a function. In the following example (`Transitions/3-dynamics.html`), each rectangle takes twice as long as the previous one to start its transition:

```
d3.selectAll("g")
        .transition()
        .delay((d,i) => 500 + 500 * i)
        .duration((d,i) => 1000 + 1000 * i*i)
        .style("opacity", 0);
```

When you chain multiple transitions, they are scheduled to run in sequence. Durations and ease functions are *inherited* but delay values are *local*. This effect is demonstrated in the following example: each transition inherits the duration of zero, but the delay between each one is one second (see `Transitions/4-chain-delay.html`):

```
d3.select("h1")
        .transition().duration(0).delay(1000).tween(...)
        .transition().delay(1000).tween(...)
        .transition().delay(1000).tween(...)
        .transition().delay(1000).tween(...)
        .transition().delay(1000).tween(...)
```

Another way to inherit durations and ease functions is to initialize the transition with a reference to an existing transition (see `Transitions/5-chain-reference.html`):

```
const ref = d3.transition().duration(0);
// ...
d3.select("h1")
        .transition(ref).delay(1000) .tween(...) // inherits duration from ref
```

Tweening and text transitions

Tweening is the process of producing intermediate animation frames. To move from blue to red or from 10 to 20, a tween operation obtains an intermediate value for each animation frame during the duration of the transition. The default *attribute* and *style* tweening uses interpolators from the *d3-interpolate* module and easing functions from the *d3-ease* module to compute the intermediate values.

The simplest way to tween is to set values for the `attr()` or `style()` attributes on a transition object that is *different* than the values set for the original selection. Attribute tweening is demonstrated in the following code. The circle has two attributes that you can tween, but only one of them is used for the transition:

```
const svg = d3.select("body").append("svg");
svg.append("circle")
    .attr("r", 30)                                 // initial value 1
    .attr("transform", `translate(${[400,300]})`)  // initial value 2
    .transition().delay(500).duration(2000)        // transition
        .attr("r", 100);                           // final value 1
```

If you run the code (`Transitions/6-attr-value.html`) you will see, after a brief delay, the circle grow over two seconds. It starts slowly, accelerates, and then slows down and comes to a stop at the new diameter. This dynamic behavior is provided by the `ease` function.

You could also tween the circle's position on the screen, adding `attr()` methods to its `cx` and `cy` attributes (which are zero by default) or interpolating the `transform` attribute, as follows (`Transitions/7-attr-transform.html`):

```
svg.append("circle")
    .attr("r", 30) // initial value
    .attr("transform", `translate(${[400,300]})`)       // initial value 2
    .transition().delay(500).duration(2000)             // transition
        .attr("transform", `translate(${[200,150]})`)   // final value 2
```

Style tweening is similar. In this example, the circle has a fill color defined in CSS, as shown in the following code:

```
circle {
    fill: red; /* initial value 3 */
}
```

The following transition changes the position, radius, and color during five seconds using a *bounce-out* easing function (`Transitions/9-style-attr.html`):

```
svg.append("circle")
    .attr("r", 30)                                    // initial value 1
    .attr("transform", `translate(${[400,300]})`)    // initial value 2
    .transition().delay(500).duration(2000)          // transition
        .ease(d3.easeBounceOut)
        .style("fill", "blue")                        // final value 3
        .attr("r", 50)                                // final value 1
        .attr("transform", `translate(${[100,500]})`) // final value.
```

As with selections, you can configure attribute and style values with a function to set values that are dependent on the current datum and index.

If you need more control, you can use the `attrTween()`, `styleTween()`, or `tween()` methods to manipulate each intermediate value and select a different interpolator. These methods usually receive an *interpolator factory* that returns an interpolator. An interpolator can be any function that receives a value between 0 and 1 and returns a value. The following code, for example, achieves the same effect as `attr("r", 50)`, but also prints intermediate values (see `Transitions/10-attr-tween.html`):

```
svg.append("text").text("").attr("transform", "translate(50,50)");

svg.append("circle")
    .attr("r", 30) // initial value
    .attr("transform", `translate(${[400,300]})`) // initial value
    .transition().delay(500).duration(2000)
        .attrTween("r", () => function(t) { // function() returns
                                    function(t)
            d3.select("text").text("t: " + t)
            return 30 + t * 50;
        });
```

The following table describes the methods that modify a selection during a transition:

Method	Description
`attr` (*name, value*)	Changes the value of an attribute. Uses `d3.interpolateNumber()`, `d3.interpolateRgb()`, or `d3.interpolateString()`, depending on the type.
`style` (*name, value, priority*)	Changes the value of a style. Uses `d3.interpolateNumber()`, `d3.interpolateRgb()`, or `d3.interpolateString()`, depending on the type.

attrTween (*name, factory*)	Changes the value of an attribute. An interpolator factory must be provided returning the interpolator function that will be invoked for each animation frame.
styleTween (*name, factory, priority*)	Changes the value of a style. An interpolator factory must be provided, returning the interpolator function that will be invoked for each animation frame.
tween (*name, value*)	Assigns a tween to a selection with the specified name and interpolator factory. It can also be used to run code during each frame. See Transitions/11-tween.html for more information.
text (*value*)	Sets the text content when the transition starts (doesn't interpolate text).
remove ()	Removes each element of the selection when the transition ends if the element has no other active (scheduled or running) transitions.

Methods of d3.transition() that modify elements

String interpolation involves numbers and dates in strings, but it doesn't interpolate characters. The text() method simply sets the text when the transition starts. If you want to animate the replacement of one text with another, you can tween opacity to create a fade in–fade out effect,as shown in the following code (Transitions/12-fadein-out.html):

```
d3.select("h1").text("Before")
        .transition().duration(1000)
          .style("opacity", 0)
        .transition().duration(1000)
          .style("opacity", 1)
          .text("After")
```

To create a cross-fading effect, you need to use two stacked elements. If they are HTML elements, you can use CSS to place both at the same position,a s shown in the following code:

```
h1 {
    position: absolute; top: 50px; left: 50px;
}
```

Create a transition to fade out the first element and remove it, while a second transition appends the second element and slowly increases its transparency, as shown in the following code (`Transitions/13-cross-fade.html`):

```
d3.select("h1")
    .text("Before")                  // previous text
    .style("color","navy")           // start: color = navy, opacity = 1
    .transition().duration(3000)     // transition 1
        .style("color", "brown")     // end: color = brown, opacity = 0
        .style("opacity", 0)
        .remove()                    // remove
d3.select("body")
    .append("h1")                    // append
    .style("color","navy")           // start: color = navy, opacity = 1
    .style("opacity", 0)
    .text("After")                   // final text
    .transition().duration(3000)     // transition 2
        .style("opacity", 1)         // end: color = brown, opacity = 1
        .style("color","brown")
```

The following diagram compares cross-fading and fade-in/out text transitions:

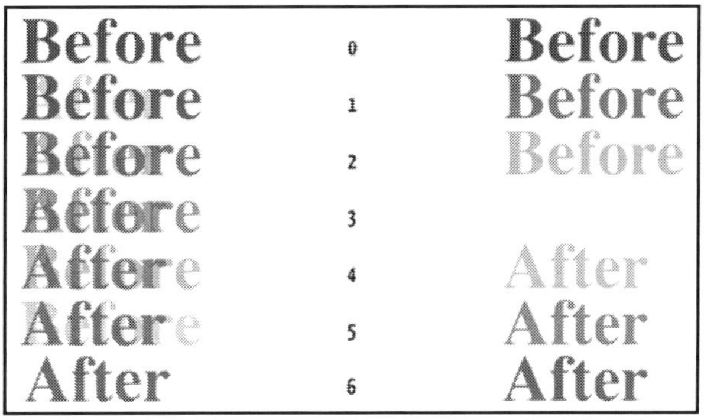

Left: cross-fading transition (Code: *Transitions/13-cross-fade.html*). Right: fade-in–fade-out transition (Code: *Transitions/12-fade-in-out.html*)

Easing algorithms

Easing functions are interpolators that change the acceleration of an animation. Most functions try to mimic real-world movement, from a static position to moving quicker (`easeIn`); from moving quicker and slowing down to a stop (`easeOut`); or starting slowly, accelerating to the middle, decelerating toward the end, and finishing slowly (`easeInOut`).

You can apply an easing function to a transition with the `transition.ease()` method and one of the 28 ease functions available in the *d3-ease* module. The default is `d3.easeCubicInOut` (or `d3.easeCubic`). The following table lists the general easing algorithms available in the *d3-ease* module:

Ease function type	Description and configuration options
`d3.easeLinear`	Linear easing: $f(t) = t$. Same as `d3.easePoly*` with *ease*.`exponent(1)`.
`d3.easePoly*`	Polynomial easing: $f(t) = t^e$. Set exponent with *ease*.`exponent(e)`. Default: *ease*.`exponent(3)`.
`d3.easeQuad*`	Same as `d3.easePoly*` with *ease*.`exponent(2)`.
`d3.easeCubic*`	Same as `d3.easePoly*` with *ease*.`exponent(3)`.
`d3.easeSin*`	Sinusoidal easing: $f(t) = sin(t)$.
`d3.easeExp*`	Exponential easing: $f(t) = 2^{10(t-1)}$.
`d3.easeCircle*`	Circular easing.
`d3.easeElastic*`	Elastic easing. Set amplitude with *ease*.`amplitude`(*amplitude*). Default is 1. Set period with *ease*.`period`(*period*). Default is 0.3.
`d3.easeBack*`	Anticipatory easing. Set overshoot with *ease*.`overshoot`(*overshoot*). Default is 1.70158.
`d3.easeBounce*`	Bounce easing.

List of easing function types available in the *d3-ease* module.

Each function, except for `d3.easeLinear`, has three possible easing behaviors, identified by their suffixes: `In`, `Out`, `InOut`. The functions with no suffixes contain the most popular behavior, which is `easeInOut` in most functions, except `easeElastic` and `easeBounce`, where it's a shortcut to their `easeOut` function. These functions are shown in the following list:

- `ease*In`: Starts slowly and ends fast.
- `ease*Out`: Starts fast and ends slowly. Equivalent to `1 - ease*In(1 - t)`.
- `ease*InOut`: Starts slowly, accelerates to the middle, slows down from the middle, and ends slowly. Scales `ease*In`, from $t = 0$ to 0.5, then `ease*Out`, from $t = 0.5$ to 1.

The following diagram contains a quick reference with visual representations of each easing function:

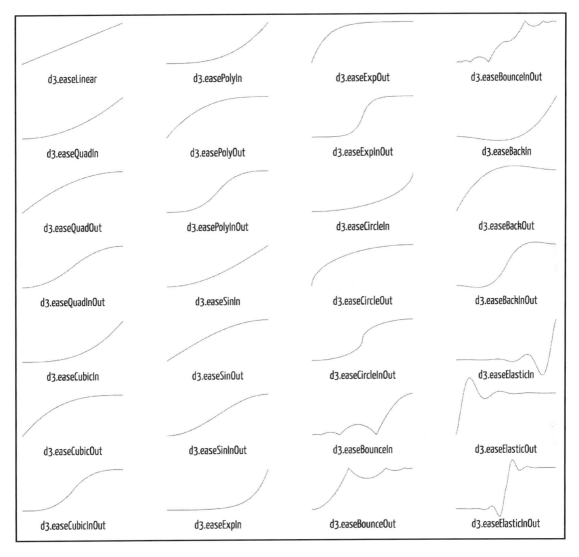

Visual representation of the 28 easing functions from d3-ease. Code: *Ease/1-ease-graphs.html.*

Also, you can see the animated version at `Ease/2-ease-animations.html`.

The best way to understand easing functions is to apply them to your code. Start with simple shapes, add a transition that changes one or two properties, such as colors, opacity, coordinates, and look at the result. For example, the following code moves a circle to the side of the screen as if it were attached to elastic or a spring (`Transitions/14-ease.html`):

```
const svg = d3.select("body").append("svg")
              .attr("width", 800).attr("height", 600);
svg.append("circle")
    .attr("r", 30)
    .attr("transform", `translate(${[400,300]})`);
    .transition().duration(5000).delay(500)
      .ease(d3.easeElastic.period(.1))
      .attr("transform", `translate(${[200,500]})`)
      .attr("r", 15);
```

You will notice a big difference by simply tuning the function's `period()` and `amplitude()`. Try replacing the function with another function, such as `d3.easeBounce`.

The official documentation provides more details about configuration options for easing functions. There is also a very good animated demo by Mike Bostock at `bl.ocks.org/mbostock/248bac3b8e354a9103c4`.

Multiple transitions

We have seen that if you call `transition()` on an existing transition chain, it will be scheduled to run as soon as the previous transition ends. For example, in following code (see `Transitions/15-sequential.html`), the circle will grow for two seconds, move down for two more seconds, and change from red (the color defined in CSS) to yellow in another two seconds:

```
svg.append("circle")
      .attr("r", 30)                                    // initial size
      .attr("transform", `translate(${[400,300]})`)    // initial position
      .transition().delay(500).duration(2000)          // transition 1
        .attr("r", 100)                                 //    final size
      .transition().duration(2000)                      // transition 2
        .attr("transform", `translate(${[600,500]})`)  //    final position
      .transition().duration(2000)                      // transition 3
        .style("fill", "yellow")                        //    final color
```

This behavior is illustrated in the following screenshot:

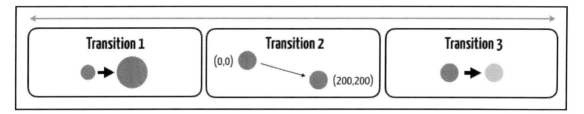

Chained transitions executing sequentially. Code: *Transitions/15-sequential.html.*

But what happens if you call them in separate selections of the same elements, as in the following code?

Let's have a look:

```
svg.append("circle")
        .attr("r", 30) // initial value
        .attr("transform", `translate(${[400,300]})`)
d3.select("circle").transition().delay(500).duration(2000) // transition 1
        .attr("r", 100)
d3.select("circle").transition().duration(2000)            // transition 2
        .attr("transform", `translate(${[600,500]})`)
d3.select("circle").transition().duration(2000)            // transition 3
        .style("fill", "yellow")
```

Run the code in `Transitions/16-interrupted.html`. The circle doesn't move and doesn't grow. Only the *last* transition happens. The first two transitions were ignored. It's easier to see what's happening if you add a small delay for the second and third transitions, as follows (see `Transitions/17-interrupted-delay.html`):

```
svg.append("circle")
    .attr("r", 30) // initial value
    .attr("transform", `translate(${[400,300]})`)
d3.select("circle").transition().delay(500).duration(2000)  // transition 1
    .attr("r", 100)
d3.select("circle").transition().delay(1500).duration(2000) // transition 2
    .attr("transform", `translate(${[600,500]})`)
d3.select("circle").transition().delay(2500).duration(2000) // transition 3
    .style("fill", "yellow")
```

The first transition starts because the others are delayed, but half a second later the second transition starts interrupting the first one, and then a second later the third transition starts, interrupting the second transition. These effects are shown in the following diagram:

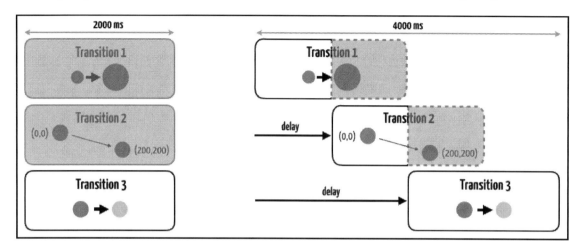

Transitions are interrupted as other transitions are started on the same selection.
Code: *Transitions/16-interrupted.html* and *17-interrupted-delay.html*.

If you set the values for each delay so that each one is the sum of the durations and delays of the previous transitions, you can avoid interruptions and obtain a sequential behavior without transition chaining, as follows (see `Transitions/18-sequential-delay.html`):

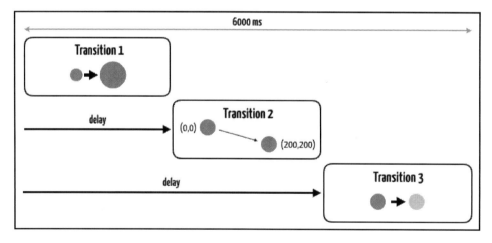

Transitions with delays set in a way that they don't interrupt one another and run sequentially. Code: *Transitions/sequential-delay.html*.

You can run multiple transitions simultaneously, but they can't be chained to one another, and must either be applied to different selections or have different names. A transition can receive a name on initialization. The following code (see `Transitions/19-simultaneous-names.html`) runs a two second animation, where the circle moves while at the same time growing and changing color:

```
svg.append("circle")
    .attr("r", 30) // initial value
    .attr("transform", `translate(${[400,300]})`);
d3.select("circle").transition("a").delay(500).duration(2000)
    .attr("r", 100);
d3.select("circle").transition("b").delay(500).duration(2000)
    .attr("transform", `translate(${[600,500]})`);
d3.select("circle").transition("c").delay(500).duration(2000)
    .style("fill", "yellow");
```

The same effect can be achieved if the transitions are attached to different selections. The following diagram shows three transitions running simultaneously:

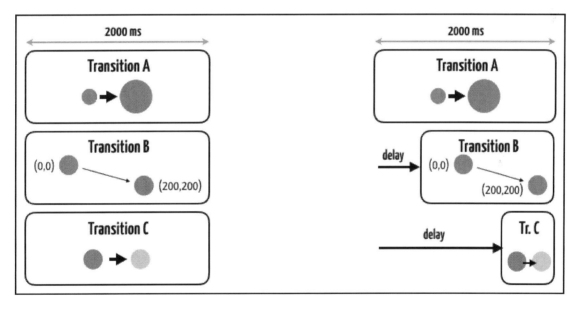

Transitions running simultaneously. Code: *Transitions/19-simultaneous-names.html* and *21-simultaneous-delay.html*

Life cycle of a transition and events

After configuration, a transition is scheduled. It may start running right away or wait until the previous transition finishes. If a delay is configured, it will also have to wait until the delay is over.

When a transition finally starts, it will call its interpolators at each animation frame. Interpolators are initialized with zero in the first frame. In subsequent frames, they are called with interpolated values that are transformed by the easing function. In the last frame, the interpolators are called with one, and the transition ends. Events are emitted during the start and end frames. The following diagram illustrates the life cycle of a single transition:

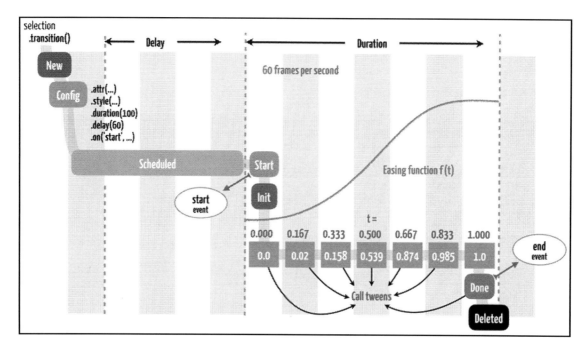

Life cycle of a single transition

If there is more than one transition running on an element, one of them must be a *named* transition. As we have seen in previous examples, multiple transitions can run on the same element only if they have different names. If a transition is created and starts running, and another transition with the same name starts running on the same element, the newer transition *interrupts* the older one as soon as it starts. The older transition will then emit an interrupt event. Other transitions with the same name and element that were created *before* the current transition but haven't yet started are cancelled, and emit a cancel event.

The following diagram describes the life cycle of three transitions with the same names applied to the same elements running simultaneously:

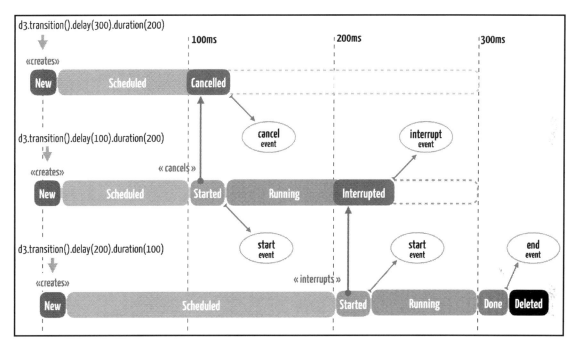

Transition life cycle when there are multiple same-name transitions. Code: *Transitions/23-transition-lifecycle.html*.

You can use event handlers to capture transition events and trigger operations when life cycle events, occur. The following table lists functions and methods related to a transition's life cycle. See `Transitions/23-transition-lifecycle.html` for examples of how to use these methods to reproduce the behavior shown in the preceding diagram:

Function or method	Description
transition.on (*types, listener*)	Types can be *start, end, interrupt,* or *cancel.* If a listener handles more than one type of event, the type names should be separated by spaces.
selection.interrupt()	Interrupts the active transition of the current selection (does not interrupt independent transitions that may be running in descendants).
d3.interrupt (*node*)	Interrupts the active transition of the specified node.
transition.end()	Returns a promise that resolves when the transition ends and rejects if cancelled or interrupted.

Functions and methods related to a transition's life cycle and events

The following code produces a cross-fading counter using chained transitions, where each digit fades as the next one appears. It uses d3.active(this) in the *start* event handler to capture the active transition, which fades out and removes the selection, while a new transition makes another element visible. It then chains another fading transition and runs forever in a recursive function (see `Transitions/26-repeat-count.html`):

```
const numbers = [0,1,2,3,4,5,6,7,8,9];
let i = 0;

d3.select("h1").text(numbers[i])
    .transition() // the first active transition
        .duration(1000)
        .on("start", function repeat() {
            d3.active(this)
              .style("opacity", 0)
              .remove();

        d3.select("body").append("h1")
          .style("opacity", 0)
          .text(() => ++i == numbers.length ?
                      numbers[i = 0] : numbers[i])
          .transition().duration(1000)
            .style("opacity", 1)
          .transition().delay(250) // the next active transition
            .on("start", repeat)
    })
```

A common mistake when chaining selections and transitions, which have methods with the same names, is accidentally calling the on() method on a *transition* object when it's meant for a *selection* object. They are completely different methods. A transition.on() listener doesn't receive native events, but only transition life cycle events such as *start*, *interrupt*, or *end*, as shown in the following code:

```
.d3.select("rect")          // Selection
  .style("fill","blue")     //    applied to selection
  .transition()             // Transition
  .style("fill","red")      //    applied to transition
  .on("click", () => {});   // Error: no 'click' event in transition
```

There is also no d3.event object in a transition event. The following code prints null on startup:

```
d3.select("rect")           // Selection
  .style("fill","blue")     //    applied to selection
  .transition()             // Transition
  .style("fill","red")      //    applied to transition
  .on("start", () => console.log(d3.event)); // d3.event is null
```

If you can't call the on() method before chaining the transition() to a selection, use selection() to get the current selection further ahead in the chain, as shown in the following code:

```
d3.select("rect")           // Selection
  .attr("fill","blue")      //    applied to selection
  .transition()             // Transition
  .attr("fill","red")       //    applied to transition
  .selection()              // Selection
  .on("click", () => console.log(d3.event)); // MouseEvent
```

Transitions make great interactive visualizations, but don't overuse them. Choose carefully which elements and attributes you wish to animate, select a simpler easing function if necessary, reduce durations, and see whether they really improve the user's experience. If you have a large dataset, you may have to optimize it, reduce the data, or use Canvas and other performance tool and techniques if your transitions run choppy. There may also be situations where you might prefer to not use them.

Timers

The *d3-timer* module is used internally by *d3-transition*. It contains functions that you might wish to use for scheduling and animations. They are similar to the `setInterval()` and `setTimeout()` functions already available in JavaScript, but are more efficient since they are based on `requestAnimationFrame()`, which applies an optimal refresh rate (about 60 frames per second) used by most modern browsers. The following table lists the most important methods in this module:

Function	Description
`d3.now()`	Equivalent to JavaScript's `performance.now()`. Returns the time elapsed since the application started.
`d3.timer` (*callback, delay, time*)	Runs a `callback` function periodically at `requestAnimationFrame` frame rates (usually 60 FPS) after a delay (default is zero) or at a specified time (default is `performance.now()`). The function returns a *timer* object that can be used to `stop()` or `restart()` the timer.
`d3.timeout` (*callback, delay, time*)	Runs a `callback` function once after a delay (default is zero). The callback is passed the elapsed *time*. Equivalent to JavaScript's `setTimeout()`.
`d3.interval` (*callback, delay, time*)	Runs a `callback` function periodically after every delay in milliseconds (default is same rate as timer). The callback is passed the elapsed time. The function returns a `timer` object that can be used to `stop()` or `restart()` the timer. Equivalent to JavaScript's `setInterval()`.

Main functions from the d3-timer module.

The following code will wait two seconds and then start `d3.timer()`, running the function that updates the text approximately 60 times every second (this is a typical frame rate, but it's actually system dependent). It will stop after reaching 10,000 (see `Timer/1-timer.html`):

```
svg.append("text").text("Wait 2 seconds and then start...")
  .attr("transform", "translate(50,50)");

const start = d3.now();
const timer = d3.timer(function() {
    d3.select("text").text(d3.now() - start)
```

```
        if(d3.now() - start >= 10000) {
            console.log("Will stop");
            timer.stop();
        }
    }, 2000); // start the timer in 2 seconds
```

To create a timer that runs at larger periods, use `d3.interval()`, which works much like JavaScript's `setInterval()`. This example will wait one second and then run the code every second. It will stop after counting after approximately 10 seconds, as shown in the following code (see `Timer/2-interval.html`):

```
.svg.append("text").text("Wait 1 second and start...")
    .attr("transform", "translate(50,50)");

const start = d3.now();
const timer = d3.interval(function() {
    d3.select("text").text(d3.now() - start)
    if(d3.now() - start >= 10000) {
        console.log("Will stop");
        timer.stop();
    }
}, 1000); // run the code every second
```

To run only once, after a delay, use `d3.timeout()`, which works like JavaScript's `setTimeout()`. This example will wait five seconds and run the function once, as shown in the following code (see `Timer/3-timeout.html`):

```
.svg.append("text").text("Waiting 5 seconds before printing delay...")
    .attr("transform", "translate(50,50)");

const start = d3.now();
d3.timeout(function() {
    d3.select("text").text(d3.now() - start);
}, 5000); // will run code in 5 seconds
```

These functions are used in several other examples in this book.

Dragging behavior

Dragging involves grabbing an object with a *mousedown* or *touchstart* event, moving the cursor *(mousemove* or *touchmove)* and dropping the object somewhere *(mouseup, touchend, or touchcancel)*. These native events are grouped in three drag events: *start*, *drag*, and *end*, that are handled by a drag behavior object.

A drag behavior is created with the `d3.drag()` function, as follows:

```
const drag = d3.drag();
```

You can then apply the drag behavior to a selection, for example:

```
drag(d3.selectAll(".square"));
```

Normally, the `call()` method is used to achieve the same result in a selection chain,as follows:

```
d3.selectAll(".square").call(drag);
```

Now you can capture drag events when you try to click and drag any of the selected objects. But first you need to configure at least one event handler.

Configuration methods

Besides event handlers, there is not much to configure for a typical drag gesture. Defaults can be used most of the time. Typically, you will configure one or more `on()` methods to control the *start-drag-end* life cycle.

The following table lists this method and two others you might wish to use:

Method	Description
on (*types, listener*)	One or more type names can be provided (separated by spaces). They can be *start*, called after a *mousedown* (or *touchstart*); *drag*, on *mousemove* (or *touchmove*); and *end*, on *mouseup* (or *touchend*). Each function receives the current *datum*, *index*, and *nodes* (which may be null if the object is not bound to a dataset). The current object can be accessed with *this*, and the `d3.event` object contains a *drag event object*, with drag-related properties.

`container` (*element*)	The container will determine the coordinate system of the drag events. In a drag-event listener, `d3.event.x` and `d3.event.y` are *relative* to this container (they are *not* the same as the coordinates obtained by a native event handler, such as *click*, and are computed from `d3.mouse` or `d3.touch`). The default container is the parent of the element to which the dragging behavior is attached.
`clickDistance` (*pixels*)	The minimum distance between *mouseup* and *mousedown* that will be considered a click event. Default is zero. A larger value can avoid accidental drags.
`subject` (*object*)	The subject is the *object* that is being dragged. It's usually captured when a drag gesture starts (for example, after a *mousedown*). This method allows a subject to be programmatically assigned to a drag behavior. The object must expose `x` and `y` properties, which are relative to the container.

Main configuration methods for the d3.drag() behavior.

The following configuration creates three handlers, one for each drag life-cycle event:

```
const drag = d3.drag()
    .on('start', function() { ... })
    .on('drag', function() { ... })
    .on('end', function() { ... });
```

In any event listener function, you can obtain a reference to the element being dragged with the `this` reference, as well as the datum, index and nodes array as the function's parameters. The `d3.event` object represents the *dragevent*, which contains the following properties:

d3.event properties	Description
x and y	The x and y coordinates of the cursor, relative to the current container (these are *not* the same coordinates you obtain from a native event handler, but equivalent to `d3.mouse`(*container*) in these methods). You can use these coordinates to move an object when a drag finishes (during the *end* event).

dx *and* dy	The *difference* between the previous and the current x and y coordinates after a drag event. You can use these coordinates to add to the coordinates of the object you are dragging and reposition it on the screen while dragging (during the *drag* event).
type	Contains the start, drag, or end string.
subject	The drag subject is the current data if the dragged object is bound to one, or the object's coordinates, if the data is null. You can also redefine the subject with the subject() configuration method.
active	The number of active gestures. It is zero at the start and end of a drag operation.
identifer	A touch ID or *mouse*.
target	A reference to the drag behavior object.
sourceEvent	The native event that triggers this event (for example, *mousemove*)

Properties of d3.event when used in a drag event listener.

The following example (see Drag/1-drag.html) demonstrates the basic use of a drag behavior to move some shapes. The data is an array of objects containing row and column coordinates and a color, created from an array:

```
const colors = [['#e41a1c','#377eb8','#4daf4a'],
                ['#984ea3','#ff7f00','#ffff33'],
                ['#a65628','#f781bf','#999999']];
const data = d3.merge(colors.map((p,i) =>
                      p.map((q,j) => ({color: q, row: i, col: j}))));
const side = 96; // side of the square
```

The following code binds the data to squares, which are drawn in a 3 x 3 grid:

```
svg.selectAll("rect.square")
    .data(data).join("rect").attr("class","square")
    .attr("x", d => 2 + 100 * (d.row + 1))
    .attr("y", d => 2 + 100 * (d.col + 1))
    .attr("width", side)
    .attr("height", side)
    .style("fill", d => d.color)
    .call(drag);     // calls the drag behavior for this selection
```

The drag behavior is configured as follows. The *start* event is used to raise the object to the front, so it won't be dragged under any objects, and to change the cursor icon (which is changed back to the default in the *end* event).

The *drag* event reads the object's current coordinates, adding `d3.event.dx` and `d3.event.dy` to obtain the new coordinates, which are updated while moving the object on the screen:

```
const drag = d3.drag()
    .on('start', function() {
        d3.select(this).raise();            // place the square on top
        d3.select(this).style("cursor", "move"); // change the cursor
    })
    .on('drag', function() {
        const xRect = +d3.select(this).attr("x"), // read coordinates
            yRect = +d3.select(this).attr("y")
        const x = xRect + d3.event.dx;    // compute new coordinates
        const y = yRect + d3.event.dy;
        d3.select(this).attr("x", x)      // update selection
        d3.select(this).attr("y", y)
    })
    .on('end', function(d,i,nodes) {
        d3.select(this).style("cursor", "auto"); // changes the cursor back
    });
```

Instead of reading the element's coordinates, we could also have used the *datum* and recomputed the coordinates (as we did in the attribute binding), or used a scale to reuse that computation. The screenshots that follow show the result before and during a dragging operation:

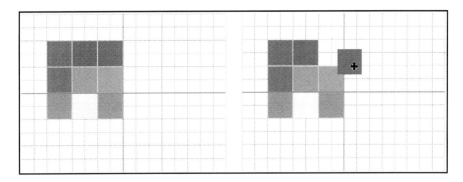

Dragging an object with the d3.drag() behavior. Code: *Drag/1-drag.html*.

Drag behavior will be used in several examples in the next chapters to move nodes in hierarchies and networks and to rotate maps in geographical visualizations.

Brushing behavior

Brushing allows the selection of a range of values in a chart, in one or two dimensions. It usually involves clicking a point on the screen with a *mousedown* or *touchstart* event, moving the cursor somewhere else (*mousemove* or *touchmove*) while drawing an area on the screen, and releasing the cursor when the area is selected (*mouseup, touchend,* or *touchcancel*). These native events are grouped in three drag events: *start, drag,* and *end* that are handled by a brush behavior object.

In two-dimensional brushes, the selection is represented as two corners of a rectangle. In one-dimensional brushes, the selection is a minimum and a maximum value. The selection rectangle can also be configured with a fixed size and allowed to move over the chart. You can also attach handles that are used to resize it. Once the brushing is done, the extent of the selection is used to compute new domains, which are used to render axes and data points.

You can create a brush behavior object using `d3.brush()`, `d3.brushX()`, or `d3.brushY()`, as follows:

```
const horizontalBrush = d3.brushX();
```

Having created this object, you can apply it to a container (for example, an SVG group), for example:

```
horizontalBrush(d3.select("g.view"));
```

Normally, the `selection.call()` method is used to achieve the same result, as follows:

```
d3.select("g.view").call(horizontalBrush);
```

You can then capture brush events by drawing or moving a selection area on the screen, but first you need to configure at least one event handler.

The following table lists the functions used to create and configure brushes from the *d3-brush* module:

Functions	Description
`d3.brush()`	Creates a two-dimensional brush.
`d3.brushX()`	Creates a one-dimensional brush for the *x* dimension.
`d3.brushY()`	Creates a one-dimensional brush for the *y* dimension.
`d3.brushSelection(node)`	Returns the current *brush selection* for a DOM node. The brush selection is an array that describes the extent of the brush. If the brush is one-dimensional, it returns an array of two elements: [*minX,maxX*] or [*minY,maxY*]. If the brush is two-dimensional, it returns an array of two-element arrays: [[*minX,minY*], [*maxX,maxY*]]. This object is normally obtained in an event handler via `d3.event.selection`.

Functions from the d3-brush module that implement brush behavior.

Configuration methods

Typically, you will configure the brushing *extent*, if your brushing area is not the same as your container, and one or more `on()` methods to handle the *start-brush-end* life cycle. The following table lists the brush configuration methods you are most likely to use:

Methods	Description
`on` (*types, listener*)	One or more type names can be provided (separated by spaces). They can be *start*, called after a *mousedown* (or *touchstart*); *brush*, on *mousemove* (or *touchmove*); and *end*, on *mouseup* (or *touchend*). Each function receives the current *datum, index,* and *nodes* (which may be null if the object is not bound to a dataset). The current object can be accessed with `this`, and the `d3.event` object contains a *brush event object*, with brush-related properties.

move (*group, brushSelection*)	Used to select a brush programmatically. The brush selection should be [*minX,maxX*] for d3.brushX(), [*minY,maxY*] for d3.brushY(), or [[*minX,minY*], [*maxX,maxY*]] for d3.brush(). The *group* is a D3 selection of \<g\> elements. A brush should already be connected to this group: run group.call(brush) or brush(group) before using this method. Calling this method with a *null brushSelection* will hide (and remove) the brush rectangle.
extent (*extent*)	Sets the brushable extent. It can be an array [[*minX,minY*], [*maxX,maxY*]] or a function that returns that array.
handleSize (*pixels*)	The invisible space outside the brushed area that you can drag and resize. The default value is 6. You may wish to increase it if you add visible resizing handles.

Main configuration methods for the d3.brush() behavior.

The following configuration creates event handlers for a two-dimensional brush, one for each brush life cycle event:

```
const brush = d3.brush()      // or d3.brushX() or d3.brushY()
    .on('start', function() { ... })
    .on('brush', function() { ... })
    .on('end', function() { ... });
```

The move() method is used for programmatic brushing. It is usually called from a selection using call(), for example:

```
d3.select("g").call(brush.move, [[100,150], [250,300]]).
```

In any event listener function, you can obtain the *datum, index,* and *nodes* arrays as the function's parameters. The brushed element is usually the view where the data is rendered, and can be accessed inside the handler with the this reference.

The d3.event object contains the *brush event,* which contains the following properties:

Properties	Description
selection	The current *brush selection* (an array that describes the extent of the brush). Returns [*minX,maxX*] if the behavior object is a d3.brushX(), [*minY,maxY*] if d3.brushY(), or [[*minX,minY*], [*maxX,maxY*]] if d3.brush().
type	Contains the string *start, brush,* or *end.*
target	A reference to the brush behavior object.
sourceEvent	The native event that triggers this event—for example, *mousemove.*

Properties of d3.event when used in a brush event listener

One-dimensional brush

Brushing can be used to zoom into the details of charts that have a lot of concentrated data. The following example adds a horizontal-axis brush to a line chart that displays global temperatures from 1880 to 2016. Only relevant code fragments are shown. You can see the full code at Brush/1-brush-x.html.

A one-dimensional *x*-axis brush is created with d3.brushX() and the default configuration, as shown in the following code. Only one listener is configured. It will handle the *end* event, calling the detail() function when the brush is done:

```
const brush = d3.brushX().on("end", detail);
```

The brush is called from the view object (<g>) that contains all the data points, as shown in the following code:

```
view.call(brush); // Call brush on the data view
```

A global domain object is created to save the domain used to configure the horizontal scale during initialization so that we can zoom back to the original domain later, as shown in the following code:

```
const domain = {}; // saves current domain
...
d3.json('../Data/monthly_json.json').then(function(result) {
    data.values = result.filter(d => d.Source == 'GISTEMP');
    scaleX.domain(d3.extent(data.values, d => d3.isoParse(d.Date)));

    // Save domains for reset
    domain.x = scaleX.domain();
```

```
    ...
}
```

A reset button will be used to restore the original scale, using the following code:

```
const reset = d3.select("body")
                .append("button")
                .text("Reset Zoom");
reset.on("click", function() {
            this.style.opacity = 0;    // hide this button
            scaleX.domain(domain.x);   // restore saved domain
            updateView();              // update axis and data with
                                          new scale
        });
```

The `detail()` function is called when the user is done defining the selection area. The selected area is represented by the array obtained from `d3.event.selection`, which contains the range of the selected data (in pixels). The data domain for this range is obtained by calling the scale's `invert()` for each range value, and then used to update the scale, and then the axes and data points (in the `updateView()` function). After the updates, the brush is hidden and a reset button (previously created in HTML) is displayed, as shown in the following code:

```
function detail() {
    if(d3.event.selection) {
        const [minX,maxX] = d3.event.selection; // the selection box

        // New domain by inverting values from the scale's range
        const newDomainX = [scaleX.invert(minX),
                            scaleX.invert(maxX)]
        scaleX.domain(newDomainX); // update scale
        updateView();              // update elements

        view.call(brush.move, null); // hides the brush rectangle
        reset.style("opacity", 1);   // Show reset button
    }
}
```

The `updateView()` method shown in the following code updates the axes and the scales used for the line generator, and then draws the points in the new domain:

```
function updateView() {
    xG.call(axisX);             // call the axis function (redraw with
                                   new scale)
    line.x(d => scaleX(d3.isoParse(d.Date))); // line function in new scale
    view.selectAll("path.line")
        .transition().duration(750)
```

```
        .attr("d", line);                    // update the line chart
    }
```

The following screenshots illustrate a horizontal brushing operation applied to the line chart. The gray rectangle shows the area to be detailed. The chart on the right shows the selected area occupying the entire view, with updated scales on the axes. The **Reset** button (not shown in the following screenshot) only appears when we have zoomed in on the chart:

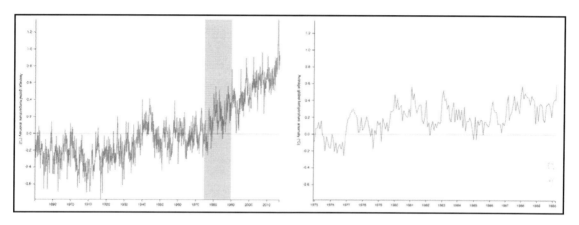

Horizontal one-dimensional brushing applied to a line chart. Code: *Brush/1-brush-x.html*

Two-dimensional brush

The next example uses two-dimensional brushing applied to the scatterplot that compares HDI and GDP that we created in Chapter 5, *Scales, Axes, and Colors*. The code is similar to the previous example, and only the relevant code fragments are shown. You can see the full code at Brush/2-brush-xy.html.

The d3.brush() function is used to create a two-dimensional brush, as shown in the following code:

```
const brush = d3.brush().on("end", detail);
view.call(brush);
```

This time, we need to save the states of both domains, since both the *x* and *y* scales will be affected, as shown in the following code:

```
d3.csv("../Data/un_regions_gdp.csv").then(function(dataset) { ...
    data.countries = dataset;

    scaleY.domain(d3.extent(data.countries, d => d.gdp)); // initial
    scaleX.domain(d3.extent(data.countries, d => d.hdi)); // setup

    domain.x = scaleX.domain(); // save initial domains
    domain.y = scaleY.domain();
    ...
}
```

The `detail()` function receives an array containing two points, which represent the corners of the selected rectangle. Each value needs to be inverted to obtain the horizontal and vertical domains, which are then used to update each scale, as follows:

```
function detail() {
    if(d3.event.selection) {
        const [[minX,minY],[maxX,maxY]] = d3.event.selection;

        const newDomainX = [scaleX.invert(minX), scaleX.invert(maxX)]
        scaleX.domain(newDomainX);
        const newDomainY = [scaleY.invert(maxY), scaleY.invert(minY)]
        scaleY.domain(newDomainY);

        updateView();

        view.call(d3.event.target.move, null); // hide the brush
        rectangle
        d3.select("#zoom-reset").style("opacity", 1); // Show reset
        button
    }
}
```

The `updateView()` function updates the axes and the data points with the new scales. The reset button updates the scales with the saved domains and calls `updateView()` to apply them to the axes and data points, as follows:

```
function updateView() {
    xG.call(axisX);
    yG.call(axisY);
    view.selectAll("circle.dot")
        .attr("cx", d => scaleX(d.hdi))
        .attr("cy", d => scaleY(d.gdp));
}
```

```
d3.select("#zoom-reset")  // this is the Reset button
    .on("click", function() {
        this.style.opacity = 0;
        scaleX.domain(domain.x);  // applies saved domain to each scale
        scaleY.domain(domain.y);
        updateView();
    });
```

The following screenshots illustrate how the brushing is applied to the scatterplot. The area selected by the rectangle in the left chart is expanded to occupy the entire view in the right chart:

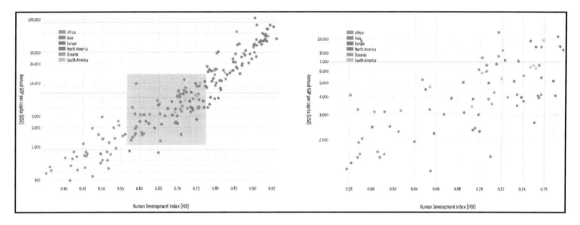

Two-dimensional brushing applied to a scatterplot. Code: *Brush/2-brush-xy.html.*

You can also programmatically create a brush with a pre-determined size, resize it as you wish, and move it over the area you want to detail. This is possible with the move() method. In this example (see Brush/3-brush-xy.html), an extra button was added to show a 200 x 150 pixel brush area at the top-left corner of the chart, using the following code:

```
d3.select("#show-brush")
    .on("click", function() {
        view.call(brush.move, [[0,0],[200,150]]); // Call brush on data view
    });
```

The user can resize the brush and move it over the area to be detailed, as shown in the following code . As soon as the box is released in any place that is not the upper-left corner, the brushing will occur:

```
function detail() {
    const s = d3.event.selection;
    if(s && s[0][0] != 0 && s[0][1] != 0) { // upper left corner
        // ... same code as before
    }
}
```

Zooming behavior

Zooming and panning are fundamental features in any web-based visualization. A large visualization, such as a map or a network diagram, might display only part of a view, requiring that the user zoom out in order to have a general view of the entire chart, zoom in to view the details, and scroll or pan to view adjacent parts that don't fit on one screen.

Zooming may involve several events and different input devices. A typical process is initiated by scrolling a mouse wheel or by performing a sequence of *mousedown* (or *touchstart*), *mousemove* (*touchmove*) and *mouseup* (or *touchend*) events. In D3, these native events are grouped into three zoom events: *start*, *zoom*, and *end* that are handled by a zoom behavior object.

A zoom behavior is created with the d3.zoom() function, as shown in the following code:

```
const zoom = d3.zoom();
```

You can then apply it to a selection, for example:

```
zoom(d3.select ("g.view"));
```

Normally, the call() method is used to achieve the same result, as shown in the following code:

```
d3.selectAll("g.view").call(zoom);
```

You can then capture zoom events or add programmatic zoom operations. In any case, you will need to set up at least one event handler.

Configuration methods

Besides event handlers, you will typically configure the extent of your zooming behaviors, since they are initially set for infinite scaling and translation. The following table contains the main configuration methods you are most likely to use. All methods return the current zoom behavior and can be chained:

Method	Description
on (*types, listener*)	One or more type names can be provided (separated by spaces). They can be *start*, called after a *mousedown* (or *touchstart*); *zoom*, on *mousemove*, *wheel*, or *touchmove*; and *end*, on *mouseup*, *touchend*, or *touchcancel*. Each function receives the current *datum*, *index*, and *nodes* (which may be null if the object is not bound to a dataset). The current object can be accessed with `this`, and the d3.event object contains a *zoom event object*, with zoom-related properties.
extent (*extent*)	Sets the *viewport extent* to a given array of two points (upper-left and lower-right). It can also be specified as a function that will be invoked for each element, with datum, index, and this reference. The default extent is [[0,0], [*width,height*]], where *width* and *height* are the dimensions of the container element. This configuration is required to enforce a translate extent.
translateExtent (*extent*)	Sets the *translate extent* to a given array of two points (upper-left and lower-right). Default allows unbounded translation in all directions. These limits are enforced when using interactive zooming and panning or the `scaleBy`, `scaleTo`, and `translateBy` methods. They are not respected by custom programmatic transforms.
scaleExtent (*extent*)	Sets the *scale extent* to a given array of two numbers, which represent the minimum and maximum allowed scale factors. The default allows unbounded scaling. Scaling limits are enforced when using interactive zooming or the `scaleBy`, `scaleTo`, and `translateBy` methods. They are not respected by custom programmatic transforms.
duration (*duration*)	The duration for double-click zooming. The default is 250 ms.
wheelDelta (*function*)	Controls the amount of scaling in response to a `WheelEvent`. It should receive a function that computes the *delta*.

clickDistance (*pixels*)	The maximum distance between the mouse positions during *mouseup* and *mousedown* events that will be considered a single click. The default is zero.

Main configuration methods for the d3.zoom() behavior.

The following configuration creates three handlers, one for each zoom life cycle event:

```
const zoom = d3.zoom()
        .on('start', function() { ... })
        .on('drag', function() { ... })
        .on('end', function() { ... });
```

In any event listener function, you can obtain the *datum, index,* and *nodes* arrays as the function's parameters. The zoomed element is usually the view where the data is rendered, and can be obtained with the this reference if you need it, but most of the time you will be manipulating with the *zoom event object,* accessible in an event handler as d3.event. It contains the following properties:

d3.event properties	Description
type	Contains the *start, zoom,* or *end* string.
transform	The zoom transform object of the current node (same as d3.zoomTransform(this)). Contains an object with three properties: x, y, and k, and several methods. For more information, read *Zoom transforms,* in this section.
target	A reference to the zoom behavior object.
sourceEvent	The native event that triggers this event (for example, *mousemove*)

Properties of a zoom event (received in zoom listeners as a d3.event)

Most of the examples in this chapter will use the following SVG image, which contains a red square (rect) and a grid, of vertical and horizontal lines (see the files in the *Zoom/* folder):

```
const width = 800, height = 600;
const svg = d3.select("body").append("svg")
        .attr("width", width).attr("height", height);

const rect = svg.append("rect").attr("x",300).attr("y",200)
        .attr("width", 100).attr("height", 100)

const exes = d3.range(0,width+1,50).map(d => [[d,0],[d,height]]);
const wyes = d3.range(0,height+1,50).map(d => [[0,d],[width,d]]);
```

```
const grid = svg.selectAll(".grid").data(d3.merge([exes, wyes]))
        .join("path").attr("class","grid").attr("d", d3.line())
        .style("stroke-width", d => d[0][0] == width/2 ||
                            d[1][1] == height/2 ? 3 : 1);
```

Interactive zoom

Interactive zooming is automatically triggered by native input events, such as *mousedown* or *touchstart*. In the following code, the zoom behavior is configured and called from a selection containing the svg object. It will affect both the square (rect) and grid since svg is their common ancestor:

```
const zoom = d3.zoom()
        .duration(1000) // duration for double-click zooming
        .on('zoom', function() {
            console.log(d3.event.transform.toString())
            svg.attr("transform", d3.event.transform);
        });
svg.call(zoom);
```

The transform property of d3.event is a transformation object with the following structure: {x, y, k}, where x and y are translation coordinates and k is the scale factor. If you call it in a string context or use its toString() method, it will return a transform string that can be used directly by a transform attribute,a shown in the following code:

```
console.log(d3.event.transform); // {x:15.914, y:16.696, k:0.824}
console.log(""+d3.event.transform); // translate(15.914,16.696)
                            scale(0.824)
```

Using a mouse, you can zoom in with double-clicks or drag the mouse or roll the wheel to zoom in and out. The duration() method was used in this example to increase the double-click zooming transition to one second (the default is 250 ms). Try the code in Zoom/1-basic.html. The result is illustrated in the following image:

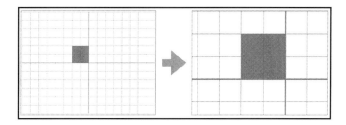

Zooming in and out using SVG transforms. Code: *Zoom/1-basic.html*.

You don't have to zoom the entire SVG. To zoom the square over a static grid, you just apply the transform to the `rect` object (see `Zoom/2-element.html`), as shown in the following code:

```
.on('zoom', function() {
    rect.attr("transform", d3.event.transform);
})
```

You could alternatively attach the zoom behavior to the `rect` object, instead of the `svg` object. The result of this transform is shown in the following screenshot:

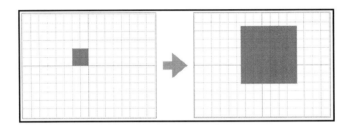

Transforming one object and leaving the others fixed. Code: *Zoom/2-element.html*.

Unless you configure *scale extents*, you can zoom in and out to infinity. *Translate extents* can also be configured, so that you don't pan your chart out of view. The following configuration uses `translateExtent()` to set the translate extent as the entire view, and `scaleExtent()` to limit zooming out to half the view size, and zooming in to five times the view size (see `Zoom/3-translate-extent.html`):

```
const zoom = d3.zoom()
        .translateExtent([[0,0],[width, height]])
        .scaleExtent([0.5,5])
        .on('zoom', () => svg.attr("transform", d3.event.transform));
```

You might configure your extent as part of a chart, for example, the area within the axes. In this case, you should also configure the *viewport extent* using the `extent()` method, and set the same values for the translate extent (see `Zoom/4-extent.html`):

```
const extent = [[0,0],[chartWidth,chartHeight]];
const zoom = d3.zoom()
        .extent(extent)
        .translateExtent(extent)
        .scaleExtent([0.5,5])
        .on('zoom', () => svg.attr("transform", d3.event.transform));
```

The following code adds a handler for the *end* event. When the user finishes zooming, the current transform is compared to the identity transform, and if it is different, the identity transform is applied programmatically, causing the zooming to be reversed (see `Zoom/5-events.html`):

```
const zoom = d3.zoom()
        .on('zoom', function() {
            console.log("zoom")
            rect.attr("transform", d3.event.transform);
            grid.attr("transform", d3.event.transform);
        })
        .on('end', function() {
            console.log("zoom.end", d3.event.transform, d3.zoomIdentity)
            if(d3.event.transform !== d3.zoomIdentity) {
                svg.transition()
                    .delay(500)
                    .call(d3.event.target.transform, d3.zoomIdentity);
            }
        })

svg.call(zoom);
```

You might use the wheel, mouse movement, or double-clicks for other operations in your code, which will conflict with zooming. In that case, you can use the `on()` method with a *null* handler to detach these gestures from the zoom behavior. For example, to turn off zooming with double-clicks, use the following code (see `Zoom/6-events-no-dblclick.html`):

```
svg.call(zoom).on("dblclick.zoom", null);
```

Or to turn off zooming with the wheel, use the following code (see `Zoom/7-events-no-wheel.html`):

```
svg.call(zoom).on("wheel.zoom", null);
```

Programmatic zoom

You can perform animated zoom transforms to scale and translate programmatically without any user interaction. This is achieved with a `zoomTransform` object, which you can create using `d3.zoomTransform(node)` or using a zoom event listener from the `d3.event.transform` object. You can then connect the transform object with a selection with the `transform()` method.

The *d3-zoom* module also includes four convenience methods that don't require the previous creation of a transform object. All these methods are listed as follows:

Method	Description
transform (*selection, transform*)	Receives a transform object with x, y, and k properties defined for translation and scaling and applies it to the selection.
translateBy (*selection, x, y*)	Translates a selection by the provided x, y coordinates.
translateTo (*selection, x, y*)	Translates a selection to the provided x, y coordinates.
scaleBy (*selection, k*)	Scales a selection by the provided relative k scale factor.
scaleTo (*selection, k*)	Scales a selection to the provided absolute k scale factor.

d3.zoom() methods for applying transforms to a selection

Most of the time, the previous methods are called from a selection using the `selection.call()` method, for example:

```
const svg = d3.select("svg");
const zoom = d3.zoom();

// instead of zoom.transform(svg, d3.zoomTransform(svg.node)); use:
svg.call(zoom.transform, d3.zoomTransform(svg.node));

// instead of zoom.translateBy(svg, 100, 200); use:
svg.call(zoom.translateBy, 100,200);

// instead of zoom.scaleTo(svg, 2); use:
svg.call(zoom.scaleTo, 2);
```

The simplest way to perform scaling and translating is to use the convenience methods. The `translateBy()` and `scaleBy()` methods apply transforms that are *relative* to the previous transform. The `translateTo()` and `scaleTo()` methods apply *absolute* transforms.

The following code fragment applies three `scaleBy()` transforms in sequence. Each transform modifies values obtained from the previous transform. Changing the order of each call will produce different results. The last transform brings the view object back to its original scale and position (see `Zoom/8-scale-by.html`):

```
const zoom = d3.zoom()
        .on('zoom', () => svg.attr("transform", d3.event.transform));

svg.transition().duration(1000).delay(500)
        .call(zoom.scaleBy, 2)      // doubles the size
        .transition().delay(500)
```

```
.call(zoom.scaleBy, 2)      // doubles the size again
.transition().delay(500)
.call(zoom.scaleBy, .25);  // shrinks to ¼ of the size
```

The following screenshots illustrate the result of each transform:

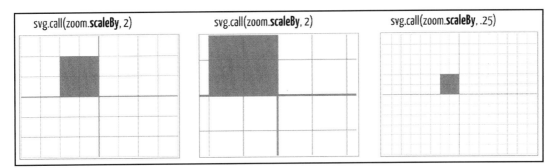

Using scaleBy() to perform relative scaling. Code: *Zoom/8-scale-by.html.*

The `scaleTo()` method operates on absolute values (previous transforms don't affect the current transform). It is used in the following code to produce the same result as the previous example:

```
svg.transition().duration(1000).delay(500)
        .call(zoom.scaleTo, 2)  // scale to twice the size
        .transition().delay(500)
        .call(zoom.scaleTo, 4)  // scale to 4x the size
        .transition().delay(500)
        .call(zoom.scaleTo, 1); // scale to 1x the size
```

The result is illustrated in the following screenshot (see `Zoom/9-scale-to.html`), as shown in the following code:

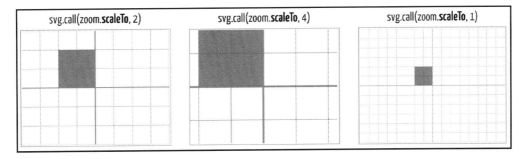

Using scaleTo() to perform absolute scaling. Code: *Zoom/9-scale-to.html.*

The `translateBy()` method moves an object relative to its previous position. The following example applies three transforms, ending with the view in its original position (see `Zoom/10-translate-by.html`):

```
svg.transition().duration(1000).delay(500)
    .call(zoom.translateBy, 100, 100)
    .transition().delay(500)
    .call(zoom.translateBy, 350, 200)
    .transition().delay(500)
    .call(zoom.translateBy, -450, -300);
```

The following screenshots illustrate the result of each one of the three transforms:

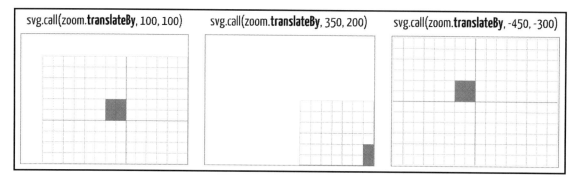

Using translateBy() to perform relative translating. Code: *Zoom/10-translate-by.html*.

The `translateTo()` method receives absolute coordinates to perform translating. The previous position of the view object is not relevant. The following code moves the view to several different positions:

```
svg.transition().duration(1000).delay(500)
    .call(zoom.translateTo, 0, 0)
    .transition().delay(500)
    .call(zoom.translateTo, 600, 200)
    .transition().delay(500)
    .call(zoom.translateTo, 400, 300);
```

The results are shown in the following screenshot (see `Zoom/11-translate-to.html`):

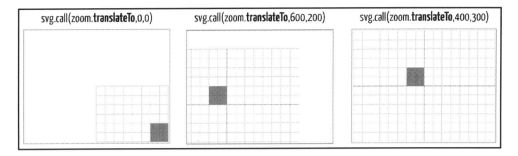

Using translateTo() to perform absolute translating. Code: *Zoom/11-translate-to.html*

To perform complex transformations, you can combine several transforms in simultaneous transitions to achieve any effect you wish. But in some cases, it may be simpler to create a reusable transform object.

Zoom transforms

A zoom transform is an object that saves state information about an object's transformed position and scale. It contains three properties:

- `transform.x`: The *translate x* coordinate. The default is zero.
- `transform.y`: The *translate y* coordinate. The default is zero.
- `transform.k`: The *scale* factor. The default is 1.

If an object wasn't been transformed yet, its zoom transform object will contain default values for each property. This object is the *identity transform*. A zoom transform can be obtained from any DOM node. It's frequently accessed as a property of the `d3.event` object in a zoom listener, described as follows:

Function or property	Description
`d3.zoomTransform`(*node*)	Creates a zoom transform object for a given DOM node. A transform object has the structure `{x, y, k}`, where `x` and `y` are position coordinates (used to translate the object along each axis) and `k` is the scale factor. In the context of an event listener, you can obtain the zoom transform using `d3.event.transform` or `d3.zoomTransform(this)`.
`d3.zoomIdentity`	This is a transform object representing the identity transform: `{x: 0, y: 0, k: 1}`.

Objects that represent a zoom transform

For example, to create a zoom transform for an SVG object you can use the following:

```
const svg = d3.select("body").append("svg");
const transform d3.zoomTransform(svg.node())
console.log(transform); // {x: 0, y: 0, k: 1}
```

You can then derive a new transform and apply it to the `svg` object using the `transform()` method as follows:

```
const newTransform = transform.scale(2); // creates a new transform
svg.call(zoom.transform, newTransform); // will run .on("zoom")
```

Transforms should be considered *immutable* and their x, y, and k properties should be considered read-only. You should always derive new transforms using methods such as `translate()` and `scale()`. These methods are described as follows:

Method	Description
`toString()`	This method is called automatically any time a transform object is used in a string context (for example, when used in a concatenation or as a method parameter that takes a string). It returns a string that can be used as the attribute value for SVG transforms,as follows: `` `translate(${this.x}, ${this.y}) scale(${this.k})` ``
`translate(x, y)`	Returns a transform with the given relative translation coordinates x, y, which are added to the coordinates of the current transform, t: xt ,yt. When chained with a `scale()` method, this method should be called first; otherwise, the scale transform will modify its coordinates.
`scale(k)`	Returns a transform with the given relative scale factor k, which is multiplied to the scale factor of the current transform, t: kt.

d3.zoomTransform() methods that return transforms and generate SVG transform strings.

The `toString()` method is called automatically any time a transform is used in a string context (such as in string concatenation). It returns a valid SVG transform string, which you can directly apply as the value of a transform attribute,as shown in the following code:

```
svg.attr("transform", d3.event.transform);
```

You can also chain `scale()` and `translate()` methods. Each one returns a new transform and provides a context for the next one. For this reason, it's important to call the `translate()` method *before* calling `scale()`, otherwise, the scale will be applied to the transform's coordinates and the string will be generated incorrectly. The following code illustrates this difference:

```
// This generates an incorrect string: translate(200,200) scale(2)
svg.attr("transform", d3.zoomIdentity.scale(2).translate(100,100));

// This generates the correct string: translate(100,100) scale(2)
svg.attr("transform", d3.zoomIdentity.translate(100,100).scale(2));
```

The following example creates six transform objects and saves references to three of them. Then they are applied to the `svg` object in a sequence of one-second transitions, with one-second delays:

```
const zoom = d3.zoom()
        .on('zoom', () => svg.attr("transform", d3.event.transform));
svg.call(zoom.transform, d3.zoomTransform(svg.node));

// 2x scale + (200,200)
const transform1 = d3.zoomTransform(svg.node()) // 1) initial transform
        .translate(-300,-200) // 2) translated initial transform
        .scale(3); // 3) transform1: translated and scaled

// .75 scale + (-100,0)
const transform2 = transform1
        .translate(-100,0) // 4) translated transform1
        .scale(0.75); // 5) transform2: translated and scaled

// zoom identity
const transform3 = d3.zoomIdentity; // 6) final transform

const t = svg.transition().delay(1000).duration(1000)
        .call(zoom.transform, transform1)
        .transition().delay(1000)
        .call(zoom.transform, transform2)
        .transition().delay(1000)
        .call(zoom.transform, transform3);
```

Each transform step is illustrated in the following screenshot. You can try the code in
`Zoom/12-transforms-svg.html;`

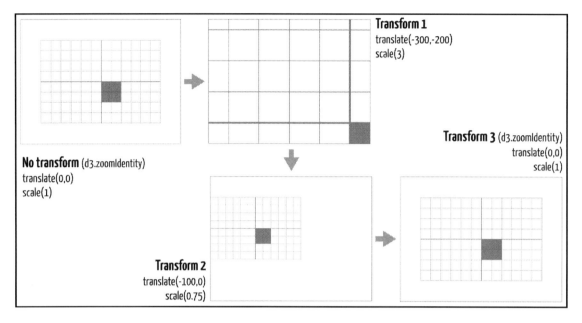

A sequence of transforms applied to an SVG element. Code: *Zoom/12-transforms-svg.html*

Canvas zooming

Zoom transforms can also be applied to Canvas contexts. The following example (see
`Zoom/13-transforms-canvas.html`) is a Canvas version of the previous example based
on SVG, and behaves in the same way. First, you need to set up a Canvas selection and
obtain the context, as follows:

```
const canvas = d3.select("body").append("canvas")
                .attr("height", height).attr("width", width);
const ctx = canvas.node().getContext("2d");
ctx.translate(margin,margin);
```

A `translate` transform was applied to the context so that it is rendered in the same place as the SVG `chart` object from the previous example.

The grid consists of a series of lines. The `context()` method is used to configure `d3.line()` so that it will generate a list of path method calls on the context when the `line()` function is called for each piece of datum:

```
const line = d3.line().context(ctx);
```

The `render()` function sets fill and stroke styles, and draws the red rectangle and the grid, as follows:

```
function render() {
    ctx.fillStyle = "red";
    ctx.fillRect(300,200,100,100);
    ctx.fillStyle = "transparent";
    ctx.strokeStyle = "gray";
    ctx.lineWidth = d => d[0][0] == chartWidth/2 ||
                    d[1][1] == chartHeight/2 ? 3 : 1;
    d3.merge([exes, wyes]).forEach(function(d) {
        ctx.beginPath();
        line(d); // call the path commands to draw each line
        ctx.stroke();
    });
    ctx.strokeStyle = "transparent";
}
render();
```

The code so far will render a static view identical to the one rendered in SVG in the previous example. Now we can implement the zooming behavior.

The configuration is identical, except for the *zoom* event listener. Before applying the transforms, you should save the current Canvas context, which will preserve the attributes and the previous transform and clear the Canvas. After translating, the `render()` function is called to draw the objects in the newly transformed Canvas, and the context is restored, as follows:

```
const extent = [[0,0],[chartWidth,chartHeight]];
const zoom = d3.zoom()
        .extent(extent)
        .translateExtent(extent).scaleExtent([0.5,5])
        .on('zoom', function() {
            ctx.save(); // save canvas context
            ctx.clearRect(-margin, -margin, width+margin*2,
            height+margin*2);
            ctx.translate(d3.event.transform.x, d3.event.transform.y);
```

```
        ctx.scale(d3.event.transform.k, d3.event.transform.k);
        render();
        ctx.restore(); // restore canvas context
    });
canvas.call(zoom);
```

The zoom behavior is attached to the canvas using the `selection.call()` method.

To apply the transform, you can move the mouse wheel for an interactive zoom, or apply programmatic zoom transforms to the `canvas` object:

```
const transform1 = d3.zoomTransform(canvas.node())
        .translate(-300,-200).scale(3);
canvas.transition().delay(1000).duration(1000)
        .call(zoom.transform, transform1);
```

Semantic zoom

The `transform` object and its `scale()` and `transform()` methods generate ready-to-use SVG transform strings and are great for *geometric zooming*, which basically increases or reduces the size of the graphical elements. But many times users expect more than just scaling when zooming in and out. When you apply an SVG transform to a shape, it affects not only its size, but also the size of its descendant elements, font sizes, and stroke widths. When zooming into a scatter plot, one-pixel dots suddenly become large circles. In a map, thin country borders can become thick rectangles.

Semantic zoom assigns meaning to each zoom level. If the data that is displayed changes when you zoom in and out, you have semantic zooming. It may be as simple as preserving stroke widths and dot sizes when scaling a scatterplot or a map, but it usually involves revealing more or less detail.

To apply semantic zoom, you may have to manipulate scale factors and translate coordinates separately, apply inverse transformations, and build new transforms from individual x, y, and k components. The following table lists several methods that are useful for implementing semantic zoom:

Method	Description
apply (*point*)	Returns a relative transformation for a point [x,y], which is expressed as [$xk + x_t$, $yk + y_t$], where k is the scale factor and [x_t,y_t] are the coordinates of the current transform, t.
applyX (*x*)	Returns a relative transformation of the x coordinate, which is expressed $xk + x_t$, where k is the scale factor and x_t is the x coordinate of the current transform, t.
applyY (*y*)	Returns a relative transformation of the y coordinate, which is $yk + y_t$, where k is the scale factor and y_t is the y coordinate of the current transform, t.
invert (*point*)	Returns the inverse transformation for a point [x,y], which is expressed as [$(x - x_t)/k$, $(y - y_t)/k$], where k is the scale factor and [x_t,y_t] are the coordinates of the current transform, t.
invertX (*x*)	Returns the inverse transformation of the provided x coordinate, which is expressed as $(x - xt)/k$ expressed as where k is the scale factor and xt is the x coordinate of the current transform, t.
invertY (*y*)	Returns the inverse transformation of the provided y-coordinate, which is $(y - y_t)/k$ where k is the scale factor and y_t is the y-coordinate of the current transform, t.

Methods that return transformations for individual points and coordinates.

These methods are applied to an existing transform, and the results are relative to the state of that transform. For example, look at the following transform ({k: 3, x: -300, y: -200}):

```
const transform = d3.zoomIdentity.translate(-300,-200).scale(3);
```

Each coordinate is multiplied by the scale factor and added to the current value, as follows:

```
const point1 = transform1.apply([-100,50]); // [-600,-50]
                                    // ([3*-100 + -300, 3*50 + -200])
const x1 = transform1.applyX(25); // -225 (-300 + 3 * 75)
const y1 = transform1.applyY(-25); // -275 (-200 + 3 * -25)
```

If you call these methods on a transform using identity transform values ($x,y = 0$, $k = 1$), they will work as getters and return the transform's attributes, as shown in the following code (see `Zoom/14-transforms-apply.html`):

```
transform.toString(); // "translate(-300,-200) scale(3)"
translate(0,0).toString(); // "translate(-300,-200) scale(3)"
scale(1).toString(): // "translate(-300,-200) scale(3)"
transform.apply([0,0]); // [-300,-200]
transform.applyX(0); // -300
transform.applyY(0); // -200
```

Inverting on 0,0 will change the signs of the x and y coordinates and divide them by the scale factor. Since $k = 3$, each coordinate will be divided by 3, as follows:

```
transform.invert([0,0]); // [100, 66.6667] // inverts coordinates and
transform.invertX(0); // 100 // divides by k = 3
transform.invertY(0); // 66.6667
```

Inverting is important for reversing a transform. In a semantic zoom, you may use it to undo transforms applied to objects that shouldn't be scaled or moved when zooming.

The *d3-zoom* module also contains two special methods that apply transforms on copies of existing scales, which can be used in the semantic zooming of Cartesian charts to update data and axes, as we did in the brushing examples. These methods are described in the following table:

Method	Description
rescaleX (*xScale*)	Returns a copy of the given continuous scale, *xScale*, with the current x transform applied to its domain.
rescaleY (*yScale*)	Returns a copy of the given continuous scale, *yScale*, with the current y transform applied to its domain.

d3.zoomTransform() methods used for rescaling.

In the following example, we will add semantic zooming to a scatter chart we created in `Chapter 5`, *Scales, Axes, and Colors*. The goal is to only zoom the object that contains the data points and update the axes so that they correctly represent the new data view. Only relevant code fragments will be shown next. You can see the full code in `Zoom/15-zoom-xy.html`.

The view configuration consists of the `svg` object, a `chart` object that contains all chart elements and is positioned inside the SVG with a small margin, and a `view` object where the data points will be drawn, as shown in the following code. This will also be the zoomable object:

```
const svg = d3.select("svg");
const margin = 75,
    width = svg.attr("width") - margin*2,
    height = svg.attr("height") - margin*2;

const radius = 4; // the radius of each dot
const format = d3.format("$,.0f");

// Clipping path to use in zoomable view
svg.append("defs")
    .append("clipPath").attr("id", "chart")
    .append("rect")
    .attr("width", width)
    .attr("height", height);
// All elements are added to this object
const chart = svg.append("g")
    .attr("transform", `translate(${[margin,margin]})`);

// The zoomable parts are added to this object
const view = chart.append("g") // the unclipped zoomable object
    .attr("class", "view")
    .attr("clip-path", "url(#chart)")
    .append("g") // the clipped zoomable object
```

The `height` and `width` constants are the height and width of the `chart` object, not of the `svg` object. This will simplify the configuration of the zoom object's viewport extent.

The `zoom` object is configured next. The current zoom transform is saved in `currentZoom` so that it can be applied to different methods. The `extent` is defined as the size of the chart object. During zooming, new scales are applied to both `axisX` and `axisY` functions (which also need to be called again from their groups' selections, `xG` and `yG`). The size of the dots doesn't change during zooming because an inverse scale transform is applied to each radius, as shown in the following code:

```
// Zoom configuration
let currentZoom = d3.zoomIdentity; // save the current zoom
const extent = [[0,0],[width, height]];

const zoom = d3.zoom()
        .scaleExtent([1, 3]) // can enlarge up to 3 times
```

```
        .extent(extent).translateExtent(extent)
        .on('zoom', function() {
            currentZoom = d3.event.transform; // calculate new zoom
transform
            // rescale positions and dots
            view.attr("transform", currentZoom); // transform view
            d3.selectAll("circle.dot")
                    .attr("r", radius/currentZoom.k) // semantic scaling

            // rescale scales and axes
            axisX.scale(currentZoom.rescaleX(scaleX));
            axisY.scale(currentZoom.rescaleY(scaleY));
            xG.call(axisX);
            yG.call(axisY);
        })
        .on('end', function() {
            if(d3.event.transform.k <= 1 + 1e-6) {
                d3.select("#zoom-reset").style("opacity", 0);
            } else {
                d3.select("#zoom-reset").style("opacity", 1);
            }
        });
svg.call(zoom);
```

The *end* event handler hides or shows the button used to zoom back to the chart's original dimensions. This button was added in HTML and the following code transforms the view back to its initial state:

```
// Button to reset zoom
d3.select("#zoom-reset")
.on("click", function() {
    this.style.opacity = 0;
    svg.transition().duration(750).call(zoom.transform, d3.zoomIdentity);
    currentZoom = d3.zoomIdentity;
});
```

Certain methods must be adapted for semantic zooming. The showDetails() method is called when the user hovers the mouse over a point. Besides showing tooltips, it increases the size of the point. In the original code, this is done by applying a larger radius value to the circle, but with zooming, that radius will be scaled as well. Applying an inverse transformation, such as the one applied in the *zoom* listener for all dots, will keep the size of the selected dot constant, in any zoom factor, as shown in the following code:

```
d3.select(this).attr("r", radius * 3 / currentZoom.k);
```

The following screenshots illustrate the effect of zooming into an area in the chart. Note that the size of the dots does not change, and the scales are adjusted to the visible data:

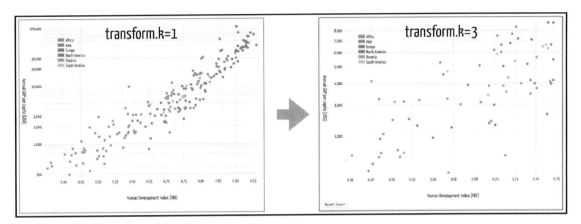

Using zooming in a scatterplot. Code: *Zoom/15-zoom-xy.html*.

You can also apply semantic zooming to a single axis. In a line chart, such as the GISS global warming line chart we used in this chapter, you only need to zoom in and out of the *x* axis, as follows:

```
const extent = [[0,0],[width, height]];
const zoom = d3.zoom()
        .scaleExtent([1, 100]).extent(extent).translateExtent(extent)
        .on('zoom', zoomed);
svg.call(zoom);

function zoomed() {
    const t = d3.event.transform;
    const newScaleX = t.rescaleX(scaleX) // rescale x-scales and x-axes
    axisX.scale(newScaleX);
    axisX.tickFormat(d => d3.timeFormat(d.getMonth() == 0 ? "%Y"
    : "%b")(d));
    xG.call(axisX);

    line.x(d => newScaleX(d3.isoParse(d.Date))) // rescale x-scale data
    d3.select(".line").datum(data.values).attr("d", line);
}
```

The following diagram shows the line chart after applying several zoom transforms. You can see and run the full code for this example from `Zoom/16-zoom-x.html`:

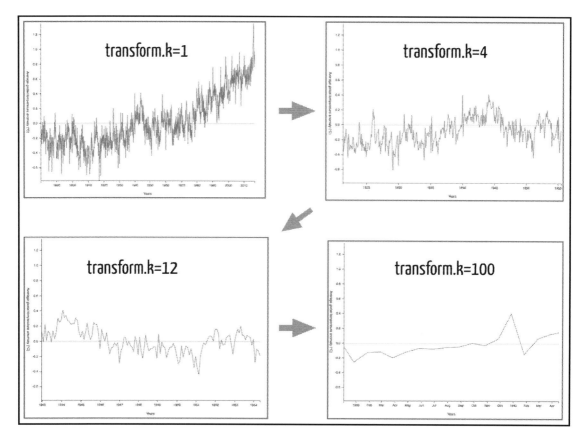

Semantic zooming used to zoom in and view details in a line chart. Code: *Zoom/16-zoom-x.html*.

Zooming and other interactive behaviors is an essential feature in any web-based data visualization. You will see many more examples in the remaining chapters of this book.

Summary

This chapter covered the fundamental libraries, functions, and methods in D3 that implement several types of interactive behaviors, which are essential in most web-based data visualizations, where interactivity is not an optional feature. You learned how to dispatch and handle native and custom events, apply and configure animated transitions, and configure drag, brush, and zoom behaviors for any chart. With this chapter, we finally covered all the basics.

In the next chapter, we will start exploring advanced charts, such as hierarchical trees and networks, and you will have the opportunity to apply much of what you learned in this and previous chapters.

References

- Module documentation, D3.js: `github.com/d3/d3-selection`, `github.com/d3/d3-dispatch`, `github.com/d3/d3-timer`, `github.com/d3/d3-transition`, `github.com/d3/d3-ease`, `github.com/d3/d3-drag`, `github.com/d3/d3-brush`, `github.com/d3/d3-zoom`.
- DOM Events, W3C: `www.w3.org/TR/2013/WD-DOM-Level-3-Events-20131105/`
- Brush and Zoom: Focus and Context, by Mike Bostock: `bl.ocks.org/mbostock/34f08d5e11952a80609169b7917d4172`
- Brush and Zoom II: Zoom to Region, by Mike Bostock: `bl.ocks.org/mbostock/f48fcdb929a620ed97877e4678ab15e6`
- Easing, by Mike Bostock: `bl.ocks.org/mbostock/248bac3b8e354a9103c4`
- Ocean temperatures: `Data/monthly_json.json`. GISTEMP Team, 2019: GISS Surface Temperature Analysis (GISTEMP). NASA Goddard Institute for Space Studies. Dataset accessed 2019-02-01 at data.giss.nasa.gov/gistemp/. Hansen, J., R. Ruedy, M. Sato, and K. Lo, 2010: Global surface temperature change, Rev. Geophys., 48, RG4004, doi:10.1029/2010RG000345.
- GDP and HDI dataset: `Data/un_regions_gdp.csv`. Compiled from several sources, including United Nations (World Population Prospects 2017: `www.un.org`) and World Bank (World bank public data. `data.worldbank.org`)

Visualizing Hierarchical Data

9

Efficient data visualizations benefit from different views of the same data, and fields sometimes can be organized in such a way as to reveal relationships with other data, forming hierarchical structures. In this chapter, you will learn how to prepare a dataset so that it can be used to represent a hierarchy, using nesting techniques and tools provided by the d3-hierarchy module.

There are many ways to represent hierarchies. In this module you will learn how to use generator functions that prepare hierarchical data so that it can be rendered as a tree or dendograms, but you can use the same data to generate other popular hierarchical visualizations, such as treemaps, circle packs, and partitions. You will learn how to create each one of them in this chapter through simple examples that are based on the same hierarchical dataset.

In this chapter, you will learn how to do the following:

- Hierarchical data
- Node-link diagrams
- Partitions
- Enclosure diagrams
- Interactive visualizations

Hierarchical data

D3 provides several layout functions that transform hierarchical data structures by adding properties and methods that facilitate their rendering as hierarchical visualizations. While D3 doesn't automatically generate hierarchical charts, it computes coordinates, angles, distances, and other values that can easily be bound to properties of SVG circles, rectangles, lines, curves, and text, using the general update pattern.

A hierarchical dataset is a recursive structure that contains objects that link to a parent node and an array of child nodes. Nodes that have no children are leaf nodes; the root node has a null parent. We created some hierarchical structures in `Chapter 4`, Data Binding with the `d3.nest()` and `d3.group()` functions. Layout functions for hierarchical visualizations provided by D3 require a specific format for the hierarchical data, and expect certain properties with standard names. This structure is provided by layout generator functions available in the d3-hierarchy module, which is included in the default bundle.

A standard hierarchical layout

The `d3.hierarchy()` generator function receives a root node from an existing hierarchical structure and transforms it by adding standard properties and methods. The resulting structure can be used with layout generator functions to create visualizations such as trees, treemaps, and partitions.

The `d3.hierarchy()` function doesn't create hierarchies from flat data. Your data should already contain a hierarchy, that is, it should at least have a node containing a set of child nodes. When generating a standard hierarchy you will need to pass a reference to the node that contains an array of child nodes. If the child nodes array is stored in a property called `children`, you just need to pass the root node reference:

```
const result = d3.hierarchy(rootNode);
```

Otherwise, you must provide an accessor function as the second argument. For example, consider the following hierarchy, which contains the tributaries of the Amazon River (obtained from the JSON data in `Data/amazon-river.json`):

```
const amazon = {
    name: "Amazon",
    length_km: 6992,
    tributaries: [
        {name: "Trombetas", length_km: 760},
        {name: "Negro",length_km: 2250,
         tributaries: [{name: "Branco",length_km: 560},
                       {name: "Vaupés",length_km: 1050}]
        },
        // ... 11 more elements
    ]
}
```

In this hierarchy, the property that contains the child nodes is not called `children`, but `tributaries`. To create a standard hierarchy an accessor function that returns the data for the `children` property is included as the second parameter, as shown below (see `Hierarchy/1-hierarchy-rivers.html`):

```
const result = d3.hierarchy(amazon, d => d.tributaries);
```

This creates the following modified hierarchical data structure stored in `result`:

```
{
   data: {name: "Amazon", length_km: 6992, tributaries: [...]},
   depth: 0,
   height: 3,
   parent: null,
   children: [
      {
       data: {name: "Trombetas", length_km: 760},
        depth: 1,
        height: 0,
        parent: (reference to root node)
      }, {
        data: {name: "Negro", length_km: "2250", tributaries: [...]},
        depth: 1,
        height: 1,
        parent: (reference to root node),
        children: [
          {data: {...}, height: 0, depth: 2, parent: h1, value: 1}
          {data: {...}, height: 0, depth: 2, parent: h1, value: 1}
        ]
      },
      // ... 11 more elements
   ]
}
```

All the original data is preserved in the `data` property, but several new properties are added for each node. These properties have standard names used by layout generators. They are all are generated at initialization except `value`, which requires an additional configuration step.

Property	Contents
data	This property contains the original data.
children	If not a leaf node, this property contains an array of references to child nodes.
parent	If not root node, this property contains a reference to the parent node.

value	The node value (which is required by several layout generator functions to compute coordinates). The *value* property is only set after a call to *count()* or *sum()*.
depth	The depth of the node in the hierarchy. Only the root has *depth = 0*.
height	The height of the node. Only leaves have *height = 0*.

Properties that are generated for each node from a hierarchical structure transformed by d3.hierarchy()

For most of the examples in this chapter will use small datasets with simple hierarchical data. Larger examples with real data are provided in the Examples/directory (from the GitHub repository for this chapter), but starting with small datasets will make it easier to understand and inspect the changes applied by that each generator function.

To demonstrate how d3.hierarchy() works we will use the simpleHierarchy object declared in the JavaScript/simple_hierarchical_data.js file. It is a hierarchical object and has the following structure:

```
const simpleHierarchy = {
    id: "root", name:"Root Level",
    children: [
        { id: "group_1", name:"First Group",
          children: [
            {   id: "subg_1", name:"First Subgroup",
                children: [
                    { id:"leaf_1",name:"First Leaf", values: [5,2] },
                    { id:"leaf_2",name:"Second Leaf",values: [1,7] },
                    { id:"leaf_3",name:"Third Leaf", values: [4,4] }]
            },
            {   id: "subg_2", name:"Second Subgroup",
                children: [
                    { id: "leaf_4",name:"Fourth Leaf",values: [9,3] },
                    { id: "leaf_5",name:"Fifth Leaf", values: [7,6] }]
            }]
        },
        { id: "group_2", name:"Second Group", children: [ /* ... */ ] },
        { id: "leaf_15",name:"Fifteenth Leaf",values: [8,8] },
        { id: "leaf_16",name:"Sixteenth Leaf",values: [3,9] }
    ]
};
```

You can access this object in any HTML file that loads its JavaScript file. Include the following at the beginning of your HTML page:

```
<script src="../JavaScript/simple_hierarchical_data.js"></script>
```

We need to transform this hierarchy so that it can be used in the layout functions. Since it already contains a property called `children` linking to the child nodes, the second parameter is not necessary:

```
const root = d3.hierarchy(simpleHierarchy);
```

Use your browser's JavaScript console to inspect the root object. You will notice that each node has the following properties: `depth`, `height`, `parent`, `children` and `data`. The `children` property was used from the original hierarchy, but all its nodes were also modified with these properties. The `data` property contains the original unmodified hierarchy. The `depth` property says how deep a node is in the hierarchy (it is zero for the root), and the `height` property informs the distance from its most distant leaf (it is zero for the leaves).

Several methods were also generated. The ones listed in the following table are used to *configure* the hierarchy. They can be used to set the `value` property or recursively generate additional properties for each node, transform and sort nodes. All these methods return the current node and can be chained together.

Method	Description
sum (function)	This method sets the *value* property for each descendant node. The property contains the sum of the values returned by each child node and their descendants. The function is called for each *d* node. This function or `count()` must be called before using a treemap, partition, or circle pack.
count ()	This method sets the *value* property for each descendant node as the sum of all the leaves. If the node is a leaf, its `value` property will be one. This function or `sum()` must be called before using a treemap, partition, or circle pack.
sort (function)	This method sorts the children of the caller node. It receives a comparator function that is called for each pair of nodes *a,b* and descendants.
each (function)	This method invokes an arbitrary function for each d node in breadth-first order (after the preceding and descending nodes).
eachBefore (function)	This method invokes an arbitrary function for each d node in pre-order traversal (after the ancestor nodes).
eachAfter (function)	This method invokes an arbitrary function for each d node in post-order traversal (after the descendant nodes).

Methods that recursively modify nodes in a hierarchy

A typical configuration is shown below:

```
const root = d3.hierarchy(simpleHierarchy)
            .count()
            .sort((a,b) => b.height - a.height || a.value - b.value)
            .each(function(d) { d.order = ++order; });
```

Let's experiment with these methods, load a page containing the `simpleHierarchy` object and then run the following code examples using the JavaScript console (this code is also available in `Hierarchy/2-methods-config.html` which prints the values so you can view them in the console).

The `value` property is required by several layout generators, and can be computed for each node with the `sum()` or `count()` methods (if it doesn't already exist). If you print the `value` property of any node after creating the hierarchy above, it will be *undefined*:

```
console.log(root.value); // undefined
```

Calling `count()` will generate a `value` property for each node in the hierarchy. Each leaf will then have `value` = **1**, and each non-leaf node will contain the sum of all its descendant leaves:

```
root.count(); // this recursively sets value property based on leaf-count
console.log(root.value); // 16 (there are 16 leaves in the hierarchy)
console.log(root.descendants().map(d => d.value)); // [16,5,9,...,1,1,1]
```

The **sum()** method selects values to be summed for each node. The following function will return **1** for each node. Leaves will contain **1**, and other nodes will contain the sum of the values of their children.

```
root.sum(d => 1);
console.log(root.value); // 24 (there are 24 nodes in the hierarchy)
console.log(root.descendants().map(d => d.value)); // [24,8,13,...,1,1,1]
```

If the node has a specific property with data that should be added, then you can use it. In this specific example, each node has a `values` array with two elements. This code will set a `value` property in each node with a cumulative sum of the first element of the `values` array of its descendants:

```
root.sum(d => d.values ? d.values[0] : 0);
console.log(root.value); // 75 (value = cumulative sum of node.values[0])
```

Since the `values` array in this hierarchy only exists in leaves, you can use the following code to implement `count()` using `sum()`:

```
root.sum(d => d.values ? 1 : 0 ); // value = leaf count: same as
root.count()
console.log(root.value); // 16
```

Using `height` or other properties that added by `d3.hierarchy` in the method above fails, since these properties may not have been added yet. But it works if you use `copy()` to make a deep copy of the hierarchy before calling `sum()`:

```
root.sum(d => d.height ? 1 : 0);        // will not generate node.value
root.copy().sum(d => d.height ? 1 : 0); // will generate node.value
```

Some hierarchical charts may need the data in some sorted order. The following code sorts sibling nodes by `height`, placing the nodes that are higher in the hierarchy first (leaves have `height` equal to zero), and by descending value:

```
root.sort((a,b) => b.height - a.height || a.value - b.value);
console.log(root.descendants()); // sorted array with all descendants
```

The `eachAfter()`, `eachBefore()` and `each()` methods allow arbitrary functions to be invoked during the traversal of the hierarchy. You can use them to transform the structure of the hierarchy, modify or add properties. The following code generates a label string for each node in a hierarchical format (e.g. 3, 3.1, 3.1.1, etc.) and stores it an a new property called `number`:

```
root.eachBefore(function(d) {
    if(!d.parent) {
        d.number = 1;
    } else {
        d.number = `${d.parent.number}.${d.parent.children.indexOf(d)+1}`;
    }
});
```

The hierarchy also contains methods that return selected data. They can be called for any node. You will use them to extract the data you need to generate visualizations. The following table lists these methods :

Method	Description
ancestors()	This returns an array with all the ancestors of the node. This is the array you will use to generate nodes for trees, clusters, treemaps, circle packs and partitions.
descendants()	This returns an array with all the descendants of the node.

leaves()	This method returns an array with all the leaves of the node.
links()	This method returns an array of link objects for each descendant node. Each link object connects a source node to a target node among its children; the format of this is *{source: node, target: child}*.
path(*target*)	Called on a source node, this method returns the shortest path to a provided target node, as an ordered list of nodes.
copy()	This method returns a deep copy of the subtree starting at the caller node. The returned node is a new hierarchy, with depth zero, and a null parent.

Methods that return selected data from a node in a hierarchy

Use your browser's JavaScript console to experiment with these methods or run `Hierarchy/3-methods-nodes.html` which contains code examples using these methods with the `root` object configured above.

The following illustration describes the nodes that are returned from each method in the preceding table:

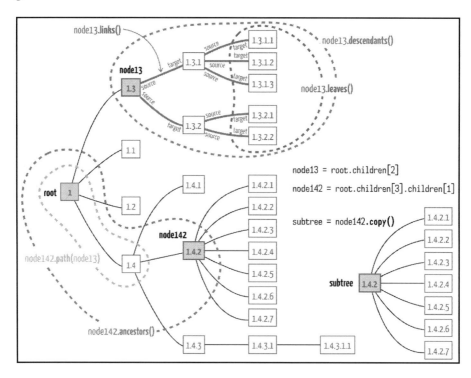

d3.hierarchy() methods that return selected nodes. Code: *Hierarchy/3-methods-nodes.html*

Creating hierarchical structures

Sometimes, hierarchical data is organized differently. For example, consider the following tabular CSV structure stored below in `refTable` (from `JavaScript/simple_hierarchical_data.js`) where the `Context` column of each entry contains a reference to the `Id` column of another entry:

```
const refTable = `Id,Name,Context,Value1,Value2
root,Root,,,,
group_1,First Group,root,,,
group_2,Second Group,root,,,
subg_1,First Subgroup,group_1,,,
subg_2,Second Subgroup,group_1,,,
subg_3,Third Subgroup,group_2,,,
subg_4,Fourth Subgroup,group_2,,,
subsubg_1,First Sub-Subroup,subg_4,,,
leaf_1,First Leaf,subg_1,5,2
leaf_2,Second Leaf,subg_1,1,7
leaf_3,Third Leaf,subg_1,4,4
```

D3 contains several tools to reorganize such structures into a hierarchical format that can be used by layout functions for different visualizations. In a previous chapter, we learned how to use the `d3.nest()` function (from the *d3-array* module). It can be used to transform some types of tabular data into hierarchies. Another tool is `d3.stratify()`, which creates a standard hierarchy from tabular data that contains link references.

The `d3.stratify()` function requires an ID and a parent ID for each node. These are configured via the accessor functions in two methods:

Method	Description
`id`(*accessor*)	This method returns the ID for each node. The default is `d => d.id`.
`parentId`(*accessor*)	This method returns the ID reference to the parent node. The default is `d => d.parentId`.

The configuration methods for d3.stratify()

The following code takes the tabular data obtained from parsing the `refTable` string and returns a standard `d3.hierarchy` structure that can be used by layout function generators:

```
const jsonTable = d3.csvParse(refTable);
const stratify = d3.stratify()
                    .id(d => d.Id)
                    .parentId(d => d.Context);
const root = stratify(jsonTable);
```

Use your browser's JavaScript console to inspect the generated result. You can run the code available in `Hierarchy/4-stratify.html`.

The Amazon River tributaries data file was originally stored in a CSV, shown in the following code:

```
Tributary,Confluence,km
Amazon,,6992
Trombetas,Amazon,760
Negro,Amazon,2250
Branco,Negro,560
Vaupés,Negro,1050
...
Iriri,Xingu,1300
Tocantins,Amazon,2639
Araguaia,Tocantins,2627
```

This is a format that can be stratified, using the `Confluence` column as the parent ID, and the `Tributary` column as the ID (see `Hierarchy/5-stratify-rivers.html`):

```
const stratify = d3.stratify()
                    .id(d => d.Tributary)
                    .parentId(d => d.Confluence);
const root = stratify(result);
```

The resulting structure is very similar to the one generated from the JSON file (actually, the only differences are the property names). Run the `Hierarchy/5-stratify-rivers.html` file and see the result in your browser's JavaScript console.

If your data doesn't fit the required structure for `d3.hierarchy` or `d3.stratify`, you might still be able to transform it. Data that has a tabular structure where each entry can be classified as one or more categories can be grouped using `d3.nest`, `d3.group` or `d3.rollup`, however you may have to perform additional transformations.

For example, if we didn't have `d3.stratify`, you could have used `d3.nest` to group rivers by their `Confluence`:

```
const nested =
   d3.nest().key(d => d.Confluence)
      .rollup(d => d.map(c => ({name: c.Tributary, length_km: +c.km})))
      .entries(result);
```

But to transform the `nested` array into a hierarchical JSON structure that can be used by `d3.hierarchy`, you need to create an object. The following recursive function performs the transformation:

```
function makeHierarchy(nested, childrenKey, item) {
    // builds root
    if(item == null || item.name == '') {
        const item = nested.filter(d => d.key == '')[0].value[0];
        return makeHierarchy(nested, childrenKey, item);
    }

    // if name is a key, it contains children
    const group = nested.filter(d => d.key == item.name)[0];
    if(group) {
        const elements = [];
        group.value.forEach(function(d) {
            const item = makeHierarchy(nested, childrenKey, d);
            elements.push(item);
        });
        item[childrenKey] = elements;
    }
    return item;
}
```

Now you can transform the nested array and generate a hierarchical object, which can then be used by `d3.hierarchy` to generate a standard hierarchy for a layout generator:

```
const hierarchy = makeHierarchy(nested, 'tributaries');
const root = d3.hierarchy(hierarchy, d => d.tributaries);
```

Of course you should always use `d3.stratify` if you can, since its much simpler. Creating a hierarchy with nesting functions is much more complex when you have to group multiple keys (see `Hierarchy/7-nest-countries.html`).

Layout generators

Once you have a standard hierarchy, you can use it co create a hierarchical visualization. There are many ways to display a hierarchy, and depending on the one you choose, you will need to perform additional computations to distribute shapes in your browser's viewport so that it renders an accurate visual representation. This involves calculating margins, applying scales and computing positions for each symbol that is bound to hierarchical data. Most of this work is done by a layout generator that takes a hierarchical dataset and computes properties for each node based on viewport parameters, such as height, width and margins.

The following table contains the five layout generator functions from the *d3-hierarchy* module that will be explored in the rest of this chapter. Each is configured to occupy an area specified in pixels, and returns a function that transforms a standard hierarchical structure, adding positioning properties to each node. These properties are used to draw rectangles, lines, circles, paths and to position text.

Function	Properties added to node	Description
d3.tree()	x, y	Creates a layout function for a tidy tree.
d3.cluster()	x, y	Creates a layout function for a dendogram.
d3.partition()	x0, x1, y0, y1 (*value* property must be set)	Creates a layout function for a partition.
d3.treemap()	x0, x1, y0, y1 (value property must be set)	Creates a layout function for a treemap.
d3.pack()	x, y, r (*value* property must be set)	Creates a layout function for a circle pack.

The generator functions for hierarchical layouts (from the d3-hierarchy module)

Unidirectional node-link diagrams

Unidirectional node-link diagrams are commonly referred to as *trees*. They display the topology of a hierarchy using marks for nodes and links. Nodes are usually rendered as dots, circles, rectangles, or some other symbol, and links are usually the lines that connect the dots. In some trees, only the leaf and root nodes are rendered, or only the links are displayed.

The following diagrams are examples of node-link diagrams created with D3. You can download the full code and data for all examples from the GitHub repository for this chapter:

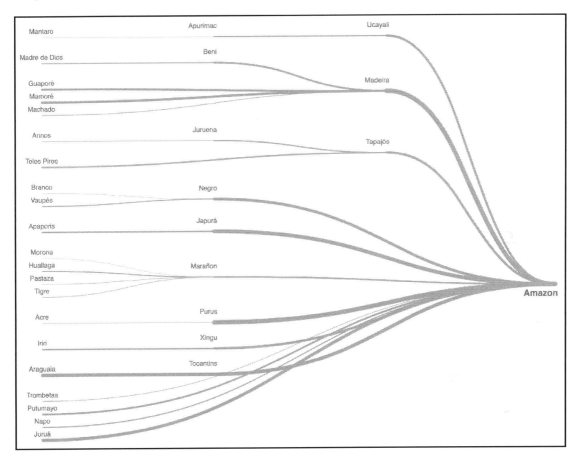

A dendogram showing the main tributaries of the Amazon river. Code: *Examples/dendogram-5-amazon-river.html.*

The next illustration is a radial dendogram displaying the names of all the countries in the Eurasian supercontinent, classified by continents (Asia and Europe) and United Nations regions. The data is from the `Data/un_regions.csv` CSV file, transformed using `d3.nest` and `d3.hierarchy`.

There are several other representations of this data in the `Examples/` folder, using trees, radial trees, circle packs, partitions and treemaps.

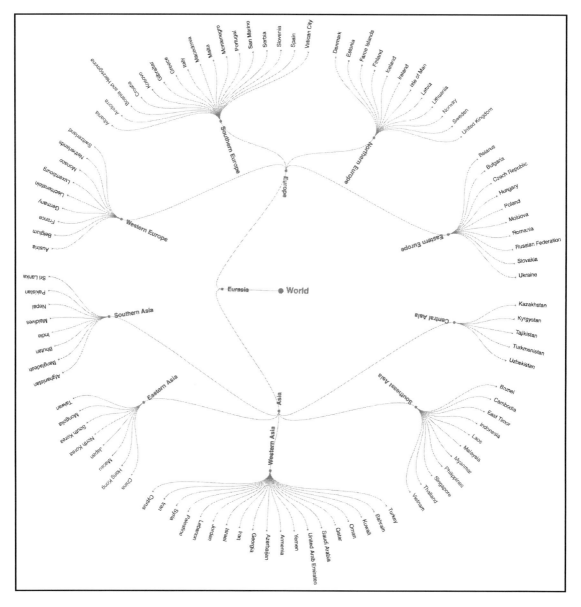

A radial tree visualization of countries in Eurasia by continent and UN region. Code: *Examples/radial-tree-1-eurasia.html*.

The following hierarchical data visualization displays the Sun, its planets and their largest satellites as nodes in a tree, using solar system data obtained from NASA compiled in the `Data/planets.json` file. The diameters of each node are proportional to the actual diameters of the Sun, planets and moons.

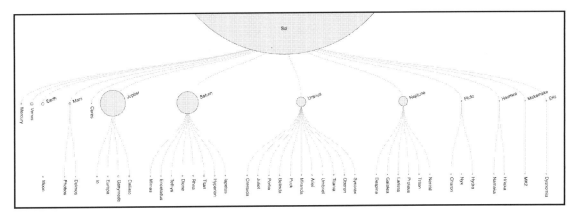

A tree visualization of the sun. planets. and selected moons. Code: *Examples/tree-5-planets.html*.

Trees and dendograms

D3 supports two different types of tree: the *tidy* tree, which renders a compact view of the algorithm by placing nodes of the same level side-by-side; and the *cluster* or *dendogram*, which places all the leaves at the same level. The following diagram illustrates both tree types rendering the same data:

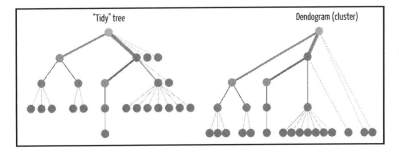

Two different tree layouts available in D3.

A tidy tree layout function is created with the d3.tree() generator function. A dendogram is created with d3.cluster(). In a tree layout, nodes of the same depth are placed side-by-side. In a cluster layout, all leaves are rendered at the last level. Tree layout functions receive hierarchical data and generate *x* and *y* coordinates for each node.

Configuration methods determine the space used by the chart and spacing between nodes of the same level. The default size for a tree is 1x1 pixels. Dimensions are specified using either the size() or nodeSize() methods. The configuration methods are listed in the following table:

Function	Description
size (*array*)	If called with an array of numbers (or a function that returns an array), this function determines the dimensions of the entire chart. The x and y coordinates for each node will be computed within the bounds provided by the array.
nodeSize (*array*)	If called with an array of numbers (or a function that returns an array), this function determines the size of each node, and ignores any limits defined by size(). The root node will be positioned at 0,0 and the coordinates for the other nodes will be computed considering the size for each node, so that the tree will be as compact as possible. If called without arguments, this function returns an array with the current node dimensions.
separation (*function*)	If a function is specified, it should return the separation between nodes (where 1 corresponds to the width of one node). The default separation is defined by the function: (a,b) => a.parent == b.parent ? 1 : 2.

The configuration methods for d3.tree() and d3.cluster() layout functions

The following code creates a layout function for a tree that will be displayed within a rectangle that is 880 pixels wide and 480 pixels tall:

```
const tree = d3.tree().size([880,480]);
```

This configuration guarantees that all coordinates of the chart will have values within those bounds, but labels and node symbols positioned at these points may be clipped out if their dimensions exceed these limits. There is also no guarantee that nodes won't overlap.

An alternative way to specify the dimension is to use nodeSize(). This method determines the space that should be occupied by each node. If the nodeSize() method is used, size() will be ignored and the root node will be positioned at 0,0.

The following code creates a function for a dendogram (cluster) with nodes that are 150 pixels tall and 50 pixels wide. If the node symbols and text are placed within these bounds, nodes and text won't ever overlap, but the size of the final tree may exceed the available space:

```
const tree = d3.cluster().nodeSize([50,150]);
```

Once the layout function is created, you can use it to generate a tree layout by passing it a hierarchical structure. The following code receives the simple hierarchy used in previous examples, generating *x* and *y* coordinates for each node:

```
const root = d3.hierarchy(simpleHierarchy); // generates hierarchy data
const tree = d3.tree().size([880,480]);     // generates layout function
const treeData = tree(root);                // generates node coordinates
```

If you print the `treeData` object in the JavaScript console, you will notice that each node now has *x* and *y* coordinates containing pixel values for each node:

```
▼hl 🔵
  ▼children: Array(4)
    ▼0: hl
      ▶children: (2) [hl, hl]
      ▶data: {id: "group_1", name: "First Group", children: Array(2)}
        depth: 1
        height: 2
      ▶parent: hl {data: {…}, height: 4, depth: 0, parent: null, children: Array(4), …}
        x: 194.11764705882354
        y: 120
      ▶__proto__: Object
    ▶1: hl {data: {…}, height: 3, depth: 1, parent: hl, children: Array(3), …}
    ▶2: hl {data: {…}, height: 0, depth: 1, parent: hl, x: 621.1764705882354, …}
    ▶3: hl {data: {…}, height: 0, depth: 1, parent: hl, x: 672.9411764705883, …}
      length: 4
    ▶__proto__: Array(0)
  ▶data: {id: "root", name: "Root Level", children: Array(4)}
    depth: 0
    height: 4
    parent: null
    x: 433.5294117647059
    y: 0
```

The console view of hierarchical data transformed by a tree layout function. Code: *Tree/1-nodes.html*.

Now let's select some SVG elements and bind them to these coordinates and draw the nodes. The following code will set the graphics context for the chart. The `chart` object allows a small margin so that circles (with less than 60 pixels in radius) can be drawn around the root coordinates without being clipped:

```
const svg = d3.select("body")
              .append("svg")
              .attr("height", 600)
```

```
                        .attr("width", 1000);
    const chart = svg.append("g")
                        .attr("transform", d => `translate(${[60,60]})`);
```

The tree's nodes can be obtained from the data object by calling the `descendants()` method (which was generated by `d3.hierarchy()`). It returns an array with all nodes, including the root:

```
    const nodes = treeData.descendants();
```

We use the `nodes` array to configure color scale. The following scale selects different colors for nodes of different `depth`, so that nodes at the same level in the tree will have the same color:

```
    const colorScale = d3.scaleOrdinal(d3.schemeCategory10)
                        .domain(d3.extent(nodes, n => n.depth));
```

Binding each node in the `nodes` array to an SVG circle will allow you to access the generated `x` and `y` properties, which can be used as the circle's origin:

```
    chart.selectAll("circle")
        .data( nodes ).
        .join("circle")
        .attr("r", 20)
        .attr("cx", d => d.x)
        .attr("cy", d => d.y)
        .attr("fill", d => colorScale(d.depth));
```

This will produce the result shown in the following image (see `Tree/1-nodes.html`):

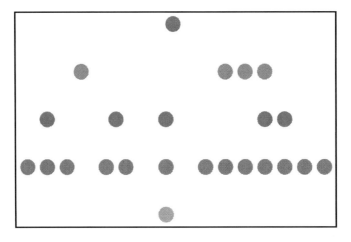

A tree visualization with nodes represented as circles: the root is positioned on top. Code: *Tree/1-nodes.html*.

Now we need to draw lines connecting each node to its parent, which can be accessed through the *parent* property of each node. This is shown in the following code where we are using a width scale so that lines arriving at nodes with greater *height* will be thicker:

```
const widthScale = d3.scaleLinear().range([1,16])
                      .domain(d3.extent(nodes, n => n.height));

chart.selectAll("line")
    .data(nodes.filter( d => d.parent))
    .join("line")
    .attr("x1", d => d.parent.x)
    .attr("y1", d => d.parent.y)
    .attr("x2", d => d.x)
    .attr("y2", d => d.y)
    .style("stroke-width", d => widthScale(d.height))
    .style("opacity", d => d.depth *.25 * .6 + .4)
```

The result is shown as follows:

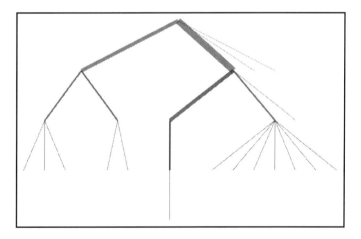

Visualization of a tree with links represented as lines between nodes and parents. Code: *Tree/2-links-from-nodes.html*

An alternative way to obtain the line coordinates is by using the `links()` method, called on the root element. It returns an array of link objects, each one containing a `source` and a `target` property with *x,y* coordinates. One advantage of using this method is that it integrates better with layout functions that generate fancy path links, which we will use later.

The following code will bind each line to a *link* object, and produce the same result (see `Tree/3-links.html`):

```
chart.selectAll("line")
    .data(treeData.links())
    .enter()
    .append("line")
    .attr("x1", d => d.source.x)
    .attr("y1", d => d.source.y)
    .attr("x2", d => d.target.x)
    .attr("y2", d => d.target.y)
    .attr("stroke-width", d => (d.target.height + 1)*(d.target.height +
1))
    .attr("stroke", "black")
    .attr("opacity", d => d.target.depth *.25 * .6 + .4);
```

By drawing the lines first, and then the circles, you will have a complete tree displaying nodes and links as shown below (see `Tree/4-tree.html`):

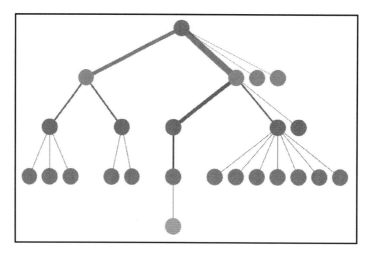

The visualization of a tree displaying nodes as circles, and links as lines. Code: *Tree/4-tree.html*.

To make the radius of the circle larger as it's higher in the hierarchy, return a value for `r` proportional to the `height` property of each node (see `Tree/5-tree-node-radius.html`):

```
.attr("r", d => (d.height + 1) * 10)
```

It's also easy to transform the tree into a *dendogram*. Just use `d3.cluster()` instead of `d3.tree()` (see `Tree/6-cluster.html`):

```
const tree = d3.cluster()
                .size([width-120,height-120]);
```

The results of these changes can be seen as follows:

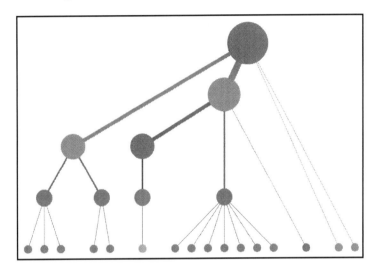

A dendogram (tree with leaf nodes at the same level) with circle radii proportional to node-height

You can place labels near or inside the nodes using the *x,y* coordinates as an anchor. Let's generate a field with text for each node. The code below adds a `number` property to each node containing a hierarchical numbering label (1, 1.1, 1.1.1, etc.):

```
root.eachBefore(function(d) {
    if(!d.parent) {
        d.number = 1;
    } else {
        d.number = `${d.parent.number}.${d.parent.children.indexOf(d) +
1}`;
    }
});
```

The `d.number` property is used below for the text contents of each node. The text is rotated and placed outside the nodes if it's a leaf (if `d.height` is zero). The font size is also scaled according to the node's height (see *Tree/8-labels.html*):

```
chart.selectAll("text")
    .data(nodes).join("text")
    .attr("x", d => d.x)
    .attr("y", d => d.y)
    .text(d => d.number) // number generated above
    .attr("transform", d =>`rotate(-90,${[d.x, d.y]}) translate(-15,5)`)
    .style("text-anchor", d => d.height != 0 ? "start" : "end")
    .style("font-size", d => 12 + widthScale(d.height));
```

Adding labels to each node is easier if each datum is bound to a group container (`<g>`) instead of a `<circle>`. The group can be translated to the node's coordinates, and have the circle appended as a child (see `Tree/9-groups-nodes.html`):

```
chart.selectAll("g")
    .data(nodes).join("g").attr("class", "node")
    .attr("transform", d => `translate(${[d.x, d.y]})`)
    .append("circle")
      .attr("r", d => (d.height + 1) * 10)
      .style("fill", d => colorScale(d.depth));
```

Now we can append a text element as a child of the group, without using the text's x or y attributes. The following code also improves the way the text is placed near or inside each node, changing its color and orientation if it's a leaf or a node with children:

```
chart.selectAll("g.node").append("text").text(d => d.number)
    .style("fill", d => d.height != 0 ? 'white' : 'black')
    .attr("transform", d => d.height == 0 ? `rotate(-90) translate(-15,5)`
                                          : "translate(0,5)")
    .style("text-anchor", d => d.height != 0 ? "middle" : "end")
    .style("font-size", d => 12 + widthScale(d.height));
```

The final result is shown in the following image. See also `Tree/10-labels-children.html` which adds a label to each node that has children, displaying the amount of descendant leaves:

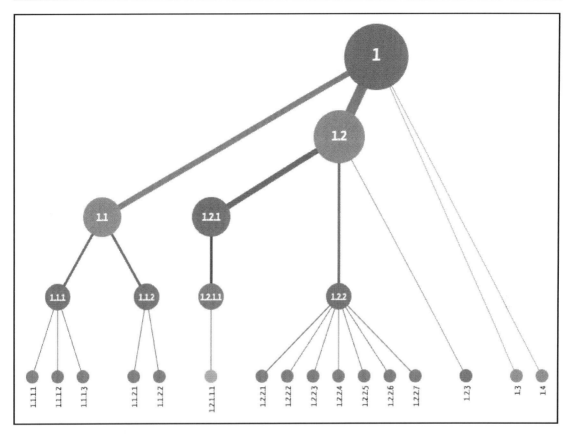

A dendogram with labels (d.height is used to rotate the labels for the leaves). Code: *Tree/9-groups-nodes.html.*

Path links

Nodes can be connected using lines created with an SVG `<path>` (instead of `<line>`) element, which allows much more flexibility and can be used to render curves. The *d3-shape* module contains three generator functions that create text contents for the `<path>` element's *d* attribute. A link generator function receives a standard link object, with two properties: *source* and *target*, each containing nodes with coordinates that are used to generate the path.

Configuration methods can be used in case the data needs to be transformed before use or if the coordinates are stored in different keys:

Function	Configuration methods	Description
d3.linkHorizontal()	.x (function) and .y (*function*)	Creates a function to generate horizontal lines. Configuration methods should be used with accessor functions for the data values of each coordinate (the *d* datum is *source* or *target*), if they aren't the default *d.x* and *d.y* .
d3.linkVertical()	.x (*function*) and .y (*function*)	Creates a function to generate vertical lines. Configuration methods should be used to swap *x* and *y* values, if necessary.
d3.linkRadial()	.angle (*function*) and .radius (*function*)	Creates a function to generate radial lines. Configuration methods specify which coordinate is the *angle*, and which is the *radius*, and make any necessary transformations.

Generator functions for path links (part of the d3-shape module)

All link generator functions also support the context() method, which takes a Canvas context. If configured with context, instead of returning an SVG path string, a call to the link function will cause it to generate a sequence of path method calls on the current Canvas context.

For example, consider the following link object (containing non-standard nodes):

```
const linkObject = {
    source: {a: 150, b: 0},
    target: {a: 50,  b: 100}
};
```

A vertical link function can be created using the following code, mapping *a* to *x*, and *b* to *y*:

```
const verticalLink = d3.linkVertical()
        .x(d => d.x)
        .y(d => d.y);
```

When the new function receives a link object as a parameter, it returns a path data string:

```
const result = verticalLink(linkObject); // "M150,0C150,50,50,50,50,100"
```

To use the function in our chart, replace `line` for `path` and all the line attributes for the `d` attribute, mapping each datum to the `verticalLink()` function:

```
chart.selectAll("path")
    .data(links).join('path')
    .attr("d", verticalLink) // d => verticalLink (d)
```

The result is shown as follows (see `Tree/10-pathlinks.html`):

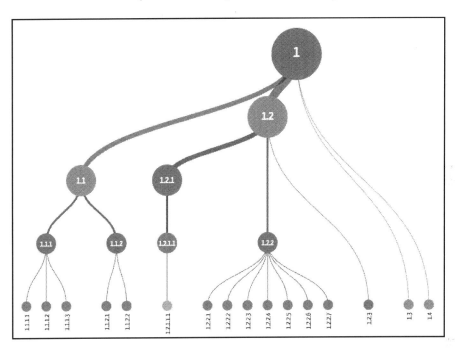

A dendogram with links represented by SVG curves. Code: *Tree/10-pathlinks.html.*

Horizontal trees

If you switch *x* for *y*, the tree will be drawn sideways, with the root on the left-hand side. The path link generator, in this case, requires configuration, since the coordinates have to be swapped:

```
const horizontalLink = d3.linkHorizontal()
        .x(function(d) { return d.y; })
        .y(function(d) { return d.x; });
```

Node elements need to be translated by using *d.y* as *x*, and *d.x* as *y*:

```
chart.selectAll("g.node")
    ...
    .attr("transform", d => `translate(${[d.y, d.x]})`)
```

But the path selection just requires the new function:

```
chart.selectAll("path")
    ...
    .attr("d", horizontalLink) // d => horizontalLink(d)
```

The text labels also no longer require the 90-degree rotation. The result, for a tidy tree, is shown as follows:

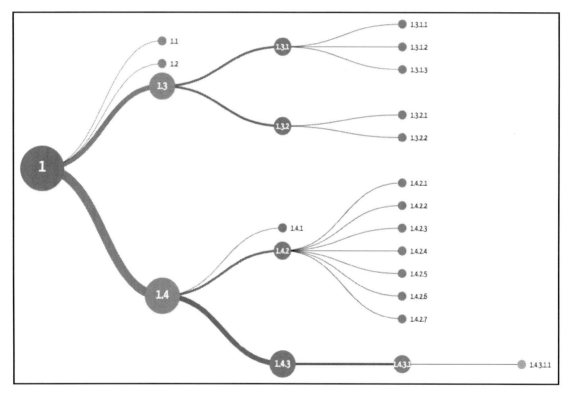

A horizontal tree. Code: *Tree/13-horizontal.html*

Using Canvas

If you have a very large tree, with thousands of nodes, you may experience performance problems because of the large amount of objects that will be created by the DOM, draining your memory resources. A common optimization procedure is to render static parts of your chart using HTML Canvas. Although you lose some interactive facilities, which are harder to implement using Canvas, the gain in performance may be worth the effort.

In this section we will create a Canvas-version of the `Tree/10-pathlinks.html` file. Although it's not a large tree that would benefit from a Canvas implementation, it's useful to demonstrate the general pattern that can be applied to larger datasets. In the `Examples/` folder you will find other examples of trees that use Canvas and mixed SVG-Canvas solutions.

We start setting up the viewport. Replace `svg` with `canvas` and append `canvas` instead of `svg`. Then obtain the Canvas context and translate it to set some margins:

```
const width = 1000, height = 600;
const canvas = d3.select("body").append("canvas")
        .attr("height", height)
        .attr("width", width);
const ctx = canvas.node().getContext("2d");
ctx.translate(60,60);
```

The code that generates the hierarchy, configures the tree, obtains nodes and links, and configures the scales is unchanged.

The path link generator needs to add a `context()` method for the Canvas context, so that its function will generate Canvas path method calls instead of returning an SVG path string:

```
const verticalLink = d3.linkVertical()
        .x(d => d.x).y(d => d.y)
        .context(ctx); // generate path commands for canvas
```

Then you can call the functions to draw links, nodes and text labels:

```
drawLinks();
drawNodes();
drawLabels();
```

Each function needs to save the current context and restore it before exiting, so that any changes to the context stay local to the functions. The `drawLinks()` draws the curves between nodes.

Since each node has a different opacity (`globalAlpha`) and line width, a new path is created for each node starting with `beginPath()`, calling `verticalLink(d)` to invoke the functions that draw the curve, and ending with `stroke()` that renders the lines:

```
function drawLinks() {
    ctx.save(); // save the current context
    ctx.fillStyle = "transparent";
    links.forEach(function(d) {
        ctx.lineWidth = (d.target.height + 1) * (d.target.height + 1);
        ctx.globalAlpha =  d.target.depth *.25 * .6 + .4;
        ctx.beginPath();
        verticalLink(d);
        ctx.stroke();
    });
    ctx.restore();
}
```

Node rendering also requires a separate path for each node, which contains a single circle (created with the `arc()` method) since they have different colors:

```
function drawNodes() {
    ctx.save();
    ctx.strokeStyle = "black";
    ctx.fillStyle = "none";
    nodes.forEach(function(d) {
        ctx.fillStyle = colorScale(d.depth);
        ctx.beginPath();
        ctx.arc(d.x, d.y, (d.height + 1) * 10, 0, 2 * Math.PI);
        ctx.stroke();
        ctx.fill();
    });
    ctx.restore();
}
```

Drawing labels applies several relative rotate and translate transforms for each node, so the context needs to be saved before each iteration, and restored after the text is drawn. Compare this code with the one used in the SVG version:

```
function drawLabels() {
    const font = 'px "Yanone Kaffeesatz", sans-serif';
    ctx.textBaseline = "baseline";

    nodes.forEach(function(d, i) {
        ctx.save(); // save current canvas state
        ctx.fillStyle = d.height != 0 ? 'white' : 'black';
        ctx.textAlign = d.height != 0 ? "center" : "end";
```

```
            const fontSize = 14 + d.height*d.height;
            ctx.font = fontSize + font;

            ctx.translate(d.x, d.y);
            if(d.height == 0) {
                ctx.rotate(-Math.PI / 2);
                ctx.translate(-15,5);
            } else {
                ctx.translate(0,5);
            }
            ctx.fillText(d.number, 0, 0);
            ctx.restore(); // recover saved canvas state
        });
    }
```

See the full code in `Tree/15-canvas.html`. Compare the result with the one produced by `Tree/10-pathlinks.html`. If you inspect the DOM of this example with your browser's development tools, you will find a single `<canvas>` object.

Radial trees

The `x` and `y` properties can be used to represent any arbitrary two-dimensional coordinate system. Using an angle as the *x* coordinate, and a radius for *y*, you can draw a radial tree in polar coordinates. The following tree layout function can be used for a radial tree with a maximum angle of 360 degrees and maximum radius of `height/2`:

```
const tree = d3.tree().size([2 * Math.PI, height/2]);
const treeData = tree(root);
```

You could also use an angle in degrees instead of radians, but it will probably need to make more conversions when using the data.

The radial effect depends on how the data is used. The following code moves the node origin's *d.y* pixels from the center (`height/2`), and then rotates them by the value in *d.x* converted to degrees clockwise (starting at the 3 o'clock position):

```
chart.selectAll("g")
      .data(nodes).join("g").attr("class", "node")
      .attr("transform", d => `rotate(${d.x * 180/Math.PI})
translate(${d.y})`)
      .append("circle")
        .attr("r", d => (d.height + 3) * 4)
        .style("fill", d => colorScale(d.depth));
```

To draw the links, you need to convert each coordinate pair from the polar to the Cartesian system. The following illustration shows how Cartesian or polar coordinates can represent a point in the SVG viewport, and how to convert between the two systems:

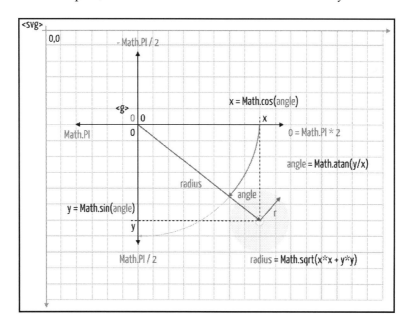

A point represented by Cartesian and polar coordinates

Since *d.x* and *d.y* contain polar coordinates, we need a function to return Cartesian coordinates

```
function cartesian([angle, radius]) {
    return [radius * Math.cos(angle), radius * Math.sin(angle)];
}
```

The function is used in the following code to draw the radial lines:

```
chart.selectAll("line")
    .data(links).join("line")
    .attr("x1", d => cartesian([d.source.x, d.source.y])[0])
    .attr("y1", d => cartesian([d.source.x, d.source.y])[1])
    .attr("x2", d => cartesian([d.target.x, d.target.y])[0])
    .attr("y2", d => cartesian([d.target.x, d.target.y])[1])
    .style("stroke-width", d => d.widthScale(d.height))
    .style("opacity", d => d.target.depth *.25 * .6 + .4);
```

The result is shown as follows:

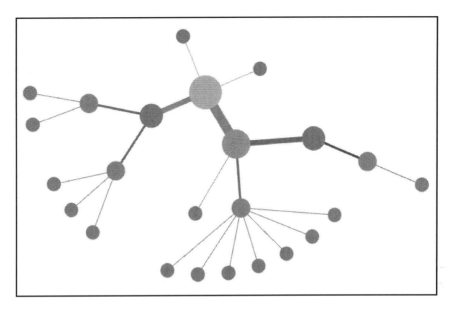

Radial tree. Code: *RadialTree/1-radial-tree.html.*

An alternative is the built-in `d3.pointRadial()` function, from the *d3-shape* module. It also converts polar coordinates to Cartesian coordinates, but the angle starts in the 12 o'clock position. To use it in the previous code, you have to add *Math.PI/2* to all angles:

```
.attr("x1", d => d3.pointRadial(d.source.x + Math.PI/2, d.source.y)[0])
.attr("y1", d => d3.pointRadial(d.source.x + Math.PI/2, d.source.y)[1])
.attr("x2", d => d3.pointRadial(d.target.x + Math.PI/2, d.target.y)[0])
.attr("y2", d => d3.pointRadial(d.target.x + Math.PI/2, d.target.y)[1])
```

If you add labels to a radial tree, you will probably need to rotate them. See `RadialTree/4-labels-translate.html and 5-labels-rotate.html` for some examples.

To create a radial dendogram, you just need to replace `d3.tree` with `d3.cluster`, as shown below (see `RadialTree/6-radial-cluster.html`)

```
const tree = d3.cluster()
                .size([200, height/2 - 50]) // radial
                .separation((a,b) => (a.parent == b.parent ?1:2)/(a.depth));
```

The configuration above uses an angle in degrees (200 degrees) and is rotated so that the chart occupies a half-circle as shown in the following screenshot:

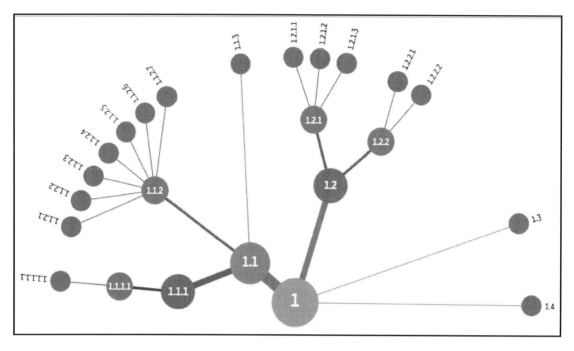

A radial dendogram using 200 degrees of a circumference. Code: *RadialTree/6-radial-cluster.html.*

If you prefer to use path links, the d3.linkRadial function generates smooth curves appropriate for radial trees. You may need, however, to configure padding and other parameters if they overlap. It seems to work better with dendograms (see RadialTree/7-pathlinks.html):

```
const radialLink = d3.linkRadial()
                    .angle(d => d.x * Math.PI/180 + Math.PI/2)
                    .radius(d => d.y);
```

The following screenshot shows a radial dendogram using `d3.linkRadial` for the link lines.

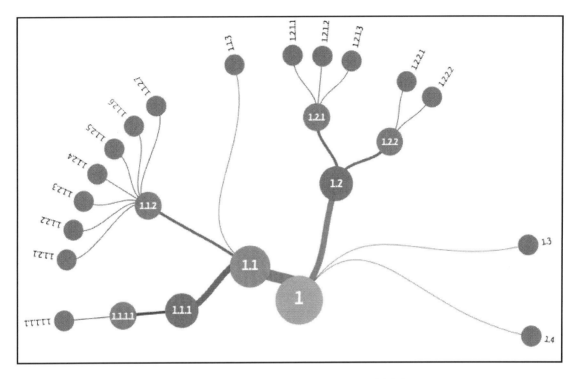

A radial dendogram using d3.linkRadial. Code: *RadialTree/7-pathlinks.html.*

Partitions

Partitions are adjacency diagrams that reveal the topology of a hierarchy by the relative placement of its nodes. Vertical partitions, or *icicle charts*, stack rectangles that represent levels in a hierarchy. At the top is a rectangle representing the root, occupying 100% of the chart's width, followed by lower levels that partition the chart's width proportionally, based on the quantitative dimension represented by each node. The leaves appear at the bottom of the chart, hanging like icicles.

Partitions can also be rendered horizontally or radially. A radial partition is called a *sunburst*, where the center represents the root, and the leaves point outward like sunrays.

The following charts are representations of the same data (the populations of countries organized by supercontinents, continents and United Nations regions) visualized as an icicle chart (without text labels) and a sunburst (with labels):

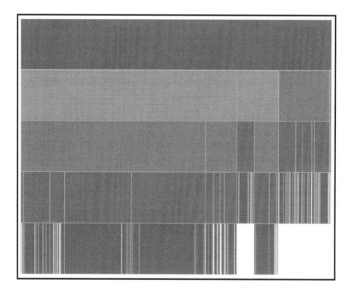

World population partitioned by supercontinents (orange), continents (green), and UN regions (purple); the countries are in red

The visualization shown below is a radial partition, or sunburst diagram, created with the same data file (`Data/un_regions.csv`), but, instead of populations, the total number of countries in each continent was used to build the chart.

This is a mostly static visualization (but it can be rotated and zoomed), so there are labels for the countries and continents:

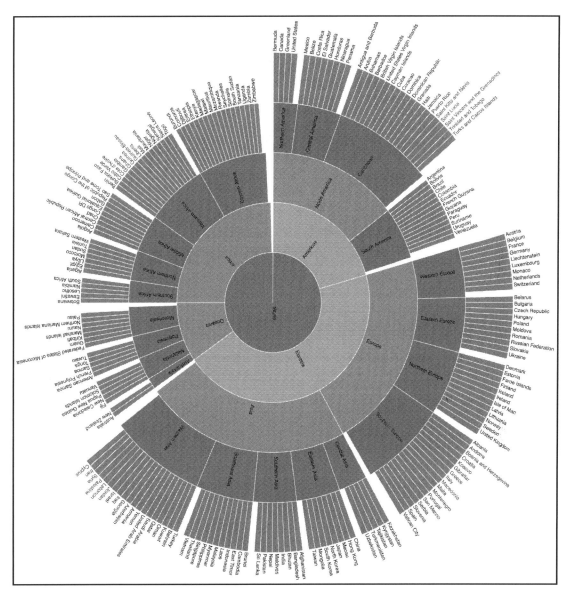

Countries by supercontinent, continent, and UN regions rendered as a radial partition or sunburst. Code: *Examples/partition-2-world-sunburst.html*.

A partition layout function is created with `d3.partition()`. Calling the function with the root node of a hierarchical dataset will generate four properties for each node: *x0, y0, x1,* and *y1*. In icicle charts, they can be used as the upper-left and lower-right corners of each rectangle. In radial sunburst charts, these properties should be mapped to the *beginAngle, innerRadius, endAngle,* and *outerRadius* properties of an *arc* layout. The configuration methods are listed in the following table:

Function	Description
`size` (*array*)	This function specifies the size of the chart. The values of all the *x0, x1, y0,* and *y1* properties will be computed within these bounds.
`round` (*boolean*)	This function enables or disables rounding. The default is false; don't use this in radial partitions with angles in radians.
`padding` (*number*)	The padding used to separate a node's adjacent children. Default is zero. In radial partitions (sunburst) padding is an angle.

The configuration methods for d3.partition()

The size of each partition depends on the *value* property of the hierarchy, which requires that either the `count()` or `sum()` method be called before using the hierarchy, (Otherwise, the value will be zero and the partition coordinates won't be computed correctly.) You might also wish to sort the nodes:

```
const root = d3.hierarchy(simpleHierarchy);
root.sort((a,b) => b.height - a.height );
root.sum(d => d.values ? d.values[0] : 0); // this or count() is required
```

If nodes don't have a value, or if the purpose of the chart is to count the children contained in each node, the `count()` method should be used instead:

```
root.count(); // same as sum(d => 1)
```

These methods can be chained, since they all return the current hierarchy.

The following code creates a new partition layout function transforming the simple hierarchy used in previous examples:

```
const partition = d3.partition()
                    .size([width - 100, height - 100])
                    .padding(2);
const partitionData = partition(root);
```

You will see the computed properties (*x0, y0, x1* and *y1*) if you log the object in the JavaScript console:

```
▼ hl ⬤
  ▼ children: Array(4)
    ▼ 0: hl
      ▶ children: (3) [hl, hl, hl]
      ▶ data: {id: "group_2", name: "Second Group", children: Array(3)}
        depth: 1
        height: 3
        number: "1.1"
      ▶ parent: hl {data: {…}, height: 4, depth: 0, parent: null, children: Array(4), …}
        value: 38
        x0: 2
        x1: 454.9866666666666
        y0: 140
        y1: 278
      ▶ __proto__: Object
    ▶ 1: hl {data: {…}, height: 2, depth: 1, parent: hl, children: Array(2), …}
    ▶ 2: hl {data: {…}, height: 0, depth: 1, parent: hl, value: 8, …}
    ▶ 3: hl {data: {…}, height: 0, depth: 1, parent: hl, value: 3, …}
      length: 4
    ▶ __proto__: Array(0)
  ▶ data: {id: "root", name: "Root Level", children: Array(4)}
    depth: 0
    height: 4
    number: 1
    parent: null
    value: 75
    x0: 2
    x1: 898
    y0: 2
    y1: 138
```

A console view of hierarchical data transformed by a partition layout function. Code: *Partition/1-data.html*.

To render a partition you need an array of `nodes`, which you can obtain with the `descendants()` method, created for each node with `d3.hierarchy()`:

```
const nodes = partitionData.descendants();
```

Icicle charts

To create an icicle chart you need to draw rectangles for each node. The `x0`, `x1`, `y0` and `y1` properties in each node contain all the data you need (see `Partition/2-icicle.html`):

```
const svg = d3.select("body").append("svg")
                             .attr("height", height)
                             .attr("width", width);
const chart = svg.append("g")
                 .attr("transform", d => `translate(${[25,25]})`);
```

```
chart.selectAll("rect")
    .data(nodes).join("rect")   // nodes = partition(root).descendants()
        .attr("x", d => d.x0)
        .attr("y", d => d.y0)
        .attr("width", d => d.x1 - d.x0)
        .attr("height", d => d.y1 - d.y0)
        .style("fill", d => colorScale(d.depth));
```

The following code places labels in the middle of each rectangle wider than 50 pixels, using *depth* to scale the fonts:

```
const fontScale = d3.scaleLinear()
                    .domain(d3.extent(root.descendants(),
                            d => d.depth).reverse())
                    .range([16,40]);
chart.selectAll("text")
    .data(nodes).join("text")
    .attr("x", d => (d.x0 + d.x1) / 2)
    .attr("y", d => (d.y0 + d.y1) / 2 + 8)
    .text(d => d.x1 - d.x0 > 50 ? d.number : '')
    .style("font-size", d => fontScale(d.depth));
```

The result is shown as follows:

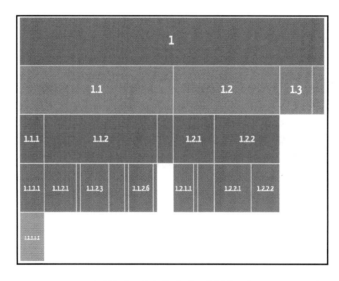

An icicle chart. Code: *Partition/3-icicle-labels.html.*

You can create a horizontal stacked partition by simply swapping **x** and **y** values when drawing the rectangles (see *Partition/4-horizontal.html*).

Sunburst diagrams

A sunburst diagram can be created using the *x* coordinates as an *angle* , and the *y* coordinates as a *radius* . The `size()` method should declare the maximum *angle* and *radius* . An *arc* layout function can be used to draw the slices:

```
const partition = d3.partition()
                    .size([Math.PI * 2, height/2-50])
const partitionData = partition(root);
const arc = d3.arc()
              .startAngle(d => d.x0)
              .endAngle(d => d.x1)
              .innerRadius(d => d.y0)
              .outerRadius(d => d.y1);
```

You might prefer to use the angle in *degrees* (which is simpler if you need to rotate using SVG transforms). In this case, you need to convert it to radians before using the *arc* function:

```
const partition = d3.partition()
                    .size([360, height/2-50]) // angle in degrees
const partitionData = partition(root);
const arc = d3.arc()
              .startAngle(d => d.x0*Math.PI/180) // must convert to radians
              .endAngle(d => d.x1*Math.PI/180)   // must convert to radians
              .innerRadius(d => d.y0)
              .outerRadius(d => d.y1);
```

Once you have the function set up, position the origin of the chart in the middle of the viewport and bind the *arc* function to each node using the *general update pattern*:

```
const chart = svg.append("g")
                 .attr("transform", d =>`translate(${[width/2,
height/2]})`);

const nodes = partitionData.descendants();

chart.selectAll("path")
     .data(nodes).join("path")
        .attr("d", arc)  // d => arc(d)
        .attr("fill", d => colorScale(d.depth));
```

You could use the *padding()* method for spacing between the arcs, but, in this type of chart, it has to be an angle. It also won't add any radial spacing between the levels, so it may be simpler to add a *stroke-width* property to the *arc* paths. The result is shown as follows:

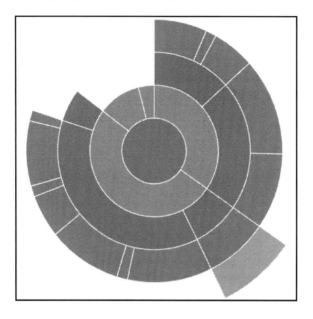

A radial partition or sunburst chart. Code: *Partition/5-sunburst-radians.html.*

Adding labels involves calculating the *centroid* of each arc and rotating the text element. The following code positions each label at the centroid with radial alignment; the chart is using angles in degrees:

```
chart.selectAll("text")
    .data(nodes)
    .enter()
    .append("text")
    .attr("x", d => arc.centroid(d)[0])
    .attr("y", d => arc.centroid(d)[1] + 4)
    .attr("transform",
        d => `rotate(${(d.x0+d.x1)/2 -90},${arc.centroid(d)})`)
    .text(d => d.number )
    .style("font-size", d => fontScale(d.height));
    .style("text-anchor", "middle");
```

The result is shown as follows:

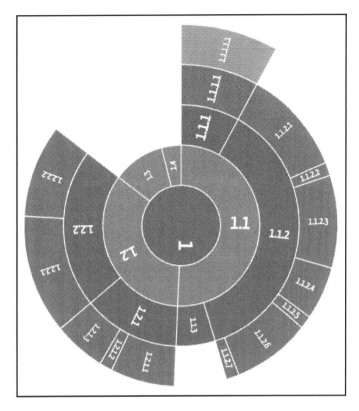

A sunburst chart with radial labels. Code: *Partition/8-sunburst-degrees-labels-radial.html.*

Additional examples with partitions are available from the GitHub repository for this chapter.

Enclosure diagrams

Enclosure diagrams reveal the topology of a hierarchy through containment. *Circle packing* places leaf nodes in circles, which represent subtrees. Their cumulative size determines the size of the enclosing circle, but the use of space in this type of chart is not very efficient. *Treemaps* use rectangles instead of circles and are more space-efficient. They also allow areas to be compared with more precision, but circle packing is usually better at emphasizing topology.

The following diagrams show the same data rendered with circle packing and treemap layouts. The full code and the data files used to generate these charts are available from the GitHub repository for this chapter:

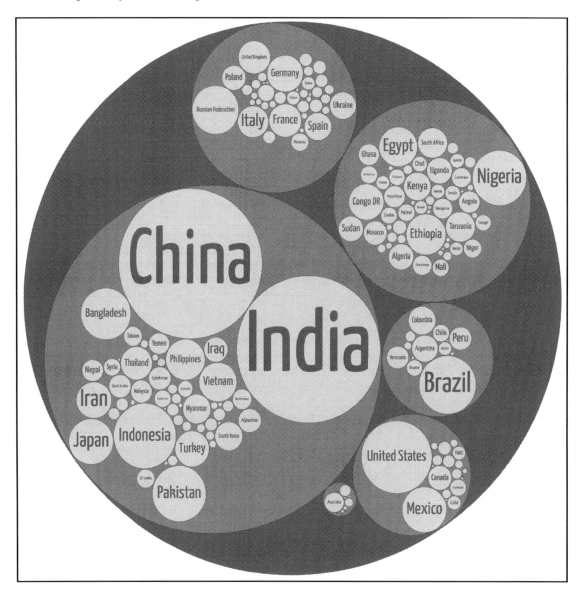

Country and continent populations (2016) visualized with circle packing. Code: *Examples/pack-2-world-by-population.html*.

A treemap visualization is shown below. It uses exactly the same data as the circle pack above, but it's easier to see details that are not visible in the circle pack, because it uses space more efficiently:

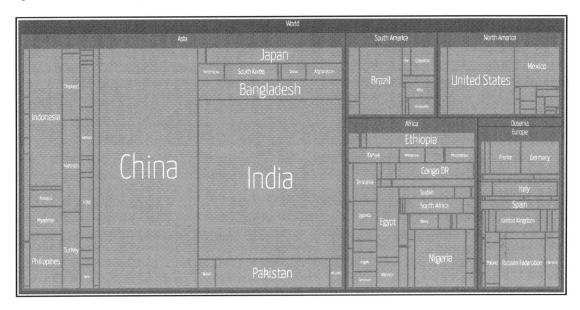

Country and continent populations (2016) visualized as a treemap. Code: *Examples/treemap-2-countries-population.html*.

Circle packing

A pack layout function is created with *d3.pack()*. Calling the function with the root node of a hierarchical dataset will generate three properties for each node: *x*, *y*, and *r*, which represent the center and radius of each circle.

The configuration methods are listed in the following table:

Function	Description
radius (*value*)	If not specified, the radius of each circle is derived from the leaf node's *value* property (computed by sum() or count()). This is the default behavior. If radius is specified (usually with an accessor function), the radius will be exactly the value provided.
size (*array*)	This function specifies the size of the chart. All the *x*, *y*, and *r* values will be computed within these bounds, unless a fixed value is specified for each radius.
padding (*value*)	This function adds space between sibling and parent nodes. The value can be a number or an accessor function that returns a number. The default is zero.

The configuration methods for d3.pack()

As with partitions, the radius of each circle depends on the value property of the hierarchy, which requires that either the count() or sum() method be called on the root object:

```
const root = d3.hierarchy(simpleHierarchy)
                .sum(d => d.values ? d.values[0] : 0);
```

The following code (Pack/1-pack.html) applies a pack layout to the hierarchy, and then obtains the descendant nodes:

```
const chart = svg.append("g")
                    .attr("transform", d => `translate(${[50,50]})`);
const colorScale = d3.scaleOrdinal(d3.schemeGnBu[5])
                        .domain(d3.extent(root, n => n.height));

const pack = d3.pack().size([width-100,height-100]);
const nodes = pack(root).descendants();
```

If you inspect the contents of the nodes array in your JavaScript console, you will notice that it added three properties to each node: x, y and r. Binding each node to a circle, and using these properties for the attributes of each circle will render the chart:

```
chart.selectAll("circle")
    .data(nodes).join("circle")
                .attr("cx", d => d.x)
                .attr("cy", d => d.y)
                .attr("r", d => d.r)
                .style("fill", d => colorScale(d.height));
```

The result is shown in the following screenshot:

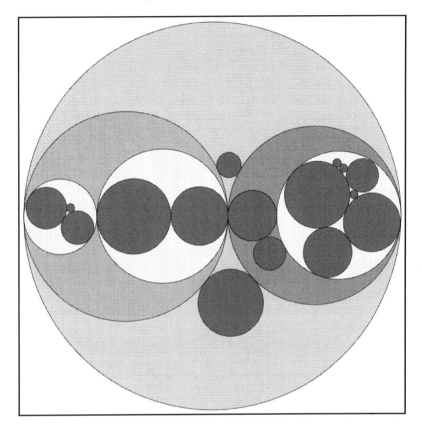

A circle pack diagram. Code: *Pack/1-pack.html.*

Instead of binding circles to each node, we can bind <g> containers. This will make it easier to add text labels, as shown in the following code (see `Pack/2-labels.html`):

```
chart.selectAll("g")
        .data(nodes).join("g")
        .attr("transform", d => `translate(${[d.x, d.y]})`)
        .each(function(d) {
            const cell = d3.select(this);
            cell.append("circle")
                .attr("r", d => d.r)
                .style("fill", d => colorScale(d.height));

            cell.append("text")
                .text(d => d.number)
                .attr("font-size", 14)
```

```
            .attr("y", d => d.height == 0 ? 3 : -d.r + 14)
            .style("fill", d => d.height ==0 ? 'black' : 'white')
            .style("opacity", d => d.r > 10 ? 1 : 0);
    });
```

The result reveals that not all nodes are represented in the chart. For example, the node 1.1.1.1.1 is directly under 1.1 and has a sibling called 1.1.3. What's missing? Let's have a look:

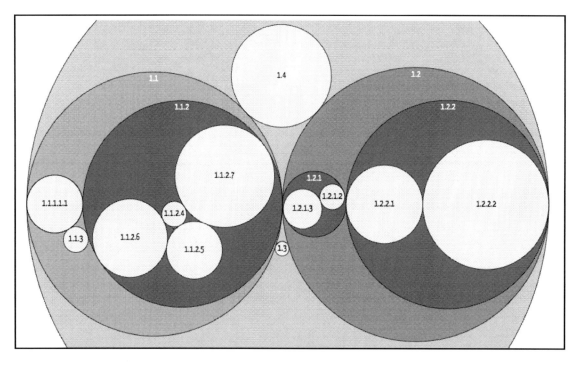

Partial view of circle pack. Code: *Pack/2-labels.html.*

If you look at the trees we created with this dataset, you will notice that this node is a single child of a node that is also a single child of its parent. Nodes that contain a single child aren't visible in a circle pack. They *are* present, but since there is no padding, the child takes up all the space. If you add some padding they will show up (see Pack/3-padding.html):

```
pack.padding(10);
```

Now you can see the hidden circles:

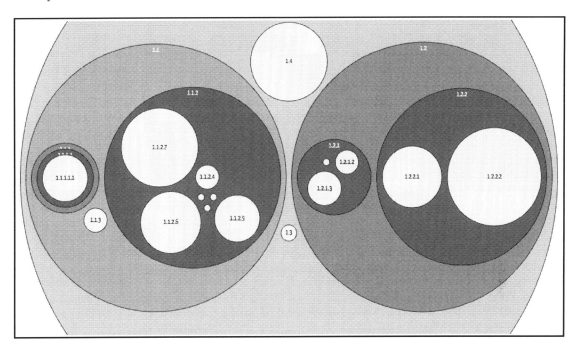

Circle pack using padding. Code: *Pack/3-padding.html.*

Padding can also be specified with a per node value using an accessor function, for example (see `Pack/4-padding-per-node.html`):

```
pack.padding(d => d.value/25);
```

The size of each circle is proportional to `d.value`, but the exact value depends on additional constraints, such as `size`. A minimum or exact value for the radius of each circle can be provided, but it may cause the chart to grow beyond the limits defined by `size()`. For example, the following configuration will set for each leaf circle a radius equal to its `value` property plus 10 pixels (which may result in a chart that is larger or smaller):

```
pack.radius(d => d.value + 5);
```

To create a circle pack that represents the count of its leaf nodes, instead of a node value, configure the hierarchy with the `count()` method on initialization:

```
const root = d3.hierarchy(simpleHierarchy).count()
```

Now each leaf has a constant radius, and the outer nodes have sizes that depend on the amount of descendants they have:

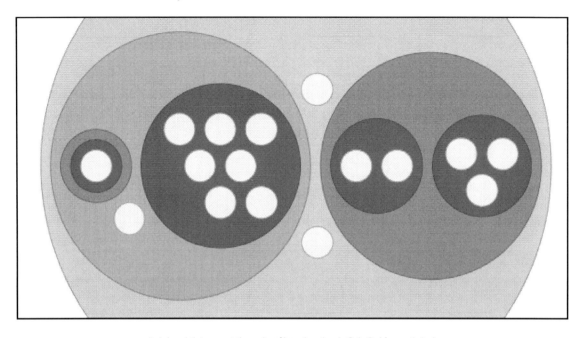

A circle pack that represents the number of leaves in each node. Code: *Pack/by-quantity.html*.

Circle packing doesn't use space very efficiently, but you can improve it a bit by removing the root node. This can be done using a data filter to include only nodes that have a `parent` (see `Pack/6-no-root.html`):

```
chart.selectAll("g")
    .data(nodes)
    .join(enter => enter.filter(d => d.parent).append("g"))
    .attr("transform", d => `translate(${[d.x, d.y]})`);
```

Treemap

The `d3.treemap()` function generates a layout function for a treemap, which should be called with the root node of a hierarchical dataset. This will generate four properties for each node: *x0, y0, y1,* and *y0,* which represent the upper-left and lower-right corners of each rectangle.

The configuration methods are listed in the following table:

Function	Description
tile (*tile*)	This function selects a tiling algorithm; see the *Treemap tiling algorithms (figure)* section.
size (*array*)	This function specifies the size of the chart. The values of all the *x0, x1, y0,* and *y1* properties will be computed within these bounds.
round (*boolean*)	This function enables or disables rounding. The default is *false*.
paddingInner (*value*)	This function sets the space between the child nodes. The default is padding(). The value can be a number (all nodes) or an accessor function (per node); this overrides padding().
paddingOuter (*value*)	This function sets the margin between the parent node and children. The default is padding(). The value can be a number (all nodes) or an accessor function (per node); this overrides padding().
padding (*value*)	This function sets both the inner and outer padding. The default is zero. With no padding, only leaf nodes will be visible.
paddingTop (*value*), paddingLeft (*value*), paddingBottom (*value*), paddingRight (*value*),	This function sets the value of the outer padding on each side of the rectangle. This overrides padding() and paddingOuter().

The configuration methods for d3.treemap()

As with partitions and circle packing, the rectangle's coordinates depend on the *value* property of the hierarchy, which requires calling count() or sum(). The following code creates a new treemap layout function and uses it to transform the simple hierarchy from previous examples:

```
const root = d3.hierarchy(simpleHierarchy)
            .sort((a,b) => b.height - a.height )
            .sum(d => d.values ? d.values[0] : 0); // required!

const treemap = d3.treemap()
        .size([width - 100, height - 100]);

const mapData = treemap(root);          // the hierarchy + computed properties

const nodes = mapData.descendants(); // the nodes array used to draw the
map
```

You should see the computed properties (*x0, y0, x1,* and *y1*) if you log the nodes in the JavaScript console view.

The following code draws a treemap:

```
const svg = d3.select("body").append("svg")
               .attr("height", height).attr("width", width);
const chart = svg.append("g")
                  .attr("transform", d => `translate(${[25,25]})`);
colorScale d3.scaleOrdinal(d3.schemeCategory10)
            .domain(d3.extent(nodes, n => n.height));
chart.selectAll("rect")
     .data(nodes)
     .join("rect")
          .attr("x", d => d.x0)
          .attr("y", d => d.y0)
          .attr("width", d => d.x1 - d.x0)
          .attr("height", d => d.y1 - d.y0)
          .style("fill", d => colorScale(d.height));
```

The result is shown as follows:

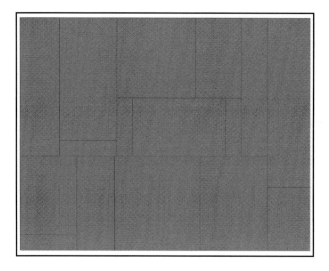

A basic treemap with no padding only shows leaves. Code: *Treemap/1-treemap.html.*

Note that only the leaf nodes are visible. The intermediate nodes will only appear if you add some padding. The following code adds different amounts of padding in different parts of the treemap, reserving space for a header and cutting the outer padding in half if the node contains a single child:

```
const treemap = d3.treemap()
        .size([width - 100, height - 100])
        .paddingInner(5)
        .paddingOuter(d => d.children.length == 1 ? 5 : 10)
        .paddingTop(50);
```

This will produce the result shown in the following screenshot:

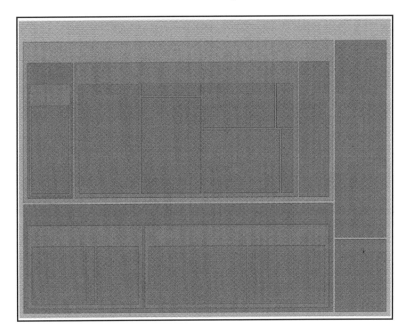

Treemap with padding reveals other levels of the hierarchy. Code: *Treemap/2-padding.html*.

Labels were previously generated for each node and stored in the d.number property (see Treemap/3-labels.html). The following code will place them in each cell:

```
chart.selectAll("text").data(nodes).join("text")
        .attr("x", d => (d.x0 + d.x1) / 2)
        .attr("y", d => d.y0 + 48 - (d.depth + 4) * 4)
        .text(d => d.x1 - d.x0 > 50 ? d.number : '')
        .style("font-size", d => fontScale(d.depth));
```

Additional styling for text and rectangles was done in CSS. The result is shown in the following code:

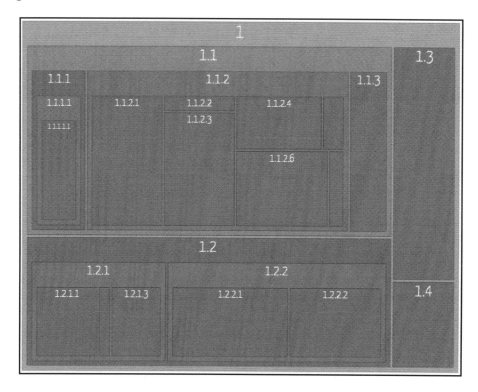

Treemaps can be configured with different tiling algorithms using the `tile()` configuration method:

```
const treemap = d3.treemap().size([width - 100, height - 100])
                            .tile(d3.treemapSquarify.ratio(1.61));
```

The following screenshot compares the different tiling algorithms available:

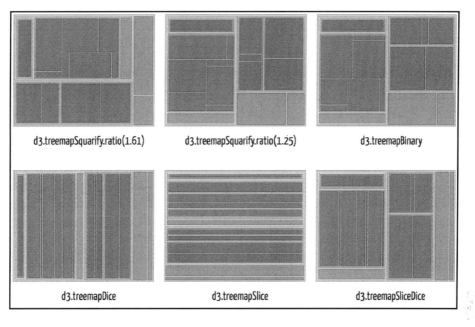

Treemap tiling algorithms. Code: *Treemap/4-tile.html*.

The d3.treemapSquarify and d3.treemapResquarify algorithms can be configured with a different aspect ratio using the ratio(*value*) method, as shown in the code above. The default is 1.61 (the golden ratio).

You can also create radial treemaps, but their practical use is very limited since they are hard to read and can introduce severe perception illusions. See an example in Treemap/5-radial.html.

Interactive visualizations

There are many ways to add interactive behaviors to hierarchical visualizations. If you have a very large tree, you may wish to zoom in to obtain details about the leaf nodes. You could implement a semantic zoom that expands the nodes as it zooms in. If you have a very complex hierarchy, with many links, you might use node and link highlighting to show a path between two nodes, or simply reveal the path between a particular node and the root. In a dynamic chart, you can also allow the user to drag nodes, add new nodes or remove existing ones.

This section describes three interactive behaviors you can add to a tree or dendogram: highlighting a path, using a subtree as the root and navigating up down a tree by expanding and collapsing nodes. Only relevant code fragments are shown, but the full code is available in the `Interactive/` folder.

Highlighting a path

The `path()` method from `d3.hierarchy()` can be used to obtain the path between two arbitrary points in a tree. The `descendants()` and `ancestors()` methods contain subtrees and or a list of nodes between the current node and the root. You can also obtain a list of leaves, or filter other nodes based on their data. Any of these sets can be revealed by highlighting in a tree visualization using a selection to turn on or off CSS classes that change the appearance of graphical elements.

This example will reveal the path from a node to the root when the mouse is over the node (see `Interactive/1-highlight.html`). It uses the following CSS to style selected nodes and links:

```
path.faded {
    stroke: lightgray;
}
path.highlighted {
    stroke: red;
}
.faded circle {
    opacity: .4;
}
.highlighted circle {
    stroke: black;
    stroke-width: 3;
}
.highlighted text {
    font-weight: bold;
}
```

The event handlers are attached to each node using the selection:

```
chart.selectAll("g")
    .data(nodes)
    .join("g").attr("class", "node")
    //...
    .on("mouseover", highlightPath)
    .on("mouseout", reset);
```

Thee `highlightPath()` and `reset()` functions are shown in the following code:

```
function highlightPath(node) {
    const steps = node.path(root); // could also be ancestors()
    const links = root.links().filter(d => steps.indexOf(d.target) >= 0);

    d3.selectAll(".node")
      .classed('highlighted', d => steps.indexOf(d) >= 0);
    d3.selectAll(".node")
      .classed('faded', d => steps.indexOf(d) < 0);

    d3.selectAll(".link").classed('faded', d => steps.indexOf(d.target) <
0)
    d3.selectAll(".link")
      .classed('highlighted', d => steps.indexOf(d.target) >= 0)
}

function reset() {
    d3.selectAll(".node, .link").classed('faded highlighted', false);
}
```

The result is illustrated by the following screenshots. The first image shows the entire chart when no mouse hovers over a node. The following other two images show the effect of hovering over the fourth and seventh leaf nodes:

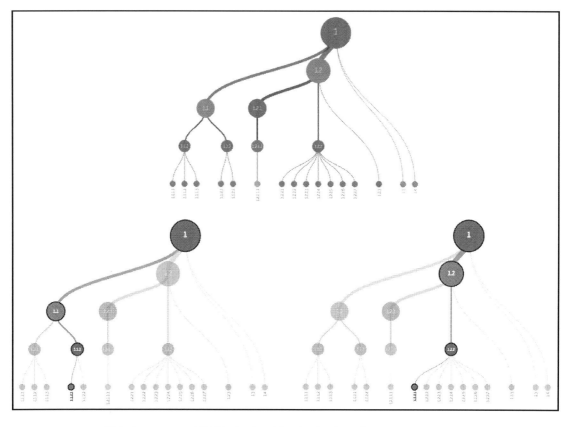

Moving the mouse over a node highlights the entire path from the node to the root. Code: Interactive/1-highlight.html.

Changing the root

If you have a very large tree, with hundreds of leaves, they might appear too small in your visualization. You could apply a zoom or brush behavior, to view a section of your visualization, but a more efficient technique may be to expand a subtree of interest, making it occupy the entire chart, as shown in the following screenshot:

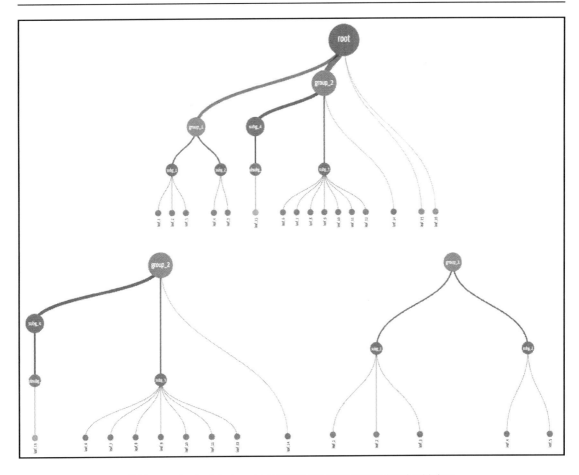

Clicking on a node makes that node a root and redraws the chart. Double-clicking redraws the original root.
Code: *Interactive/2-change-root-tree.html*.

This behavior can be implemented by changing the root that is used to render the tree. The following code adds event listeners to each node that call a `changeRoot()` function that changes the current root:

```
chart.selectAll("g.node")
    // ...
    .on("click", changeRoot)
    .on("dblclick", () => changeRoot(root))
```

The `changeRoot()` function is called on initialization to render the initial tree, but if called with a node, as in the event listener, it will redraw the chart using that node's descendants and links as the data. A double-click also calls the root, restoring the visualization to show the full tree:

```
changeRoot(root);

function changeRoot(d) {
    const treeData = tree(d);
    draw(treeData.descendants(), treeData.links());
}
```

The `draw()` function contains all the code that binds the data and renders the chart:

```
function draw(nodes, links) {
    chart.selectAll("path").data(links).join("path")
    // ...

    chart.selectAll("g.node").data(nodes, d => d.data.id)
        // ...
        .classed("leaf", d => !d.children) // add this class if leaf
        .on("click", changeRoot)
        .on("dblclick", () => changeRoot(root))
}
```

The leaf nodes are ignored for mouse events using CSS:

```
.leaf { pointer-events: none; }
```

See the full code for this example in `Interactive/2-change-root-tree.html`.

Navigating a subtree

If you have a very large tree, you may prefer not to display it all on the screen, but allow the user to reveal child nodes on demand as they navigate down the hierarchy. The following example contains a tree where each node displays the amount of children it contains if it's not a leaf. When these nodes are clicked, they expand their hierarchy to the next level to show all child nodes. Any child nodes that also contain a number can be clicked, expanding the hierarchy further down, as shown below:

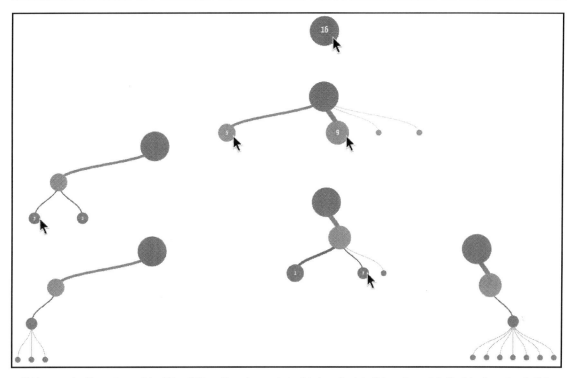

Clicking on a node with a number reveals its children. Children with numbers can also be clicked revealing their children and so on. A double-click collapses the node. Code: *Interactive/3-tree-navigate.html.*

This example adds an additional property (`expand`) in each node of the hierarchy that is used to control collapsing and expanding. It initially contains the `depth`:

```
root.each(d => d.expand = d.depth); // add to control expanding nodes
```

The tree is created with a `draw()` function that computes nodes and links, and renders the chart. Initially, only the root node is shown:

```
draw(tree(root));
function draw(d) { ...}
```

A `toggle()` function either expands or collapses a node showing its children. It increments the `d.expand` property of the node to expand it, and resets the property on all descendants during collapse:

```
function toggle(d) {
    if(d.expand <= d.depth) { // expand
        d.expand = d.depth == MAX_DEPTH ? MAX_DEPTH : d.expand + 1;
    } else { // collapse
```

```
                d.descendants().forEach(k => k.expand = k.depth)
        }
        draw(d);
    }
```

After changing these properties, the `draw()` function is called. It uses these properties to filter nodes and links so that only the hierarchy from the root to the clicked node and its descendants is shown:

```
function draw(d) {
    const nodes = treeData.descendants()
                    .filter(n => n.ancestors().indexOf(d) >= 0 ||
                            n.descendants().indexOf(d) >= 0)
                    .filter(n => n.depth <= d.expand);

    const links = treeData.links()
                    .filter(k => k.target.depth <= d.expand)
                    .filter(k => k.target.ancestors().indexOf(d) >= 0 ||
                            k.target.descendants().indexOf(d) >= 0)
    // links
    chart.selectAll("path")
        .data(links).join("path")
        // ...
    // nodes
    chart.selectAll("g.node")
        .data(nodes, d => d.data.id) // this key function is required!
        // ...
}
```

Note that a key function is required as the second parameter of the `data()` method in the node binding, since nodes may be added and removed out of array order.

The `toggle()` function is registered as a *click* event handler on all nodes except leaves. See the complete code in `Interactive/3-tree-navigate.html`.

This section only showed interactive examples with trees and dendograms. Think about what kinds of interactive behaviors you could apply to circle packs, treemaps or partitions, and try to implement one as an exercise.

Summary

In this chapter, you learned several different strategies to display hierarchical data, and how to use layout generator functions available in D3 to easily bind your data to SVG graphics. You learned how to transform tabular data into a hierarchical structure that can be used by the layout functions, and several useful methods to extract nodes, links, and other derived data from these structures.

Through several examples using the same hierarchical dataset, you learned how to create a tidy tree, a dendogram, a vertical partition, a sunburst chart, a circle pack, and a treemap. You also learned how to change a layout's default configuration, employ alternative rendering techniques, and display the charts in different orientations.

Interactivity is an important feature of hierarchical charts and was not covered in this chapter. Examples of interactive hierarchic charts, as well as zooming and panning features will be explored in the next chapter.

References

- Module documentation, D3.js: `github.com/d3/d3-hierarchy`
- Object Constancy, by Mike Bostock: `bost.ocks.org/mike/constancy/`
- Amazon River tributaries dataset: `Data/amazon-river.csv`. Compiled from several sources, including Wikipedia.
- Planetary data: `Data/planets.json`. Compiled from Solar System data obtained mainly from NASA (JPL) and other public sources.
- Demographic dataset: `Data/un_regions.csv`. Compiled from several sources, including United Nations (World Population Prospects 2017: `www.un.org`) and World Bank (World bank public data. `data.worldbank.org`)

Visualizing Flows and Networks

10

In the last chapter, you learned how to create visualizations of hierarchical data: unidirectional connected node networks. In this chapter, we will explore the visualization of other types of networks, which may contain disconnected nodes and sub-networks, allowing for directional flows as well as cycles.

A simple graph connecting lines to points can be drawn with basic D3 tools that you already learned how to use, but it's always much easier if a generator function calculates the coordinates for us. D3 provides several of those functions for popular network visualizations, revealing different aspects of connected graphs, with emphasis on either the nodes, links, or layout.

This chapter will describe the standard data structures used for network data and show how to apply them to create different topologies for network graphs, using three modules from the D3 repository: *d3-chord*, to create circular chord/ribbon diagrams, *d3-sankey*, to represent weighted flows using horizontal ribbons between automatically positioned nodes, and *d3-force*, a complete force integration engine that dynamically positions nodes in network diagrams. You will also learn how to add interactive features, such as node highlighting; node dragging; finding, adding, and removing nodes; and zooming.

An outline of this chapter is as follows:

- Network visualization
- Graphs and data structures
- Adjacency diagrams
- Chord diagrams
- Sankey diagrams
- Arc diagrams
- Node-link diagrams with force-directed simulations

Network visualization

A network is a collection of *nodes* connected by *links*. Its main purpose is to describe relationships between data. The structure that describes how nodes are connected is called a *topology*. Examples of regular topologies are *lines* (nodes connected to one another in a sequence), *rings* (nodes connected in a cycle), *stars* (nodes connected to a central node) and *trees*. Real-world networks usually are a combination of all these.

Network visualizations can be used for any kind of connected system, which may be abstractions of physical real-world systems such as roads, flight routes, subway systems, or abstract relational structures, like social networks, migration flows; and hierarchies. Visualizations can reveal different aspects of these networks, such as the importance of some connections in relation to others, the number of connections that enter and leave a node, and topological aspects of a network.

The two main types of visualizations used for networks are *matrix* and *node-link* diagrams.

Matrix visualizations lay out the nodes in a table, with the same nodes as rows and columns, revealing links where they cross.

Node-link visualizations employ graphical symbols for nodes, connecting them with lines or curves. The main issue in this kind of visualization is where to place the nodes, which results in many different strategies for laying out nodes in a two-dimensional space. There is no best solution. The choice depends on the size of your data, the number of nodes and links, and the details that you wish to show or hide.

Here is a short list that may help you choose the ideal layout for your data:

Adjacency matrices: A square grid of nodes, represented as perpendicular lines that cross at a point revealing the link. This layout is best when comparing the weight of relationships is more important than topology. It's the ideal chart when there are many link crossings, since links are reduced to points. A typical visualization is a *heatmap*, where diverging hues, saturation, lightness, or opacity reveal the weight of each link.

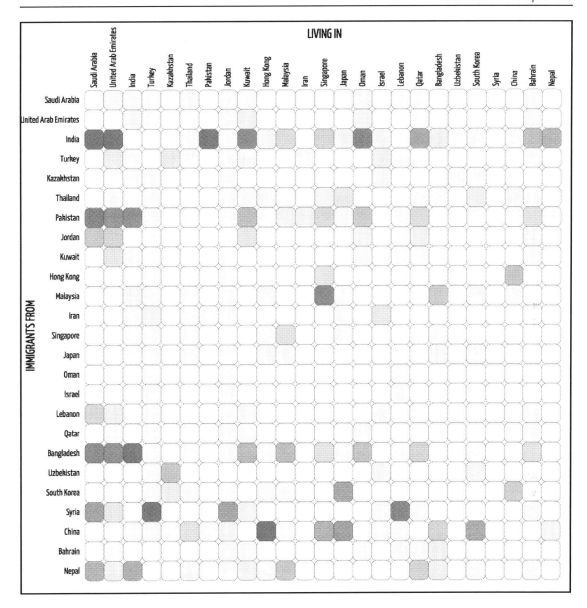

Direct placement: You don't have to compute node positions if you already know them. In a geographically localized system such as a transportation network or a power distribution system, you can use latitudes and longitudes to place the nodes. But this can also make it harder to perceive other aspects of the network. Abstracting spatial positions usually improves visualization.

Subway maps, for example, focus on stations (nodes) and connections (links), ignoring most geographical information (except cardinal orientation).

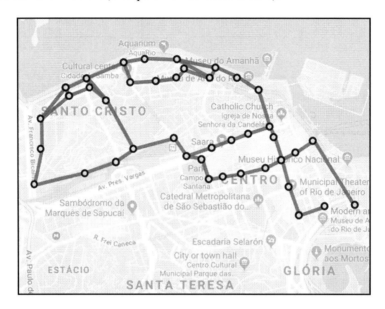

Geometrical layouts: Nodes are placed along a line, a circle, a grid or another regular shape. Links are straight lines, curves, or arcs between the nodes. A popular layout is the *arc diagram*, good for small, directed networks: nodes are placed on an axis and are connected by arcs spanning above or below the axis, depending on their direction. Circular layouts, such as *chord diagrams* place points on a circumference connected by lines or curves that cross the circle. They can be more compact than arc diagrams, but aren't as good for showing link direction. The fixed geometry of these charts also makes it harder to perceive topological aspects of the network.

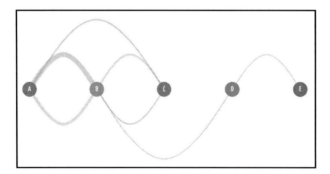

Chord/ribbon diagrams divide a circle into arcs (nodes) connected by semi-transparent ribbons. Each ribbon represents a pair of links. Link weight is encoded in the width of each end of the ribbon. They are very popular and make beautiful visualizations, but may be hard to read without interactive highlighting and tooltips.

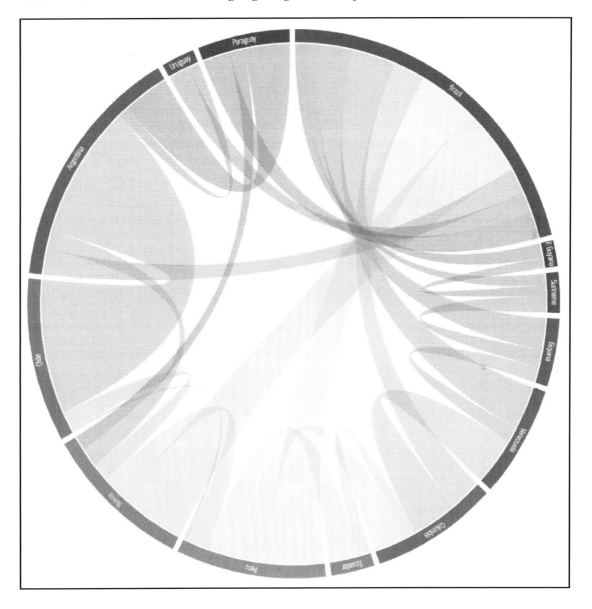

Flow and proportion layouts: This type of chart places nodes on a grid, while links are variable-width ribbons flowing from one node to another, sometimes splitting and joining in with other nodes. *Sankey* diagrams and *Parallel Sets* are the most popular charts of this type. They are great to visualize *flows*, but can also show *proportion, distribution* and other relationships. Flow diagrams don't allow cycles. *Sankeys* are **directed acyclic graphs (DAGs)** or sets of unconnected trees (forests), which are undirected but acyclic

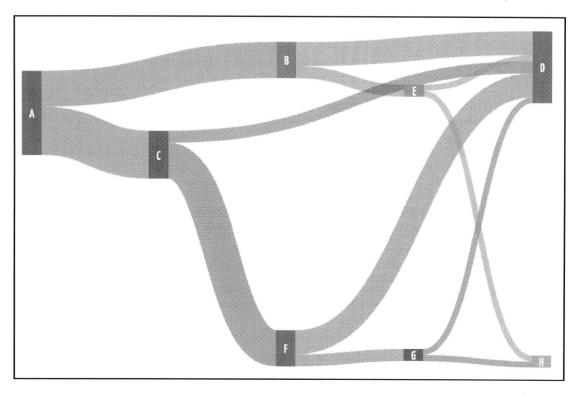

Force-directed networks: An iterative process to find the best places to position the nodes can avoid node overlapping, minimize link crossings and display topological details. This is the best alternative for large networks, and to reveal general aspects of topology, clusters, and node centrality. Although it may be difficult to access information from individual nodes and links, some improvement can be obtained using interactive resources, such as tooltips, highlighting, zooming and dragging.

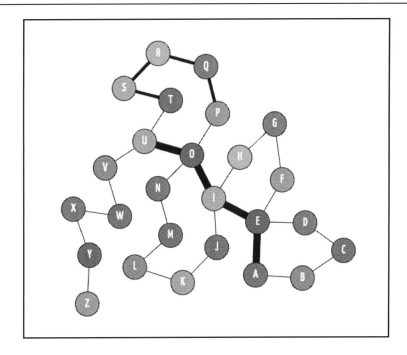

D3 provides generator functions for chord diagrams (in the *d3-chord* module), *Sankey* diagrams (*d3-sankey*) and force-directed graphs (*d3-force*). The *d3-sankey* module is not part of the default bundle and must be imported separately. In this chapter, we will also create generator functions for other chart types.

Graphs and data structures

In mathematics, networks are called *graphs*, nodes are called *vertices*, and links are called *edges*. In computer science (and in the D3 libraries) these terms are often used interchangeably. You don't have to be fluent in graph theory to create network visualizations, but it's good to know the basic terms and concepts, since it will help you choose the best network layout for your data.

A *directed* graph or network is one where each connection between two nodes has a specific direction (moving from A to B is not the same as moving from B to A). In an *undirected* (or symmetrical) graph, there is no difference. For example, a graph showing flight connections between countries is directed, since the number of flights leaving a country is not necessarily equal to the number of flights entering it. But a graph where the connections between countries represent the extension of their common border is undirected, since that value is not affected by the direction of travel.

An edge that connects a node to itself is a *loop*. In a chart that compares migrations between continents, loops can be used to represent migrations *within* each continent.

Even if a connected graph contains no loops, it can still contain *cycles*. If you follow a path through a *directed* graph without cycles, it may split into separate links at a node and join again later, but never return to a previously visited node. This type of graph is commonly used for unidirectional flows:

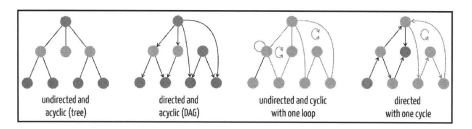

Graphs used to represent some of the network structures we will explore in this chapter

The number of links that enter or leave a node is the node's *degree*, which measures the relative importance of a node in a network. For example, in a road network you can quickly identify the most important cities by observing the amount of roads that cross it. The importance of a link can be represented by its *weight*; for example, a multi-lane highway compared to a single lane road.

To create a graph, you first need to obtain the data and convert it into a connected data format. The most popular data structures used to store network data are *adjacency matrixes* and *node-link structures*. You might find CSV and JSON data in these formats, but may still need to do some pre-processing to convert the data into a standard format used by the generator functions. The next sections will describe the two main data structures used by layout generator functions in D3.

Adjacency matrices

An adjacency matrix is common way to represent links between nodes in a network. It's a square matrix with n rows and n columns representing the same nodes (*vertices*), where each element represents a link (*edge*) between nodes in one direction. With n^2 elements, it can be used for directed graphs containing self-referencing loops. With all zeros on its diagonal, the remaining $n*(n-1)$ values represent a *directed* graph without loops (all edges connect *different* vertices). *Undirected* graphs (including trees) are represented by symmetric or triangular matrices with $n*(n-1)/2$ distinct values.

Networks are usually represented as *weighted* adjacency matrices, where each element not only reveals if the two nodes are connected or not, but contains information about the connection itself. Compare the matrices below with the previous illustration showing different graph types:

	A B C D		A B C D		A B C D		A B C D		A B C D
A	0 0 1 2	A	0 0 1 1	A	1 3 3 9	A	0 3 1 0	A	0 3 1 0
B	9 0 0 1	B	1 0 0 1	B	4 2 5 1	B	3 0 2 5	B	0 0 2 5
C	0 3 0 7	C	0 1 0 1	C	0 3 0 1	C	1 2 0 1	C	0 0 0 1
D	0 0 0 0	D	0 0 0 0	D	1 0 0 1	D	0 5 1 0	D	0 0 0 0
	directed weighted		directed non-weighted		directed with loops		undirected (symmetric)		undirected (triangular)

When matrices are used to represent networks, each element (vertex) is a link (edge) between adjacent nodes.

A simple adjacency matrix that we will use in some examples in this chapter is shown as follows. The labels array is used to label each row and column (see `Adjacency/1-matrix.html`):

```
const matrix = [
    [0, 6, 2, 0, 0],
    [8, 0, 5, 0, 0],
    [0, 1, 0, 0, 0],
    [0, 1, 0, 0, 1],
    [0, 0, 0, 0, 0]
];

const labels = ['A', 'B', 'C', 'D', 'E'];
```

Node-link structures

Another common way to represent a network is with a pair of arrays: a list of *nodes* and a list of *links* (also called an adjacency list). Each link contains references to its adjacent nodes, and may contain a value, if weighted. We generated node-link structures in the previous chapter using `d3.hierarchy` to represent *rooted trees* (which are connected undirected graphs with a single root and no cycles).

The matrix data shown in the last section could be represented as the *list* structure shown below (see `Adjacency/2-node-link.html`):

```
const edges = [
                {source: 0, target: 1, value: 6},
                {source: 0, target: 2, value: 2},
                {source: 1, target: 0, value: 8},
                {source: 1, target: 2, value: 5},
```

```
                    {source: 2, target: 1, value: 1},
                    {source: 3, target: 1, value: 1},
                    {source: 3, target: 4, value: 1} ];

    const nodes = [{node: 'A'},{node: 'B'},{node: 'C'},{node: 'D'},{node:
    'E'}];
```

Since there is a distinction between `source` and `target` properties, this structure can also be used for directed graphs. Each contains a reference to an element in the `nodes` array, using the array element's index as the identifier. This is usually the default, but you could also choose a property from each object in the `nodes` array and configure it as the unique identifier. Many layout generator functions require data in this format. Others require an adjacency matrix. You can convert a matrix into a list of links with node index references using the code below:

```
function matrixToLinks(matrix) {
    const links = [];
    for(let s = 0; s < matrix.length; s++) {
        for(let t = 0; t < matrix.length; t++) {
            if(matrix[s][t]; != 0) {
                links.push({source: s, target: t, value: v});
            }
        }
    }
    return links;
}
```

In case you have an array of nodes and a list of links you can obtain an adjacency matrix with this code:

```
function linksToMatrix(nodes, links) {
    const matrix = [];
    for(let s = 0; s < nodes.length; s++) {
        const line = [];
        for(let t = 0; t < nodes.length; t++) {
            const link = links.filter(k => k.source == s && k.target == t);
            line.push(link.length != 0 ? link[0].value : 0);
        }
        matrix.push(line);
    }
    return matrix;
}
```

You can include this library in your code when you need to convert from one type of structure to the other.

Most layout functions provided by D3 will automatically replace the `source` and `target` node *identifiers* of each link object with references to the actual node objects. In the following sections we will use data in these formats to create different network visualizations.

Adjacency diagrams

The simplest way to visualize an adjacency matrix is to plot the matrix as a table, using colors or other highlighting techniques to emphasize the weight of each connection, producing a *heatmap* visualization. This can be easily done with HTML tables, but SVG offers more flexibility and interactive resources. D3 does not, however, provide a layout generator function in D3 to plot adjacency heatmaps, but it's not difficult to create one.

As an example, consider the following CSV data (see `Data/sa_borders.csv`) containing a triangular adjacency matrix, where each element represents the border between two South American countries or its coastline with the Atlantic or Pacific oceans:

```
Country,Atlantic,Pacific,Brazil,French Guyana,Suriname,Guyana,Venezuela,↵
        Colombia,Ecuador,Peru,Bolivia,Chile,Argentina,Uruguay,Paraguay
Atlantic,0,0,,,,,,,,,,,,,
Pacific,0,0,,,,,,,,,,,,,
Brazil,7491,0,0,,,,,,,,,,,,
French Guyana,378,0,730,0,,,,,,,,,,,
Suriname,386,0,593,510,0,,,,,,,,,,
Guyana,459,0,1606,0,836,0,,,,,,,,,
Venezuela,2800,0,2200,0,0,789,0,,,,,,,,
Colombia,1760,1448,1644,0,0,0,2341,0,,,,,,,
Ecuador,0,2337,0,0,0,0,0,708,0,,,,,,
Peru,0,2414,2995,0,0,0,0,1494,1420,0,,,,,
Bolivia,0,0,3423,0,0,0,0,0,0,1212,0,,,,
Chile,0,6435,0,0,0,0,0,0,0,168,942,0,,,
Argentina,4989,0,1261,0,0,0,0,0,0,0,942,6691,0,,
Uruguay,660,0,1068,0,0,0,0,0,0,0,0,0,541,0,
Paraguay,0,0,1365,0,0,0,0,0,0,753,0,2351,0,0
```

This data is an undirected graph and can be rendered as a square grid, symmetrically duplicating the values above and below the center diagonal, or as a concise triangle, reducing the non-data-ink of the chart. Different color scales, distinguishing borders from coastlines, highlight the strength of each connection, which represents the extension in thousands of kilometers. These two strategies are illustrated below:

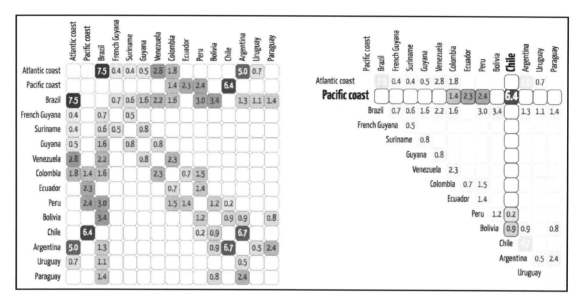

Two different ways to display adjacency matrices. comparing coastlines and borders between South-American countries.
Code: *Examples/adjacency-5-borders-sa-symmetrical.html* (left) and *adjacency-6-borders-sa-triangular.html* (right)

Data visualizations of a *directed* adjacency matrix are shown below. The data, obtained from the United Nations data portal, compares migration stock (number of immigrants) between over 200 locations. Both charts were created from the same data file (`Data/migrations_2017_continent.csv`), filtered by continent. The center diagonal is only zeros, since the data does not consider migration within the same country, but the matrix is not symmetrical and the connections between countries can be represented by two elements, since migration to and from a country may have different values.

The edges are color-coded and additional information is available with tooltips.

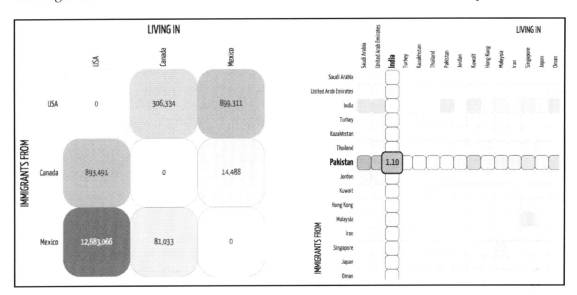

Visualizations created from directed adjacency matrices showing distribution of local immigrants per country. Left: Within North America. Code: *Examples/adjacency-4-migrations-na.html*. Right: Within Asia (in millions). Code: *Examples/adjacency-2-migrations-asia.html*

These charts are interactive. You can load them in a browser and try them out. You can find them in the `Examples/` directory of the GitHub repository for this chapter.

Creating a simple adjacency diagram

You can create a heatmap that displays node adjacencies by binding a matrix to a square grid of shapes and using the value of each element to change the appearance of its corresponding shape. In this section you will learn how to create a reusable layout function that will make this work easier by previously calculating the coordinates for each node.

Consider the following data as an example (see `Adjacency/1-matrix.html`).

```
const matrix = [
    [0, 6, 2, 0, 0],
    [8, 0, 5, 0, 0],
    [0, 1, 0, 0, 0],
    [0, 1, 0, 0, 1],
    [0, 0, 0, 0, 0]
];

const labels = ['A', 'B', 'C', 'D', 'E'];
```

The layout function should receive this data as input and produce an array of objects, containing the original data and additional properties. These properties will be:

- x and y : The x and y coordinates of an SVG rectangle
- w and h: The `width` and `height` attributes of an SVG rectangle

You can adjust the coordinates for other shapes, such as circles or points, of course. The layout function also requires an output range, which can be provided with a `size()` method. For example, to fit the chart in a 700x500 pixel area you might call the generator function like this:

```
const matrixLayout = adjacencyMatrix().size([700,500]);
```

Once you have the layout function, you can call it providing the data:

```
const result = matrixLayout(labels, matrix);
```

And expect as the result a 25-element array with the following structure. The resulting array has *x,y* coordinates for *all* rectangles in the grid, and additional data for the ones that contain values.

```
[
  {"x":0,"y":0,"w":120,"h":120},
  {"source":"A","target":"B","value":6,"x":120,"y":0,"w":120,"h":120},
  {"source":"A","target":"C","value":2,"x":240,"y":0,"w":120,"h":120},
  // 21 more lines
  {"x":480,"y":480,"w":120,"h":120}
]
```

The generator function we described above is not provided by D3, but you can implement it with the code shown as follows (this is a simplified version of the implementation in `JavaScript/dvj-all.js`):

```
function adjacencyMatrix() {
    let w = 1, h = 1;

    function layout(nodes, sourceMatrix) {
        const len = nodes.length;
        const resultMatrix = [];
        for(let s = 0; s < sourceMatrix.length; s++) {
            for(let t = 0; t < sourceMatrix.length; t++) {
                const v = +sourceMatrix[s][t];
                const rect = {x: t*w/len, y: s*h/len, w: w/len, h: h/len};
                if(v > 0) {
                    const edge = {source: nodes[s],
                                  target: nodes[t],
                                  value: value = v};
```

```
                    resultMatrix.push(Object.assign(edge, rect));
            } else {
                    resultMatrix.push(Object.assign({}, rect));
            }
        }
    }
    return resultMatrix;
}

    layout.size = function(array) {
    return arguments.length ? (w=+array[0], h=+array[1], layout) : [w,h];
    }
    return layout;
}
```

Having transformed the data, we now can use the data-binding tools provided by D3 to position the grid and labels using the coordinates that were generated (see `Adjacency/1-matrix.html`):

```
chart.selectAll("rect")
        .data(data).join("rect")
        .attr("x", d => d.x)                         // using d.x
        .attr("y", d => d.y)                         // using d.y
        .attr("height", d => d.h*.95)                // using d.h
        .attr("width", d => d.w*.95)                 // using d.w
        .attr("rx",d => d.w/4)                       // using d.w
        .attr("ry", d => d.h/4)                      // using d.h
        .style("fill", d => d.value ? color(d.value) : 'white');

chart.selectAll('text.source')
        .data(data.filter(d => d.x == 0))
        .enter()
        .append("text").attr("class",'source')
        .attr("y", d => d.y + d.h/2 + 7)             // using d.y and d.h
        .attr("x", -15)
        .text((d,i) => labels[i]);

chart.selectAll('text.target')
        .data(data.filter(d => d.y == 0))
        .enter()
        .append("text").attr("class",'target')
        .attr("x", d => d.x + d.w/2)                 // using d.x and d.w
        .attr("y", -10)
        .text((d,i) => labels[i]);
```

Styles for the rectangles and text were configured in CSS:

```
rect {
    stroke: black;
}
text {
    text-anchor: middle;
}
text.target {
    text-anchor: end;
}
```

The following code adds labels for each side of the table:

```
chart.append("text")
        .attr("transform", `rotate(-90,${[0,height/2 - margin/2]}) ↵
                        translate(${[0, height/2 - margin/2 - 30]})`)
        .text("FROM");
chart.append("text")
        .attr("transform",`translate(${[width/2 - margin/2, -35]})`)
        .text("TO");
```

The result is shown as follows:

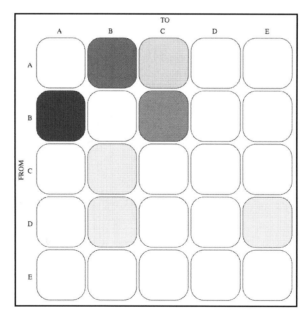

A simple heatmap created from an adjacency matrix using a custom layout generator function.
Code: *Adjacency/1-matrix.html*.

Try creating an adjacency diagram with a larger dataset. You will see that it will automatically adjust to fit in the smaller area. The examples that were shown at the beginning of this section used this same layout function.

You can make the chart interactive by adding row and column highlighting when moving the mouse over a cell (see `Adjacency/3-highlight.html`). This improves legibility and may be a mandatory feature if you have a large table. You will first need to add CSS classes that will be turned on and off during mouse events:

```css
.faded {
    opacity: .3;
}
.highlight {
    font-weight: bold;
    font-size: 120%;
}
rect.highlight {
    stroke-width: 3px;
}
```

The following code captures mouse events on all rectangles redirecting them to event handler functions:

```
chart.selectAll('rect').on('mouseover', highlight).on('mouseout', fade)
```

The `fade()` and `highlight()` functions receive the current datum and add or remove CSS classes from rectangles and text elements, changing their appearance based on the data they contain.

```javascript
function highlight(d) {
d3.selectAll("rect").classed('faded',k => !(k.x == d.x || k.y == d.y));
d3.selectAll("rect").classed('highlight',k => k.x == d.x ||k.y == d.y);
d3.selectAll("text.source").classed('highlight', k => k.x == d.x);
d3.selectAll("text.target").classed('highlight', k => k.y == d.y);
}

function fade(d) {
    d3.selectAll("rect, text").classed("faded highlight", false);
}
```

The result, when moving the mouse over the *B to C* link, is shown as follows:

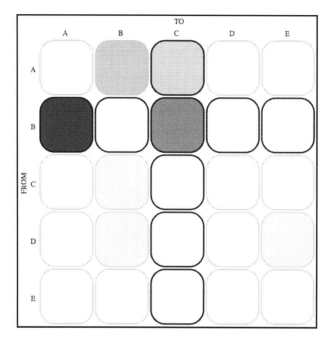

The adjacency diagram with an interactive feature highlighting the nodes connected to a link.
Code: *Adjacency/3-highlight.html*

You can further improve the chart, for example, by displaying the link's value when the mouse is over a cell, or drawing a tooltip somewhere in the chart with extra information (see `Adjacency/4-tooltip.html`). Additional examples using adjacency matrices are available in `Examples/` directory.

Chord diagrams

A *chord diagram* is a graphical method of displaying matrix data, where nodes are distributed in a circular layout. Nodes are points radially positioned on the edge of a circumference, while links are lines that cross the circle to connect the points. It's also called a *radial network diagram*. It's a good choice for small datasets of undirected data with few connections, since directed links arriving and leaving a pair of nodes will overlap. The undirected matrix shown in the previous section, comparing border extensions of 13 countries, can be efficiently rendered as the following chord diagram:

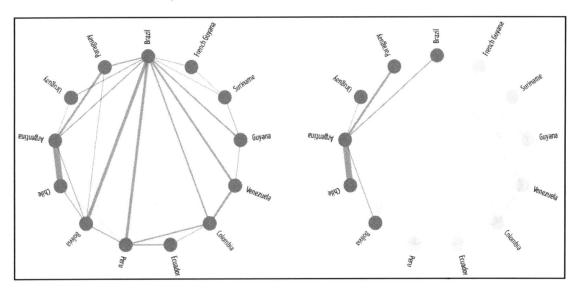

A simple circular layout (non-ribbon chord diagram) showing South American countries (nodes) that have common borders.
The width of each line (link) is proportional to the extension of the border. Code: *Examples/circle-1-borders-sa.html*.

D3 doesn't include layout generators for this kind of simple chart (the one used to create the charts above is available in `JavaScript/dvj-all.js`) but features a more sophisticated type of chord diagram that divides the circle into arcs using curved *ribbons* to connect them. This chart supports directed graphs by allowing different ribbon widths at each end. *Chord/ribbon* diagrams are actually more popular than the non-ribbon chord diagrams.

The following example is a chord/ribbon version of the previous chart. Since the flow is undirected and symmetrical, both ends of a ribbon will have the same width. To highlight which countries make up the borders of each other country, this chart applies a gradient to the ribbons so that the color at each end reflects the color of the opposite node.

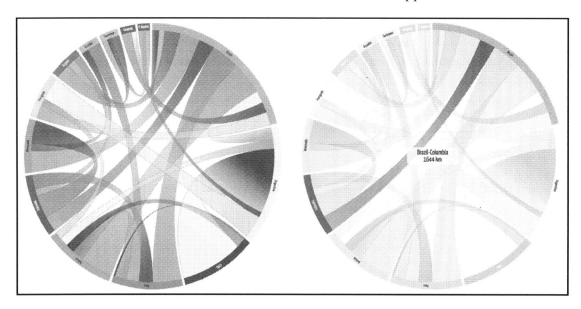

Chord diagram showing the relative extensions of borders between countries in South America. Tooltips and highlighting can be used to obtain details about selected connections. Code: *Examples/chord-4-borders-gradient.html*.

This second example shows the relative number of immigrants among selected countries (based on the same data used for the adjacency matrix examples). The ribbons connect country of residence to country of origin. The origin determines the color of each ribbon. Unlike the previous chart, this one contains asymmetric bidirectional connections so the ribbon-ends have different widths.

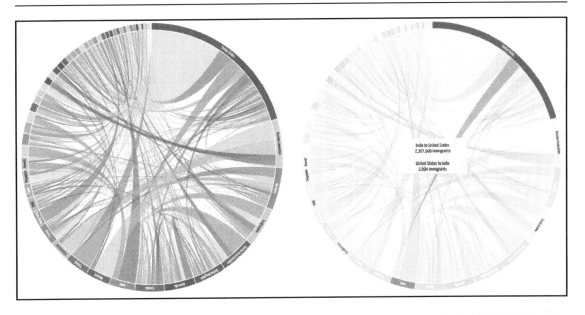

A directed chord diagram showing the relative amount of immigrants in each country linked to their country of origin. The dataset was filtered to include only the 50 countries with greatest immigrant population. Code: *Examples/chord-6-migrations.html*.

Where in the previous chart interactivity is optional, this chart is not very useful without it. You can see that one quarter of the immigrants in the United States come from a single country, but the chart doesn't provide enough resolution to discover which country it is unless you move the mouse to highlight the link and read the tooltip. It may be too much information for this type of layout.

Chord diagrams are best for undirected networks or directed networks where all links are bidirectional. Since a single ribbon always represents a pair of links, if one is missing or zero, the ribbon width on that end will be zero. Nodes that only receive target links produce arcs of zero radians, and vanish from the chart. These diagrams are usually a bad choice for trees or unidirectional topologies.

You can try out these and other examples running the code available in the `Examples/` folder.

Creating a chord/ribbon diagram

Chord/ribbon diagrams can be created in D3 using the generator functions from the *d3-chord* module, which is part of the default D3 bundle. The module contains two layout generator functions: the d3.chord() layout generator and d3.ribbon() shape generator described in the table below. A typical chord diagram also uses the d3.arc() shape generator (from *d3-shape*) to render nodes.

Function	Description
d3.chord()	Returns a chord layout generator function. The layout function receives a matrix as input returning an array of *chord* objects (links) and an array of *groups* (nodes).
d3.ribbon()	Returns a ribbon path generator function. The function receives a chord object and uses its properties to generate an SVG path string for a ribbon, or a sequence of canvas path commands if configured with the context() method, providing a Canvas context.

Generator functions for chords and ribbons.

It's easier to understand with a simple example. Consider the following adjacency matrix data (see Chord/1-ribbon.html):

```
const matrix = [
    [0,3,3,3,0,0,0,2,4],
    [3,0,5,0,0,0,0,0,0],
    [8,5,0,6,0,0,4,0,0],
    [9,0,8,0,9,0,0,0,0],
    [0,0,0,9,0,8,0,0,0],
    [0,0,0,0,9,0,7,8,0],
    [0,0,9,0,0,7,0,7,0],
    [3,0,0,0,0,8,6,0,7],
    [4,0,0,0,0,0,0,9,0]
];
```

The first step is to convert this data using a chord layout. If your data is in a different format, you will need to convert it to an adjacency matrix first (see Chord/9-from-nodelink.html for a chord diagram created from a node-link array converted into an adjacency matrix).

A chord layout function is created below using d3.chord(). The padAngle() method for d3.chord() is used to add spacing between groups (represented by nodes). It receives an angle in radians.

```
const chord = d3.chord().padAngle(.3);   // generates a chord() function
```

To generate the chord data, call the chord function with the `matrix` as input:

```
const chords = chord(matrix);
console.log(chords); // View the generated data in your console!
```

View the result in your browser's JavaScript console. For an $n * n$ adjacency matrix received as input, the output will be an array k objects (*chord* objects), where k is the number of non-zero elements of the matrix, and a second array of n objects (*group* objects), in the `groups` property:

```
chords:  [ {...}, {...},..., {...} ] // 14 objects
chords.groups: [ {...}, ..., {...} ] // 9 objects
```

Each object in the chords array has the following structure:

```
{source: {...}, target: {...}}
```

And *each* `source` or `target` contains an object with the five properties listed below, used to draw ribbons:

- `index`: the *row* index of the input matrix
- `subindex`: the *column* index of the input matrix
- `value`: the value originally stored in `matrix[row][column]`
- `startAngle` and `endAngle` (computed angles in radians for one of the ribbon sides).

Each object in the `groups` array contains four properties, used to draw arcs that represent nodes:

- `index` (the *row* index of the input matrix),
- `value` (the sum of the values of the row),
- `startAngle` and `endAngle` (computed angles in radians for the group).

Now that we have a chord data structure, we can use it with the `d3.arc()` and `d3.ribbon()` shape generators to render a chord/ribbon diagram.

Groups are rendered as arcs, so their `startAngle` and `endAngle` should be provided as input to an *arc* layout function (see `d3.arc()` in Chapter 7, *Shape and Layout Generators*).

A ribbon function is created as follows . The `radius()` method for `d3.ribbon()` sets the radius of the circular chart. This radius is used for all ribbons:

```
const ribbon = d3.ribbon().radius(700); // generates a ribbon() function
```

The `ribbon()` function above will generate an SVG path string using the provided `radius`. Four other properties are obtained from each chord object: the `startAngle` and `endAngle` from each `source` and `target` nodes. To generate the SVG path string for the ribbon, you need to bind SVG path elements to the `chords` array and call the `ribbon()` function for each datum. This is shown in the following code.

```
const color = d3.scaleSequential(d3.interpolateRainbow)
                .domain([0,matrix.length]);
const chart = svg.append("g")
                 .attr("transform",
                       `translate(${[width/2+margin/4,
height/2+margin/4]})`);

chart.selectAll('path.ribbon')
      .data(chords).join("path").attr("class",'ribbon')
      .attr("d", ribbon)      // calls the ribbon function for each datum
      .style("opacity", .3)
      .style("fill", d => color(d.source.index));
```

The expected result is shown as follows:

Drawing semitransparent ribbons in a chord/ribbon diagram. Code: *Chord/1-ribbon.html*.

The next step is to draw the nodes. In this case we bind SVG `<path>` elements to the `chords.groups` array and call the following `arc()` function for each datum:

```
const arc = d3.arc().innerRadius(radius+2).outerRadius(radius+30);

chart.selectAll('path.arc')
```

```
    .data(chords.groups)
    .join("path").attr("class",'arc')
    .attr("d", arc)      // calls the arc function for each datum
    .style("fill", d => color(d.index));
```

The result is shown as follows:

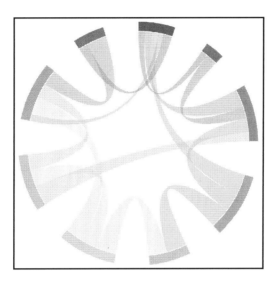

Drawing arcs as nodes in a chord/ribbon diagram. Chord/2-nodes.html.

Labels can be added using the nodes from the headers array and the `index` property of each group. The following code uses the arc's centroid to position the text (see `Chord/3-labels.html`):

```
chart.selectAll("text")
    .data(chords.groups).join("text")
    .attr("x", d => arc.centroid(d)[0])
    .attr("y", d => arc.centroid(d)[1])
    .text(d => headers[d.index])
    .attr("transform", d => `rotate(${(arc.endAngle()(d) +
    arc.startAngle()(d))*90/Math.PI}, ${arc.centroid(d)})`);
```

You can increase or reduce the `padAngle()` and sort the ribbons in several ways using configuration methods for the `d3.chord()` function, listed in the table as follows:

Function	Description
`padAngle(angle)`	The angle in radians between adjacent groups (nodes). Default is zero.
`sortGroups(comp)`	Receives a comparator to sort groups (nodes, rows).
`sortSubgroups(comp)`	Receives a comparator to sort subgroups (links, columns) within each group.
`sortChords(comp)`	Receives a comparator to sort chords (affects the order in which they overlap).

Configuration methods for the *d3.chord()* layout generator function.

For example, this code will sort the groups by descending value (see `Chord/4-sort-groups.html`):

```
const chord = d3.chord()
        .sortGroups((a,b) => d3.descending(a,b));
```

You can also sort the ribbons within each group (see `Chord/5-sort-subgroups.html`):

```
const chord = d3.chord()
        .sortGroups((a,b) => d3.descending(a,b))        // sorts nodes
        .sortSubgroups((a,b) => d3.descending(a,b)); // sorts ribbons
```

When there are many data connections, it can be difficult to follow the ribbons. You can improve readability with interactive features, for example, you can fade out other nodes and links to focus on the selected data. The following functions select unselected arcs and ribbons and apply a CSS class that reduces their opacity (CSS is not shown).

```
function highlightNode(node) {
    d3.selectAll("path.arc").classed("faded", d => !(d === node));
    d3.selectAll("path.ribbon")
      .classed("faded", edge => !(edge.source.index === node.index));
}
function highlightRibbon(edge) {
    d3.selectAll("path.arc")
      .classed("faded", node => !(node.index === edge.source.index
                               || node.index === edge.target.index))
    d3.selectAll("path.ribbon").classed("faded", d => !(d === edge));
}
function fade(node) {
    d3.selectAll("path").classed("faded", false);
}
```

To call them, they must be registered as event handlers for mouse events. See the full code in `Chords/6-highlight.html`. The result is shown below.

```
d3.selectAll("path.arc").on("mouseover", highlightNode)
                        .on("mouseout", fade);
d3.selectAll("path.ribbon").on("mouseover", highlightRibbon)
                           .on("mouseout", fade);
```

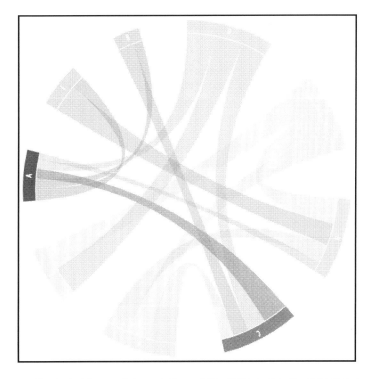

Readability of a chord diagram can be improved with arc and ribbon highlighting. Code: *Chord/6-highlight.html*.

The `d3.ribbon()` and `d3.arc()` functions can both be initialized with a HTML Canvas context using the `context()` method. This will make each generator function call a sequence of Canvas path functions instead of returning an SVG string. This can improve the performance when drawing chord diagrams with lots of data, but it also makes it more complicated to select individual ribbons for the interactive behaviors. See `Chord/8-canvas.html` for a Canvas-rendered version of this chart.

Additional examples are available in the *Examples/* folder, which include chord diagrams with additional features such as arc labels, tooltips and different highlighting effects, and Canvas implementations.

Sankey diagrams

In a *Sankey* diagram, lines or arrows of variable widths represent quantities *flowing* from one *stage* (node) to another. The chart is a *directed acyclic graph* (DAG). After reaching a stage, a flow may split or join other flows that arrive from previous stages, but never return to a previously visited stage. In most Sankey charts nodes are placed on a vertical grid, uniformly spaced, while curves flow through them. Nodes are usually represented as rectangles or vertical lines and sometimes hidden, to reveal only the flows.

Charles J. Minard's dramatic representation of Napoleon's attempt to invade Russia in 1812, uses a Sankey chart to reveal the tragic the fate of the French soldiers while they marched from Kovno (present-day Kaunas, Lithuania) to Moscow and back. The nodes are placed on geographical locations and the chart is also linked to a line chart with below-zero temperatures at each point.

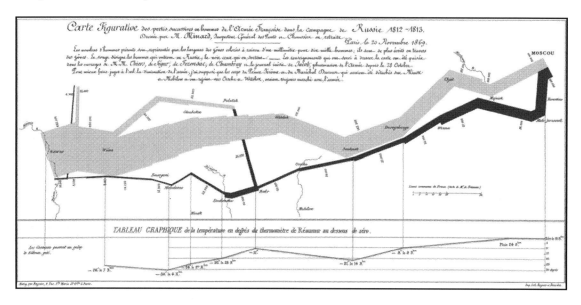

Figurative map of the successive losses of men of the French Army in the Russian campaign 1812-1831. by Charles M. Minard in 1869.
Source: Wikimedia.

The D3v5 distribution features a non-standard module for creating Sankey charts with horizontal links and automatically computed node positions. The following chart was generated using this library and the same data used by Charles Minard.

It only moves in one direction and does not contain temperatures or geographical data, but adds up the total amount of losses and survivors as final stages.

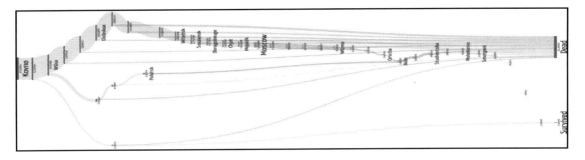

A Sankey diagram of Napoleon's march to Moscow and back inspired by the chart by Charles Minard. Code: *Examples/sankey-1-minard.html*

In the next example each node is a political organization (country or group of countries) and each link represents an event where the organization either splits into smaller units, or gains new members. It shows the effects of the fall of the Berlin Wall, the end of the European Community, the formation of the European Union, and the collapse of Yugoslavia and of the Soviet Union. The width of each link is proportional to the area of each country or group (except Russia, which was reduced so that it would fit).

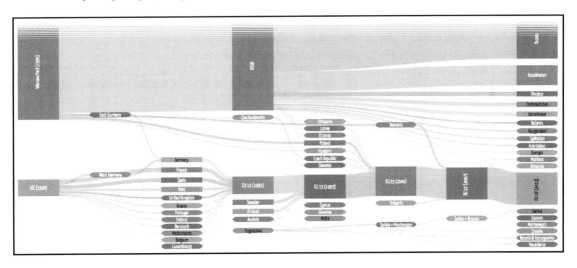

A Sankey diagram revealing political changes in Europe and the USSR from 1990 to 2008. Code: *Examples/sankey-3-europe-ussr.html*.

In both these diagrams, the position of all nodes and links were computed automatically using D3's Sankey algorithm. The full code for these charts and other Sankey examples are available in the `Examples/` folder. The CSV and JSON data is available in the `Data/` folder.

Creating a Sankey diagram

You can create a Sankey diagram using the *d3-sankey* module, which is not part of the default bundle. That means you have to import the module separately. If you use NPM, run:

```
npm install d3-sankey
```

You can also import it directly to an HTML page using the `<script>` tag and the library's CDN URL:

```
<script src="https://unpkg.com/d3-sankey"></script>
```

A Sankey layout function requires a *node-link data structure*, which consists of two datasets: one containing a list of nodes, and a second one containing an adjacency list of link objects identifying the source and target nodes for each link. If your data is in another format you will have to convert it (see the `JavaScript/dvj-all.js` file for conversion functions). The Sankey layout function receives this data as input and adds Cartesian coordinates for each node and link.

The layout function is created with the `d3.sankey()` generator function, where you can configure the width of each node, vertical padding between nodes, number of iterations for node placement, and other properties using the methods listed as follows:

Configuration method	Description
`size` (*array*)	Sets the size of the chart with an array containing *bottom-right x,y* coordinates for the view (same as *width* and *height* if the chart is positioned at 0,0). Default is [1,1]
`extent` (*array*)	Sets position and size of the chart with an array containing two sub-arrays, with the *top-left* and *bottom-right x,y* coordinates for the view. Default is `[[0,0], size()]`.
`iterations` (*number*)	The number of iterations to calculate node placement. Default is 32.
`nodeId` (*function*)	In link objects, `target` and `source` properties locate the corresponding node by their index in the `nodes` array. This method can be used to override this behaviour, returning a different node property as the ID.
`nodeAlign` (*function*)	Configures horizontal node alignment. There are four functions: `d3.sankeyJustify` (default), `d3.sankeyLeft`, `d3.sankeyCenter` and `d3.sankeyRight`.

nodeWidth (*number*)	The default width of each node (this value will be used to generate the x0 and x1 properties for each node). Default is 24.
nodePadding (*number*)	Minimum vertical spacing between nodes at the same level. If this value is too large, the chart may not appear if there is not enough vertical space. Default is 8.
update (*graph*)	After dragging a note and changing its vertical position, this will update the values in the graph (y0 and y1) so that the links can be automatically repositioned.

Configuration methods for d3.sankey() layout functions

The following code creates a sankey() layout function with vertical padding of 50 pixels between each node. All nodes are 30 pixels wide (the height will be computed by the algorithm). The chart has an origin at 50,50 and is 600 pixels wide, 400 pixels tall and uses default alignment (d3.sankeyJustify).

```
const sankey = d3.sankey()
                .nodePadding(50)
                .nodeWidth(30)
                .extent([ [50, 50], [600, 400] ])
                .iterations(100);
```

Two other methods described in the following table, are used to provide the data the function needs to generate layout coordinates. These coordinates are properties that are also listed as follows:

Function	Properties added to each object	Description
nodes (*array*)	sourceLinks, targetLinks value, index depth, height x0, x1, y0, y1	Receives an array of objects, representing the nodes and adds several layout properties to each object. The properties sourceLinks and targetLinks allow navigation to links that arrive and leave each node. The x0, x1, y0 and y1 properties are the coordinates of a rectangle with a width of nodeWidth() and height computed by the algorithm based on the value property. If called without arguments, this method will return the current nodes array.

links (*array*)	y0, y1 width, index	Receives an array of link objects. Each object has the format {source: *nodeID*, target: *nodeID*, value: *number*}, where the default *nodeID* is the array index of a node in the nodes array. You can change the default ID accessor with the nodeId() method. If called without arguments this method will return the current links array.

Data methods for d3.sankey() layout functions (can also be set as parameters when calling the function)

You can also call the function with an object containing the input data as an object:

```
const graph  = sankey({nodes: nodes, links: links});
```

The transformed nodes and links can then be retrieved through the nodes() and links() functions:

```
const sankeyNodes = graph.nodes();
const sankeyNodes = graph.links();
```

We will now demonstrate how to create a Sankey chart using a simple step-by-step example. The following code will generate data for the nodes (a node can be any object, but not a simple string):

```
const nodes = ['A','B','C','D','E','F','G','H'].map(n => ({node: n}));
```

In the links array, all links must move forward, that is, the target index should always be larger than the source index). Link cycles are not permitted, nor are they detected: they will simply hang the application. Each target and source should contain an ID for the corresponding nodes array object. The array index is used as default (but you can override this with the nodeId() method if necessary). We will use the following array:

```
const links = [
    {source: 0, target: 1, value: 3},
    {source: 0, target: 2, value: 4},
    {source: 1, target: 3, value: 2},
    {source: 1, target: 4, value: 1},
    {source: 2, target: 5, value: 3},
    {source: 5, target: 6, value: 1},
    {source: 5, target: 3, value: 2},
    {source: 2, target: 3, value: 1},
    {source: 6, target: 3, value: .5},
    {source: 4, target: 3, value: .5},
    {source: 6, target: 7, value: .5},
```

```
        {source: 4, target: 7, value: .5},
    ];
```

In case you are using real world data (CSV or JSON files), you probably will need to transform your data into this standard format. If you have an adjacency matrix, you can use the `dvj.matrixToLinks()` function from `JavaScript/dvj-all.js`. Be sure to check the data for any cycles.

The following code initializes a `sankey()` function and calls it with the data above to generate the `graph` object. If you list the contents of this object in the JavaScript console, you will notice that each node and link objects now contain several new properties.

```
const sankey = d3.sankey().nodePadding(300)
                    .extent([[50, 50], [700, 450]])
                    .iterations(100);
const graph = sankey({nodes: nodes, links: links});
```

Now you can select some SVG elements and bind them to these coordinates and draw the nodes. This code will set the graphics context for the chart:

```
const color = d3.scaleOrdinal(d3.schemeCategory10).domain([0,
nodes.length]);
const chart = d3.select("body")
                    .append("svg").attr("height",550).attr("width",800)
                    .append("g");
```

And the following code will draw the nodes and labels:

```
chart.selectAll('g.node')
        .data(graph.nodes).join("g")
        .attr("transform", d => `translate(${[d.x0, d.y0]})`)
        .attr("class", "node")
        .each(function(d,i) {
            d3.select(this).append("rect")
                .attr("width", d.x1 - d.x0)
                .attr("height", d.y1 - d.y0)
                .style("fill", color(i))
            d3.select(this).append("text")
                .attr("x", (d.x1 - d.x0)/2)
                .attr("y", (d.y1 - d.y0)/2 + 2)
                .text(d.node);
        });
```

The code for the links should be placed *before* the code for the nodes, so that the SVG rectangles are drawn over the SVG link paths. D3 provides a Sankey horizontal link generator function that creates a path string. You can call it when setting the path's d attribute:

```
chart.selectAll('path.link')
    .data(graph.links).join("path")
    .attr("class", "link")
    .attr("d", d3.sankeyLinkHorizontal())
    .style("stroke-width", d => d.width)
    .style("stroke", d => color(d.source.index));
```

The result (which also added text labels placed on the nodes) is shown in the following screenshot. See the full code in Sankey/Sankey-1.html.

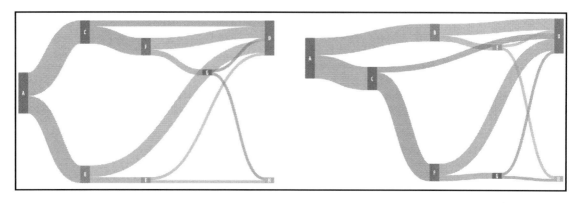

Left: A default-aligned (d3.alignJustify) Sankey diagram. Right: A right-aligned (d3.alignRight) Sankey diagram. Code: Sankey/2-align.html.

You can change the appearance of the chart by changing configuration parameters or alignment. The nodeAlign() method accepts four different algorithms, for example (see Sankey/2-align.html):

```
sankey.nodeAlign(d3.sankeyRight)
```

Other adjustments can be made tweaking with the number of iterations, node padding and data. If you are not satisfied with the automatic rendering, you can assign fixed values to position the nodes vertically, then call sankey.update(graph) to redraw the links at the new positions. You can do this interactively by dragging nodes (see Sankey/4-drag-nodes.html). Other Sankey examples are available in the Examples/ folder.

Arc diagrams

Arc diagrams are linear layouts that place nodes along a horizontal axis connected by arcs. They are good for networks that don't have many nodes or connections, or sequential topologies with few orthogonal links (e.g. train networks). They are also better than chord layouts to represent directional flows, since links in opposite directions span arcs on different sides of the axis.

The following example is another version of Minard's *Russian Campaign* chart. Each node is a location and the arcs are troops. The width of each line is the number of troops marching between each location. The ochre-colored arcs above the axis are advances, and the gray arcs below the axis are retreats.

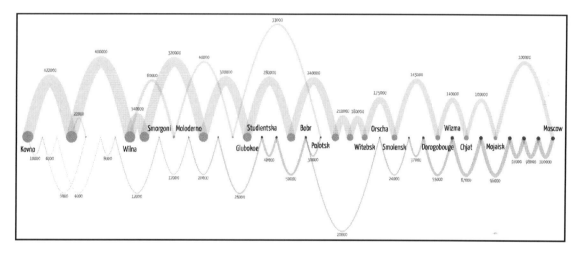

An arc diagram created from the same data as Charles Minard's famous Russian Campaign chart. Code: *Examples/arc-8-minard.html*.

D3 doesn't provide any generator function for arc diagrams, but you can use the one provided in the `JavaScript/dvj-all.js` library, which receives a standard node-link structure. You can configure it providing the horizontal width of the chart and it will add `x` coordinates that you can use to position each node. To use it, include the JavaScript library in your code:

```
<script src="JavaScript/dvj-all.js">
```

Let's use it to create a linear arc diagram for the following data (see `Linear/1-arc-diagram.html`):

```
const nodes = [{node:'A'},{node:'B'},{node:'C'},{node:'D'},{node:'E'}];

const edges = [
    {source: 'A', target: 'B', value: 16},
    {source: 'A', target: 'C', value: 2},
    {source: 'B', target: 'A', value: 8},
    {source: 'B', target: 'C', value: 4},
    {source: 'C', target: 'B', value: 1},
    {source: 'D', target: 'B', value: 1},
    {source: 'D', target: 'E', value: 1}
];
```

If your data is structured as a matrix, use the `dvj.matrixToLinks()` function (from the same library) to convert it to a node-link structure (see `Linear/4-from-matrix.html`).

The following code creates the layout function:

```
const arcLayout = dvj.arcDiagram().width(800);
```

Then you can generate the layout object from the `nodes` and `edges` arrays:

```
const data = arcLayout(nodes, edges);
```

The following code declares a `widthScale` to adjust the value of each link to a range used for the `stroke-width` of each arc. A `color` scale assigns a different color for each node:

```
const chart = d3.select("body").append("svg")
             .attr("width",800).attr("height",600)
             .append("g").attr("transform", `translate(${[400,300]})`);
const widthScale = d3.scaleLinear()   // for the stroke width
                   .range([2,10])
                   .domain([0, d3.max(edges, d => d.value)]);
const color = d3.scaleOrdinal(d3.schemeCategory10)
              .domain([0, nodes.length]);
```

This function returns the links in the `data.links()` method. The `dvj.curve()` function (see `JavaScript/dvj-all.js`) is used to generate an SVG path string that draws a curve from the link data:

```
chart.selectAll("path")
       .data(data.links()).join("path")
       .attr("d", dvj.curve()) // generates a curve for each link
       .style("stroke-width", d => widthScale(d.value))
       .style("stroke", d => color(d.source.i));
```

The nodes are obtained with `data.nodes()`. The following code uses the generated x properties to position each circle and text label in the center (CSS is not shown):

```
chart.selectAll('circle')
        .data(data.nodes()).join('circle')
        .attr('cx', d => d.x)
        .attr('r', 15)
        .style("fill", (d,i) => color(i));

chart.selectAll("text")
        .data(data.nodes()).join("text")
        .attr("x", d => d.x)
        .text(d => d.node);
```

The result is shown as follows:

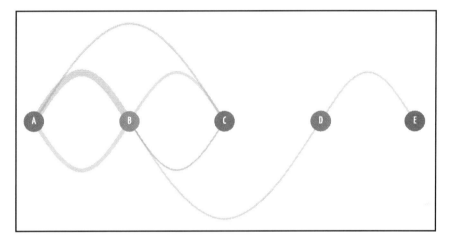

A simple arc diagram created with a custom generator function (see *JavaScript/dvj-all.js*). Code: *Linear/1-arc.html*

Adding more data to an arc diagram can quickly make it unreadable. Interactivity is usually a required feature in these charts. You can use node highlighting to show a node's connections, or link highlighting to reveal which nodes are connected by the selected links. See `Linear/3-highlight-letters.html` for an example using a small dataset. Additional arc diagram examples with interactive node and connection highlighting in larger datasets are also available in the `Examples/` folder.

Node-link diagrams with force-directed simulations

Force-directed simulations solve the problem of deciding where to place the nodes of a network diagram by integrating different forces that iteratively enforce positioning constraints. The process can be used to create not only node-link diagrams, but also clustered bubble charts and word clouds, and to reveal patterns in large scatterplots. They are great to show topology in link-node systems.

A force simulation layout function receives an array of nodes, one or more constraints configured in force algorithms, and runs for a finite number of iterations or until the simulation reaches a stable state. At each iteration, computed x and y coordinate positions are assigned for each node.

You can create static charts by running several iterations of the simulation in the background, and then using the computed final node positions to render the chart. The Sankey algorithm works this way. But it's not more complex to create an animated simulation, where intermediate coordinates are used to produce a dynamic visualization.

The duration of an animated simulation is controlled by an internal timer that, at each iteration, logarithmically decrements a value (the *alpha*) that converges towards a limit (the *alpha target*). The simulation stops when *alpha* reaches a threshold (the *minimum alpha*) before the target. The animation lasts for a finite number of iterations. *Velocity* values are computed for each node during each iteration, and are then applied to its x and y positions. Velocities also decrement logarithmically, making the simulation decelerate smoothly towards stability.

The following bubble chart was created using a force-directed simulation. The bubbles represent countries linked by continent, and their area represents the total number of immigrants. Links and positioning forces are attracted towards each other and around chosen centers in the chart. A collision detection force avoids node overlapping.

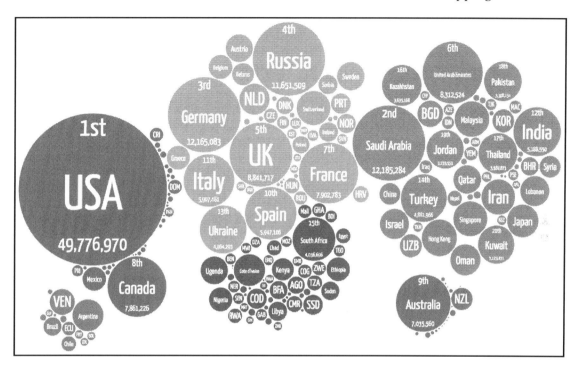

A force-directed bubble chart displaying the population of immigrants in each country (generated from data in CSV format obtained from the United Nations data portal). Code: *Examples/force-static-7-bubble-continents-migrants-position.html.*

This second example is a network diagram representation of the data structure (triangular matrix) containing borders between South American countries that we have used in different chart examples throughout this chapter. The area of each node is proportional to the land area of each country, and the width of the links is proportional to their common borders.

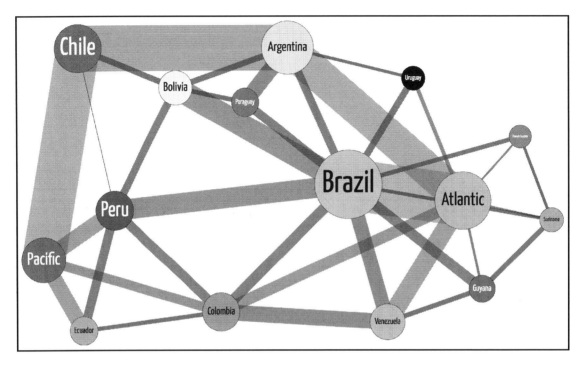

A force directed undirected symmetrical network with weighted links that reveal the extensions of coastlines and borders in the South American continent. Code: *Examples/force-dynamic-11-links-borders-sa.html*.

These examples are animated interactive charts with highlighting and dragging behaviors. You can download them from the `Examples/` folder and try them out.

Creating a force-directed network diagram

The *d3-force* module contains most of the API you will need to create force-directed diagrams. It's included in the default bundle, which already provides all required dependencies.

To create a new force simulation you need to provide the `d3.forceSimulation()` function with an *array of nodes* (containing any objects, even empty ones, but not plain strings). Several positioning properties will be added to each node. Once you create a simulation it starts immediately, but nothing will happen unless you initialize it with one or more *force algorithms*. If you wish to animate the simulation, you should also register a handler for *tick* events. These tasks are performed by the methods listed as follows:

Method	Description
`nodes` (*array*)	Overrides the default nodes *array* (optional parameter) used by the simulation. If called without parameters, returns the current *nodes* array used by the simulation.
`force` (*key, algorithm*)	Adds a *force algorithm* to the simulation. This method is usually called multiple times to add different force functions and configurations. The *key* can be used to replace an existing force algorithm with a new function or configuration or to remove it by declaring *null* as the second parameter.
`on` (*event, handler*)	Binds an event handler to a simulation event. There are two possible event identifiers: *tick*, which is called at every simulation tick, and *end*, called when the simulation is done.

Main initialization methods for a d3.forceSimulation()

Let's create a simple example (see `Force/no-force.html`). We will use the following nodes array:

```
const nodes = [
    {node: 'A', value: 79},
    {node: 'B', value: 15},
    {node: 'C', value: 24},
    {node: 'D', value: 44},
    {node: 'E', value: 125},
    {node: 'F', value: 22},
    {node: 'G', value: 20},
    {node: 'H', value: 64},
];
```

A new simulation can be created with the code shown below. It starts producing ticks immediately.

```
const sim = d3.forceSimulation(nodes);
```

If you now view the `nodes` array in your browser's JavaScript console, you will notice that each node has gained *five* new properties. They represent the array `index` of the node plus four computed absolute and relative Cartesian positions. The following table lists and describes all properties that are generated for each node. Only `fx` and `fy,` used to override computed values, are not generated by the simulation.

Function	Description
index	The *index* of each node.
x, y	The current *x,y* coordinates of the node. New positions are computed from the current alpha value and decay rate at every tick by adding values from vx and vy. If fx or vy are present, their values replace any values stored in x or y.
vx, vy	The current horizontal and vertical velocities of the node. The values are zero if the simulation is finished. New values are computed from the current alpha value and velocity decay rate at every tick and added to x and y.
fx, fy	The fixed *x,y* coordinates of each node. These values are not changed by the algorithm and can be used to place nodes in a fixed position. If present, their values are copied to x and y (unless they are null).

Properties that are added to each object in the nodes array used by a d3.forceSimulation().

Although the simulation is already running, the values of `vx` and `vy` in all nodes are zero. They should contain relative node distances between iterations. The value is expected to be zero when the simulation ends, which a few seconds after it starts. But in this case they are zero because we haven't yet attached any forces. Without forces, no positions are ever changed and the nodes don't move.

But the `x` and `y` properties *do* have assigned values, so before attaching any forces, let's bind these nodes to circles we can view where they are positioned on the screen (see `Force/1-no-force.html`):

```
const nodes = [...];
const color =
d3.scaleOrdinal(d3.schemeCategory10).domain([0,nodes.length]);
const svg = d3.select("body").append("svg")
            .attr("width",400).attr("height",400);
const chart = svg.append("g").attr("transform", `translate(${[200,200]})`);

const sim = d3.forceSimulation(nodes);
```

```
chart.selectAll("circle")
        .data(nodes).join("circle")
        .attr("r", 15)
        .attr("cx", d => d.x)
        .attr("cy", d => d.y)
        .style("fill", (d,i) => color(i))
```

The result is shown in the following. Note that the nodes were initialized around a central position (this is called a *phyllotaxis* arrangement):

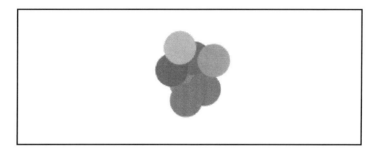

Nodes clustered in phyllotaxis arrangement (default where there are no forces attached). Code: */Force/1-no-force.html*.

To view the effects of the simulation we will now add a listener to track *tick* events and update the circle positions whenever a tick occurs:

```
sim.on("tick", d => chart.selectAll("circle")
                            .attr("cx", d => d.x)
                            .attr("cy", d => d.y);
```

The simulation runs with 300 iterations (default) but the nodes don't move. To change that situation we will add a *force*. Since the nodes are all clustered together we need a *repulsion* force to move them apart. The d3.forceManyBody() function provides electrostatic-like repulsion as default (but can also be used for gravity-like attraction). The following code will add this repulsion force to the simulation (see Force/2-dynamic.html).

```
sim.force("manybody", d3.forceManyBody());
```

Now you can reload the page and see the results. The circles will quickly dash apart and slowly decelerate until the simulation ends at tick number 300. The following illustrations shows a static representation of several moments during a force animation (see `Force/3-static.html`):

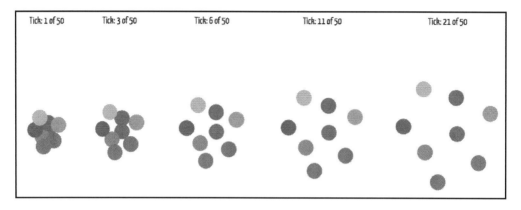

A simple force simulation with a single repulsion force after some iterations. Code: *Force/3-static.html*.

Sometimes you just want to compute the final coordinates for each node without any animation. You can do that by stopping the animation as soon as it starts, and then calling `tick()` until the simulation reaches a desired stable state.

The following code runs the same simulation manually, obtaining a static layout after 50 iterations and using it to draw the nodes at their final position:

```
const sim = d3.forceSimulation(nodes)
        .force("manybody", d3.forceManyBody()) // configure force
        .stop(); // stop the simulation as soon as it starts

for(let i = 0; i < 50; i++) {  // generate 50 ticks
    sim.tick();
}
chart.selectAll("circle")
     .data(nodes).join("circle")
     .attr("r", 15)
     .attr("cx", d => d.x)
     .attr("cy", d => d.y)
     .style("fill", (d,i) => color(i))
```

To see this in action, run the `Force/3-static.html` which calls the `tick()` method every half-second, or `Force/4-interactive.html` where ticks are created at every button press.

Forces

Besides `d3.forceManyBody()`, D3 contains six other force algorithms that compute node positions and velocities. A typical simulation combines the effects of several forces, and each force can be configured with a unique behavior. Some forces cause nodes to repel or attract, while others resolve specific positioning constraints, such as moving in a certain direction or keeping a certain distance apart. The following illustration gives a general view of the force algorithms available in D3:

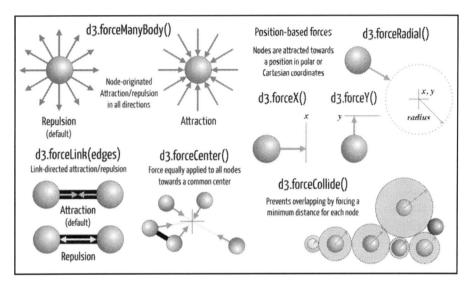

Force algorithms available in D3 version 5.

The following table lists the force algorithms and their configuration methods. Functions that receive one or more parameters can be called without parameters and configured using methods. Methods accept scalar values and most of them also accept callback functions that can be called per-node.

Function	Configuration methods	Description
`d3.forceCenter(x,y)`	`.x(x)`, `.y(y)`: overrides parameters.	A centering force that is applied equally to all nodes, pulling them towards a center position. Default = 0,0. Values can be provided by x,y parameters or `.x()` and `.y()` methods. They must be numbers, not functions.

d3.forceX (*x*)	.x (*x*): overrides *x* parameter. .strength (*value*): a non-negative value between 0 and 1.	A positioning force towards a line perpendicular to the *x*-axis. Position and strength can be configured per-node or for all nodes (default = 0.1).
d3.forceY (*y*)	.y (*y*): overrides *y* parameter. .strength (*value*): a non-negative value between 0 and 1.	A positioning force towards a line perpendicular to the *y*-axis. Position and strength can be configured per-node or for all nodes (default = 0.1).
d3.forceRadial ()	.radius (*radius*), .x (*x*), .y (*y*): overrides default parameters. .strength (*value*): a non-negative value between 0 and 1.	A positioning force towards the edge of a circle with provided *radius* (default = 1) and *center* (0,0). Position and strength can be configured per-node or for all nodes (default = 0.1).
d3.forceCollide ()	.radius (*radius*): overrides default. .strength (*value*): a non-negative value between 0 and 1. .iterations (*integer*): number of iterations per tick (default: 1)	A force that pushes nodes away until distance is equal or larger than the sum of their collision radii. Collision *radius* (default = 1) and *strength* (default = 0.7) can be configured per-node or for all nodes. More iterations speed up collision resolution.
d3.forceLink ()	.links (*links*): overrides default. .id (*function*): the acessor for the node ID (default is index) .distance (): space between nodes .strength (*value*): a negative or positive value. .iterations (*integer*): number of iterations per tick (default: 1)	A directed force along the link that connects two nodes. This force requires an array of link objects and affects both connected nodes. A positive strength causes *attraction*. A negative strength causes *repulsion*. The default strength (attraction) is inversely proportional to the degree (number of connections) of least connected node. More iterations speed up resolution.

d3.forceManyBody()	.strength(*value*): overrides default. .distanceMin(): min distance between nodes (default: 1) .distanceMax(): max distance between nodes (default: Infinity) .theta(value): threshold value for the simulation (default: 0.9)	A force that simulates gravity or electrostatic repulsion (based on the Barnes-Hut astrophysics algorithm). It affects all nodes, in all directions. A positive strength causes *attraction*. A negative strength causes *repulsion*. Default is -30. Performance is improved setting upper and lower limits to distanceMax() and distanceMin(). A higher theta() increases speed, but lowers accuracy.

Force algorithms and configuration methods.

Besides the methods listed above, all forces support initialize(nodes), which updates the *nodes* array when necessary (for example interactive charts where nodes can be added or removed dynamically).

The best way to understand how forces work is to first apply them in isolation, experiment with their configuration parameters, and then try them out with other forces. In each of the examples that follow, a single force is applied to a set of nodes, revealing its effect after a finite number of iterations.

We saw d3.forceManyBody() in action in the previous example, using the default value for its strength() method (-30), which makes nodes repel each other. A positive value will make nodes attract. You can also change the intensity of the strength or apply the force differently to individual nodes.

The following illustration shows the effect of a single `d3.forceManyBody()` applied to a group of nodes.

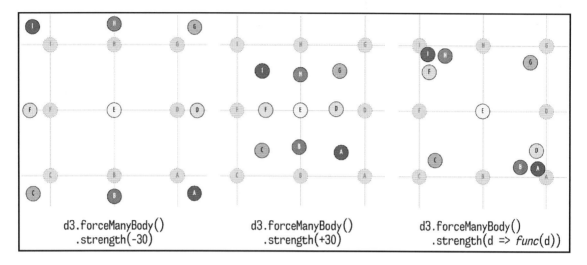

Effects of simulations configured with a single force of the type d3.forceManyBody(), acting on nodes with previous positions indicated by the gray circles, after 300 iterations. Code: *Force/ManyBody/*.html*

You can view the source code and experiment with these examples running the files in the `Force/ManyBody/` folder.

You will only see `d3.forceCollision()` in action if nodes are close enough to violate its minimum radius constraint. This constraint will keep circles from overlapping if it is equal or larger than the sum of the radii of the neighboring circles. The value may be a constant if all nodes have equal radius, or a function returning a different value for each node. This force is usually combined with forces that attract nodes, such as `d3.forceLink()`, `d3.forceManyBody()` or positioning forces.

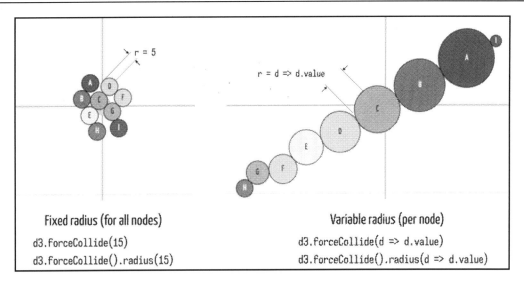

Effects of simulations configured with a single force of type d3.forceCollide(). acting on nodes
previously positioned in the center. after 300 iterations. Code: *Force/Collide/3-strength.html and 4-variable-radius.html*

These and other examples with `d3.forceCollision()` are available in the
`Force/Collide/` folder.

Positioning forces used in isolation attract nodes towards a coordinate axis or a
circumference. By adding both `d3.forceX()` and `d3.forceY()` to a simulation, you can
integrate forces that will attract nodes to a specific point. The following illustration shows
the effect of a single one of these forces applied to a set of nodes.

You can also configure the *strength* of the force but it only works well with positive values between 0 and 1.

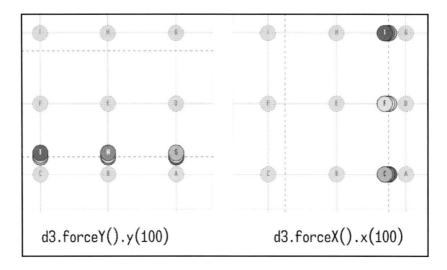

Effects of simulations configured with a single force of type d3.forceX() (left) and d3.forceY() (right)
acting on nodes with previous positions indicated by the gray circles, after 300 iterations. Code: *Force/PositionXY/1-x.html and 2-y.html*

Even if there is no opposing force, you can't guarantee that the nodes will really end up exactly in the expected position. The computation depends on many factors, including strength and number of iterations. If the strength and iterations are low enough, the simulation may have finished before the nodes reach their destination. With other forces interacting, it becomes even more difficult to preview exactly where the node will be placed.

Additional examples with `d3.forceY()` and `d3.forceX()` are available in the `Force/PositionXY/` folder.

The d3.forceRadial() function is a positioning function that attracts nodes towards a circumference defined by *x,y* center coordinates (default is 0,0) and a *radius* (default is 1). The following illustration shows its effects when applied in isolation to a group of nodes.

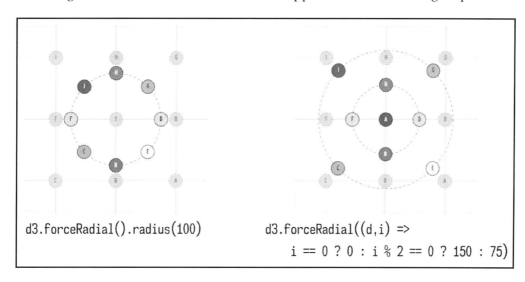

```
d3.forceRadial().radius(100)          d3.forceRadial((d,i) =>
                                        i == 0 ? 0 : i % 2 == 0 ? 150 : 75)
```

Effects of simulations configured with a single force of type d3.forceRadial() acting on nodes with previous positions indicated by the gray circles. after 300 iterations. Code: *Force/PositionRadial/1-radial.html* and *2-radial-2.html*

You can experiment with these examples running the files in the Force/PositionRadial/ folder.

Node-link network diagrams can be created using d3.forceLink(), which requires a standard adjacency list (with source and target properties) referring to objects in the *nodes* array. Links cause *directed* repulsion or attraction (default) between nodes, and can be used to reveal clusters, degree centrality and other topological aspects of a chart. The following illustration shows the effect of link forces applied in isolation to a set of connected nodes. The effect will be very different if other values for strength() are applied.

The gray lines indicate how the nodes were connected before the force was applied.

Effects of simulations configured with a single force of type d3.forceLink() acting on nodes with previous positions and links indicated by gray circles and lines, after 300 iterations. Code: *Force/Link/2-sequential.html and 6-strength-per-link.html*

Link forces can also add additional constraints for node distance and number of iterations. The `distance()` method tries to keep a specific distance between nodes, and the `iterations()` method (also used in collide and positioning forces) can help the function converge faster towards resolution (at a performance cost).

These and several other examples with `d3.forceLink()` are available in the "Force/Link" folder.

While a simulation runs, nodes may be pushed off-screen changing the network's center of gravity. The `d3.forceCenter()` function provides a force that is applied *uniformly* on all nodes, keeping them attracted to a chosen center of gravity. Unlike all other forces, it doesn't deform the existing node structure.

The following illustration compares `d3.forceCenter()` with positioning forces `d3.forceX()` and `d3.forceY()`.

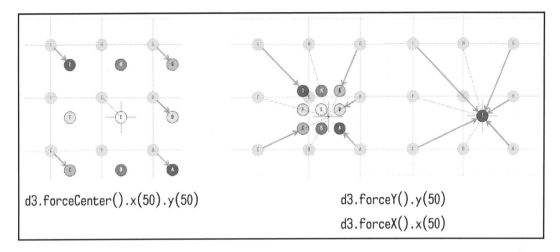

d3.forceCenter().x(50).y(50)   d3.forceY().y(50)
                                       d3.forceX().x(50)

A simulation configured with a single force of type d3.forceCenter() compared to a simulation with two positioning forces of type d3.forceX() and d3.forceY() with the same center. after 150 and 300 iterations. Code: *Force/Center/2-center-xy.html* and *PositionXY/3-xy-center.html*.

Typical simulations contain different forces with competing constraints that are resolved after a finite number of iterations. The following code combines five different forces to attract a set of linked nodes to the edges of an ellipse (see `Force/Combinations/link+collide+position+radial.html`):

```
d3.forceSimulation(nodes)
  .force("center", d3.forceCenter())
  .force("link", d3.forceLink(links).iterations(5).distance(1))
  .force("collide", d3.forceCollide(15))
  .force("radial", d3.forceRadial(200).strength(.1))
  .force("y", d3.forceY().strength(.05))
  .on("tick", redraw);
```

The process is illustrated in the screenshots below, showing where the nodes are placed in several iterations from the initial *phyllotaxis* arrangement to the 300th tick.

The final result can be very different if you make small adjustments in the properties of each force, especially `iterations()`, `strength()` and link `distance()`:

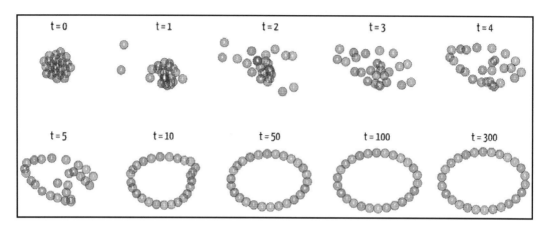

Applying a combination of forces to linked nodes. Code: *Force/Combinations/link+collide+position+radial.html*.

Try experimenting with the examples in the `Force/` folder, which includes several simple simulations with forces in isolation and combinations. Change their values and see what results you get. You can also run the "Force/App/1-forces.html" D3 application (shown in the following screenshot), where you can select different forces and see their effects.

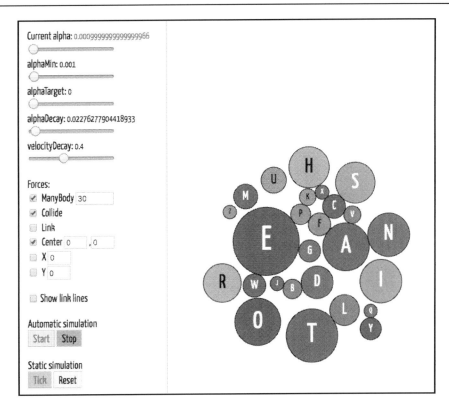

Run the Force/Interactive-Alpha/interactive-force.html application and experiment with different
features of the d3-force library. Code: *Force/App/1-forces.html*

Simulation dynamics

You can configure the duration and dynamics of a simulation by changing its *alpha* value,
decay rates, thresholds and limits. The methods that allow these configurations are listed in
the following table:

Method	Description
stop()	Stops the simulation. To update positions in this state it is necessary to call `tick()`.
restart()	Restarts an existing simulation, maintaining current position and alpha values. This method will only restart the simulation if the `alpha()` value is set to a value higher than `alphaMin()`.

`tick()`	Explicitly causes a *tick* event, moving the *alpha* value closer to the *alpha target*, calls each force with the new alpha, decrements each node's velocity and increments its position with the new velocity. This method is used in static simulations and ignores the *alpha minimum*.
`alpha()`	*Alpha* is a value between 0 and 1 that is decremented or incremented at each *tick* (by the *alpha decay* rate) so that it moves closer to an *alpha target* value. In automatic simulations, it usually reaches a threshold (*alpha minimum*) before the target, stopping the simulation. This method sets or returns the current alpha during a simulation. It can be a value between 0 and 1. The initial value is 1. It is decremented by the *alpha* decay rate at each tick.
`alphaMin()`	Sets or returns the *alpha minimum* used as a threshold in automatic simulations. When the current *alpha* is equal or less than the *alpha minimum*, the simulation ends. Default is 0.001.
`alphaDecay()`	Sets or returns the *alpha decay* rate at each tick. The default rate is approximately 0.023 and is calculated so that the simulation will finish in 300 iterations, considering the default values for *alpha minimum* (0.001) and *target alpha* (0).
`alphaTarget()`	Sets or returns the *alpha target* for this simulation. During the simulation, *alpha* tends to a limit (of its logarithmic function) which is the *alpha target*. If it is greater than *alpha minimum*, the simulation runs forever. Default is zero.
`velocityDecay()`	During the simulation, node velocities are decremented by the *velocity decay* rate, which can be any number between 0 and 1 (default is 0.4). This rate decelerates node position changes as the simulation approaches its end.

Methods of d3.forceSimulation() used to configure the global dynamic behavior of the simulation.

The relationship between alpha controls is shown in the following chart, which you can run as a dynamic application in `Force/App/2-alpha-linear.html`.

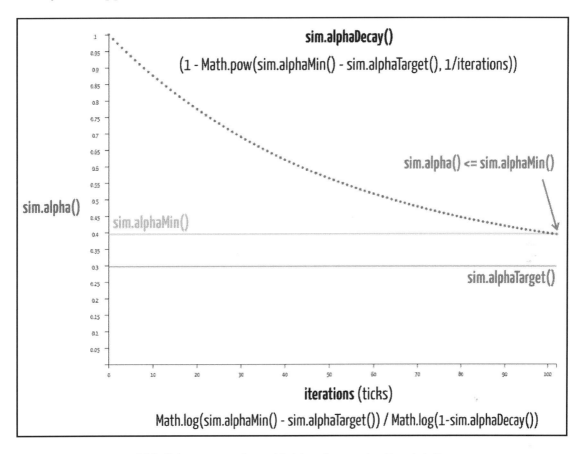

Relationship between parameters that control simulations and compute node positions and velocities.
Code: *Force/App/2-alpha-linear.html*

The chart shows the decay of the current alpha during 300 iterations (default) until it reaches the alpha minimum and stops. Try moving the alpha minimum below the alpha target to see the simulation run forever. You can change these values during a simulation, so that a simulation runs longer in certain situations (e.g. when adding, removing nodes or dragging nodes).

Interactive highlighting

Although network visualizations can reveal important topological information, many times it is difficult to identify individual nodes and their connections. With interactive highlighting you can select groups of nodes and links and hide them so that the relevant parts of the diagram stand out.

In this example (see `Force/Interactive/1-highlight.html`) we will configure node highlighting with these two CSS classes:

```
.faded { opacity: .2 }
.highlight { stroke-width: 3 }
```

The `highlightNode()` function below receives a node and adds the `.highlight` class to the SVG circle that is bound to it, making its stroke wider. Additionally, it selects all remaining nodes except the ones the current node links to, and fades them. It does the same with the lines that represent links. The `fade()` function simply removes these classes, returning the selection to its original appearance.

```
function highlightNode(node) {
    d3.selectAll("circle").classed("highlight", d => d === node);
    d3.selectAll("circle").classed("faded", d => !(d === node
        || links.filter(k => k.source == node)
                .filter(m => m.target == d).length > 0
        || links.filter(k => k.target == node)
                .filter(m => m.source == d).length > 0));
    d3.selectAll("line").classed("faded", edge => !(edge.source === node
                                                  || edge.target === node
)));
}
function fade() {
    d3.selectAll("circle, line").classed("faded highlight", false);
}
```

To activate the highlighting behavior when the user hovers over the node, these methods are registered as *mouseover* and *mouseout* event handlers for all circles:

```
chart.selectAll("circle")
    .on("mouseover", highlightNode)
    .on("mouseout", fade);
```

The result is shown as follows:

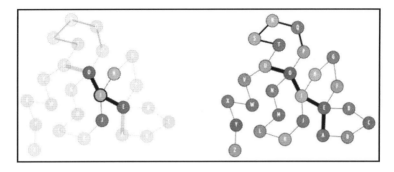

Interactive node highlighting can improve visualization in large network diagrams. Code: *Force/Interactive/1-highlight.html*.

Dragging nodes

By dragging nodes the user can change the layout of a network after all the nodes are placed. You can use dragging to make a specific node stand out from the hairball, or adjust the layout of the entire chart so that its topology can be viewed from different angles.

To implement drag-and-drop behavior in D3, you need to generate a drag behavior function, which is called by the selection that will activate it. Drag behavior functions were introduced in Chapter 8, *Animation and Interactivity*. To configure node dragging for an active force simulation, we will need handlers for all three drag events: *start*, *drag*, and *end*, as follows:

```
const nodeDragged = d3.drag()
    .on("drag", function(d) {
        d.x = d3.event.x;
        d.y = d3.event.y;
    })
    .on("start", function() {
        if(sim.alpha() <= sim.alphaMin()) { // reheats the simulation
            sim.restart();
        }
        sim.alphaTarget(sim.alphaMin() + .1)
    })
    .on("end", () => sim.alphaTarget(0));
```

The simulation is *reheated* so that the changes can be observed in real time. There are many ways to reheat a simulation. Here we changed the *alpha target* to a value greater than *alpha minimum*. This makes the simulation temporarily run forever, since it will never reach the target. When dragging is done we change it back to zero.

To connect the drag behavior to each node, call it from a node selection, as follows:

```
chart.selectAll('g.node').call(nodeDragged);
```

Now you can run the code and drag a node. You will notice that it also pulls several other nodes and affects the entire simulation. If you can't deform the chart much, try reducing the strength of the forces. The full code for this example is in `Force/Interactive/2-drag.html`.

Fixing nodes to a position

Dragging the node to a position doesn't keep it there forever, since the simulation is still running and its *x* and *y* coordinates are still being modified. But you can *override* that behavior by setting the final coordinates in the `fx` and `fy` properties (fixed coordinates) instead of `x` and `y` (see `Force/Interactive/3-drag-fix.html`):

```
d3.drag().on('drag', function(d) {
        d.fx = d3.event.x;
        d.fy = d3.event.y;
        console.log(sim.alpha())
})
```

If any of `fx` or `fy` properties is present in a node, the simulation will copy their values to `x` and `y`, ignoring `vx` and `vy`. Now if you drag a node, it remains in its final position and no longer is affected by the rest of the simulation. You can then move all nodes to any position you wish. To resume the original behavior, remove these properties or assign *null* values to them.

Adding and removing nodes

If you add or remove nodes from a network while a simulation is running, the forces must reevaluate the positions of all nodes, since the original constraints may no longer be valid. When adding or removing nodes, besides updating data arrays and SVG data bindings (using `join()` or `enter()` and `exit()` selections), you also need to update the simulation object and the forces involved with the new data. And, if you want to watch the network rearranging itself, you will also need to reheat the simulation (like we did when implementing the dragging behavior.)

In the example that follows we will add two event handlers. One will be activated when the user clicks directly on a node, removing it. The other will be called when the user clicks anywhere else in the view port, creating a new node at that position and linking it to the *nearest* existing node.

To find the nearest node you can use the `find()` method, described as follows:

Function	Description
`find(x, y, radius)`	Returns the node nearest to the point at *x,y*. If a a *radius* is provided as the third argument, it will only return the nearest node if it is located within that radius, or *undefined* if there is no node in that range. See `Force/Interactive/5-find.html`.

Method of d3.forceSimulation() for locating a node based on its current position.

In this example, we have to deal with several event-handling issues (see `Chapter 8`, *Animation and Interactivity*). Since both actions for adding and removing nodes are triggered by clicks, it is necessary to discover where the click happened, control event bubbling and clickable surfaces.

To add a node, the user will click in the empty space between existing nodes. Since nodes are descendants of the SVG `<g>` object represented by the `chart` selection, placing the 'click' listener there seems like a good idea. The problem is that `<g>` objects are not clickable surfaces. They won't capture any clicks unless they occur on a descendant `<line>` or `<circle>`.

One solution to this problem is to create a rectangle with the same dimensions as the view and append it as the first child of the `<g>` object, which will place it behind all elements. If the rectangle is transparent, you will also need to configure the CSS property `pointer-events:all` so that events can be captured (this is only necessary if the rectangle is transparent).

A simpler solution is to attach the click listener to the `svg` object, instead. We will have to deal with a different coordinate system, but D3 will help us with that:

```
svg.on('click', addNode);
```

In a *click* event, you can obtain the absolute coordinates of the mouse click from `d3.event.x` and `d3.event.y`, but the nodes were appended to the `chart` selection, which has a different coordinate system:

```
const offsetX = margin/2 + width/2, offsetY = margin/2 + height/2;
const chart = svg.append("g")
                 .attr("transform", `translate(${[offsetX,offsetY]})`);
```

If we had placed the handler in the `chart` object, we could obtain relative coordinates by using `d3.mouse(this)`, but since the handler was placed in the `svg` object, we need to get the coordinates from `d3.mouse(chart.node())`. Using these coordinates, we can find the nearest node:

```
const nearest =
        sim.find(d3.mouse(chart.node())[0], d3.mouse(chart.node())[1]);
```

This code is used in the `addNode()` function, shown as follows. It locates the nearest node, pushes it into the `nodes` array, updates the data bindings, the simulation, and the link force, and reheats the animation:

```
function addNode() {
  // 1) Find the nearest node to the point where the mouse was clicked
    const nearest = sim.find(d3.mouse(chart.node())[0],
                             d3.mouse(chart.node())[1]);

    // 2) Create new nodes and links
    const newNode = {
node: nearest.node + (links.filter(n => n.source == nearest).length+1),
      value: 1
    };
    const newLink = {
      source: nearest.index,
      target: nodes.length-1, value: 2
    }

    // 3) Update the data
    nodes.push(newNode);
    links.push(newLink);

    // 4) Update the simulation
    sim.nodes(nodes); // update simulation with new nodes
    sim.force("link")
        .links(links)        // binds new links to simulation
        .initialize(nodes); // update nodes with new links

    // 5) Update SVG data bindings
    chart.selectAll('line.')
```

```
        .data(links)
        .join("line") // same as enter().append("line")
        .attr("x1", d => d.source.x)
        .attr("x2", d => d.target.x)
        .attr("y1", d => d.source.y)
        .attr("y2", d => d.target.y)
        .style('stroke-width', d => d.value * d.value)

    chart.selectAll("g.node").raise()
        .data(nodes).join("g").attr("class", "node")
        .each(function(d,i) {
            d3.select(this).append("circle")
                .attr("r", 15)
                .style("fill", color(i))
            d3.select(this).append("text")
                .text(d => d.node)
        })
        .on("click", removeNode)   // a handler to remove the node
        .call(nodeDragged);        // the dragging behavior

    // 6) Reheat simulation
    if(sim.alpha() < .05) {
        sim.alpha(.05);
        sim.restart();
    }
}
}
```

Note the steps required to update the preceding simulation. First, nodes are updated, and then, after the links are added to the simulation, the initialize() method is called so that the nodes get updated, as well.

To remove the node when clicking on it, a listener has to be added to the node selection:

```
chart.selectAll("g.node").on("click", removeNode);
```

If you click on a node, the click event will be handled by the removeNode() function, but it will also be received by the addNode() method, which will create a new node shortly after the node is removed!

This effect is caused by event bubbling, which propagates the event to all ancestors. Since the SVG element has a click event handler, it will also process the event. This behavior can be prevented adding the following code to the removeNode() function:

```
d3.event.stopPropagation();
```

The node can be removed with a call to `d3.select(this).remove()` (or even `this.remove()`, since the DOM also supports this method), but removing the links requires updating the data selection. Calling `join()` (or `exit().remove()`) after updating will compare the data with the existing elements and remove the `<line>` elements that aren't bound:

```
d3.selectAll("line") // update SVG elements: remove links
   .data(links, d => d.source.node + '-' + d.target.node)
   .join();
```

The full `removeNode()` function is listed as follows:

```
function removeNode(d) {
    d3.event.stopPropagation(); // event won't propagate to ancestors

    // 1) Update data
    nodes.splice(d.index, 1); // remove from nodes array
    for (let i = 0; i < links.length;) { // remove links from links array
        if(links[i].source == d || links[i].target == d) {
            links.splice(i, 1);
        } else {
            ++i;
        }
    }

    // 2) Update simulation
    sim.nodes(nodes);          // update simulation with new nodes
    sim.force("link")
          .links(links)        // update simulation with new links
          .initialize(nodes);  // update nodes with new links

    // 3) Update SVG data bindings
    d3.select(this).remove();        // update SVG elements: remove node
    d3.selectAll("line")             // update SVG elements: remove links
          .data(links, d => d.source.node + '-' + d.target.node)
          .join(); // same as exit().remove()

    // 4) Reheat simulation
    if(sim.alpha() < .05) {
        sim.alpha(.05);
        sim.restart();
    }
}
```

The new nodes are labeled with a name derived from the nearest node they are linked to, and if you remove a node that connects two sub-networks, they will split into individual networks, as follows:

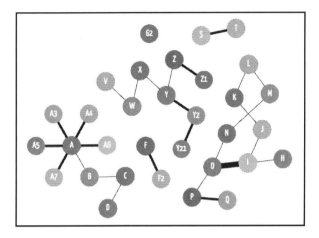

The force simulation after several nodes were added and removed. Code: *Force/Interactive/4-edit.html.*

Canvas rendering

Force simulations frequently have thousands of nodes, and this can make it run choppy or freeze your browser. One of the main optimization strategies you can use is to draw the simulation using HTML Canvas, instead of SVG. This will make it harder to add interactive features, such as highlighting and dragging, because you won't be able to use selections. But the gain in performance may be worth the trouble.

The following example is an implementation of the last example using Canvas. First, you need to obtain the Canvas context and translate it to the middle of the chart. Since we can't use CSS, the default `strokeStyle` and `lineWidth` properties are also set for the context:

```
const canvas = d3.select("body").append("canvas")
                .attr("width",width).attr("height",height);
const ctx = canvas.node().getContext("2d");
ctx.translate(width/2,height/2);
ctx.strokeStyle = "black";
ctx.lineWidth = 1;
```

There is no change in the simulation code. This is the same simulation used in previous examples:

```
const sim = d3.forceSimulation(nodes);
sim.force("link", d3.forceLink(links).iterations(15));
sim.force("manybody", d3.forceManyBody().strength(100))
sim.force("collide", d3.forceCollide(30));
sim.on("tick", draw);
```

The `draw()` function contains all the Canvas code, which was divided into three functions: `drawLinks()`, `drawNodes()`, and `drawText()`, which draws the labels in the nodes. The canvas is cleared each time the method is called, and the context is saved before and restored after each drawing function is called, so that the global context settings are maintained:

```
function draw() {
    ctx.clearRect(-width/2,-height/2,width,height);

    ctx.save();
    drawLinks();
    ctx.restore();

    ctx.save();
    drawNodes();
    ctx.restore();

    ctx.save();
    drawText()
    ctx.restore();
}
```

The links should be drawn first, since they are behind the nodes. They are just straight lines. The context's `lineWidth` is set for each link, since it is data-dependent. This code draws the line as a single path:

```
function drawLinks() {
    ctx.fillStyle = "transparent";
    ctx.beginPath();
    links.forEach(function(d) {
        ctx.lineWidth = d.value * d.value;
        ctx.moveTo(d.source.x, d.source.y)
        ctx.lineTo(d.target.x, d.target.y);
    });
    ctx.stroke();
}
```

To draw a circle in Canvas, you need to use the context's arc() command in a path. Each circle is a different path, so beginPath(), stroke() and fill() must be in the loop:

```
function drawNodes() {
    nodes.forEach(function(d,i) {
        ctx.fillStyle = color(i);
        ctx.beginPath();
        ctx.arc(d.x, d.y, 15, 0, 2 * Math.PI);
        ctx.fill();
        ctx.stroke();
    });
}
```

Text properties are set for the context and each text is drawn at the center of each node:

```
function drawText() {
    ctx.fillStyle = "white";
    ctx.font = '14px "Yanone Kaffeesatz", sans-serif';
    ctx.textAlign = "center";
    ctx.textBaseline = "middle";
    nodes.forEach(function(d,i) {
        ctx.fillText(d.node, d.x, d.y);
    });
}
```

The result is practically identical to the SVG version. The full code is in Force/Canvas/1-canvas.html. If you run this example, you may not notice any gain in performance, because this dataset is very small, but try some larger examples, such as the ones in the Examples/ folder, and you will see the difference.

Zooming in and out

Some network charts are dense hairballs, where the details about each individual node aren't as important as the general topology they reveal. But sometimes, you might be curious to obtain information about a specific node that stands out in a dense network chart, or to have a closer look at the center of the cluster and look for patterns that aren't obvious from the general view. In such cases, you may consider adding a zoom feature to the chart.

You just need to add the behavior and apply it to the objects that contain the elements you wish to zoom. For example, this code (see `Force/Interactive/6-zoom.html`) adds basic zooming functionality to the charts we have created in the previous examples:

```
const zoom = d3.zoom()
    .on('zoom', function() {
        chart.attr("transform",
            d3.event.transform.translate(offsetX, offsetY).scale(1));
    });
svg.call(zoom);
```

Now you can add more nodes and zoom out to see the entire chart, as follows:

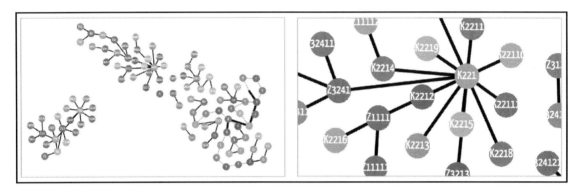

Adding a zoom behavior to a node-link diagram. Code: *Force/Interactive/6-zoom.html.*

You can improve this example with semantic zooming, for example, preserving the width of the lines and only showing the text labels when the scale factor reaches a certain level.

Summary

In this chapter, you learned how to create visualizations of relational data using D3, starting from the two basic data structures used by most layout generator functions in D3: *adjacency matrixes* and *adjacency lists*. You also learned how to convert between the two structures and how to create a simple generator function to plot adjacency matrix visualizations. A comparative chart was provided to describe different types of network visualizations and to help you choose the best one for your data.

We also provided step-by-step examples, showing you how to create simple node-link visualizations using functions from three D3 libraries: the *d3-chord* module, used to create circular chord/ribbon diagrams for multidirectional flows and associations; the *d3-sankey* module, to create *Sankey* diagrams for unidirectional flows; and the *d3-force* module, to create interactive network simulations with automatic node placement. You also learned how to apply some interactive features, such as node highlighting, which can make complex charts more readable, and also how to drag, add, and remove nodes in a force-directed simulation.

You have now used most of D3's modules and features. In the next and last chapter, we will explore one of the most popular features in D3: geographical visualizations.

References

- Module documentation, D3.js: `github.com/d3/d3-chord`, `github.com/d3/d3-sankey`, `github.com/d3/d3-force`
- Arc Diagram, by Yan Holtz: `www.data-to-viz.com/graph/arc.html`
- Borders and coastlines of South America: `Data/sa_borders.csv`. Dataset compiled from several sources, including Wikipedia.
- Migration Stock datasets. Compiled from several sources, including United Nations (World Population Prospects 2017: `www.un.org`) and World Bank (World bank public data. `data.worldbank.org`).
- Dataset created from Minard's sources used in his Russian Campaign chart obtained and adapted from `www.datavis.ca/gallery/re-minard.php`: `Data/minard-steps.csv`.
- European political borders dataset: compiled from Wikipedia: `Data/EuropeUSSR_1990_2010_nodes.csv`.

11
Visualizing Geographical Data

In this chapter, you will learn how to process geographical data using files in standard vector formats for web-based **geographical information systems (GIS)**, such as GeoJSON and TopoJSON. You will then use these to render interactive map visualizations using D3.js. You will learn how to display this data using a map projection of your choice and decorate it with graticules, meridians, parallels, labels, and thematic data that's been extracted from the files. You can choose the projection that best fits the purpose of your map from a very large collection of projection functions that are available in the *d3-geo*, *d3-geo-projection*, and *d3-geo-polygon* modules. Combining it with other data files, you can create dot distributions, bubble charts, flow diagrams, choropleths, and other thematic maps.

This chapter explores most of the functions from the *d3-geo* module, which contains tools for operations in planar and spherical geometry. You will use them to calculate bounds, centroids, distances and areas, to center coordinates, scale and rotate a projection, for fitting, clipping and other transformations. You will also learn how add zooming and panning behavior to your map using mouse controls, brushing, fitting to object bounds, panning a projected map and rotating a projection.

What you will see in this chapter includes the following:

- Geographical information systems
- How to make a thematic map
- GeoJSON geometries
- TopoJSON
- Graticules, circles and lines
- Projections
- Spherical geometry
- Zooming, brushing and rotating
- Using Canvas

Geographical information systems

A *Geographical Information System*, or GIS, is a system that stores, presents, and allows manipulation of spatial or geographic data. GIS applications are built on databases and contain a rich graphical user interface that manipulates multiple layers of geographic data in vector and raster formats.

GIS existed way before the Web was born. The first desktop GIS product was *MapInfo Pro*, released in 1986. One of the most popular products is *ArcGIS*, by *Esri*, the company that created the popular *Shapefile* format (`.SHP`), which is a *de facto* standard in the field. Free and open-source solutions include *PostGIS* (based on the *Postgres* database and used by many GIS applications), *GRASS GIS* and *QGIS*, which runs in Mac, Windows and Linux. They all support the *Shapefile* format as well as open web standards like *GeoJSON* and *TopoJSON*. GIS applications are also available as cloud services. They can be feature-rich applications such as *QGIS Cloud* (*qgiscloud.com*), which is also free, or simple tools that focus on specific tasks, such as *MapShaper* (*mapshaper.org*).

GIS data formats

Geographical data can be stored in any file. It may be a simple CSV file with a list of cities and their latitudes and longitudes, a complex vector *Shapefile* with high-resolution outlines for all the political divisions in a country, or even a raster TIFF file with elevation levels for a volcano. Many public data portals, map services and mapping applications distribute geographical data in popular raster and vector formats. The most popular formats include:

- **GeoTIFF**: A TIFF raster format containing embedded georeferencing information, frequently used in terrain relief and bathymetry maps
- **Shapefile (SHP)**: A *de facto* (and somewhat open) standard by *Esri* for vector data used in GIS applications, supported as a native vector format in most GIS applications
- **Geography markup language (GML)**: A XML-based standard for geographical data from **OGC (Open Geospatial Consortium)**
- **Keyhole markup language (KML)**: Another OGC standard, also XML-based, similar to GML. This is the vector format used in Google Earth

- **GPS exchange format** (**GPX**): An XML-based standard for GPS applications. You can extract data from a GPS in this format, convert it to GeoJSON and use D3 to overlay the path on a map
- **GeoJSON**: A JSON-based open standard for vector data maintained by the **Internet Engineering Task Force** (**IETF**) with specification published as RFC 7946
- **TopoJSON**: An efficient extension of GeoJSON that encodes topology

JSON and XML-based data formats can be parsed and loaded into JavaScript and used by D3. The others are easily converted into usable formats. There is a huge online library called **GDAL**: **Geospatial Data Abstraction Library** (`gdal.org`) with APIs in many languages and command line tools to that support all these formats and convert between them. Conversion tools are also present in most GIS applications. **MapShaper** (`mapshaper.org`) is a popular online tool that imports and exports between Shapefile, GeoJSON, TopoJSON, and other formats, and can also be used to optimize and repair files.

You can draw your own maps using a GIS application, but there are many places where you can download maps for free. Public portals provided by international organizations and governments of many countries and their political divisions provide free detailed vector data files with border outlines, natural features, roads, and thematic data. Many of the examples used in this chapter used data files adapted from the maps available at `naturalearthdata.com`.

But many data files are enormous. Before using them you might still have to reduce their size, eliminating information you don't need or extracting selected data such as latitudes and longitudes. For CSV files you can always use simple tools, such as Excel, but to edit GIS files you will probably need to use a GIS application, GDAL tools or write your own scripts.

Thematic maps

Thematic maps are among the most popular data visualizations. Unlike *reference maps*, which usually focus on political and natural features, *thematic maps* focus on a particular theme, such as population density and distribution, amount of rainfall, migration flows, etc.

A thematic map doesn't always need any country outlines. The map shown in the following screenshot is a *dot distribution* displaying towns and cities with at least 1000 inhabitants. The only data used was a CSV file with latitudes, longitudes and populations. The dots were positioned using a conic projection scale.

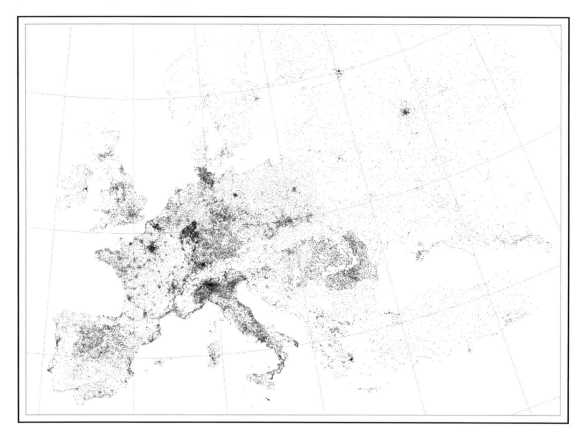

Dots projected with a conic conformal projection revealing human presence. Each dot is a town with at least 1000 inhabitants. Code: *Examples/dot-cities-europe.html*

A *flow or network map* connects geographically located nodes. Railroad and subway networks, road maps, electrical distribution systems are some examples. The map below on the left was created with two data files: one containing New York City borders and coastlines, and another with coordinates for the subway lines. The map on the right is a D3 version of the main diagram in Minard's famous *Russian Campaign* chart, which we explored in previous chapters.

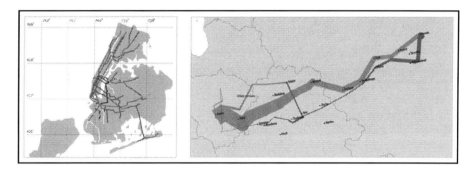

Examples of flow and network maps. Left: New York subway. Code: *Examples/network-ny-subway.html*
Right: Minard's flow chart of Napoleon's Russian campaign. Code: *Examples/network-minard.html*

Another popular thematic map is the *choropleth*, which uses colors or shades to encode information. Variations in opacity, hue, brightness or saturation are used to communicate a larger or smaller magnitude of a variable. You can use a choropleth to compare data between countries or regions, such as population, population density, HDI, GDP, electoral polls, etc. But choropleths can also be a source of misperception, since shades and colors are quantized and spread uniformly over an area, ignoring how the data is actually distributed in that space. A *graduated dot map*, in this case, may be a better option.

The three maps below show exactly the same data: relative number of deaths caused by traffic accidents in Brazil in 2017. In the first choropleth, the data is distributed in 27 states. The second choropleth and the third graduated dot map show the data in 5570 municipalities. Although the second choropleth displays the areas in areas of municipalities with more relative accidents in bright red, they are too small to grab the viewer's attention, but using bubbles they stand out in the graduated dot map.

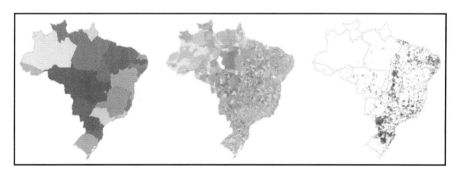

Three thematic maps of the same data: deaths caused by traffic accidents in Brazil in 2017. relative to population. The first two are choropleths. The third is a graduated dot map.
Code: *Examples/choropleth-1.html, choropleth-2.html, graduated-dots.html*

One big advantage of Web-based visualizations is that you don't have to commit to a single projection or rendering strategy. You can allow the user to switch from a choropleth to a graduated dot map, choosing colors for best contrast, filtering out unnecessary data and hiding unwanted layers, offering the best of both worlds.

GIS is not limited to the Earth. You may find GeoJSON files containing data for the surface of the Moon and Mars. Geographic projections can also be applied to the sky to locate stars, planets and artificial satellites, since astronomical coordinate systems also use parallels and meridians. In a geocentric equatorial system, latitude is called *declination*, and longitude is **right ascension (RA)**. The prime meridian is the spring equinox and the celestial equator is a projection of the Earth's equator. If you have a CSV containing the *declination* and *RA* of each star, you can use D3 to plot a map of the sky.

The screenshots shown below illustrate extra-terrestrial maps created with D3. The map of Mars was created with contour data of surface features projected on an orthographic projection. The map of the sky uses a stereographic projection. The stars positions were included from the Hipparcos catalog, and the positions of the Sun, Moon and planets were computed for a specific date.

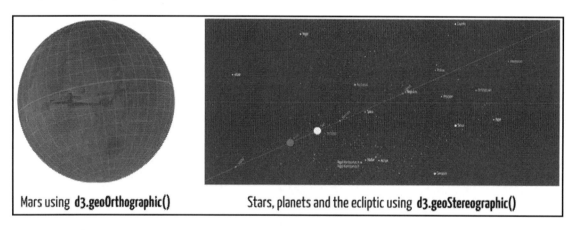

Mars using **d3.geoOrthographic()**   Stars, planets and the ecliptic using **d3.geoStereographic()**

Left: map of mars created from a GeoJSON file containing surface contours (Examples/mars.html). Right: map of the sky using Hipparcos catalog data for the stars and position of planets on a certain date (*Examples/sky.html*).

All the maps shown in this section were created with D3. The full code and the data files (or their links, if unmodified) can be downloaded from the GitHub repository for this chapter.

How to make a thematic map

You can use D3 to create maps of any place you wish, real or imaginary, using any data that contains locations expressed in spherical coordinates. There are many details to cover, so we will begin in this section with a quick step-by-step tutorial on map-making with D3, and then proceed in the sections that follow to cover the details. The files that contain the full code for the examples in this section are in the `MapMaking/` folder of the GitHub repository for this chapter.

GeoJSON

GeoJSON is an open standard format (IETF RFC 7946) for geographical information systems (GIS), supported by most GIS applications, GPS software and Web-based mapping applications. Many public data portals provide geographical data in GeoJSON or derived formats such as TopoJSON. GeoJSON files contain geographical coordinates for points and shapes. You can use GeoJSON to draw maps using vector graphics.

GeoJSON is a JSON format. You already know how to load JSON files and extract their data, so it shouldn't be hard for you to load a GeoJSON file, access its properties and plot its coordinates in a Cartesian grid. You may recall that we already did that in `Chapter 4`, *Data Binding* (see the section called *Drawing a map with SVG*) using GeoJSON coordinates to draw SVG polygons and display a map of the world.

The GeoJSON specification describes a standard JSON structure representing geographical geometries and features. A typical GeoJSON data file stores the data inside a single object of one of its standard data types: `FeatureCollection`, `GeometryCollection`, `Feature` or `Geometry`.

Most of the GeoJSON files we will use in this chapter contain a `FeatureCollection` object, with the general structure shown in the following code snippet. Its data in stored the `feature` property: an array of *Feature* objects, each containing `properties` and `geometry` members:

```
{
    "type":"FeatureCollection",
    "features":[
      {
        "type":"Feature",
        "id": "MDG",
        "properties":{ "name": "Madagascar" },
        "geometry":{
          "type":"Polygon",
```

```
         "coordinates":[
           [
             [44,-25],[43,-22],[45,-20],[44,-18],[45,-16],[47,-15],
             [49,-12],[50,-15],[47,-25],[45,-26],[44,-25]
           ]
         ]
       }
     },    { "type":"Feature", ... } // ... more feature objects
   ]
 }
```

There are several GeoJSON files in the `Data/` directory. The preceding code is from `Data/africa-madagascar.geojson`.

A *feature* is anything that can be represented in space. Objects of type *Feature* may contain a `properties` object, which can be empty, and must contain a *geometry* object, which is a GeoJSON shape object with geographical coordinates for a specific shape type. Features usually also contain an `id` member.

The *properties* object can contain any non-spatial attributes related to the shape. For example, if the shapes represent countries, it may contain data such as country codes, population, administrative name, etc. If you need to add any data to a feature, you should add it to the *properties* object.

An optional `id` property is usually located outside the *properties* object. It should be used to uniquely identify a feature object within a feature set.

Drawing a map with D3

Although it's not difficult to draw a map using the D3 tools we already know, the *d3-geo* module makes it much easier to create sophisticated maps. You can quickly render data from a GeoJSON file with just a few lines of code. It also contains functions to convert between Cartesian and geographical systems and you can choose among over one hundred different map projections.

The *d3-geo* module is part of D3's default bundle. If your project includes the full *d3.js* library you don't have to load anything else. It contains 15 popular projections (from over 100 projections available in two other optional D3 modules).

The main shape generator in the *d3-geo* module is the `d3.geoPath()` function. It returns a function that takes a GeoJSON object and creates a path within the bounds dictated by a map projection function. The generated string can be passed to the `d` attribute of a `<path>` element. This function and its main configuration methods are listed as follows:

Function	Description
`d3.geoPath` (*projection, context*)	Creates a layout function which generates a path from a GeoJSON object. This function is normally called without parameters, since these can be set with the configuration methods in this table.
`geoPath.projection` (*projection*)	A `geoPath` requires a projection object in order to convert geographical coordinates into pixels and project spherical coordinates to a flat surface. You can choose among over a hundred different projections. The default `null` projection is an identity transform and will consider latitudes and longitudes as pixel coordinates, without any transformation.
`geoPath.context` (*canvasCtx*)	If a canvas context is set, instead of returning an SVG path string the layout function will return a list of canvas path operations.
`geoPath.pointRadius` (*radius*)	`Point` and `MultiPoint` GeoJSON objects are rendered as small circles (using path commands). This method configures the radius of these circles.

Generator function for geographical paths and main configuration methods

For all examples of this section you will use the `Data/world-lowres.geojson` file to render the shapes of the world's countries. It contains a `FeatureCollection` with a single *Feature* per country. It's structure is similar to the smaller file shown before, but much larger. Each *Feature* contains an *id* with the country's ISO-3166 alpha-3 three-letter code, and a *properties* object with its administrative *name*. These *properties* and the id are non-standard. If you use a different GeoJSON file for the country outlines, they may be different.

Let's start from scratch with the following HTML page (it doesn't contain any code you haven't seen before):

```
<!DOCTYPE html>
<html lang="en">
<head>
    <script src="https://d3js.org/d3.v5.min.js"></script>
    <style>
```

```
            .country {
                fill: gray;
                stroke: white;
                stroke-width: .5;
            }
        </style>
    </head>
    <body>
    <script>
        const width = 960;     // standard width and height for most maps
        const height = 500;
        const FILE = "world-lowres.geojson"; // the file we will use

        const svg = d3.select("body").append("svg")
                .attr("width", width).attr("height", height);
    </script>
    </body>
    </html>
```

The first step is to create a `geoPath` generator function using `d3.geoPath()`. It renders shapes in SVG as <path> elements by default (they can also be rendered as HTML Canvas paths, if you initialize `geoPath` with a Canvas context). A `geoPath` function takes a GeoJSON object as its parameter and returns an SVG path string with pixel coordinates calculated for the view port according to a geographical projection. Before using a `geoPath`, you should at least initialize it with a map projection algorithm (otherwise latitudes and longitudes will be treated as pixel coordinates, and your map will be rendered mostly off-screen, and no taller than 90 pixels).

The following code configures a `geoPath` with the Mercator projection:

```
// choose a projection
const projection = d3.geoMercator();
// create a path generator function initialized with the projection
const geoPath = d3.geoPath().projection(projection);
```

Now you can load the map:

```
const map = {}; // store global objects here

d3.json('../Data/' + FILE).then(function(shapes) {
    map.features = shapes.features; // array containing the features
    draw();
});
function draw() {}
```

The `features` array is our dataset, so each `<path>` element will be bound to a different GeoJSON `Feature` object. The `d` attribute for each `<path>` will be generated calling `geoPath(feature)` for each feature. It will locate the `geometry` array inside the feature and use it to generate the path string:

```
function draw() {
    svg.selectAll("path.country") // CSS styles defined above
        .data(map.features).enter()
        .append("path").attr("class","country")
        .attr("d", geoPath)
}
```

Open the file in a browser and you will have the world before your eyes:

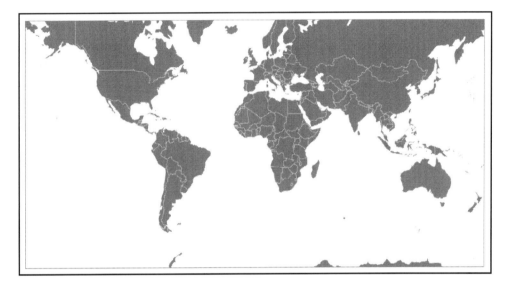

A GeoJSON world map rendered in SVG with D3. Code: *MapMaking/1-geojson.html*.

Making a choropleth

To create a choropleth we need to combine shape data, obtained from the GeoJSON file, with thematic data, usually obtained from other sources unless it's already in your Features' properties object. In this example we will load a CSV file with population, area and HDI data compiled from United Nations and World Bank public databases (See `Data/un_regions.csv`).

Replace the d3.json().then() block from the previous code with the following code, that uses Promise.all(). Everything should work as before.

```
Promise.all([
    d3.json('../Data/' + FILE),              // the shapes file
    d3.csv('../Data/un_regions.csv')         // the thematic data file
]).then(function([shapes, thematic]) {
    map.features = shapes.features;
        draw();
});
```

We don't need all the columns in the CSV file. Using a second argument in d3.csv() we can process each row as it loads and return an object containing only the data we need, converting the values that are numbers in the process. To do that, replace the d3.csv() block above with this one:

```
d3.csv('../Data/un_regions.csv', function(row) { // the thematic data file
    return {
        population: +row.Pop_2016,
        area: +row.Area_km2,
        hdi:  +row.HDI_2017,
        code: row.Code
    }
})
```

Initially we will create a choropleth to compare *populations*, but we also included area and HDI data because we can use them later.

Now you need to add the CSV data to the GeoJSON data, so that all data is kept in a single dataset. This requires that each GeoJSON feature be linked to a corresponding CSV row with the data for that feature. The link, in this case, is the feature's id property: the country's ISO-3166 alpha-3 code, which is also present in each CSV entry. Iterate through each feature from the shapes array, filter the corresponding row from the thematic array and then add the data to the feature's properties member as follows:

```
.then(function([shapes, thematic]) {
    map.features.forEach(function(d) { // each feature (country)
        const entry = thematic.filter(t => t.code == d.id)[0];
        if(entry) {
            d.properties.population = entry.population;
            d.properties.hdi = entry.hdi;
            d.properties.area = entry.area;
        }
    })
    map.features    = shapes.features; // save data in global context
```

```
        draw();
    });
```

You will also need a scale for the color scheme. Since we are using areas, a square root scale should be used (for the same reason, we should also be using an *equal-area projection* instead of Mercator, but you can change that later). Add the code that follows as a top-level declaration:

```
const popScale = d3.scaleSequentialSqrt(d3.interpolateReds);
```

Then configure the domain inside the `then()` block, before calling `draw()`:

```
popScale.domain([0, d3.max(map.features,
                    d => d.properties.population)])
```

The `draw()` function is practically unchanged, but now a different `fill` is computed for each country:

```
function draw() {
    svg.selectAll("path.country")
        .data(map.features).enter()
        .append("path").attr("class","country")
        .attr('d', geoPath)
        .style("fill", d => popScale(d.properties.population))
}
```

The final result is shown in the following screenshot:

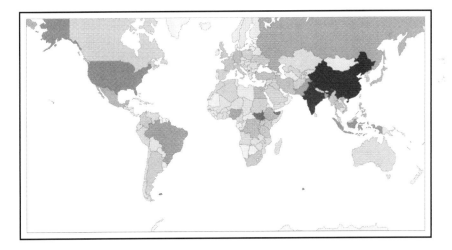

Choropleth comparing populations of the world's countries. using an exponential color scale (d3.scaleSequentialSqrt). Darker countries are more populated. Code: *MapMaking/2-choro-pop.html.*

Since you have the area of each country, you can calculate the average population density dividing population by area. The new property should be added to the GeoJSON `properties` object (after inserting the other data), so that it can be easily accessed later.

```
d.properties.density = entry.population / entry.area; // new property
```

The new property is used to configure the scale:

```
popScale.domain(d3.extent(map.features, d => d.properties.density))
```

Now you can change the *fill* style value, so that it returns a color for population density:

```
.style("fill", d => popScale(d.properties.density))
```

The result is shown in the following screenshot. The `d3.interpolateBlues` was used as the scale's color scheme. The choropleth reveals that although China has more people, it's less dense than India:

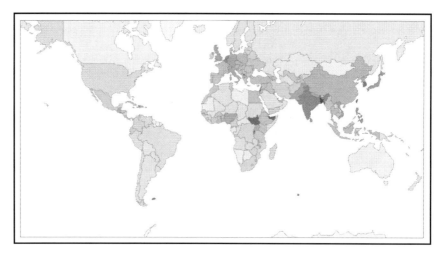

Choropleth revealing population density per country. Code: *MapMaking/3-choro-density.html*.

A **Human Development Index** (**HDI**) choropleth would probably look better in a *diverging* color scheme, where the extreme highs and lows appear as different colors. To use such a scheme, you need to express the domain as `[minValue, 0, maxValue]`. The median value that divides HDI categories *low* and *medium* can be used as the central value:

```
const threshold = 0.555;
const hdiScale = d3.scaleDiverging(d3.interpolateBrBG)
                   .domain([-threshold, 0, 1-threshold]);
```

If there is any HDI value that is zero or below in the CSV file, we shall redefine it as `undefined` when copying the properties to the GeoJSON object:

```
d.properties.hdi = entry.hdi > 0 ? entry.hdi : undefined;
```

The following fill style will apply the scale to the HDI minus the `threshold` value,

```
.style("fill", d => d.properties.hdi ?
                hdiScale(d.properties.hdi - threshold): 'gray')
```

The resulting map is shown in the following screenshot. Higher HDI increases towards dark green, lower HDI increases towards brown. Places with no data, such as Antarctica, South Sudan and Somaliland appear gray. You can now quickly detect where HDI is highest and where it is lowest:

Choropleth using a diverging color scheme and scale to reveal countries with higher (darker green) and lower (darker brown) Human Development Indexes (HDI). Code: *MapMaking/4-choro-hdi-div.html.*

The *United Nations Development Program* places countries into five categories of HDI: *very low, low, medium, high, very high*. These categories can be color-coded using a *threshold scale*, as follows:

```
const thresholds = [0, .350, .555, .7, .8, 1],
      colors = ["gray", "brown", "red", "orange", "olive", "darkgreen"];

const hdiScale = d3.scaleThreshold().domain(thresholds).range(colors);
```

We reserved the gray color for countries that have an HDI of *undefined* or zero. The fill is defined as:

```
svg.selectAll("path.country").style("fill", d =>
hdiScale(d.properties.hdi))
```

The result is shown in the following screenshot:

HDI choropleth showing categories: Very low (brown): <0.350. low (red): < 0.555. medium (orange): < 0.700.
high (olive): <0.800 and very high (dark green): >= 0.800. Code: *MapMaking/5-choro-hdi-cat.html*.

Adding tooltips

You might be interested in knowing the name of a country that has a particular HDI and its precise value. We can't place all that data on the world map since it would be unreadable, but we can add a tooltip that reveals the data as the mouse hovers over the country. Let's do it. First create some CSS styles for the tooltip:

```
#tooltip {
    pointer-events: none;
}
#tooltip rect {
    fill: white;
    fill-opacity: .7;
```

```
        stroke: black;
        stroke-width: .5;
    }
    #tooltip text {
        font-family: "Yanone Kaffeesatz", "Arial Narrow", sans-serif;
        font-size: 12px;
        text-anchor: middle;
    }
```

To inform the category linked to each HDI value, add the following array:

```
const labels = ["No data","Very Low","Low","Medium","High","Very High"];
```

The tooltip is created as a hidden group containing a rounded rectangle and two lines of text:

```
svg.append("g").attr("id", "tooltip").style("opacity", 0) // hidden
    .each(function(d) {
        d3.select(this).append("rect")
          .attr("height", 40)
          .attr("width", 150)
          .attr("rx", 5)
          .attr("ry", 5)
          .attr("x", -75)
          .attr("y", -20)
        d3.select(this).append("text").attr("y", -5)
        d3.select(this).append("text").attr("y", 15);
    })
```

Mouse hover handlers are registered for each country object, using `selection.on()`:

```
svg.selectAll("path.country")
    .on("mouseenter", showTooltip)
    .on("mouseleave", hideTooltip)
```

The event handler methods are shown below. The `showTooltip()` method moves the tooltip to the place where the mouse is positioned and makes it visible, updating the text elements with data obtained from the selected object:

```
function showTooltip(d,i) {
    const label = labels[colors.indexOf(hdiScale(d.properties.hdi))];

    const tooltip = d3.select("#tooltip")
            .attr("transform", `translate(${[d3.event.x, d3.event.y]})`)
            .style("opacity", 1);

    tooltip.select("text:first-of-type").text(d.properties.name)
    tooltip.select("text:last-child")
```

```
                 .text(`HDI: ${d.properties.hdi} (${label})`)
    }

    function hideTooltip() {
        d3.select("#tooltip").style("opacity", 0)
    }
```

Now, when your mouse hovers over a country, its HDI information will be displayed:

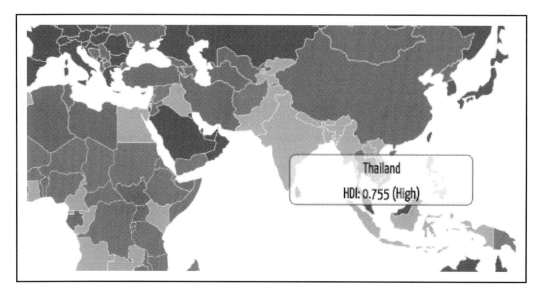

HDI choropleth with tooltips. Code: *MapMaking/6-tooltip.html.*

Adding graticules to a map

Graticules are the parallel lines used in maps that represent the positions of selected longitudes and latitudes. The d3.geoGraticule10() method returns a GeoJSON object for parallels and meridians with 10° spacing between them. The geoPath(d) function will transform it into an SVG path data string.

```
    function drawGraticules() {
        svg.append("path").attr("class","graticule")
            .datum(d3.geoGraticule10())
            .attr("d", geoPath) // transforms the graticule into a path string
    }
```

You can then set the style using CSS:

```
.graticule {
    fill: none;
    stroke: green;
    stroke-width: .25
}
```

Call the `drawGraticules()` function *before* calling `draw()`, so that they appear *behind* the continents. The result applied to the first map in this section is shown in the following screenshot:

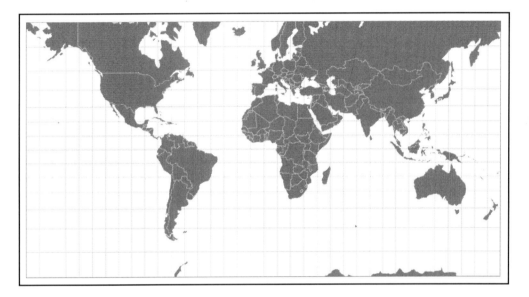

Default graticules representing parallels and meridians. Code: *MapMaking/7-graticule-div.html*.

Simple SVG zooming and panning

You can quickly add simple zooming and panning to any map or chart with using the `d3.zoom()` behavior. First, create an SVG group as a container for the zoomable map:

```
const globe = svg.append("g");
```

Then append the countries and the `graticule` to this object (they were previously appended on the SVG):

```
globe.selectAll("path.country") ...
globe.append("path").attr("class","graticule") ...
```

You also need a component to capture the zoom events. It can be a background rectangle as follows:

```
const rect = svg.append("rect").style("fill", "none")
        .attr("pointer-events", "all")
        .attr("width", width)      // svg width
        .attr("height", height)    // svg height
        .call(zoomBehavior);
```

The `zoomBehavior()` function is created by `d3.zoom()`:

```
const zoomBehavior = d3.zoom()
        .translateExtent([[0,0],[width, height]]) // limits translations
        .scaleExtent([1, 30]) // limits the zooming extent
        .on('zoom', () => globe.attr("transform", d3.event.transform));
```

After adding this code to any of the previous examples, you should be able to zoom in, zoom out and pan the map. The full code is available in `MapMaking/8-zoom.html`. In the end of this chapter you will learn other zooming techniques that are more suited for maps.

Now you should know how to make a simple thematic map with D3. In the next two sections we will learn about the file formats that contain data for shapes: GeoJSON and its extension TopoJSON, since they will be used in all other examples of this chapter.

GeoJSON geometries

The most important object in a GeoJSON feature is the `geometry` object. It contains two properties: `type` and `coordinates`. The coordinates array is a collection of *positions*, which are `[longitude, latitude]` pairs (in this order). The specific structure of the coordinates array depends on the *type* of the shape.

Primitive geometries

There are three standard shapes in GeoJSON, which can be represented by `primitives` or `multipart` geometries. Primitive shapes are listed as follows:

Function	Description
Point	A *single position*, which is a 2-element array of the form: `[longitude, latitude]`, where `longitude` and `latitude` are floating point numbers in the ranges `[-180,180]` for `longitude`, and `[-90,90]` for `latitude`. Example: `{ "type": "Point", "coordinates": [36.8484, 174.7633] }`

LineString	An array of *two or more positions*. A line or open path with a single beginning and end. Example:
	
	`{`
	  `"type":"LineString",`
	  `"coordinates":[`
	    `[-17,16],[-16,17],[-14,17],[-13,16],[-12,15],[-12,13]`
	    `]`
	`}`

Polygon	A collection of one or more *linear rings*: a sequence of *at least four positions*, where *the first and last positions are identical*. Linear rings are the boundaries of closed shapes (for example, countries). Winding order is important: if a *Polygon* contains holes (for example, lakes), their linear rings rotate in the opposite direction of the nearest outer boundary (for example, country boundaries are counterclockwise, lakes are clockwise, islands in lakes are counterclockwise, and so on). Example:
	
	`{`
	  `"type":"Polygon",`
	  `"coordinates":[`
	    `[ [34,31],[34,27],...,[29,31],[34,31] ],` `// outer`
	    `[ [35,-12],[34,-9],...,[35,-12],[35,-12] ],` `// hole`
	    `[ [29,-4],[29,-6],[31,-9],[30,-6],[29,-4] ]` `// hole`
	    `]`
	`}`

GeoJSON standard types: primitive geometries

The primitive GeoJSON shape types are illustrated in the following screenshot:

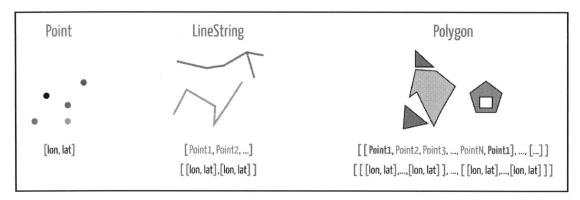

Examples of GeoJSON primitive types. The illustrations show five distinct *Points*, three distinct *LineStrings*, and four distinct *Polygons*. One of the polygons contains a hole.

Note that although a `LineString` requires only two *positions*, it can (and usually does) contain many more. Positions of different shapes may match, but that doesn't connect them in any way. In the illustration above the same position is part of the green and red *LineStrings*, but each is part of a different feature object and can have their own properties.

Multipart geometries

Multipart geometries group primitive geometries in a single feature. `MultiPoint` can be used to represent positions that belong together, sharing the same properties and never treated as individual points (e.g. a star cluster in a map of the sky). A `MultiLineString` represents multiple lines that always are treated as a single entity (e.g. a river basin with unnamed tributaries). A `MultiPolygon` can group a collection of shapes (e.g. a country and its islands) and treat it as a single feature object with the same properties.

GeoJSON's types for multipart geometries are listed in the following table:

Function	Description
MultiPoint	An array of Point objects. The *coordinates* member of a MultiPoint is an array of *positions*. Example: `{ "type": "MultiPoint", "coordinates": [[32,-17],[32,-18]] }`

MultiLineString	An array of LineString objects. Example:
	<pre>{
	    "type":"MultiLineString",
	    "coordinates":[
	      [[31,31],[31,30],[32,2],[33,1],[33,0]],
	      [[33,16],[34,14]]
	    ]
	}</pre>

MultiPolygon	An array of Polygon objects. In the MultiPolygon below there are two polygons. The first one consists of two *linear rings*:
	<pre>{
	    "type":"MultiPolygon",
	    "coordinates":[
	      [[[34,31],[34,32],[33,32],[34,31]], // polygon 1
	        [[35,-12],[36,-12],[35,-14],[35,-12]]], // polygon 1
	      [[[44,-25],[43,-22],[45,-20],[44,-25]]] // polygon 2
	    ]
	}</pre>

GeoJSON standard types: multipart geometries

The multipart geometries supported in GeoJSON are illustrated in the following screenshot:

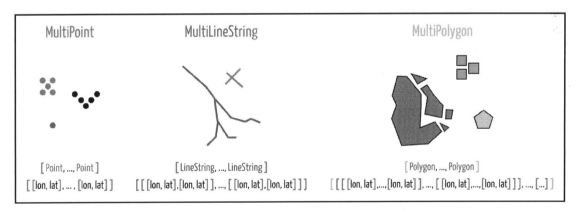

Examples of GeoJSON multipart types. The illustrations show three distinct *MultiPoint* objects, two *MultiLineStrings* and three *MultiPolygons*.

Drawing geometries as paths

We have already used GeoJSON do draw a world map containing over 200 geometries, but they were all either `Polygon` or `MultiPolygon`. Let's try rendering the other types. The simplified GeoJSON file as shown (`Data/africa-simple.geojson`) contains four different geometry types: `MultiPolygon`, `LineString`, `MultiLineString` and `Point`, each one inside a separate `Feature`.

```
{"type":"FeatureCollection",
  "features":[
    { "type":"Feature",
      "properties":{},
      "geometry":{
        "type":"MultiPolygon",
        "coordinates":[
          [[[34,31],...,[34,31]], [[35,-12],...,[35,-12]],
            [[32,-2],...,[32,-2]], [[29,-4],...,[29,-4]]],
          [[[44,-25],...,[44,-25]]]
        ]
      }
    },{"type":"Feature",
      "properties":{ "id":"river1", "name":"Nile" },
      "geometry":{
        "type":"MultiLineString",
        "coordinates":[[[31,31],...,[33,0]], [[33,16],...,[37,12]]]
      }
    },{ "type":"Feature",
      "properties":{ "id":"river2", "name":"Congo" },
      "geometry":{
        "type":"LineString",
        "coordinates":[[12,-6],...,[29,-9]]
      }
    },
    // ... many more features with LineString or MultiLineString geometries
    {
      "type": "Feature",
      "properties": { "id": "city1", "name": "Lagos" },
      "geometry": {
        "type": "Point",
        "coordinates": [3,7]
      }
    },
    // ... many more features with Point geometries
    }
  ]
}
```

You really don't have to do anything different to draw `LineStrings` and `Points`. The `d3.geoPath()` function also takes care of that for you, but you might wish to choose an outline color for the lines, and make sure their fill is *none*.

For this example, CSS will only be used to set the color for the strokes:

```
.continent { stroke: white }
```

Since the `d3.geoPath()` generator will render lines as paths, they need to be identified so that their `fill` style is configured to *none*. You can create a simple JavaScript function to identify lines:

```
function isLine(d) {
    return d.geometry.type == 'LineString' ||
            d.geometry.type == 'MultiLineString';
}
```

The `geoPath` function will automatically render points as circular paths, with radius configured by the `pointRadius()` method. The following code draws all the features and uses scheme-selected colors for points and shapes (see the complete code in `GeoJSON/3-lines-africa.html`):

```
const color = d3.scaleOrdinal(d3.schemeCategory10);
const svg = d3.select("body").append("svg")
                .attr("width", 960).attr("height", 500);
const geoPath = d3.geoPath().projection(d3.geoMercator()).pointRadius(3);
d3.json('../Data/africa-simple.geojson').then(function(data) {
    svg.selectAll("path.continent")
        .data(data.features).enter()
        .append("path").attr("class","continent")
        .style("fill", (d,i) => isLine(d) ? "none" : color(i))
        .attr("d", geoPath);
})
```

The result is shown as follows:

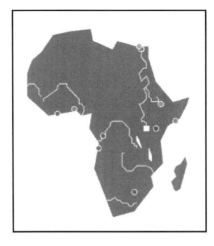

A simple GeoJSON file containing Polygons. LineStrings and Points rendered by D3.
Code: *GeoJSON/1-lines-africa.html*

Drawing points and text

The function created with `d3.geoPath()` only generates path strings, so they are only good for `<path>` elements. If you want to draw points using other shapes, such as `<circle>` and `<rect>`, you need to translate every pixel position from geographical to pixel coordinates. This is easily done with the path's `projection` function. Projections work like two-dimensional scale functions, initialized with a default pixel range of `[900,500]`:

```
const projection = d3.geoMercator();
const pixels = projection([100,-50]); // returns [746.94, 484.58]
```

For this example the data needs to be split into separate datasets so that continent outlines, rivers and cities can be treated differently. They are filtered by their `geometry.type`:

```
const rivers = data.features.filter(d => d.geometry.type=='LineString'
                                          ||
d.geometry.type=='MultiLineString');
const continent = data.features.filter(d => d.geometry.type=='Polygon'
                                          ||
d.geometry.type=='MultiPolygon');
const cities    = data.features.filter(d => d.geometry.type=='Point');
```

Now configure some CSS styles for the text and each class:

```
text {
    font-family: "Yanone Kaffeesatz", "Arial Narrow", sans-serif;
    font-size: 10px;
    text-anchor: middle;
    alignment-baseline: hanging;
}
.continent {
    fill: #94923c;
}
.river {
    fill: none;
    stroke: aquamarine;
}
.city circle {
    fill: yellow;
    stroke: black;
}
```

Since the river and continent outlines are rendered as paths in the same projection, the `geoPath` function call is reused with identical syntax in each selection (only the data is different):

```
svg.selectAll("path.continent").data(continent).enter()
        .append("path")
        .attr("class","continent")
        .attr("d", geoPath)

svg.selectAll("path.river").data(rivers).enter()
        .append("path")
        .attr("class","river")
        .attr("d", geoPath)
```

The location of a point representing a city is obtained with the `projection` function configured for the `geoPath`. It converts *Point* coordinates in `[longitude,latitude]` format to `Cartesian [x, y]` coordinates according to the projection. These coordinates can be used by an SVG `translate` transform to place the points:

```
svg.selectAll("g.city")
    .data(cities)
    .enter()
    .append("g")
    .attr("class","city")
    .attr("transform", }
            d => `translate(${ [geoPath.projection()(d.geometry.coordinates)]
})`)
```

```
    .each(function(d) {
        d3.select(this)
          .append("circle")
          .attr('r', 3);
        d3.select(this)
          .append("text")
          .attr('y', 2)
          .text(d.properties.name);
    });
```

The result is shown in the following screenshot. The full code is in `GeoJSON/2-points-africa.html`:

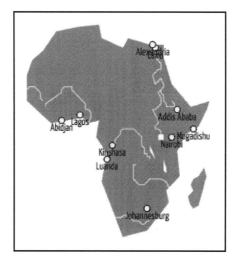

Using a projection function to position cities and text labels. Code: *GeoJSON/2-points-africa.html*.

You should try these examples with other GeoJSON files. If your code doesn't use anything from the `properties` object, it should work with few or no changes.

TopoJSON

TopoJSON extends GeoJSON by encoding *topology*, that is, relationships between individual shapes. Instead of storing the coordinates of each shape, TopoJSON stores line segments (called *arcs*) that are used to build the shapes, removing duplicates that occur when two shapes share a common border. This eliminates redundancy and results in a file that is much smaller and more efficient. TopoJSON makes it easier to compute neighboring shapes, merge all shapes into one and create a mesh from shape outlines. This can considerably reduce the amount of objects in a Web page, making it more memory-efficient.

TopoJSON files aren't as popular as GeoJSON, but you can easily generate one using command-line or online tools. D3 supports TopoJSON through a JavaScript library with methods that generate GeoJSON data from TopoJSON.

The following code reveals the structure of a simple TopoJSON file (Data/africa-simple.topojson) generated from a GeoJSON file (Data/africa-simple.geojson). It has half the size of the original file. Larger GeoJSON files can result in TopoJSON files that are 80% smaller:

```
{
  "type":"Topology",
  "objects":{
    "africa-simple":{
      "type":"GeometryCollection",
      "geometries":[
        {"type":"MultiPolygon","arcs":[[[8],[9],[10],[11]],[[12]]]},
        {"type":"MultiLineString","arcs":[[0,1],[2]],
         "properties":{"name":"Nile"}},
        {"type":"LineString","arcs":[3],"properties":{"name":"Congo"}},
        // ... more LineStrings
        {"type":"Point","coordinates":[3,7],"properties":{"name":"Lagos"}},
        // ... more Points
      ]
    }
  },
  "arcs":[
    [ [31,31],...,[33,16] ],
    [ [33,16],...,[33,0] ],
    // more arc arrays...
  ],
  "bbox":[-17,-35,51,37]
}
```

TopoJSON is available from `github.com/topojson`, where it is distributed as a collection of three different modules that can be installed via `npm`:

- `topojson-server`: Contains command line tools to generate TopoJSON from GeoJSON. Install this package if you have GeoJSON files you wish to convert to TopoJSON.
- `topojson-simplify`: Functions for additional simplification.
- `topojson-client`: Functions to convert TopoJSON into GeoJSON, merge geometries, create meshes, compute neighbors and other tasks.

You can also install the full `topojson` bundle, which includes all three modules.

To use TopoJSON with `d3-geo` we only need `topojson-client`. It can be included in an HTML file using a CDN such as `unpkg`:

```
<script src="https://unpkg.com/topojson-client"></script>
```

Its main functions are listed as follows:

Function	Description
`feature` (*data, object*)	Returns the GeoJSON `feature` for a specified *object* from the topology data, which are properties of the `objects` member in a TopoJSON file. Their name is application-dependent. The result is a standard GeoJSON `FeatureCollection` where each object in the `geometries` property is included in a separate `Feature`.
`merge` (*data, geometries*)	Merges all objects in the *geometries* array into a single object. The result is a single GeoJSON `MultiPolygon` representing the union of all *Polygon* and `MultiPolygon` objects, with common borders removed.
`mesh` (*data, object, filter*)	Creates a mesh from the outlines and borders of the object. If object is not specified, it will create a mesh from the entire topology. The result is a single GeoJSON `MultiLineString`. A filter can be provided to remove specific arcs from the mesh.
`neighbors` (*geometries*)	Returns an array containing a list of arrays, each representing an object. The elements of each array contain the `indexes` of its neighbors in the `neighbors` array (see example below).

Main functions from the *client-topojson* module

This section contains some code examples that demonstrate how to use the functions above, but you should also try running the complete examples. Their full code is available in the `TopoJSON/` directory.

Obtaining GeoJSON features

A TopoJSON file contains one object of type `Topology` with an `objects` member, which may contain one or more `geometry` objects. This property is not an array: geometry objects are *referenced by name* and you need to know the name of the geometry object you wish to use. Most files contain a single object and you can discover its name by simply inspecting the source code. You can also run the following code and obtain a list (See `Tools/list-geom-objects.html`):

```
d3.json('../Data/africa-simple.topojson').then(function(data) {
    const geoms = [];
    for(const key in data.objects) {
        geoms.push(key);
    }
    const keys = geoms.join(); // a list of geometry object names
}
```

The data file above contains a single geometry object: `africa-simple`.

To use a TopoJSON file in code that expects GeoJSON features, you need to extract the `features` object stored in the geometry object using the `topojson.feature()` function. It takes two arguments: the TopoJSON data and a selected geometry object, and returns a GeoJSON `FeatureCollection` containing a GeoJSON `Feature` for each geometry object, including the `properties` object. After loading this file, you can extract the GeoJSON data as shown in the following code (See `TopoJSON/1-features-africa-simple.html`):

```
d3.json('../Data/africa-simple.topojson').then(function(data) {
    const object  = data.objects["africa-simple"];
    const geodata = topojson.feature(data, object); // FeatureCollection
    ...
```

Now you can render the data just as before, obtaining the array of features with `geodata.features` and using it as your dataset:

```
svg.selectAll("path.continent")
    .data(geodata.features)
    .enter()
    .append("path")
    .attr("class","continent")
```

```
    .style("fill", (d,i) => isLine(d) ? 'none' : color(i))
    .attr("d", geoPath);
```

This should produce exactly the same result as `GeoJSON/3-lines-africa.html`.

To explore TopoJSON's `merge()`, `mesh()` and `neighbors()` operations in the next examples we shall use a considerably larger data file: `Data/africa.topojson`. It doesn't contain cities or rivers but includes the `Polygon` and `MultiPolygon` shapes of several adjacent countries and properties, which are better to illustrate how TopoJSON works. See the full code in `TopoJSON/2-features-africa-countries.html`. It contains practically the same code as the last example, but renders several countries on the screen in different colors.

A second version of these examples using simple squares instead of country borders is also provided. It uses the `Data/border-example.topojson` file, which is very simple. An example of the `features()` function with this file is available in `TopoJSON/3-features-shapes.html`.

Merging geometries

The `merge()` function takes an array of geometries as the second argument, returning a single GeoJSON `MultiPolygon` with the `union` of all the objects in a geometry collection:

```
const polygon = topojson.merge(data, object.geometries)
```

Since a single object is returned, you can bind it to a path using `selection.datum()`:

```
svg.append("path").datum(polygon).attr("d", geoPath);
```

The result is a map with a single shape created from all shapes combined, and no internal divisions. In this example you will see the entire continent of Africa, without any country borders. The full code is available in `TopoJSON/4-merge-africa.html`. See also `5-merge-shapes.html` that contains the same code using another TopoJSON file containing simple shapes.

You don't have to merge the entire dataset. Since this data file contains a `subregion` property that groups several countries, we can use it to filter which geometries to include:

```
const geometries = data.objects['africa'].geometries;
                        .filter(d => d.properties.subregion=="North
Africa");
const polygon = topojson.merge(data, geometries)
```

This was used in the interactive map shown below. It draws a semitransparent merged shape over a group of objects when the mouse hovers any member of the group. It only contains the shapes with the same `subregion` property as the clicked shape.

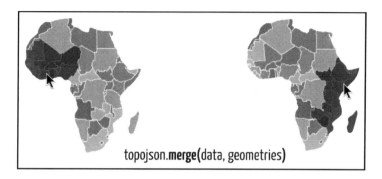

topojson.**merge**(data, geometries)

Using *topojson.merge( )* to draw a *MultiPolygon* containing the union of several shapes.
Code: *TopoJSON/6-merge-africa-regions.html*

Creating a mesh

The `topojson.mesh()` function returns a mesh of the entire topology, which includes outlines and borders between shapes.

```
const geomesh = topojson.mesh(data);
```

A mesh is a `LineString` rendered as a single path. It should not have any `fill` style, only *stroke*.

You can also filter the objects you want to mesh based on whether they share or not the same *arcs*. This can be used to separate the outline of a topology (for example the coastlines of the continent) from the internal borders. The filter takes two arguments that will be identical if an arc is used by a single geometry, and different if they are shared.

```
const borders =
    topojson.mesh(data, data.objects['africa'], (a,b) => a !== b

const outline =
    topojson.mesh(data, data.objects['africa'], (a,b) => a === b )
```

The effect is illustrated below. You can see the complete code is in the files `TopoJSON/7-mesh-africa.html`, `9-mesh-africa-borders.html` and `10-mesh-africa-outline.html`.

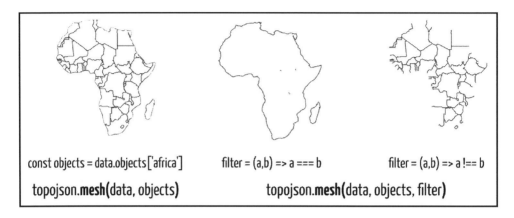

Using topojson.mesh() to create outlines and a mesh of internal borders.
Code: *TopoJSON/7-mesh-africa.html, 9-mesh-africa-borders.html* and *10-mesh-africa-outline.html.*

See also the examples using a data file with simple shapes in `TopoJSON/8-mesh-shapes.html` and `11-mesh-shapes-outline.html`.

In a large dataset, the use of `merge()` and `mesh()` combined with drawing the shapes on a Canvas can significantly improve the performance of an interactive animated map.

Discovering neighbors

Since adjacent shapes share common borderlines in TopoJSON, it's easy to compute their neighbors. The `topojson.neighbors()` function receives an array of geometries and returns an array of arrays with the neighbors of each shape:

```
const neighbors = topojson.neighbors(object.geometries);
```

Each array inside the main array represents a shape, and their contents are array-indexes of the shapes that have common borders with them. This is made clearer in the following illustration, which compares an array of neighbors with the rendered shapes. You can see the code and run this example in `TopoJSON/13-neighbors-shapes.html`:

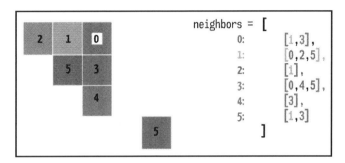

A neighbors array generated with *topojson.neighbors()*. Code: *TopoJSON/13-neighbors-shapes.html*.

With the *neighbors* array, you can select a specific shape by its index and then retrieve the indexes of its neighbors. In the following code (from `TopoJSON/12-neighbors-africa.html`) event handlers were added to highlight a shape and its neighbors on mouse hover:

```
svg.selectAll("path.country")
        .on('mouseover', showNeighbors)
        .on('mouseout', showAll);

function showNeighbors(d,i) {
    d3.selectAll('.country')
       .classed('faded', (k,j) => !(map.neighbors[i].includes(j) || k ===
d))
       .classed('highlighted', k => k === d);
}

function showAll(d) {
    d3.selectAll('.country')
            .classed('faded', false)
            .classed('highlighted', false);
}
```

These styles change the colors and opacity of the shapes when activated:

```
.faded {
    opacity: .3;
}
```

```
.highlighted {
    fill: black;
    stroke-width: 2
}
```

The result is shown in the following screenshot, where hovering over a country will reveal the countries that have borders with it.

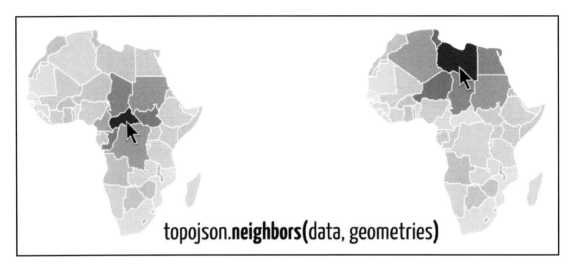

Using *topojson.neighbors( )* to discover shapes that have common borders.
Code: *TopoJSON/12-neghbors-africa.html.*

Converting GeoJSON to TopoJSON

Many GIS applications and online tools convert GeoJSON to TopoJSON. MapShaper (mapshaper.org) is very simple to use, and supports big GeoJSON files. You can also install the *topojson-server* in your computer with NPM:

```
npm install -g topojson-server
```

Now you can call the geo2topo command-line application and transform GeoJSON files into TopoJSON. The simplest way to do it is to use:

```
geo2topo source.geojson -o target.topojson
```

The transformation can be tuned by applying a quantization parameter. This may be necessary if your input data is messy and there are gaps between adjacent borders. The parameter is a number, usually a power of ten. Very low values will produce a pixelated map. Higher values allow more points per dimension but also use more memory. Typical values are 1000, 1e4, 1e6, and so on.

```
geo2topo source.geojson -q 1e4 -o target.topojson
```

There are many other functions available, mostly for simplification. They can be used to filter parts of a topology, calculate areas and bounding boxes, remove coordinates and apply transforms. Command-line versions of *mesh* and *merge* are also available and can be used to pre-process a file before using it.

Graticules, circles and lines

Graticules in geographic coordinate systems have the same function as axes in Cartesian coordinate systems. They add context to a map with lines representing parallels of latitude and meridians of longitude. Graticules should be discrete as to provide sufficient context for the data without getting in the way. They are usually rendered with thin semitransparent lines over or behind the data shapes.

You can generate GeoJSON shapes for graticules using the `d3.graticule()` function. It creates a `MultiLineString` with concentric parallels and meridians that can be rendered with a `geoPath` function. The following code draws gray, pixel-wide graticules lines on an SVG object using the `projection` function configured for the `geoPath`.

```
svg.append("path")
        .datum(d3.geoGraticule()) // returns a single MultiLineString
        .attr("d", geoPath)       // generates the path string
        .style("fill", "none")       // CSS styles for the graticule
        .style("stroke", "gray");
```

There are several methods that can be used to configure graticules, by filtering unwanted lines, limiting the graticule's extent, and adjusting the angular distance between each line. There are also methods to obtain the graticules as an array of `LineStrings` or to compute an outline of the extent. These are listed in the following table.

Functions and methods	Description
d3.geoGraticule()	Returns a geometry generator function for creating graticules. The default shape draws minor meridians and parallels for every 10° in the default extent [[-180,-80], [180,80]].
d3.geoGraticule10()	Same as `d3.graticule()`.
.lines()	Returns an array of GeoJSON *LineString* objects, one for each meridian or parallel. You can use this method to render individual lines or position labels on graticules.
.outline()	Returns a *Polygon* object representing the outline of the graticule's extent. You can use this to fill the background of a map, or draw a border around it. To add a border around the entire projected globe you can also use a *{type: Sphere}* object.
.precision()	Sets the precision for the graticule. The default is 2.5°.
.extent(array)	Configures the extent of the graticule. Receives an array containing [longitude, latitude] pairs to set the range in each direction. The default is [[-180,-80],[180,80]] for the *minor* extent (configurable with `.extentMinor()`) and [[-180,-90],[180, 90]] for the *major* extent (configurable with `.extentMajor()`). Setting new values with `.extent()` affects both minor and major extents.
.step(array)	Receives a pair of non-negative angles in degrees representing relative longitudes and latitudes. The default is [10,10] for minor steps extent (configurable with `.stepMinor()`), and [90,360] for the major steps extent (configurable with `.stepMajor()`). Setting new values with `.step()` affects both minor and major steps.

Functions and methods used to configure graticules

The following illustration shows the graticules produced by several configurations of `d3.graticule()` rendered with an orthographic projection. The first image is the result of the code shown above. To apply different styles to selected lines you can generate different graticule objects and overlay them, as shown in the fifth image in the following screenshot (see full code in the `Circles/` folder).

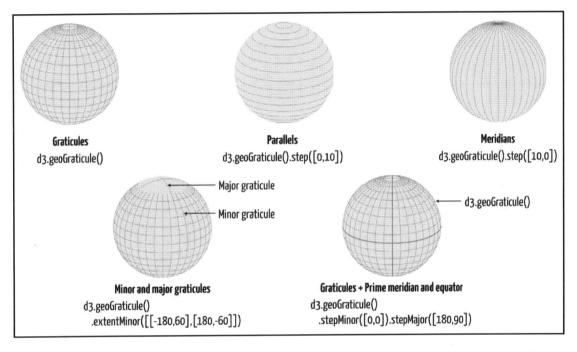

Graticules
d3.geoGraticule()

Parallels
d3.geoGraticule().step([0,10])

Meridians
d3.geoGraticule().step([10,0])

Major graticule
Minor graticule

Minor and major graticules
d3.geoGraticule()
.extentMinor([[-180,60],[180,-60]])

d3.geoGraticule()

Graticules + Prime meridian and equator
d3.geoGraticule()
.stepMinor([0,0]).stepMajor([180,90])

The *d3.graticule()* function generates GeoJSON shapes that draw parallels and meridians. The code that generates these images are in *Circles/1-meridians.html, 2-parallels.html, 3-graticules.html, 4-graticules-extent.html* and *6-graticules-equator.html*.

Lines and outlines

You can add any parallels or meridians to a map by filtering graticule lines with `step()` and `extent()`. The following illustration shows the code used to create a detailed area within a larger map, and standard parallels for the tropics and polar circles.

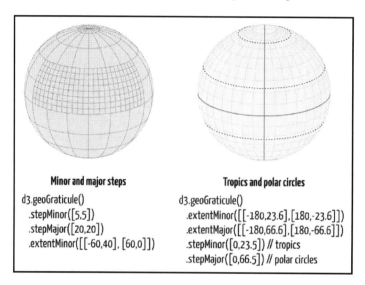

Standard parallels and areas with different graticules density can be configured using step and extent configuration. Code: *Circles/5-graticules-step.html* and *7-graticules-tropics.html*.

Instead of circles, you can also draw lines and polygons on a map using simple GeoJSON geometries. Another way to draw the equator is to pass a `LineString` as the datum:

```
const equator =
{type:"LineString",coordinates:[[-179.9,0],[0,0],[179.9,0]]}

svg.append("path").datum(equator).attr("d", geoPath)
    .style("fill", "none").style("stroke-width", 3);
```

But this won't work for any parallel or meridian, since D3 interpolates straight lines as great circles (see the *Projections* section). The `Circles/10-linestrings.html` contains an example using resampled lines.

The `lines()` method returns an array of `LineStrings` instead of a single `MultiLineString`. You can use it to apply the *general update pattern* and render the graticule as multiple *path* objects. This can be used to filter graticules or use their coordinates to place labels (see `Circles/13-graticules-labels.html`).

The outline() method is useful to obtain the outline of an area decorated with graticules. You can use it to draw a background or border around this area. With maximum extent(), you can draw an outline around the entire projection, but a better option is the {type: "Sphere"} object, which also outlines the projection but won't split at the anti-meridian (outline() will). The {type: "Sphere"} object is also better for clipping on the globe. The following illustration shows the difference between the two methods.

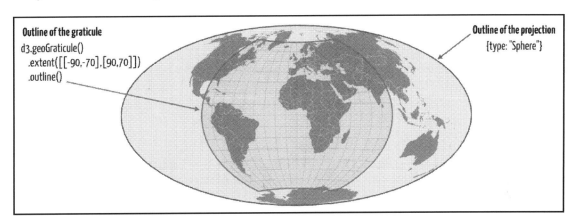

Comparing the shape generated by the *graticule.outline()* method and {type: "Sphere"}. Code: *Circles/8-graticules-outline.html*.

Drawing circles

The d3.geoCircle() function draws a circle on the surface of a sphere, using the coordinates of its center and radius. It can be used to draw hemispheres and spherical caps. The shape only appears as a circle on the surface of the sphere, but may be distorted into an elliptical form, lines or curves, depending on the projection used. The following table describes this function and its configuration methods.

Function and methods	Description
d3.geoCircle()	Creates a circle generator function that returns a GeoJSON Polygon approximating a circle on the surface of a sphere.
.center (*coords*)	Coordinates of the center of the circle on the surface of the sphere.
.radius (*radius*)	The radius of the circle, specified in degrees. Should be a value between 0 and 90. Default is 90, which represents a hemisphere.
.precision()	Sets the precision for the circle approximation. The default is 6°.

Surface circle generator function *d3.geoCircle()* and configuration methods

All the standard parallels and meridians drawn on the maps below as well as the circle that separates night and day at 6 AM GMT during the summer solstice were created using `d3.geoCircle()`. Circles are distorted by different projections. The same code was used to create for both maps as shown in the following screenshot. The only difference is the projection used.

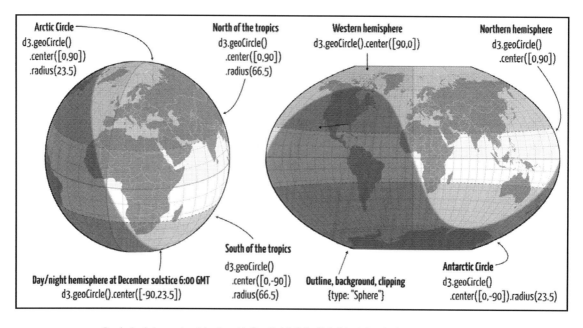

Drawing hemispheres and parallel regions with *d3.geoCircle()*. Code: *Circles/9-hemispheres.html and 9-hemispheres-2.html.*

Unlike straight lines, circles do not require resampling. In a regular *Mercator* projection, any circle perpendicular to a meridian or parallel will appear on the map as a straight line (or as a rectangle, if filled). It will become a curve if slanted or if rendered in a projection where meridians or parallels are curves. Smaller circles may appear as ellipses.

A grid of circles can be drawn on a map to create a tool that is used to compare geographical projections called *Tissot's indicatrix*. It shows distortions in different projections revealing how and where they occur. The function below can be used to create an array of circles for this purpose (see the full code in `JavaScript/tissot.js`):

```
const tissot = {};
tissot.makeIndicatrix = function(radius, stepLon, stepLat, maxLon, maxLat)
{

    if(!stepLon) stepLon = 10; // defaults
    if(!stepLat) stepLat = 10;
```

```
        if(!maxLon) maxLon = 180;
        if(!maxLat) maxLat = 80;
        if(!radius) radius = 2;

        const circles = [];
        for(let lon = -maxLon; lon < maxLon; lon += stepLon) {
            for(let lat = -maxLat; lat <= maxLat; lat += stepLat) {
                const circle = d3.geoCircle()
                        .center([lon, lat])
                        .radius(radius)
                        .precision(1);
                circles.push( circle() );
            }
        }
        return circles;
    }
```

Tissot's indicatrix is usually rendered with orange circles. The following CSS styles will be used to render the circles (CSS/tissot.css).

```css
.indicatrix {
    fill:orange;
    fill-opacity: .5;
    stroke: black;
    stroke-width: .5;
}
```

Finally, the code fragment in the following code snippet, applied to an existing SVG map, will render *Tissot's indicatrix* for the projection configured in the map's geoPath:

```
svg.selectAll("path.indicatrix")
        .data(makeIndicatrix(1.5, 20, 10, 180, 90)).enter()
        .append("path")
        .attr("d", geoPath)
        .attr("class","indicatrix");
```

The result for a cylindrical *Plate Carree* projection is shown in the following screenshot:

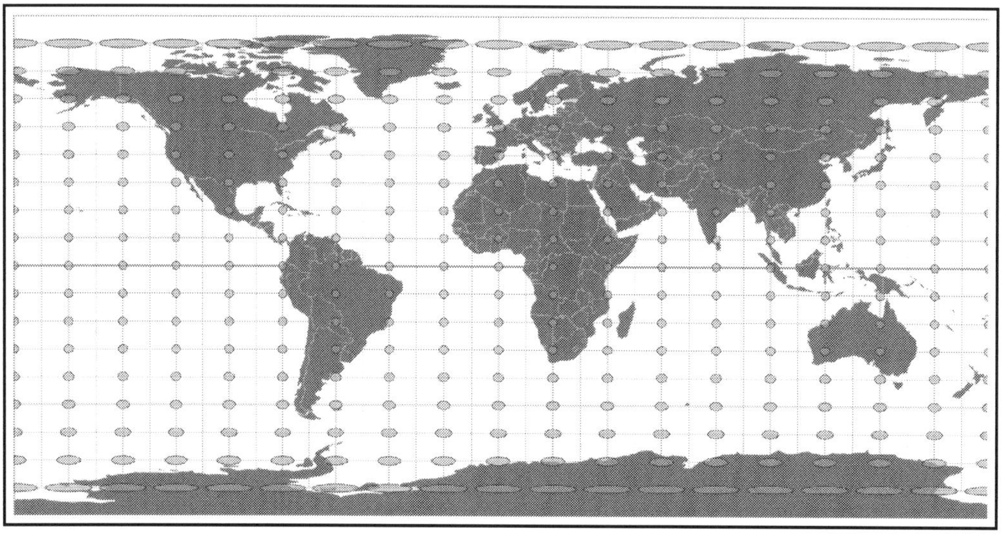

Tissot's indicatrix applied to en equirectangular (Plate Carree) projection. showing where
and how shapes are distorted in this projection. Code: *Circles/14-tissot-indicatrix.html*.

Projections

Projections are functions that transform latitudes and longitudes on the surface of a sphere or ellipsoid into positions on a plane. In order to represent the Earth, the sky, the moon, a planet or any spherical shape on a plane, you need a projection. Humans have used geographical projections for millennia (the oldest projections date over 2,500 years ago) for many different purposes. There is no limit to the amount of projections that can be invented.

Types of projections

The three basic cartographical projections project the surface a sphere or ellipsoid onto a *developable surface*: any surface that can be flattened onto a plane without stretching or compressing. These surfaces are: the *plane*, the *cylinder* and the *cone*, illustrated in the following screenshot:

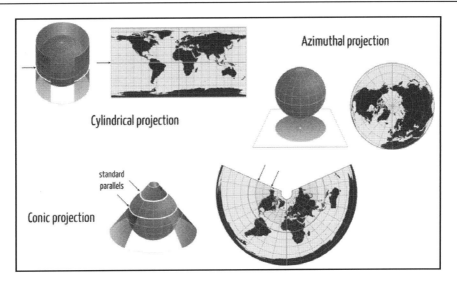

Typical azimuthal. cylindrical and conic projections of a sphere on a developable surface.

There are many ways to project a sphere onto these surfaces. They can touch the surface at one *tangent point* (a pole, in polar azimuthal projections) or a *tangent line* (the equator, in normal cylindrical projections; a parallel, in conic projections). They can also cross the surface producing a *secant circle* (in azimuthal projections), or *secant lines* (in conic and cylindrical projections). Azimuthal projections also differ in where the projection originates.

In normal azimuthal projections the lines are traced from the surface of the sphere, but the Gnomonic projection starts at the center of the earth, and the Stereographic projection from a central point in the opposite side of the sphere.

The *aspect* of a projection describes the angle between the axis of the sphere and the surface. Azimuthal maps of the world are more common in the polar aspect (the axis is perpendicular), cylinders are normally parallel to the sphere's axis and cones are centered in the axis, but transverse and oblique aspects are also possible.

There are also many projections that don't fit any of these definitions. Some don't project onto a developable surface, others are mathematical functions that try to strike a balance between different properties to achieve minimum distortion. They usually have names that relate to properties of the basic projection they are derived from: *pseudocylindrical, pseudoconic, polyconic*, and so on.

Choosing a projection

Probably the first consideration to be made when choosing a projection is the *purpose* of the map. Do you plan to use it for navigation? Do you plan to compare quantitative data represented as areas or lines? Is preserving shapes, angles and patterns important? What about direction and distance?

To choose a projection, it is useful to classify them according to the spatial properties that they preserve. A projection will always distort the projected subject in one way or another, but some properties may be preserved when distortion increases for others. A good projection is one where the properties of interest suffer the least distortion. Properties that can be represented on a projected map include:

- Distance
- Direction
- Bearing
- Area
- Shape and angle

Maps used in navigation, for example, may require equal distances or constant bearings. *Bearing* is a way to express direction as an angle measured from a meridian in relation to the north position (0°). A constant bearing is maintained when you travel along a *rhumb line* (also called a *loxodrome*). Any straight lines between two points in a Mercator cylindrical projection are rhumb lines, since they maintain a constant angle in relation to the meridians.

There is no such thing as a straight line on the surface of a sphere or ellipsoid. The *shortest distance* between two points and the *line of constant bearing* are both curves.

The shortest path between two points on the surface of a sphere is the *arc of a great circle*. The *great circle* (also called *orthodrome*) is any circle dividing a sphere into two equal hemispheres. The equator and meridians are both rhumb lines and great circles, but if you travel along any oblique great circle, the bearing changes at every point on the line. Great circle arcs appear as curves in a Mercator projection, but are projected as straight lines in a Gnomonic projection, where rhumb lines are curves.

The following maps compare rhumb lines and great circles showing both paths between London and Los Angeles (an actual flight path is usually chosen somewhere in between them, since it depends on factors like flight regulations, winds, climate and politics).

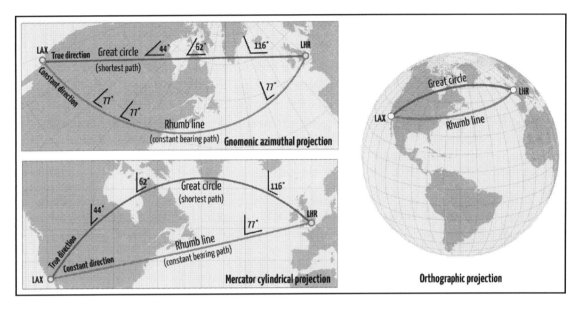

A path between two points on the surface of a sphere is represented differently. depending on the projection.
Code: *Path-Geometry/4-loxodrome-*.html*

Straight lines in D3 are automatically drawn as great circles. If you need to draw a rhumb line between two points, you need to resample the GeoJSON object, adding intermediate points so it can be interpolated. There is no such function in the current D3 distribution (version 5.8.2) but you can use the `resample()` function available from `github.com/d3/d3-geo-projection/issues/75` (by Mike Bostock). It was used to produce the illustrations above (see the files in `Path-Geometry/4-loxodrome-*.html`).

Conformal, equal-area and equidistant projections

Mercator is considered a *conformal* projection because it preserves local shapes and angles (but distances and areas may be distorted). These projections are commonly used in navigation and weather maps. It's the projection used in Google Maps.

Although azimuthal projections show true distances from a central point, there exist no projections that preserve distances between arbitrary points. *Equidistant* projections are projections that have equally spaced parallels. There do exist, however, projections that preserve distance between *two* selected points, as the *two-point equidistant* projection (see the `d3.geoTwoPointEquidistant` projection) and others that *minimize* distortions near three or more selected points, like the *Chamberlin* trimetric projection (see `d3.geoChamberlin()`).

Thematic maps such as choropleths (which encode quantitative values in shapes) and dot distributions should minimize area distortion, since the area influences the perception of quantity. Using a Gnomonic or the Mercator projection for these maps (as we did in the beginning of this chapter) is not recommended. *Equal-area* projections employ different strategies to minimize area distortion. The areas that appear in these projections are proportional to their actual size on the surface of the sphere.

General-purpose maps, such as atlases, usually try to balance area and shape distortions and use *compromise* projections that cannot be classified as conformal, equal area or equidistant.

D3 provides a collection of over one hundred ready-to-use projections you can choose. Many are configurable and allow the creation of derived or new projections. The most popular ones (about 15) are available in the `d3-geo` module, which is part of the default bundle. Others are in the `d3-geo-projection` and `d3-geo-polygon` modules.

The following table compares popular projections classified by type and the property that they preserve. All, except `d3.geoCylindricalEqualArea()`, are in the `d3-geo` module.

	Equidistant (preserves local distances)	Equal area	Conformal (preserves angles)
Azimuthal	`d3.geoAzimuthalEquidistant`	`d3.geoAzimuthalEqualArea`	`d3.geoStereographic`
Cylindrical	`d3.geoEquirectangular` (Plate Carree)	`d3.geoCylindricalEqualArea` (Secant, parallels at ±38.58°)	`d3.geoMercator`
Conic	`d3.geoConicEquidistant`	`d3.geoConicEqualArea`	`d3.geoConicConformal` (Tangent, parallel at 30°)

D3 functions for classic projections of a sphere on the plane. cylinder and cone classified by the spatial properties they preserve.

The following illustration compares the three classic azimuthal projections and different spatial property preservation strategies. *Tissot's indicatrix* (see previous section) is used to reveal the nature of distortion in each projection and to highlight points where distortion increases or diminishes.

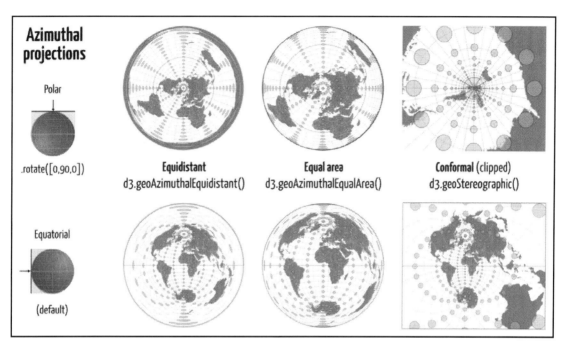

Equidistant. equal-area and conformal azimuthal projections. Code for the maps are in Projections/1-main-projections.html.

The `projection.rotate()` method can be used to change the *aspect* of a projection (how the axis of the sphere is aligned with the projection surface). It takes an array with three angles and can rotate the globe in a three-dimensional grid. For most projections, the default alignment is parallel to the axis of the sphere. A polar projection can be obtained using the following:

```
projection.rotate([0,±90,0]); // +90 = south pole, -90 = north pole
```

The next image compares several cylindrical projections.

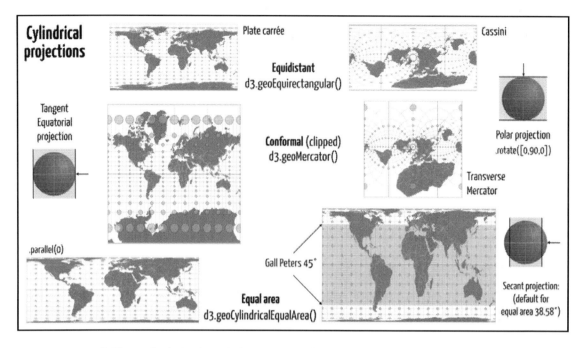

Equidistant. conformal and equal-area cylindrical projections. Code for the maps are in Projections/1-main-projections.html

The same `projection.rotate()` method was used above to create the `transverse` forms of the projections. *Secant* projections, where the projection surface slices the sphere, are configurable in some projection functions with the `parallel(angle)` method. They are a common strategy to reduce distortion. The *Gall-Peters* projection above is created from the `d3.geoCylindricalEqualArea()` function using:

```
d3.geoCylindricalEqualArea().parallel(45);
```

The following image compares some conic projections and functions available in D3.

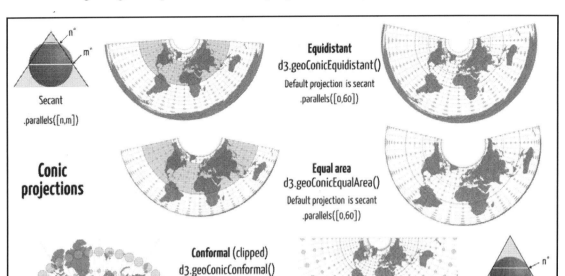

Equidistant. equal-area and conformal conic projections. Code for the maps are in Projections/1-main-projections.html.

Secant conic projections can have two different *parallels*. If the value is the same, the result will be a tangent projection. If identical values of opposite signs are used, or if both values are zero, the function will generate a cylindrical projection:

```
d3.geoConicConformal().parallels([15,45]); // Lambert's Conformal Conic
```

One preconfigured variation of the d3.geoConicEqualArea() is d3.geoAlbers(), which is designed for minimal distortion for the continental United States. A composite version (d3.geoAlbersUsa()) is also available, including Alaska and Hawaii.

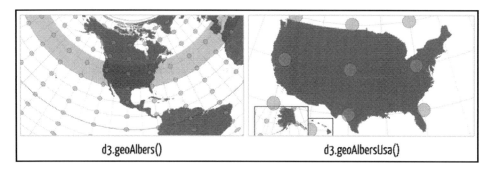

The US-centric *Albers* projection is a d3.geoConicEqualArea()with standard parallels at 29.5° and 45.5° N.
The composite version includes Alaska and Hawaii with minimum distortion. Code: Projections/2-conic-albers.html.

In the *orthographic* projection, deformations follow perspective and seem not to exist when the globe is perceived as a three-dimensional object. It only shows one hemisphere. The projection.rotate() method can be used to show hidden areas and is perceived as rotating the globe and not the projection.

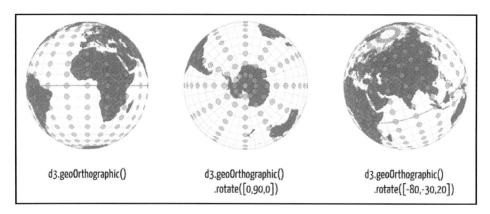

Orthographic projections in different rotations. Code for the maps are in Projections/1-main-projections.html.

Besides several compromise projections (like *Robinson, Winkel Tripel, Mollweide*), D3 also includes functions for *interrupted* projections (with default cuts usually at the oceans), *polygonal* projections (that can be folded and assembled as polygons), and *quincuncial* projections (that can be used as tiles). Examples of these last two are shown in the following screenshot:

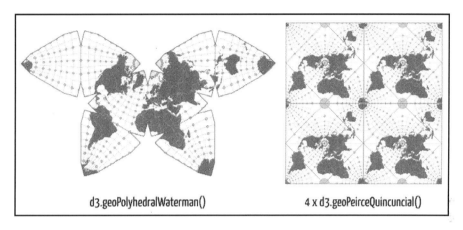

The world in a polyhedral projection and four world tiles in a quincuncial projection. Code: *Projections/3-other-projections.html*

You can explore selected D3 projections clicking the links with their names in `Projections/1-main-projections.html` and `3-other-projections.html`. See also the documentation and samples from the `d3-geo-projection` and `d3-geo-polygon` module.

Using a projection

A projection is like a two-dimensional scale function. To use it, first create a function:

```
const projection = d3.geoMercator();
```

Now you can pass it to a `geoPath`, or use it to convert spherical coordinates into pixels and back:

```
const geoPath = d3.geoPath();
geoPath.projection(projection);

const pixels = projection([-45,23]); // convert location to pixels
const coords = projection.invert(pixels); // and back
```

Once a geoPath is configured with a projection, you can render it The standard viewport has a default dimension of 900x500 pixels. You don't have to make your map fit that area, but you should be aware of it since the methods that transform the projection in the viewport assume these default values.

You can configure a projection with methods that change its position in the viewport, scale, clip, rotate, etc. Specific projections may have additional methods (for example, the `parallels()` method in conic projections). The most important methods supported by all projections are listed in the following table.

Method	Description
rotate (*[yaw,pitch,roll]*)	Rotates the sphere in three directions *before* projecting. Each element corresponds to the rotation of an axis. This can be used to create oblique and transverse projections. For example, rotating the Mercator projection with [0-90,0] will result in a Transverse Mercator projection.
center (*[lon,lat]*)	Sets the geographical center reference for planar transforms. Default is [0,0] is placed at the viewport origin (default [480,250]). This is the reference origin for `angle()`, `translate()` and `scale()`. Unlike `rotate()`, this method affects the *projected* map. Ignored if any of the `fit()` methods are used.
angle (*angle*)	Rotates the *projected* map on its center by an *angle*. Default is 0°. The map is not constrained by the viewport and may be clipped when rotating.
translate (*[x,y]*)	Sets the viewport origin and translates a projected map within the view port (position in pixels). Default is [480,250], which corresponds to the center of a standard [900,500] viewport; `translate([0,0])` will place the geographical center of the map at the upper-left corner of the viewport. Ignored if any of the `fit()` methods are used.
scale (*factor*)	Scales the map by a factor. The value and the default are projection-dependent. The default scale for the Mercator projection is 153, which clips out Antarctica and northern parts of America and Asia in a standard 900x500 viewport. To fit the entire map (clipped as a square) map in this viewport you need to scale below 80. Ignored if any of the `fit()` methods are used.

clipAngle (*angle*)	Performs *small-circle* clipping. Used in infinite azimuthal projections, such as Gnomonic (which is usually clipped at half-circle or less). Angle in degrees.
clipExtent (*extent*)	Performs *view port* clipping. Used in infinite cylindrical projections, such as Mercator (clipped at ±85° latitude). Extent in pixels: [[*minX,minY*],[*maxX,maxY*]]
fitExtent (*extent, object*)	Fits the object to an extent in pixels: [[*minX,minY*],[*maxX,maxY*]]. The *object* can be any GeoJSON object. Use {type: "Sphere"} to fit the entire globe. If this method is used, center(), scale() and translate() are ignored.
fitSize (size, object)	Fits the object in an area of specified size in pixels: [*width,height*]. Same as fitExtent([[0,0], [width,height]], object). The *object* can be any GeoJSON object. Use {type: "Sphere"} to fit the entire globe. If this method is used, center(), scale() and translate() are ignored.
fitWidth (*value, object*), fitHeight (*value, object*)	Fits the object to the specified width or height, maintaining aspect ratio and positioning at top or left. The *object* can be any GeoJSON object. Use {type: "Sphere"} to fit height or width of the the entire globe. If these methods are used, center(), scale() and translate() are ignored.
invert (*coords*)	Receives an array of spherical coordinates [*longitude, latitude*] and returns an array of planar pixel coordinates [*x,y*] for the standard viewport (900x500).
precision (*value*)	Smaller values increase the quality of the projection, but also consume more resources. The default is 0.7. You may wish to increase the precision when you zoom in, as imprecise rendering may become evident at larger scales.

Some of the methods used to configure any projection in D3 (specific projections may have additional methods)

Moving, rotating and scaling a projected map

A projected map has two centers: the *geographical center* is expressed in [*longitude,latitude*] and determines the point in the map that will be aligned with the other center, the *viewport center*, expressed in [*x,y*] pixel coordinates. The geographical center is controlled by the `center()` method, and defaults to [0°,0°], which is where the prime meridian crosses the equator. The viewport center is controlled by the `translate()` method, and defaults to [480,250], which is the center of the default 900x500 viewport. The centers are always connected, that is, the default location [0°,0°] is shown at the default position [480,250], which is the center of the viewport. If you change the viewport center using *translate([0,0])*, the center of the map will move to the upper-left corner of the viewport, leaving only the lower-right quarter of the map visible. If you change the geographical center using *center([78,22])*, the map will be translated so that new geographical position occupies the center of the viewport. You can also rotate the projected map in the viewport with the `angle()` method. It will rotate around the geographical center. The `scale()` method scales the map by a certain factor that is projection dependent. These methods are illustrated in the sequence of screenshots as follows:

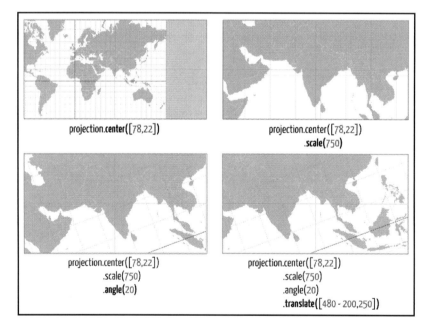

Transforming a projected map inside a viewport. The red lines cross at the center of the viewport. Code: Projection-Geometry/9-view-*.html.

Fitting a projection in a viewport

When zooming, you may wish to *fit* an object (for example, a country) in a rectangle. You can do that with one of four methods that fit GeoJSON objects within an *extent* (upper-left and lower-right coordinates), a rectangle *size* (height and width), or only a *height*, or a *width*. You can use this when you configure your projection and fit the entire globe (using `{type:"Sphere"}` as the GeoJSON object, or in other parts of your code when you filter an object to zoom in to. For example, this function receives a GeoJSON object and zooms to a bounding box that fits it:

```
function zoom(object) {
    const boundingObject = {
        type: 'MultiPoint', coordinates: d3.geoBounds(object)
    };
    projection.fitSize([width, height], boundingObject);
    render(); // updates the projected shapes
}
```

We will explore this function in a section dedicated to zooming strategies at the end of this chapter.

The fitting methods will ignore any configuration previously defined with `center()`, `scale()` or `translate()`. The following illustration illustrates their effect on a full map and on shapes that are taller or wider.

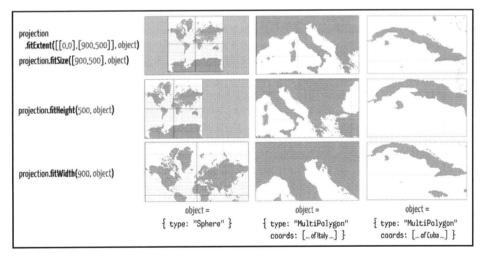

Using different methods to fit the globe and smaller GeoJSON objects in a rectangle. Code: *Projection-Geometry/6-fit-*.html*.

Rotating the sphere inside a projection

You can use `projection.angle()`, `center()` or `translate()` methods to move a *projected* map on the screen in order to focus on a specific object, but that won't change its distortion or relative position in the map. If you wish to show uninterrupted flight lines over the Pacific ocean or display Antarctica with minimum distortion you need to use `projection.rotate()`. This method rotates the sphere *before* projecting.

The `projection.rotate()` method takes a single argument: a three-element array containing the axis-angle representation of a rotation. Each angle is a 0 to 360° rotation along a perpendicular axis in a three-dimensional Euclidean space, as illustrated in the following screenshot:

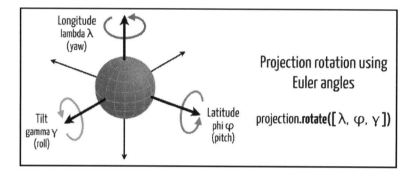

Projection rotation using three perpendicular axes: normal (yaw), transverse (pitch) and longitudinal (roll).

With `projection.rotate()` you can change the *aspect* of a projection so that your area of interest is in the center of least distortion. You need it to create a pole-centered projection. If you have an orthographic projection that shows only one hemisphere, you need it to view the other sides. You can also produce animations by changing the value of one or more axes and redrawing the map. The following illustration shows the effects of applying `projection.rotate()` to the Mercator and orthographic projections.

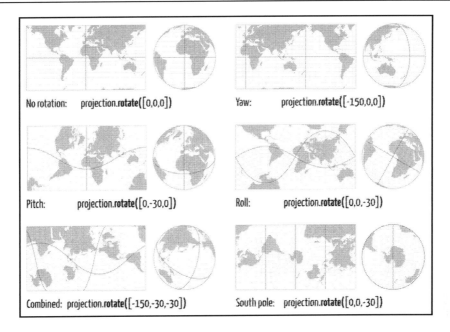

Rotating a sphere in relation to its projected surface. Code: *Projection-Geometry/5-rotate-*.html*.

The following code changes the *yaw* angle in a loop, simulating the rotation of the earth on its axis:

```
const projection = d3.geoOrthographic(); // try a different projection!
const geoPath = d3.geoPath().projection(projection);
const map = {};

d3.json('../Data/' + file).then(function(data) {
    map.topology = data.objects[key];
    map.features = topojson.feature(data, map.topology).features;
    map.merged = topojson.merge(data, map.topology.geometries)
    map.mesh = topojson.mesh(data, map.topology)

    svg.append("path").attr("class", "background")
        .datum({type: "Sphere"}).attr("d", geoPath);
    svg.append("path").attr("class","graticule")
        .datum(d3.geoGraticule10()).attr("d", geoPath)
    svg.append("path").attr("class","continents")
        .datum(map.merged).attr("d", geoPath);
    svg.append("path").attr("class","borders")
        .datum(map.mesh).attr("d", geoPath);

    let i = 0;
    d3.interval(function(d) { // this creates an animation loop
```

```
        if(i == 180) i = -180;
        geoPath.projection().rotate([i++,0,0])
        svg.select(".graticule").attr("d", geoPath)
        svg.selectAll(".continents").attr("d", geoPath)
        svg.selectAll(".borders").attr("d", geoPath)
    }, 100)
});
```

The code is in `Animation/rotating-earth.html`. Try it with other projections! If you use a Mercator projection you should see the continents sliding to the right. A nice exercise would be to add a shadow on the sphere to simulate day and night. See examples in the *Animation/* folder.

Clipping

There are many ways to clip an area: you can scale a map so that the parts that don't fit in the viewport get clipped out, you can filter out unwanted features and adjust the graticule's extent, or you can perform SVG or Canvas clipping using geometric shapes. There are also two `d3-geo` methods that perform clipping using map coordinates. The first, `clipAngle()`, clips the sphere by an angular distance from a center point on the surface *before* projection,. The second, `clipExtent()`, clips the *projected* map using pixel coordinates of a bounding rectangle.

For example, to clip the sphere by a radius of 20 degrees around London, you should configure the projection as follows (`Projection-Geometry/7-clipping-small-circle.html`):

```
const projection = d3.geoOrthographic() // try other projections!
.rotate([2,-52,0]) // rotates to center London
.clipAngle(20); // clips a radius of 20 degrees
```

Clipping the projected map using a 150x150 pixel rectangle located at the same center will include the same countries (`Projection-Geometry/7-clipping-viewport.html`):

```
const width = 960, height = 500;
const projection = d3.geoOrthographic()
.rotate([2,-52,0]) // rotates to center London
.clipExtent([[width/2 - 75,height/2 - 75],[width/2 + 75, height/2 + 75]]);
```

The results are illustrated below. The original globe is shown as a reference.

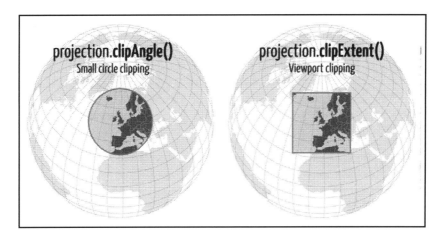

Reference maps showing the original projection and shaded areas showing the effects of two kinds of clipping.
Code: *Projection-Geometry/7-clipping-*.html.*

The `geoOrthographic()` projection has default angle clipping at 90°, but you can override this. If you want to create a semitransparent globe where you can see the opposite side, configure the projection to *increase* the `clipAngle()`:

```
const projection = d3.geoOrthographic().clipAngle(180);
```

See a complete example in `Projection-Geometry/7-clipping-orthographic.html`.

Clipping to the sphere

Some projections in D3 require *clipping to the sphere* because, due to how the projection is applied, features may be rendered *outside* the outline of the sphere. This is true for all interrupted projections and for some others. Polygonal projections from the `d3-geo-polygon` module don't require clipping.

Clipping to the sphere uses a special GeoJSON object:

```
{type: "Sphere"}
```

It doesn't take any additional arguments and can be used in functions that accept GeoJSON geometries.

The simplest way to clip to a sphere is to create a clipping mask from a {type: "Sphere"} object. In SVG you can do this with a <clipPath> element containing a <path> that describes the clipping path. This is usually defined in an SVG <defs> header. Then you can apply the *clip-path* attribute to graticules, shapes, backgrounds, and any path elements that use a data string generated by the *geoPath* function.

The following listing (Projection-Geometry/7-clipping-orthographic.html) uses this technique to clip to the sphere a map created with *Goode's Homolosine* interrupted projection. A clipping mask is created and appended to a <defs> header block, using {type: "Sphere"} as the datum and a geoPath configured with the projection so that the spherical is generated according to the projection. The clipPath element requires an ID so that the shapes that apply the clipping can reference it:

```
const projection = d3.geoInterruptedHomolosine()
                      .fitExtent([[10,10], [width-20, height-20]],
                                 {type: "Sphere"});
const geoPath = d3.geoPath().projection(projection);

const svg = d3.select("body").append("svg")
              .attr("width", width).attr("height", height);

svg.append("defs")
   .append("clipPath")
   .attr("id", "clip") // creates the mask
     .append("path")
     .datum({type: "Sphere"}) // shape of mask is projected sphere
     .attr("d", geoPath);
```

Now you can apply the mask to each path that needs to be clipped with the *clip-path* attribute:

```
svg.append("path").attr("class","background")
        .datum({type: "Sphere"})
        .attr("clip-path", "url(#clip)") // clipping
        .attr("d", geoPath);
svg.append("path").attr("class","graticule")
        .datum(graticule())
        .attr("clip-path", "url(#clip)") // clipping
        .attr("d", geoPath);
```

The result, before and after clipping, is shown in the following screenshot:

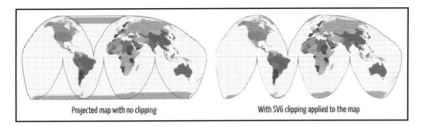

Clipping to the sphere is necessary in interrupted projections. Code: *Projection-Geometry/7-clipping-sphere.html.*

If your `geoPath` is configured to draw on a Canvas context, you can use Canvas clipping to achieve the same effect above.

CSS clipping and masking can also be used for additional clipping layers not affected by projections. There are also other graphical clipping methods that were not mentioned here. See the references at the end of this chapter for some links.

Spherical geometry

The `d3-geo` module contains methods and functions for spherical math operations, which can compute areas and distances, find centroids and bounds of an object in spherical or planar coordinates. Operations in planar geometry occur in the viewport domain and use pixel coordinates. They are methods of the `d3.geoPath()` object. Corresponding operations in spherical geometry are top-level functions. They all operate on GeoJSON objects. The following table compares them:

Planar geometry	Spherical geometry	Description
`geoPath.area(object)`	`d3.geoArea(object)`	Computes the *area* of a shape. The planar `area()` method computes a visible (non-clipped) area of the *projected* shape in square pixels. Different projections and aspects will result in different values. The spherical `d3.geoArea()` function computes the area in square radians (steradians), and is projection-independent.

geoPath.measure (*object*)	d3.geoLength (*object*) d3.geoDistance (*a,b*)	Computes the *length* of a line. The planar measure() method computes the visible (non-clipped) length of a line in pixels. If the shape is a *Polygon* or *MultiPolygon*, it will return the sum ot the perimeters of each linear ring. The length may differ between projections and aspects of the same projection. The spherical d3.geoLength() function computes the length in radians and is projection-independent. The d3.geoDistance(a,b) function returns the length between two points, expressed as [*longitude,latitude*].
geoPath.bounds (*object*)	d3.geoBounds (*object*)	Returns the bounding box for an object. The planar bounds() method returns an array in the format [[*minX, minY*],[*maxX,maxY*]], with coordinates that are affected by projection, aspect and clipping. The spherical d3.geoBounds() function returns an array in the form [[*minLng,minLat*],[*maxLng,maxLat*]] and is projection-independent.

`geoPath.centroid(`*object*`)`	`d3.geoCentroid(`*object*`)`	Returns the *centroid* for an object. The planar `centroid()` method retuns an array [*x,y*] with the coordinates for the centroid, which is affected by clipping, aspect and projection. The spherical `d3.geoCentroid()` function returns an array [*longitude,latitude*] and its position is projection-independent.

geoPath methods for planar geometry and top-level D3 functions for spherical geometry compared

Measuring distances

The length of objects can be measured with three functions/methods:

- `geoPath.measure(`*object*`)`, returns a measure in pixels
- `d3.geoLength(`*object*`)` returns a measure in radians (which can be used to calculate the actual distance in kilometers or miles)
- `d3.geoDistaince(`*a,b*`)` is equivalent to `d3.geoLength()` but takes two position arrays instead of a GeoJSON object

If the object is a *LineString,* these functions return its length, as expected. If the object is a *MultiLineString,* the value returned is the sum of the lengths of all the segments. If it's a *Polygon* or *MultiPolygon,* the sum of the perimeters of all linear rings will be returned (including the perimeter of the holes, if any). The object can also be a GeoJSON *Feature* that contains any of these geometries.

The following illustration compares, in two different projections, the values returned by planar and spherical length measuring functions applied to *LineStrings* that contain two points. Straight lines are automatically interpolated as arcs of a great circle. They appear as curves in the Mercator projection with increasing distortion toward the poles. This distortion is greatly reduced in an equidistant projection:

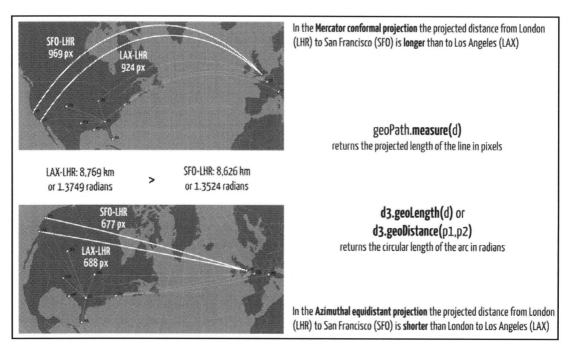

Comparing distances measured in pixels and in radians using different projections. Code: *Path-Geometry/4-measure-*.html*.

You can use the value in radians to calculate the actual distance in kilometers, dividing the length of the arc by the average circumference of the Earth (see `Path-Geometry/4-measure-*.html`):

```
const object = {
    id: "LHR-LAX",
    type: "LineString",
    coordinates: [[-0.46, 51.47], [-118.41, 33.94]]
};
const radians = 2 * Math.PI; // total radians in a circumference (180 deg)
const earth = 40075; // circumference of the earth in km
const km = d3.geoLength(d) / radians * earth;
```

Calculating areas

Areas are calculated using the `geoPath.area(object)` method, which returns a value in square pixels, or `d3.geoArea(object)`, which returns a value in square radians (steradians), that can be used to obtain the actual area in square kilometers or square miles. They each take a GeoJSON object.

Areas in square pixels and steradians should be proportional in an equal-area projection of the globe. Conformal projections, like Mercator, distort area in order to preserve shapes. In a Mercator projection, Greenland appears with a projected area superior to South America, but in reality it is smaller than the Democratic Republic of the Congo, which is 15 times smaller in the same projection, as illustrated below. With an equal-area projection, `geoPath.area()` returns proportional values for D.R. of Congo and Greenland. With `d3.geoArea()` you get proportional values in *any* projection.

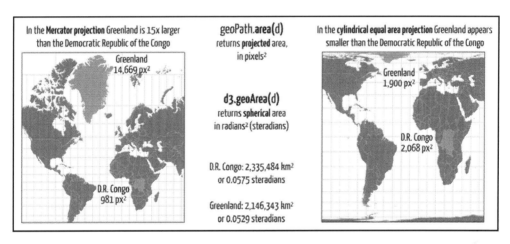

Comparing areas measured in square pixels and square radians (steradians) in different projections. Code: *Path-Geometry/3-area-*.html*.

You can use the value in steradians to calculate the actual area in km2, dividing the length of the arc by the average circumference of the Earth (See `Path-Geometry/3-area-*.html`):

```
const object = {
    id: "Greenland",
    type: "MultiPolygon",
    coordinates: [[[[-43.7062,59.9028], ...]]]
};
const steradians = 4 * Math.PI; // total steradians in a perfect sphere
const earth = 510072000; // area of the earth in square km
const sqkm = d3.geoArea(d) / steradians * earth;
```

Centroids and bounds

Bounds are the limits of the rectangle that contains the entire shape, and are an important measure for selecting and zooming to shape boundaries. Centroids are the center of gravity of a shape, and are useful for placing labels or symbols near the middle of the shape. Centroids and bounds may be computed on the sphere, before the projection occurs, or on the projected plane.

Planar centroids and bounds are computed with `d3.geoPath()` methods. The `geoPath.centroid(object)` method returns an array with pixel coordinates [*x*,*y*] for the *projected* planar centroid of a shape. The `geoPath.bounds(object)` method returns pixel coordinates of two opposite corners of a rectangle that contains the projected object, in an array with the following structure:

```
[ [minX, minY],[maxX, maxY] ]
```

Bounds and centroids of a projected shape depend on the projection used, clipping and rotation. If you need projection-independent bounds and centroids, you should use the *spherical* top-level functions `d3.geoCentroid(object)` and `d3.geoBounds(object)`, which return the centroid or bounds of a shape on a sphere expressed in longitudes and latitudes.

The spherical bounds are the corners of a four-sided polygon, with sides parallel to the meridians and parallels of the sphere. The function returns an array with the following structure:

```
[ [minLon, minLat],[maxLon, maxLat] ]
```

Centroids and bounds may not always be where you expected. Some GeoJSON files that group the overseas departments, states or provinces of a country in a single *MultiPolygon* will have bounds and centroids of an area containing all shapes. For example, in some maps, the centroid of France lies in Spain and the bounds extend over the Atlantic Ocean because French Guyana (which is a department of France) is part of the same *MultiPolygon*. To fix that, you would need to edit the original GeoJSON file, or filter individual geometries.

You can also convert bounds and centroids to planar pixel coordinates and back to geographical coordinates using the `projection.invert()` function:

```
const centroid = geoPath.centroid(d); // pixels
const geoCentroid = d3.geoCentroid(d); // geoCoords
const centroid2 = projection(geoCentroid); // pixels
const geoCentroid2 = projection.invert(centroid); // geoCoords
```

The illustration that follows contains a summary of the four functions that D3 provides to calculate bounds and centroids. These examples are interactive. You can run the code examples in `Path-Geometry/1-centroid*.html` and `2-geobounds*.html`.

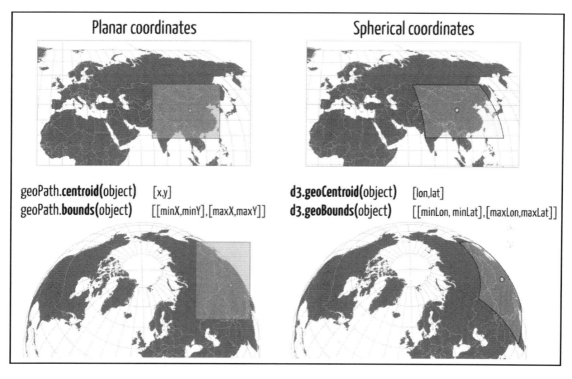

Obtaining bounds and centroids using planar and spherical coordinates. *Path-Geometry/1-centroid*.html and 2-geobounds*.html.*

Interpolation, rotation and containment

Three other *d3-geo* functions and methods are worth mentioning here, since they encapsulate the complexity of very useful operations, such as point interpolation, rotation and containment. They are described in the following table.

Functions	Description
`d3.geoInterpolate`(*a,b*)	Returns an interpolator function between two points *a* and *b*. Each point is an array of the form [*longitude,latitude*]. The interpolator function receives a value between 0 and 1 and returns the corresponding point on the great circle arc that passes between *a* and *b*.

d3.geoRotation (*[yaw,pitch,roll]*)	Returns a rotation function that receives a [*longitude,latitude*] point and returns the new [*longitude,latitude*] after the rotation is applied. An invert ([longitude,latitude]) method can be used to obtain the original point from one that was rotated.
d3.geoContains (*object, point*)	Returns *true* if a point, expressed as an array of [*longitude,latitude*] is contained in a GeoJSON object.

Other useful functions for spherical math

The d3.geoInterpolate (*a,b*) function returns an interpolation function that you can use to obtain any point on a line. For example, to place a label in the middle of a great circle arc, which appears as a curve in a Mercator projection, you can't use a centroid, since it won't be located on the curve, but you can use an interpolator to obtain the position of a point in the middle of the curve.

You first need to create an interpolator function from the two points:

```
const line = {
    type: "LineString",
    coordinates: [[-0.46, 51.47], [-118.41, 33.94]]
};
const interpolator =
d3.geoInterpolate(line.coordinates[0], line.coordinates[1]);
```

Now you can obtain any point on the curve, passing a value between the beginning (0) and the end (1) of the curve. To obtain the coordinates of the point in the middle of the line, you can use:

```
const geoMiddle = interpolator(0.5);
```

In case you need pixel coordinates, you just need to apply the projection function:

```
const middle = projection(geoMiddle);
```

You can use an interpolator to animate an object that travels along the curve, for example, to show a small plane moving on the line from Los Angeles to London (see Path-Geometry/7-interpolate.html).

The `geoRotation(coords)` function returns a rotation function that you can use to place an object anywhere on the sphere using 3-axis rotation. For example, the following code will create a rotation function that will rotate the sphere 20 degrees in different axes and directions:

```
const rotation = d3.geoRotation([20,-20,20]);
```

Now you can apply the function to any position, and obtain a new rotated position:

```
const position = [0,0];

const newPosition = rotation(position); // returns [26.0334, -10.6631]
```

You can also obtain the inverse coordinates and discover what would be the original position if the current position were the result of a rotation:

```
const previousPosition = rotation.invert(position); // returns [-20, 20]
```

With these functions, you can make very cool animations by moving objects on the sphere (see `Path-Geometry/6-rotation.html`).

The `d3.geoContains(object, point)` function will return *true* if a position is contained inside a GeoJSON object, which is usually a *Polygon* or *MultiPolygon*. You can use this, for example, to highlight a country that contains a selected city. The function below receives a GeoJSON object containing a *Point* representing a city, then selects all countries applying a highlighting class to the ones that contain it:

```
function showCity(city)
    d3.selectAll(".country")
        .classed("highlight",
                    country => d3.geoContains(country, city.coordinates))
}
```

This code is used in `Examples/africa-chamberlin-trimetric.html` example, where hovering the mouse over a city shows the name of the city and highlights its country. See also `Path-Geometry/5-contains.html`.

Zooming, brushing and rotating

Maps can contain a lot of information, much more than a viewer can grasp. If you fill a map with all the information you have, it becomes unreadable. Web-based maps should be interactive. A typical viewer expects to zoom in for details, zoom out for context, and pan when necessary. At the beginning of this chapter we added simple SVG zooming and panning to a map with the *d3.zoom()* behavior and SVG transforms. In this section we will explore other techniques that take advantage of the three-dimensional nature of maps to achieve the best zooming and panning experience.

Brushing, or zoom to bounding box

One way to zoom in to an area in a map is to draw a box, clip the box and expand it so that it fits the viewport. Once you have the coordinates of this bounding box, you can use clipping and the fitting methods from *d3-geo* to zoom in.

First you need to save the initial values for the projection's *scale* and *translate*, to be able to restore the original values and zoom back to the full map. This is done in the following code, which sets up a SVG viewport, creates a projection and saves its state:

```
const width = 960, height = 500;
const svg = d3.select("body").append("svg")
            .attr("width", width).attr("height", height);
const globe = svg.append("g").attr("class","globe");

const projection = d3.geoMercator().scale(80),
scale = projection.scale(), // saves current scale
translate = projection.translate(), // saves current translate
geoPath = d3.geoPath().projection(projection);
```

The mechanism to draw the selection box is provided by the d3-brush module, which is part of D3's default bundle. The code below creates a new brush that will call the zoom function when the selection is done:

```
const brush = d3.brush()
.extent([[0,0], [width,height]]) // max size of brush
.on("end", zoom);
```

You have to register the brush in some higher-level object. In this example we will use the SVG:

```
svg.call(brush);
```

The bounding box of the selection is stored in the selection property of the *brush.end* event that is captured. A *selection* contains an array with the format [[*minx*, *minY*], [*maxX*, *maxY*]]. The zoom() method retrieves this object using d3.event.selection and places the geographical coordinates in a GeoJSON object, so we can use a fitting method:

```
function zoom() {
    const selection = d3.event.selection;
    if(selection){
        const boundingObject = {
            type: 'MultiPoint',
            coordinates: [projection.invert(selection[0]),
                          projection.invert(selection[1])]
        };
        projection.fitSize([width, height], boundingObject);
        render();
        svg.call(brush.move, null);
    }
}
```

Once you have the GeoJSON object, all you have to do is pass it to fitSize() or fitExtent() to automatically zoom to the bounding box. The last line hides the drawing box calling *brush.move* with *null*. After updating the projection, the render() method updates the SVG objects:

```
function render() {
    globe.selectAll("path.country").attr("d", geoPath);
    globe.selectAll("path.graticule").attr("d", geoPath);
    globe.selectAll("path.background").attr("d", geoPath);
}
```

To zoom out, you can use a single mouse click and restore the original state.

```
svg.on("click", function() {
    d3.event.stopPropagation();
    projection.scale(scale).translate(translate)
    render();
});
```

The screenshots below show the process of drawing the box and zooming. The code above omits details such as drawing graticules and shapes, but you can see the full code in `Interactive/2-brush+zoom.html`.

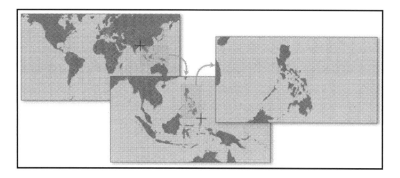

Zooming to a bounding box drawn on the screen with *d3.brush*. *Code: Interactive/2-zoom-to-bounding-box.html*.

Zoom to object

You don't have to draw a bounding box if you are only interested in zooming to a specific object. You can simply pass the object to `fitExtent()` so that it occupies all the available space. This is used in the next example, where the user clicks on a country and it scales to fit the viewport. Since we also use clicks to zoom out, we need a flag to keep track of the current state:

```
let zoomed = false;
```

Each shape will be a source for click events. The appropriate action will be selected depending on the state of *zoomed*:

```
d3.selectAll(".country")
.on("click", d => zoomed ? zoom(d) : unzoom())
```

The `zoom()` method is very simple. All you have to do is call `fitSize()` or `fitExtent()` with the current GeoJSON feature:

```
function zoom(object) {
    projection.fitSize([width, height], object);
    render();
    zoomed = true;
}
```

The `unzoom()` function performs zoom out restoring the original scale and translate positions:

```
function unzoom() {
    d3.event.stopPropagation();
    projection.scale(scale).translate(translate);
    render();
    zoomed = false;
}
```

This will work well for almost all countries, but will seem to fail for countries that cross the anti-meridian: Russia, USA and Fiji. The reason is because the bounding box for these countries wraps around the anti-meridian, making it almost as wide as the globe, as shown in the following screenshot:

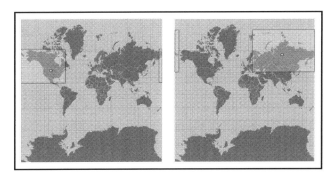

Bounding boxes for countries that cross the anti-meridian (resampled and fixed for the anti-meridian). Code:Interactive/*3-zoom-to-object-mercator.html*.

We can use a different projection, such as:

```
const projection = d3.geoOrthographic();
```

But it doesn't really solve the problem, since the globe doesn't rotate. It only works for countries near the center of the map, but if you click on a country near the edges, it appears but with a large distortion:

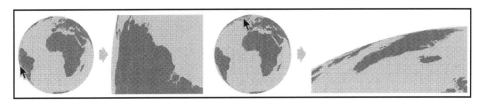

Zooming in to object in the orthographic projection without rotating the globe. Code: Interactive/*3-zoom-to-object.html*.

We need to *rotate* the globe and move the selected country in the center before clicking. That would guarantee minimal distortion. Even better would be to have the application rotate automatically to the best position, and then zoom in. We will do this next.

Rotate and zoom to object

This function creates a `d3.geoRotation()` function from the projection, and then uses it to obtain the three rotated coordinates of the centroid. It then rotates the projection using these coordinates so that the object's centroid is in its center:

```
function rotateToView(object) {
    const rotate = d3.geoRotation(projection.rotate()),
        centroid = d3.geoCentroid(object);

    const rotation = rotate(centroid);

    const lambda = projection.rotate()[0] - rotation[0],
        phi = projection.rotate()[1] - rotation[1],
        gamma = projection.rotate()[2];

    projection.rotate([lambda, phi, gamma]);

    const epsilon = 1e-6;
    if(Math.abs(rotation[0]) >= epsilon || Math.abs(rotation[1]) >= epsilon){
        return rotateToView(object);
    }
    return rotation;
}
```

Now we can add these methods to the zoom function, which first rotates the globe so the country is placed in the center of the projection, and then fits it in the available space:

```
function zoom(object) {
    rotateToView(object);
    projection.fitExtent([[50,50],
    [width-50, height-50]], object);
    render(object.id);
}
```

The function calls `render()` with an id, which you can use to filter data and show details that probably wouldn't fit in the full map. This is called a *semantic zoom*. In this example we just changed the color and added a label to the country, but you could use it to show towns, internal borders and other details.

The result is shown below. See the full code in `Interactive/4-zoom-to-geobounds-rotate.html`.

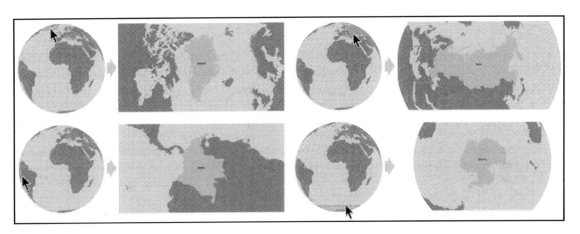

Zooming in to object bounds using the orthographic projection with rotation to centroid before zoom.
Code: Interactive/4-rotate-and-zoom-to-object.html.

Zooming with drag and rotate

This strategy is similar to the SVG zoom and pan we used in the first example at the beginning of this chapter, but instead of using *translate()* to pan the projection, here we rotate the globe *before* projecting. As a result, there is no risk of reaching the edges of the map, and you can easily zoom in to the Bering Strait and show Chukotka and Alaska in the same view.

We just need to save the current scale, since we won't be using translate:

```
const scale = projection.scale()
```

And we will also need to keep track of the current zoom transform, which will be used for the panning. You can initialize it with *d3.zoomIdentity*, which contains the following object:

```
{x: 0, y: 0, k: 1}
```

Now set up a zoom behavior and register it. We will limit the scale extent to 15, because this solution also has some serious limitations (in the next section you will discover how to fix it):

```
const zoom = d3.zoom()
            .scaleExtent([1,15])
            .on('zoom', zoomMap)
svg.call(zoom);
```

There are three angles that can be controlled in `rotate()`, but calculating relative rotations involving all three is no trivial task. We will try with a simple naïve solution using only two angles, one for longitudes and another for latitudes. It works as long as you don't zoom in too much and keep the globe upright.

First, create scales for each angle:

```
const lambda = d3.scaleLinear()
            .domain([-width, width])
            .range([-180, 180])

 const phi = d3.scaleLinear()
            .domain([-height, height])
            .range([90, -90]);
```

Then in the `zoomMap()` function, discover if the user is moving the mouse (to pan/rotate) or rolling the wheel (to scale). After each rotation the `currentTransform` should be updated with the data in the zoom *transform* object, available in the method as `d3.event.transform`. After each scale, the zoom transform object is updated.

```
function zoomMap() {
    var t = d3.event.transform;

    if (d3.event.sourceEvent.type === "mousemove") {
        projection.rotate([lambda(t.x), phi(t.y)]);
        currentTransform.x = t.x;
        currentTransform.y = t.y;
    } else {
        projection.scale(scale * t.k)
        t.x = currentTransform.x;
```

```
            t.y = currentTransform.y;
        }

        render();
    }
```

Now you can rotate the globe and zoom in and out! See the full code in `Interactive/naive.html` and try using it with other projections.

Quaternion dragging and zooming

If you tried the previous solution, you should have noticed that, the more you zoom, the harder it is to keep track of the mouse when you pan. If you turn the globe upside down, the mouse moves in one direction and the globe in the other! That's the cost of ignoring that third angle in our rotation vector.

A good solution needs to keep the mouse at the same point on the sphere during the entire dragging process. The simplest way to achieve this requires a different representation for rotations: the *quaternion*. A quaternion, or *versor*, is a 4-dimensional vector that can be used to model rotations in 3D space. It can be represented as an expression of the form: $w + xi + yj + zk$, where w, x, y, and z are real numbers and i, j, and k represent perpendicular unit vectors. The result of the multiplication of two quaternions, each representing a rotation along an axis, is a new quaternion that is equivalent to the application of the two rotations in sequence. This makes it much easier to apply relative rotations using all three axes.

So quaternions are definitively the way to go, but the *projection.rotate()* method gives us Euler angles. We need to convert them to quaternions, do the transformations and then convert back to Euler angles. You also need to implement quaternion vector multiplication. All this is made simple with the *versor.js* library, by Mike Bostock and Jason Davies, available from `github.com/Fil/versor`. You can include it in your page using:

```
<script src="https://unpkg.com/versor"></script>
```

In the `versor.js` library, a quaternion is a 4-element array in the form $[w,x,y,z]$. Rotations are three-element arrays following the same convention used in the `projection.rotate()` method: $[yaw, pitch, roll]$.

The library's main methods are listed in the following table:

Functions and methods	Description
versor (*euler*)	Returns the unit quaternion for the euler rotation angles. The *euler* array must have the format [λ, φ, γ], where λ, φ, γ are angles in degrees [0-360°]
versor.rotation (*q*)	Returns the euler rotation angles for the given quaternion *q*. The *q* array must have the format [*w,x,y,z*], where *w,x,y,z* are real numbers.
versor.cartesian (*[lng,lat]*)	Returns 3D cartesian coordinates [*x,y,z*] for the given spherical coordinates.
versor.multiply (*q0, q1*)	Returns the quaternion product of *q0* and *q1*.
versor.delta (*v0, v1, alpha*)	Given two quaternions *v0* and *v1*, returns the *rotation delta*: a rotation quaternion between two cartesian points on the sphere. The alpha paramemeter is optional and allows interpolation. Default is 1. Range is [0,1].

Main functions and methods of the versor.js library

You can obtain a quaternion for an existing angle with:

```
const q0 = versor([0,0,0]); // result: [1,0,0,0]
```

And convert a quaternion back to Euler angles with:

```
const euler = versor.rotation(q0); // result: [0,0,0]
```

A *quaterniondelta* returns a quaternion that represents relative rotation (between two points). If you multiply another quaternion by this value, you will rotate it by the same angle and axis:

```
const q1 = versor([0,45,0]);                // [0.924, 0, 0.383, 0]
const delta = versor.delta(q0, q1);         // [0.981, 0, 0.195]
const v = versor([-20,45,0]);               // [0.91,-0.16,0.377,0.066]
const product = versor.multiply(v, delta);  // [0.819, -0.17, 0.547, 0.034]
```

Let's use this library to drag the globe. First set up a *d3.drag* behavior with handlers for *drag.start* and *drag.end*. A *state* object should be created to store the initial rotation states used by both methods.

```
const drag = d3.drag()
          .on("start", dragStart)
          .on("drag", dragging);

  const globe = svg.append("g")
          .attr("class","globe")
          .call(drag);

  const state = {}
```

The `dragStart()` function gets the pixel coordinates from the mouse event and converts it to spherical coordinates. Then it uses these coordinates to save a quaternion with the initial mouse rotation (*v0*). It also saves the current projection rotation (*r0*) and it corresponding quaternion (*q0*):

```
function dragStart() {
    const mouse = projection.invert(d3.mouse(this));
    state.v0 = versor.cartesian(mouse);
    state.r0 = projection.rotate();
    state.q0 = versor(state.r0);
}
```

The `dragging()` function rotates the projection to the current position (which will change during dragging), and obtains a quaternion of the new mouse position (*v1*). The rotation between the previous mouse position (*v0*) and the new one (*v1*) is computed with `versor.delta()`, which is then used to generate a quaternion for the globe's rotation (*q1*) from multiplication (quaternion multiplication is *not* commutative: the order is important). Finally, the `versor.rotation()` method is used to convert the quaternion back into Euler angles that can be used in the projection's rotation function:

```
function dragging() {
    projection.rotate(state.r0);
    const mouse = projection.invert(d3.mouse(this));
    const v1 = versor.cartesian(mouse);

    const mouseDelta = versor.delta(state.v0, v1);
    const q1 = versor.multiply(state.q0, mouseDelta)
    projection.rotate(versor.rotation(q1));

    render();
```

```
    }
```

Now you can move the globe upside down, and in any direction, and the mouse will always be connected to a point on the globe. You can see the full code and run this example from `Interactive/drag-1-versor.html`.

The previous example only implements a dragging behavior. To zoom you just need to switch to zooming behavior configuration and add scaling. Replace `d3.drag()` with `d3.zoom()`, shown as follows:

```
const zoom = d3.zoom()
    .scaleExtent([.5,40])
    .on("start", zoomStart)
    .on("zoom", zooming);

  const globe = svg.append("g")
    .attr("class","globe")
    .call(zoom);
```

The `zoomStart()` method is identical to `dragStart()`:

```
function zoomStart() {
    const mouse = projection.invert(d3.mouse(this));
    state.v0 = versor.cartesian(mouse);
    state.r0 = projection.rotate();
    state.q0 = versor(state.r0);
}
```

We no longer have to distinguish mouse and wheel events, so the only difference between the `zooming()` method and the `dragging()` method we used before is a line of code to invoke `projection.scale()`:

```
function zooming() {
    projection.rotate(state.r0);
    const mouse = projection.invert(d3.mouse(this));
    const v1 = versor.cartesian(mouse);

    const mouseDelta = versor.delta(state.v0, v1);
    const q1 = versor.multiply(state.q0, mouseDelta)

    projection.rotate(versor.rotation(q1));
    projection.scale(scale * d3.event.transform.k); // add this line
    render();
}
```

Now you can rotate and zoom. You can see the full code and run this example from `Interactive/drag-2-versor-zoom.html`.

Inertia

When you move the mouse the globe starts spinning, and when you stop, it stops immediately. Perhaps you wish it would react more naturally, slowing down until stopping. You can include this behavior using a simple plugin created by Philipe Rivière called *inertia.js*, documented at `github.com/Fil/d3-inertia`. You don't have to implement any methods, just include the *versor.js* and *inertia.js* libraries in your page:

```
<script src="https://unpkg.com/versor"></script>
<script src="https://unpkg.com/d3-inertia"></script>
```

And add a single line in your code. In many of the examples we created in this section, you can add:

```
d3.geoInertiaDrag(svg, () => render(), projection);
```

The `d3.geoInertiaDrag(view, render, projection, options)` function takes three or four parameters:

- **view**: a graphics container. Can be an SVG object or a Canvas
- **render**: a function with the code to update the map during drag and zoom
- **projection**: the projection object used to render the map (must support `invert()`)
- **options**: array with configuration options, described in the plugin's documentation

If you already have a method that renders your map after updates, you just need to add this line to your code and it automatically adds the inertial behavior. Try adding this to any map you created in this chapter, including other projections. See also a full working example in `Interactive/8-inertia-drag.html`.

Using Canvas

You may have noticed that dragging and zooming are sometimes slow and choppy. One of the main reasons this happens is the large amount of objects in memory. A large dataset can create hundreds of thousands of objects, draining your memory resources and freezing your animations.

But if you configure a path with the *context()* method and an HTML Canvas context, it will no longer generate an SVG path string, but a sequence of calls to HTML Canvas path methods.

The same dataset that creates thousands of SVG objects creates a single Canvas, which uses much less resources. On the other hand it's much harder to select object in a Canvas, apply styles and create interactive maps.

The following example is a Canvas-version of the map you created in the beginning of this chapter. Replace the code that creates and configures the SVG for one that creates and configures a Canvas and obtains a context:

```
const context = d3.select("body").append("canvas")
                .attr("width", width).attr("height", height)
                    .node().getContext("2d");
```

Initialize the *geoPath* with a projection and the context:

```
const projection = d3.geoMercator();
 const geoPath = d3.geoPath().projection(projection).context(context);
```

We can't use the *general update pattern* here, since HTML Canvas doesn't deal with individual objects that can be appended or removed. To draw a collection of shapes, you have to loop through each object, begin a new path and call the `geoPath()` function for each object, which generates Canvas path commands that will draw each shape.

Replace the old `draw()` function with the one shown below, which calls each feature in a loop, initiates a path with `context.beginPath()`, and then calls the `geoPath()` function. The styles also need to be configured as context properties.

```
function draw() {
    map.features.forEach(function(d) {
        context.beginPath();
        geoPath(d);
        context.fillStyle = 'gray';
        context.strokeStyle = 'white';
        context.lineWidth = .5;
        context.fill();
```

```
            context.stroke();
        });
    }
```

If you have graticules and other shapes that use the *geoPath* you also need to convert them to Canvas. The code for this example is in `MapMaking/9-canvas.html`.

Summary

In this chapter you explored one of D3's coolest features: geographical maps and projections, which is part of the *d3-geo* module.

Throughout this chapter we explored the main GIS data formats for Web-based vector maps: GeoJSON and TopoJSON. You learned how to read a GeoJSON file and display its shapes using `d3.geoPath()`, how to use a projection to place GeoJSON positions on a map, how to obtain GeoJSON features from TopoJSON data, merge shapes, create meshes and discover neighboring shapes. You also learned how to add graticules to a map, standard parallels, draw lines and circles.

A large section was dedicated to projections, one of the main features of the *d3-geo* module. D3 supports over a hundred projection functions in the *d3-geo-projection* and *d3-geo-polygon* modules. You learned how to distinguish different types of projections and how to select them based on how they distort the original features.

A large part of *d3-geo* is dedicated to spherical mathematics. We covered the main functions that you can use to calculate distances, areas, centroids and bounds, find points in a shape, interpolate over a line and capture a rotation function. We also explored functions that scale, rotate and translate globes and projections, using those functions to create interactive zoom, pan, drag and rotate behaviors.

We finished this chapter with a brief introduction to Canvas rendering, which is an important optimization technique supported by all shape generation tools in D3.

References

- Module documentation, D3.js: `github.com/d3/d3-geo`, github.com/d3/d3-geo-projection, `github.com/d3/d3-geo-polygon`.
- GeoJSON specification: `tools.ietf.org/html/rfc7946`.
- TopoJSON specification: `github.com/topojson/topojson-specification`.
- Shapefile specification: `www.esri.com/library/whitepapers/pdfs/shapefile.pdf`.
- GDAL: Geospatial Data Abstraction Library: `www.gdal.org`.
- Natural Earth Public Domain Map Dataset. `naturalearthdata.com`.
- MapShaper Editor for Map Data: `mapshaper.org`.
- Geojson.io GeoJSON editor: `geojson.io`.
- African cities: `Data/africa-1500-cities.csv` compiled from GeoNames geographical database: `www.geonames.org`. `Data/africa-10-cities.geojson` compiled from Wikipedia.
- African GeoJSON maps: `Data/africa.geojson`, `Data/africa-simple.geojson`, `Data/africa-rivers.geojson`, `Data/africa-madagascar.geojson`. Obtained from naturalearthdata.org and transformed using GIS tools (QGIS, geojson.io and MapShaper).
- GeoJSON map of the world with 245 countries adapted from map generated from naturalearthdata.com and transformed using GIS tools: `Data/world-lowres.geojson` and `Data/world-medres.geojson`
- GDP and HDI dataset: `Data/un_regions_gdp.csv`. Compiled from several sources, including United Nations (World Population Prospects 2017: `www.un.org`) and World Bank (World bank public data. data.worldbank.org)
- Shapes file in GeoJSON created with geojson.io: Data/border-example.geojson.
- Selected airport coordinates compiled from Wikipedia: Data/airports-busiest.csv.
- Resampling (to draw rhumb lines), by Mike Bostock: github.com/d3/d3-geo-projection/issues/75
- Inertia plugin, by Philippe Riviere: github.com/Fil/d3-inertia
- Rotate the World, by Jason Davies: www.jasondavies.com/maps/rotate/
- Three-Axis Rotation, by Mike Bostock: `bl.ocks.org/mbostock/4282586`
- Interactive Orthographic, by Mike Bostock: `bl.ocks.org/mbostock/3795040`
- Versor Dragging, by Mike Bostock: `observablehq.com/@d3/versor-dragging`

Other Books You May Enjoy

If you enjoyed this book, you may be interested in these other books by Packt:

Learn Chart.js
Helder da Rocha

ISBN: 9781789342482

- Learn how to create interactive and responsive data visualizations using Chart.js
- Learn how to create Canvas-based graphics without Canvas programming
- Create composite charts and configure animated data updates and transitions
- Efficiently display quantitative information using bar and line charts, scatterplots, and pie charts
- Learn how to load, parse, and filter external files in JSON and CSV formats
- Understand the benefits of using a data visualization framework

Hands-On Data Visualization with Bokeh

Kevin Jolly

ISBN: 9781789135404

- Installing Bokeh and understanding its key concepts
- Creating plots using glyphs, the fundamental building blocks of Bokeh
- Creating plots using different data structures like NumPy and Pandas
- Using layouts and widgets to visually enhance your plots and add a layer of interactivity
- Building and hosting applications on the Bokeh server
- Creating advanced plots using spatial data

Leave a review - let other readers know what you think

Please share your thoughts on this book with others by leaving a review on the site that you bought it from. If you purchased the book from Amazon, please leave us an honest review on this book's Amazon page. This is vital so that other potential readers can see and use your unbiased opinion to make purchasing decisions, we can understand what our customers think about our products, and our authors can see your feedback on the title that they have worked with Packt to create. It will only take a few minutes of your time, but is valuable to other potential customers, our authors, and Packt. Thank you!

Index

Made in the USA
Monee, IL
17 October 2020